And the Sun Shines Now

Adrian Tempany is a Liverpool supporter and a journalist who has written for the *Guardian*, the *Observer*, *The Times* and the *Financial Times*.

And the Sun Shines Now

How Hillsborough and the Premier League Changed Britain

ADRIAN TEMPANY

FABER & FABER

First published in 2016
by Faber and Faber Limited
Bloomsbury House
74–77 Great Russell Street, London WC1B 3DA

Typeset by Ian Bahrami
Printed in England by CPI Group (UK) Ltd, Croydon, CR0 4YY

A CIP record for this book
is available from the British Library

ISBN 978-0-571-29511-1

FSC
www.fsc.org
MIX
Paper from
responsible sources
FSC® C101712

2 4 6 8 10 9 7 5 3 1

For Deb, always

Contents

Acknowledgements

If there's a page in any book that readers are likely to skip, it's probably this one. Skip this, however, and you might as well go straight to the end of the book, for the 400 pages in between could not have been written without the help of the following people.

Thanks, first, to my friend David Williams, a superb writer and journalist who gave me the inspiration for this book as long ago as 2010.

Thanks to my agent, Mark Stanton of Jenny Brown Associates, for showing faith in me at the outset, and for his wise advice and encouragement along the way.

At Faber, I'd like to thank my editor Lee Brackstone, a genuine football fan, for his vision and passion; Ian Bahrami, my copy-editor, for his exceptionally keen eye and instinctive feel for the book; Anne Owen, my managing editor; and Rachel Alexander and Sophie Portas in publicity, for giving this a nudge in all the right places.

Huge thanks to everyone who agreed to an interview: every quote in this book was given to me directly, unless stated otherwise – and every contributor gave his or her time willingly and freely. Hopefully, through your voices, I've managed to capture something of the spirit of the real football family.

Special thanks must go to Professor Phil Scraton, for his expertise on Hillsborough and its aftermath, and for his invaluable contribution to the campaign for truth and justice; Andy Burnham, Peter Snape, Chris Bryant and Steve Rotheram, for their generosity and candour; Stuart Dykes and Jens Wagner, for their invaluable assistance in Gelsenkirchen and Hamburg; the directors of Schalke 04, who welcomed me into their club with such warmth and honesty; Rogan Taylor and Dave Boyle, for their insight and sheer quotability; the staff at the Tottenham Hotspur Foundation; Chris Platts, lecturer in sport development at Sheffield Hallam University, for his assistance with the chapter on children's play and their relationship to football; and to Supporters Direct and the Football Supporters' Federation – and in particular Antonia Hagemann and Michael Brunskill.

Most of the following people are not quoted in the book, but their help was vital. Many thanks to…

Jerry Andrews, Philip Bernie, Mike Bracken, Peter Carney, Ian Colledge, David Conn, Alex Eckhout at the Premier League, Tony Edwards, Simon Elliott, Nick Garnett, Owen Gibson, Dan Gordon, Ken Green at the University of Chester, David Hall, Roy Hattersley, Chris Horrie, the late Katy Jones, Damian Kavanagh, Ursula Kenny, Robert Knight at the British Psychological Society, Simon Kuper, Peter Marshall, Nicola McMillan, Steve Melly, Kevin Miles, Judith Moritz, Sean O'Brien, Anna Pallai, Dr Martyn Pickersgill at Edinburgh University, Keith, Jan and Bryan Pilgrim, Martin Polley at Southampton University, Ian Preece, Peter Rankin, James Robinson, Jancis Robinson, Erik Samuelson at AFC Wimbledon, Gavin Sandercock at Essex University, Scouse Not English, Mike Shallcross, Jim Sharman, Ben Shave, John Sherar, Christian Spooner at GMG Radio, Mark Stuart at

Nottingham University, Alan Sutherill, Toby Syfret and Enders Analysis, Matthew Tetlow at HESA, Tony Trueman at the British Sociological Association, Rhys Williams, and Trevor Williams – so sadly missed.

Huge thanks to my family for a priceless head start in life – a happy, normal childhood.

Thanks to Anne Williams, for her strength and dignity in the face of decades of cynicism, and to those fellow Reds who shared the most painful of memories in the first chapter of this book. We walk on . . .

Most of all, thanks to Deb – for your unfailing faith, and humour, and love, and for being the best thing that ever happened.

Editor's Note

It is not unusual for books to be acquired by publishers on the promise and outline of a proposal. Faber did that back in 2011, contracting Adrian Tempany to write the book you are now holding. Adrian delivered a draft of a previous version of this book in the summer of 2013 and we were set to publish in March 2014, 25 years after the Hillsborough disaster, at which he was present.

A month or so before publication, with the book to some degree already in bookshops, the hands of reviewers and early champions, we were advised to withdraw it and postpone publication or risk being accused of contempt of court, as the second inquest opened. In the first few months of 2016, Adrian made substantial changes to the body text of the original (unpublished) edition of *And the Sun Shines Now*. Specifically, Chapters 9, 10 and 11 were in need of radical updating, as the situation in the Bundesliga had developed in the two-year hiatus between the original publication date and actual publication. The final chapter was written after the verdict on the second hearings was delivered on 26 April 2016.

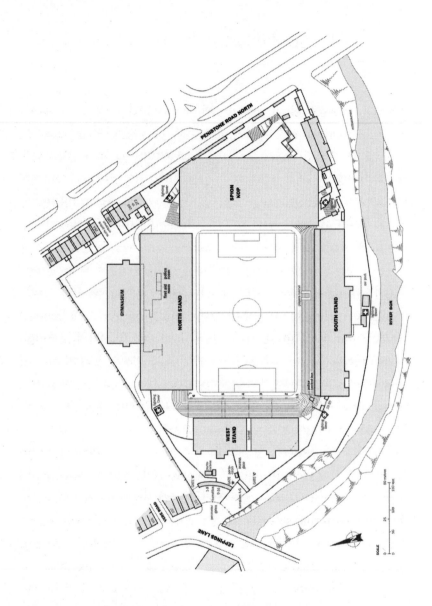

Map of Hillsborough stadium on 15 April 1989 (courtesy of the Hillsborough Inquests – www.hillsboroughinquests.independent.gov.uk)

1 : Sorry, Lad . . . I Can't Move

The 1980s began eight months early. On 4 May 1979, Margaret Thatcher arrived at Downing Street, fumbling the spirit of St Francis of Assisi and promising to fix a broken nation with the husbandry of a grocer's daughter. In the decade that followed, she defeated and embraced South American dictators, broke Britain's most powerful unions, and went toe to toe with the IRA. But even Margaret Thatcher was powerless to write the epitaph for the decade that was unquestionably hers, and which would unravel as it began, eight months early.

On 15 April 1989, 96 people were fatally injured on a football terrace at an FA Cup semi-final in Sheffield. The Hillsborough disaster was broadcast live on the BBC; it left millions of people in shock, and English football in ruins. In the weeks that followed, Britain embarked on an unprecedented period of soul-searching over its national sport.

The bare facts were appalling: 79 of the dead were aged 30 or younger; 37 were teenagers; the youngest was a ten-year-old boy. These, overwhelmingly, were Thatcher's children. Many of them died, on that sunny spring day, covered in their own excrement and urine. The coroner at the original inquests recorded that most had died of traumatic or crush asphyxia. Many spent their last moments throwing up, or crying. Some were trampled beneath dozens of pairs of designer trainers, worn by people who were trying desperately to escape, and trying desperately not to stand on their heads. Others made it onto a faded football pitch, only to die on an advertising hoarding.

On the evening of the disaster, as bereaved relatives began their unimaginable journey to Sheffield, journalists at a press conference at South Yorkshire Police headquarters now asked the question on the lips of most people in Britain that Saturday night: 'Who was responsible for this?'

In 2009, the country was asking that question again. Twenty years after the biggest disaster in British sport, much of the public were still in the dark about what really happened at Hillsborough. But in March and April 2009, as the 20th anniversary approached, survivors, the bereaved and sympathetic journalists took to the airwaves, the press and the internet to demand the truth. Such was the outcry, the Labour government set up the Hillsborough Independent Panel, a nine-strong committee charged with reviewing all of the remaining documented evidence on the disaster. While the recent inquests in Warrington have delivered the ultimate verdict on the tragedy (and are considered in depth in Chapter 12), this was the moment of truth.

For fully two decades, much of the 'wisdom' around Hillsborough had held that it was an accident. Even if it wasn't, then it was inevitable: fans were just like that. Stadiums were like that. Football, in the 1980s, was like that. But Hillsborough was not an accident, and it was not inevitable. Indeed, so many decisions throughout the decade conspired to cause the disaster that, according to the Hillsborough Independent Panel, the crush in 1989 was 'foreseeable'.

If there was unwillingness on the part of the public to

acknowledge what really went on at Hillsborough, it was seldom more apparent than at the stadium itself. For 20 years, many Sheffield Wednesday supporters remained aggrieved that their home ground was synonymous with such an appalling tragedy. Some campaigned to have the stadium renamed Owlerton, its name until 1914. Others would maintain that the disaster was nothing to do with their unfortunate club, referring to it still as 'the Liverpool fans disaster'. But, in 1989, Hillsborough was in a wretched condition. As the Hillsborough Independent Panel reported, the safety of supporters admitted onto the Leppings Lane was 'compromised at every level'.

Supporters had first to pass through an insufficient number of turnstiles, which were also too slow, leading to bottlenecks at the outer gates. Then, access to the Leppings Lane terrace was poorly signposted. The only entrance to pens 3 and 4, behind the goal, was via a tunnel built on a one in six downward gradient: this failed to meet the safety recommendations in the *Guide to Safety at Sports Grounds* (aka the *Green Guide*). So too did the seven gates in the perimeter fence of the terrace, which were the only means of emergency egress onto the pitch – they were too narrow, and had given cause for concern within the fire service. And the configuration of crush barriers in pen 3 left a lengthy, uninterrupted diagonal channel, which allowed substantial crowd movements to go unchecked.

Part of the reason the danger went unnoticed by Sheffield Wednesday's own supporters was that the central pens in the Leppings Lane terrace were reserved for away supporters. Wednesday spent the first four seasons of the decade in the Second Division, and rarely would the Leppings Lane be full. Even after they were promoted to the top flight in 1984/5, only

Man Utd, Everton and Liverpool brought a sizeable away support (Wednesday wouldn't play their city rivals, Sheffield Utd, until the autumn of 1989). But on the three occasions on which Hillsborough hosted an FA Cup semi-final between 1981–88, with near-capacity crowds, there were problems.

In 1988, John Aldridge scored a smart volley to give Liverpool a 2–1 win over Nottingham Forest at Hillsborough and book their place in the Cup Final. Millions of *Match of the Day* viewers saw the goal, but hundreds of Liverpool fans on the Leppings Lane, barely 20 feet away, did not. The ball came over from the left wing, Aldridge's right foot connected, and then . . . All they saw were the fans in front of them leap up, and they heard a roar around the ground. Some experienced a frightening crush in pens 3 and 4, behind the goal. As they made their way out of Hillsborough, many were heard to say: 'There's something wrong with that terrace. The view's terrible.'

This is not an apocryphal story: I was one of those supporters. In the weeks that followed, Liverpool fans wrote to Peter Robinson, the club's chief executive, to complain about the poor state of the terrace. Another fan wrote to the FA, to 'protest in the strongest possible terms at the disgraceful overcrowding that was allowed to occur in the Leppings Lane terrace area . . . The whole area was packed solid to the point where it was impossible to move and where I, and others around me, felt considerable concern for my personal safety.'*

In 1987, Leeds Utd's FA Cup semi-final with Coventry City was delayed by 15 minutes on the advice of the police match commander, after late-arriving Leeds fans, held up at police

---

* The FA later claimed they could find no trace of the letter.

checkpoints, found themselves in a bottleneck at the Leppings Lane turnstiles. And in 1981, 38 Spurs fans were injured on the Leppings Lane terrace while watching their FA Cup semi-final against Wolves. This was no minor incident: the injuries included broken arms, a broken leg and crushed ribs, after the Leppings Lane's capacity was exceeded by over 400. The South Yorkshire Police averted disaster by shutting off the tunnel and allowing 150 fans to climb over the fence and sit beside the pitch. Following the match, Assistant Chief Constable Goslin told the Sheffield Wednesday chairman, Bert McGee, that there had been 'a real chance of fatalities'. McGee replied: 'Bollocks! No one would have been killed.'

Shortly afterwards, the South Yorkshire Police notified Sheffield Wednesday that they believed the 10,100 capacity of the Leppings Lane was set too high. But the club dismissed their concerns: Sheffield Wednesday blamed the near-disaster on poor policing.

Thus began a decade of piecemeal renovation of the stadium and fitful liaison between the organisations charged with ensuring it met safety regulations. The 1975 Safety of Sports Grounds Act stipulated that any stadium with a capacity of more than 10,000 spectators for football should have a safety certificate, and that it was the responsibility of a local authority to issue this certificate. Hillsborough, with a capacity of 54,000, sat squarely within this category. Between 1978 and October 1988, the ground saw a series of structural modifications, but the stadium's safety certificate, issued in December 1979, was not updated in line with these alterations.

That Spurs fans avoided fatalities in 1981 was due in no small part to the fact that the Leppings Lane was still one open terrace – it had not been divided into pens. This allowed Spurs supporters to move sideways and escape the crush.

However, in late 1981 the West terrace (which combined with the adjoining, raised Northwest terrace to form the Leppings Lane) was carved into three pens. The fitting of radial fences should have seen the total capacity of the Leppings Lane reduced by 100, but the original figure of 10,100 was retained. Sheffield Wednesday and the club's structural engineers, Eastwoods, also considered introducing turnstiles to count the number of spectators entering both the West terrace (capacity: 7,200) and the Northwest terrace (2,900). The proposal was shelved. Now, with no means of monitoring the number of spectators in each section, and with an out-of-date calculation of safe capacity, the club was operating with an invalid safety certificate.

In July 1985, the central pen of the Leppings Lane was further divided by a new radial fence into two pens – numbered 3 and 4. But a proposal for monitoring the number of fans on each terrace was declined a second time, on the grounds of anticipated cost. While Sheffield Wednesday spent £340,000 on safety measures that summer, in response to the fire at Valley Parade, this oversight would prove disastrous.

With an irony so bitter as to be almost indigestible, the club's annual accounts for 1985/6 record instead that: 'A new computerised accounting system was introduced from 1 June 1985 that produces more detailed information analysed between the different activities of the club to give the Board of Directors better information on which to base their decisions.'

*

The following year, 1986, was a historic one for Liverpool FC. Kenny Dalglish's side became only the third in the 20th century to do the Double, following Arsenal and Spurs. Across the Pennines, Sheffield Wednesday and the South Yorkshire Police had settled their differences over the Spurs scare, and the club was ready once more to stage FA Cup semi-finals. Few gave consideration to the fact that Hillsborough was operating week in, week out without a valid safety certificate.

According to Lord Justice Taylor, ultimate responsibility for a certificate lay not with Sheffield Wednesday but with the local authority. As Taylor found:

> Section 8(1) of the 1975 [Safety of Sports Grounds] Act requires the holder of the certificate before carrying out any proposals to alter or extend the stadium or any of its installations while a Safety Certificate is in operation to give notice of those proposals to the local authority . . .
> The Club complied with the requirement. Having received notice of the alterations to the pens and the barriers, the local authority ought, in my view, to have amended the Safety Certificate accordingly. They did not do so.

The local authority in question was Sheffield City Council, which assumed responsibility for the safety certificate in 1986, when South Yorkshire County Council was abolished.

Taylor recorded that David Bownes, Sheffield City Council's chief licensing officer, 'knew very little' about football grounds. He had read the report passed to him on handover by South Yorkshire County Council, and he presumed everything was running smoothly.

In fairness to Bownes, he had indicated that the ground's

safety certificate was giving him cause for concern. This led to a call for a new certificate, work on which was begun in June 1986. But when Forest and Liverpool came to Hillsborough for their FA Cup semi-final in April 1988, the new draft had still not been finalised. A final draft was circulated on 30 March 1989, ten days after the FA had given Hillsborough the green light for its third successive semi-final.

In the days following Liverpool's FA Cup quarter-final win over Brentford, in March 1989, Peter Robinson phoned the FA at Lancaster Gate, requesting that Old Trafford stage the semi-final, in light of complaints from Liverpool supporters the previous year; failing this, he urged that if Hillsborough were to be selected, Liverpool should be allocated the Kop and Forest the Leppings Lane. Graham Kelly, the FA's chief executive, did not pass on Robinson's concerns when the Match and Grounds Committee sat to approve the venue. There seemed little point: the South Yorkshire Police were opposed to the idea, and as Kelly would explain to Lord Justice Taylor, 'the staging club and the FA are really bound to accept the view of the police'.

However, the police Operational Order for 1989 neglected to mention the serious crushing in pens 3 and 4 in 1988. Sheffield Wednesday similarly failed to notify the FA of any problems – they later denied knowledge of a crush the previous year. For their part, the FA failed to properly consider whether Hillsborough was a suitable venue for 54,000 neutral supporters, and they did not consult Sheffield Wednesday, or Sheffield City Council.

Nonetheless, two days after the disaster, on 17 April 1989, dazed but on the defensive, Graham Kelly told the BBC's *Newsnight*: 'There was a lot of planning went into the match in conjunction with the club and in conjunction with the police.'

The FA appear to have succumbed to a disease running rife in Britain in the 1980s. It was identified by Lord Justice Sheen, who chaired an inquiry into the sinking of a Townsend-Thoresen ferry on departure from Zeebrugge, in Belgium, in March 1987. Sheen blamed the tragedy, in which 193 passengers and crew drowned or died of hypothermia, on a 'disease of sloppiness' at every level of the Townsend-Thoresen shipping line. The ferry had set off while its bow doors were still open, and its car decks had flooded, causing the ship to capsize. For weeks, it lay off the coast of Belgium on its side. While Townsend-Thoresen moved quickly to remove their distinctive 'TT' logo from the wreck, the ship's name was tilted to the sky for the world to see: *Herald of Free Enterprise*.

Between Zeebrugge and the end of the decade, Britain was hit by a succession of disasters. As Iain McLean and Martin Johnes describe in *Aberfan: Government and Disasters*, between 1966 and 1979 there had been five disasters in the UK with a death toll greater than 30; between 1985 and 1989 alone there were ten.

After Zeebrugge came the King's Cross fire, in November 1987: 31 people died after a discarded match ignited a fire beneath an escalator at one of London's busiest underground stations. The blaze was fuelled by debris on the underside of the wooden stairs, which had not been cleaned since the 1940s. In July 1988, 167 people were killed on the Piper Alpha oil rig in the North Sea, after a gas leak ignited flames a hundred metres high. Piper Alpha's operator, Occidental, was found guilty of inadequate maintenance and safety procedures. In December 1988, 35 people died in a rail crash at Clapham, in south London, after incorrect wiring work caused a signal to show green when it should have shown red. An inquiry found that a major safety project had been delegated to mid-level technical staff. Poorly supervised, and tired after months of voluntary seven-day-week shifts, they were tasked with re-signalling the busiest railway junction in Britain.

Terrorists killed 270 people when a bomb exploded aboard a PanAm jet over Lockerbie in December 1988. The following month, 47 died at Kegworth, when a technical fault brought down a plane beside the M1, in Leicestershire. Purley is almost a forgotten footnote, and yet five people died in a train crash here in March 1989. On releasing the train driver, after he had served four months of a 12-month sentence for manslaughter, Lord Latham said that 'something about the infrastructure of this particular junction was causing mistakes to be made'. Before the year was out, Hillsborough and the sinking of the *Marchioness* on the River Thames would claim the lives of 147 others.

If Britain appeared to be falling apart at the seams, it was easy to argue that the rot had set in at the top – that as deregulation of state assets gathered pace, and investment lagged behind profiteering, the Tories' laissez-faire agenda had been interpreted as a licence to disregard public safety. However, Professor David Parker, the UK government's official historian of privatisation, told me: 'I've not seen any evidence of a desire among the Thatcher governments to pare back health and safety. Public spending fell in the 1980s as a percentage of GDP [from 44.6 per cent to 39.1 per cent], but that came about not through

actual cuts in public spending but because Thatcher managed
to restrict the growth in public spending to a rate lower than
the growth in GDP.' However, as Parker notes, 'The cutbacks
in the early '80s fell largely in capital expenditure, which can
be deferred.'

Thus, investment in society's infrastructure, or hardware,
was often postponed. A similar thinking appeared to prevail at
Hillsborough. In 1978, safety assessors found that the ground
failed to meet the minimum standards recommended in the
Green Guide. So between 1978 and October 1988, Sheffield
Wednesday received £430,000 from the Football Trust to invest
in 21 safety projects, plus a grant of £595,000 for the improvement of the huge Spion Kop – over £1 million worth of ground
improvements paid for by someone else. But, in 1985, the club
declined the means to manage the safe influx of supporters into
their away end because it might be too expensive.

Out there in the country, on the boats, rigs and railways,
the disease of sloppiness was rampant. Perhaps it was under-
standable, in this context, that on 16 April 1989, after 94 people
were pronounced dead in a football stadium without a valid
safety certificate, Graham Kelly told *Newsnight*: 'There was no
reason, up until six minutes past three yesterday, to doubt the
adequacy of all the arrangements for the safety of everybody
concerned.'

The *Herald of Free Enterprise* capsized a few months before
Thatcherism reached its high-water mark. After their re-election
in June 1987, the Tories appeared invincible: here was a prime
minister who had won a war, survived a bomb and defeated
the miners. Now, with a majority of 102, Mrs Thatcher was

determined to press home the economic and social reform she had been incubating during her first, turbulent two terms. And it was now that she gave her most enduring message to the British people. In the autumn of 1987, in an interview with *Woman's Own*, the prime minister said: 'There is no such thing as society. There are individual men and women, and there are families.'

With society dismissed as a relic, Britain was introduced to TINA – the idea that There Is No Alternative to the market. It was during this third Thatcher government that privatisation gathered pace: there were share flotations in electricity, water and steel, BP, Rolls-Royce and British Airways, to follow the deregulation of the City of London, or 'Big Bang', in 1986. Britain had become a flexible place to live and do business: its people were no longer reliant on or restricted by the old sureties; the citizen was reimagined as the consumer-stakeholder.

But one group of people remained largely out of reach. Football supporters were not rushing to join the new, blue Jerusalem. While English teams dominated Europe from 1977– 82, their supporters had turned the country into a pariah state. After a decade of sporadic violence, English football reached its nadir at the European Cup final in May 1985. At the decrepit Heysel stadium in Brussels, 39 people – mostly Juventus fans, but neutrals too – died when a wall collapsed during running battles with Liverpool supporters. The FA moved swiftly to ban English clubs from European football.

It would be absurd to deny that hooliganism was a problem in the 1980s. But in 1984/5, and for the first time in decades, attendances at grounds across England had been showing a small but steady increase. Lord Justice Taylor concluded that this sprang from a confidence among 'the decent majority of spectators that violence in the ground is under control'.

In the House of Commons, Denis Howell, the former Labour sports minister, tried to impress upon the government the notion that hooliganism was only a weekend manifestation of deep-rooted social frustration. He might have pointed to the fact that in 1985/6, when all eyes were turned to 'the English disease', arrest rates at football matches fell 51 per cent from the previous season.

There was scope for further improvement, if the appetite were there. In the late 1980s, football was contributing around £200 million a year to the Exchequer (around £400 million in today's money). But Howell was up against a government, and its media supporters, who had declared war on football. In 1985, the *Sunday Times* railed that the national game was 'a slum sport played in slum stadiums, and increasingly watched by slum people who deter decent folk from turning up'. There could be no place for this: society was out, the market was in; Britain was moving on, and football must too. In March 1989, a month before Hillsborough, Tory peer Lord Onslow boasted that the government was determined to deal with the 'members of the yob class' who attended football matches.

These were not rogue voices. As Kenneth Clarke MP later admitted, by the late 1980s Thatcher had grouped football supporters alongside militant trade unions and the IRA as 'the enemy within'. The process of introducing Britain to TINA necessitated nothing less than social and economic confrontation. By 1989, the unions had been tamed, and the IRA had found Thatcher bombproof. Football supporters were left in no doubt that there could only be one winner.

Now, Colin Moynihan, the former Olympic coxswain and minister for sport, was tasked with speeding up the introduction of the Football Spectators Bill, which would require football fans to carry identity cards to every league, cup and international match played in England and Wales. Despite fierce opposition to the Bill – driven largely by the Football Supporters' Association – the Tories' course was set. One further indiscretion among English football supporters and the Bill, surely, would become law.

In the meantime, the police would be asked to contain this enemy within.

When the FA faxed its request for the use of Hillsborough to Sheffield on 20 March 1989, the experienced match commander, Chief Superintendent Brian Mole, was in command of F Division, whose remit included Hillsborough. However, Mole was due to be removed from his post on 25 March, against his will. Either no one in South Yorkshire thought to inform the FA of this, or the alarm bells failed to ring at Lancaster Gate.

Chief Superintendent Mole's transfer, to Barnsley, was highly controversial; for years, the South Yorkshire Police passed it off as part of a routine reshuffle. Others believed the transfer was ordered by the Home Office, compelled to act after an initiation prank played by officers under Mole's command had backfired spectacularly.

In his seminal account of the disaster, *Hillsborough: The Truth*, Professor Phil Scraton reported how, in October 1988, a police probationer was ordered to 'a suspected break-in' in the Ranmoor district of Sheffield. When the probationer, Ian Bailey, arrived at the scene, he was seized by masked men who handcuffed him, put a gun to his head and pulled down his trousers. Terrified, he saw something pointed at his face, and a flash: fortunately, it was just a camera. His attackers put away what turned out to be air pistols and took off their masks. Horrified to find that his assailants were fellow officers enjoying an initiation prank, Bailey threw up over himself.

Bailey's father was outraged, and his complaint is thought to have landed, eventually, in the home secretary's in-tray. On 25 March 1989, Chief Superintendent Brian Mole was forced to relinquish command of F Division and move to Barnsley. Barely a week after the FA accepted the South Yorkshire Police's conditions for hosting the semi-final at Hillsborough, the experienced match commander was replaced by David Duckenfield. He had not policed the ground in a decade.

On 22 March 1989, Duckenfield was due to meet Mole and other officers for a handover briefing. Inspector Frank Brayford, now retired, claims that Duckenfield didn't turn up. Duckenfield insists he was present, but that Mole was so disgruntled by his move to Barnsley that he essentially blanked him. The minutes of the meeting have disappeared. What isn't in doubt is that Duckenfield adopted Mole's operational order, with one striking difference: the number of police personnel (mostly at the Leppings Lane end) would be reduced from the previous year – by no fewer than three inspectors, five sergeants and 58 constables.

On 29 March, Duckenfield met with his own planning team, and made only a few minor amendments to the Order. Unfortunately, as Professor Scraton discovered, no mention had been made at Mole's handover meeting of the crushing that had occurred in pens 3 and 4 of the Leppings Lane at the previous year's semi-final. Scraton also found that an earlier warning had gone unheeded. In June 1986, an inspector had written to a senior officer about the serious danger of a bottle-neck forming outside the Leppings Lane, around the turnstiles. He stated that 'the redesigned turnstiles do not give anything like the access to the ground . . . needed by away fans'.

In early April, Chief Superintendent Duckenfield went to Hillsborough to familiarise himself with the stadium. But the matches he attended were a poor dress rehearsal for an FA Cup semi-final: Wimbledon and then Millwall contributed to gates of just 15,777 and 18,358. Despite visiting the rear of the Leppings Lane terrace – the outer concourse and turnstiles – Duckenfield did not acquaint himself with the pens. Perhaps, as far as the chief superintendent was concerned, there was no need: he was under the impression that the management of supporters inside the stadium was the responsibility of Sheffield Wednesday's match stewards.

As Forest and Liverpool fans arrived in Sheffield on 15 April 1989, the South Yorkshire Police were themselves in high spirits: they were looking forward to the game, enjoying the spring sunshine and confident they were dealing with two sets of well-behaved supporters. Many officers later attested that they would have worked the shift for nothing. There seemed little that could possibly go wrong. And yet the Operational Order for the day was a plan in keeping with the sentiments of the prime minister and Lord Onslow, for the predominant mindset it had encouraged among the South Yorkshire Police was not one of owing a duty of care to the fans, but of containing the threat of hooligans – an enemy.

The Operational Order that Duckenfield distributed among the 1,122 police officers under his command that day gave a general strategic overview; there was also a detailed account of the responsibilities of every 'serial' (or unit of police officers – typically, eight to ten PCs reporting to one sergeant and an inspector). As Professor Scraton reported in *Hillsborough: The Truth*:

> Twenty-one officers were given responsibility for policing the perimeter track . . . They were instructed to pay 'particular attention to prevent any person climbing the fence to gain access to the ground'. The gates in the perimeter fences were to remain 'bolted at all times . . . with no one allowed access to the track from the terraces without the consent of a senior officer'.

As Scraton notes, this latter instruction 'was in capitals and underlined'.

Twenty officers and two sergeants were deployed to police the Leppings Lane terrace. Their instructions were to enforce ground rules concerning alcohol, missiles, banners and weapons. No mention was made of crowd management or safety.

Moreover, Chief Superintendent Duckenfield was about to take charge of over 50,000 people without a clear idea who was responsible for their safety inside the stadium. Duckenfield believed the management of the crowd was the responsibility of the club; both Sheffield Wednesday and the FA would later tell Taylor that the responsibility lay with the police.

Just after midday, 10,000 people were heading for the Leppings Lane terrace. The South Yorkshire Police had deployed almost a third of its entire force to the match. And yet there was nothing in Duckenfield's Operational Order advising his officers how to prevent a bottleneck around the outer concourse near the turnstiles, how to identify whether the pens were exceeding capacity, or when to close the tunnel to the Leppings Lane.

The police were at the ground early. At just after 10 a.m., Chief Superintendent Duckenfield held a briefing in the North Stand. He was followed by Superintendent Marshall, who would take control of the area to the rear of the Leppings Lane, around the turnstiles. Intelligence briefings followed, and by 10.30 a.m. the police had dispersed to their posts. For the next few hours, the build-up passed without incident: the turnstiles opened just after midday, and a steady stream of supporters arrived, emptying off the trains at Sheffield Midland and Wadsley Bridge, or arriving by coach and car. At around midday, Chief Inspector Creaser asked Superintendent Murray if the pens on the Leppings Lane were to be filled one at a time. Murray replied that all the pens would be opened at the same time. The fans, he said, would be free 'to find their own level'.

I was one of many thousands to arrive at the stadium at about 1.30 p.m. We had parked the car a mile or so from Hillsborough, and as the four of us walked down to the ground, it was just as I remembered it from the previous year: dreary, dated, ramshackle.

At around 2 p.m. I walked down the tunnel and onto the Leppings Lane. A cold, sinking sense of familiarity crept over me. I didn't like this terrace, and the Kop looked magnificent. Still, the pitch was the colour of a ripening lime, and the sun was flickering over the hills around the city. From the Leppings Lane, the stadium certainly looked impressive. I squinted for signs of Liverpool supporters mingling peaceably among the Forest fans on the Kop, and thought I saw a knot to the far left, in the corner. My brother, a Forest fan, was on the Kop; I was already looking forward to buying him a consolation beer tonight. To the right of the pitch was the South Stand, home to the press box, the dugouts and the police control room. Inside, David Duckenfield and his officers had a clear view over the West Stand and the Leppings Lane.

As I emerged from the tunnel leading to pen 3 and into the sunshine, I remember thinking: 'Where would you rather be on a day like this?' The previous year, I had stood towards the front third of the terrace and got lost in a surge. Now, I leant idly on one of the crush barriers, drinking in the sight of a big Victorian stadium filling up on FA Cup semi-final day. The other Liverpool supporter from my car made his way towards the front, and the blue perimeter fence. I was happy where I was: the atmosphere was excitable, tense, expectant. A beach ball was launched into the air. I moved slightly this way and that as the sun moved across the terrace, and chatted briefly with lads who came and went in search of a better 'spec'.

At 2.30 p.m., Chief Superintendent Duckenfield, positioned in the control room with Superintendent Murray, noticed a severe build-up of fans outside the turnstiles on Leppings Lane. Many Liverpool supporters had been held up by roadworks coming across the Pennines and by intermittent police checks around Sheffield. Now, the crush outside the gates was becoming a serious concern, but the fans were in good time, nonetheless. Printed on their tickets was the instruction: 'Please take your place 15 minutes before kick-off.' They were early.

Peter Rankin, a 19-year-old biology undergraduate from Liverpool, had seen problems developing half an hour earlier, when he arrived at 2 p.m., with his friend Brian. 'I was immediately concerned about the scenes at the entrance to the Leppings Lane,' Rankin remembers. 'There was a large crowd gathered in a funnel-like entrance system, and no one seemed to be managing the situation. We asked a policeman how else we could get into the ground with our tickets; he pointed back to the crowd and said that was our only way in. Reluctantly, we joined the back of the crowd, and over the next 45 minutes we slowly edged forwards towards the turnstiles . . .'

Duckenfield's officers had not put a queuing system in place. And they were now dealing with the problems inherent in the stadium's design: the West Stand and the North Stand together held 24,256 spectators, who were expected to pass through just 23 turnstiles. The rest of the stadium held 29,800 spectators, who were able to pass through 60 turnstiles. Thousands of people were now edging towards the narrow apron of land set off Leppings Lane road, a concourse no bigger than a few tennis courts. Duckenfield radioed Superintendent Marshall outside. Marshall replied: 'With half an hour to kick-off we should get them all in on time.'

Inside, on the Leppings Lane, it was getting strangely uncomfortable in pen 3. I had been leaning on a crush barrier, but it was getting tight now, so I shrugged a couple of people off my back and pushed my way under. Ten minutes later, it would have been too late. By then, at about 2.40 p.m., the crowd around me were wheezing and heaving and settling slowly, grudgingly, like cement. My feet were wrapped up in a slight surge, and for half a minute or so I moved softly on the back of other people's legs, before finding solid ground again. But I was now towards the front third of the terrace, and no longer able to move freely. People were starting to jockey for position, using elbows, knees, even heads. 'Sorry, lad, sorry, but . . . I can't move.' Gradually, people around me began to sweat; others were pleading with the people behind them for room. The response was the same: 'I can't move.'

I remember thinking, 'This is ridiculous. My head is tilted into a channel of sky. How are we going to see the game like this?' Over in pen 4, to my left, Damian Kavanagh, a 20-year-old from Skelmersdale, was experiencing similar difficulties. 'I was always taught in a tight crowd to keep my arms up,' he says, 'with my fists towards my throat. I was doing that now.'

Outside, the build-up of fans was almost beyond control. Police radio contact was breaking up, and officers were starting to panic. In pens 3 and 4, the crowd was getting tighter. Hands were pressed on my back, and feet against my legs. Someone's breath was blowing hot on my hair. Rival chants were bouncing the length of the stadium, but no one was coming to help.

On the concourse outside, the police had lost control. Mike Bracken, a 20-year-old from Merseyside, was in serious distress. 'The police just did not appear to have a plan,' he wrote in the *Guardian*, in 2009. 'Unable to move my arms and facing a metal gate, I saw others begin to struggle.'

At that precise moment, 2.47 p.m., Superintendent Marshall, engulfed in the crowd not far from Bracken, was 'having to shout to make himself heard on the radio'. Fearing fatalities, Marshall radioed Duckenfield and asked him to open a large concertina gate to relieve the pressure on the turnstiles. Duckenfield refused. 'It would have defeated the objectives of the Operational Order,' he later explained to Lord Justice Taylor. 'Drunken fans may get in . . . people who had got missiles, or people who were without tickets.'

By now, Mike Bracken was screaming at a policeman to open the exit gate he was crushed against. 'I was sweating and panicking, then I felt the gate open briefly and I fell through it. Moments later, it closed again.' The gate had been opened momentarily to eject a fan from the stadium, but Bracken was through it, and safe. 'I think I was the second person to get through,' he recalled. 'The calmness inside on the inner concourse, compared with the bedlam outside, was staggering.'

Outside, tempers were fraying. Police officers and supporters were desperately passing children over the turnstiles. It was just over ten minutes until kick-off, and there were thousands of people still to get through the turnstiles. Inside, the central pens had been bursting for nearly 15 minutes. By now, my legs, my backside, my arms and my chest were numb. I could move my eyes, my mouth and my head, but no more. I was now paralysed from the neck down. My right foot seemed to move involuntarily, until I realised that it wasn't on the ground but planted on another man's calf. Around me, people were passing out.

A photo taken from the North Stand – directly opposite the police control room in the South Stand, but giving a similarly panoramic view – shows how pens 3 and 4 were dangerously overcrowded and that the pens either side of them were sparsely populated; some fans in pen 5 were sat on the terrace reading newspapers.

One of Hillsborough's glaring safety deficiencies was about

to turn an emergency into a catastrophe. There was only one tunnel leading from the inner concourse to the Leppings Lane terrace, and above it stood a sign marked 'STANDING'. It appeared to be the only access to the entire terrace, and yet that tunnel led only to pens 3 and 4; access to the wing pens 2 and 5, via other routes, was poorly signposted. Moreover, every ticket for the entire Leppings Lane had the letter B printed on it, the same letter that was marked on the sign above the tunnel. To most supporters arriving on the concourse, it seemed the only route into the stadium.

And yet, by ten to three, people already in pen 3 were sweating, swearing and hyperventilating. Some were crying. Hundreds were screaming for help from the police across the fence, but still no one was coming. The players seemed to be on the pitch – there was a roar around the ground. But around me people were now turning blue. They were within feet of me, and yet I literally couldn't lift a finger to help them. It felt as if every part of my body was being compressed and stretched at the same time. My lungs were burning and freezing in alternate breaths. A voice behind me: 'Open the fucking gate!'

At 2.52 p.m., someone did open the gate. But it wasn't the gate in the perimeter fence that would have allowed people to escape onto the pitch; it was exit gate C, back out by the turnstiles. At around 2.50 p.m., Superintendent Marshall had repeated his request that Chief Superintendent Duckenfield allow the exit gates to be opened. 'Open the gates,' he shouted down his radio, 'or someone is going to be seriously injured or killed.'

Mike Bracken was now on the inner concourse between exit gate C and the tunnel leading to pens 3 and 4. Sweating and in distress, he was recovering with a carton of Kia-Ora when the exit gate was drawn back. Around 2,000 people now moved towards him and straight for the tunnel to pens 3 and 4. With no police officers deployed to seal the tunnel, Bracken did his best to steer the fans away. 'Don't go down there, lads,' he begged the supporters coming towards him, 'it's gonna be packed!' They passed him without comment, into the tunnel. CCTV footage shows many of them clearly relieved to be out of the crush on the outer concourse and happily, calmly, walking to their deaths. 'Every day since, I have wondered if I could, and should, have done more,' Bracken says.

Now, he hurried from the tunnel entrance to the steps at the side of the Leppings Lane terrace: the scene across the pens, slightly below that which greeted Duckenfield in the control room, left Bracken in a state of shock. Recovering, he ran to the gates of the South Stand, shouting 'People are going to die!' at police and Sheffield Wednesday club officials. 'They looked at me in silence,' he says.

Those 2,000 fans that Bracken had tried to turn back were now compressed in a narrow tunnel, with a one-in-six downward gradient, and ploughed into pens 3 and 4. Peter Carney, a 30-year-old from Liverpool, was walking down the tunnel when 'Whoosh! This surge came and I was off my feet,' he remembers. 'I was just . . . thrown into the stadium. I actually entered the ground with my back to the pitch.'

Peter Rankin and his friend Brian were also heading for pen 3. 'But as we entered the inner concourse, I looked down the tunnel and I could see a steep slope leading to a terrace that already looked full,' Rankin recalls. 'The crowd appeared to be moving abnormally: people were getting carried around in circles and were struggling to stay on their feet. I went over to two stewards by the steps that led to the upper part of the stand, and I asked them if we could go up the steps. One of them looked at our tickets and pointed towards the tunnel. I said, "It looks packed in there," and he shrugged his shoulders.'

Brian went down the tunnel, entered the crowd in pen 3 and got swept away. Peter stopped at the end of the tunnel: 'I was really anxious now, but I saw Brian turn around in the pen and signal to me to join him. I managed to reach him, but the pressure was getting worse and worse. A few minutes before the game kicked off, I said to Brian, "We need to go, now."'

The momentum of the crowd had carried Peter and Brian far enough across pen 3 that they could now climb over the radial fence into the relatively empty pen 2. It also carried dozens of others around Peter Carney nearly as far as the perimeter fence at the front of pens 3 and 4. Around 12 feet from that fence, it felt like someone had hit me between the shoulder blades with a hammer. But I was fortunate: I was hit square in the back and driven forward; some of those around me were clipped on the shoulder and went down. People cried out and passed out almost immediately. The screaming was unbearable. Crushed for nearly 15 minutes now, I was still conscious, but starting to fade. The man beneath me, on whose legs I had been standing, had been silent for a while. Pens 3 and 4 were meant to hold 2,200 people; there were now more than 3,000 of us in there.

Over in pen 4, Damian Kavanagh had managed to climb above the crowd and crawl over the heads and shoulders of people to the fence, about 20 feet away. 'As I was trying to get out through the gate and onto the pitch this copper was wrestling me. "You fucking twat!" he shouted, and he tried to push me back into the pen. "No dice, mate," I said. He threw me on the track beside the pitch, but I was like . . . fine, fine, I was out. You never argued with the police, but there was no way I was going back in that pen.'

In pen 3, it was bedlam. A crush barrier towards the front buckled and gave way. Peter Carney remembers that 'There was a gap in the crowd all of a sudden, which was weird. It was like, "What the fuck's that?" The people leaning on the barrier had gone down as it buckled, the people leaning on their backs went down too, and there was a third row went down on top. There was a stack of bodies.'

That crush barrier went down with a loud snap, but I didn't see it. I was losing my peripheral vision, and my breathing. Every minute or so, 50 or 60 people would wheel as one under the pressure from behind; as they moved, impaling someone's chest or ribs on metal or flesh or bone, a voice would cry out, then fall silent. The crowd would settle again, helpless and exhausted, trying to draw breath and scream. But the energy was already building up again somewhere behind. We girded ourselves for the movement, tried to arch paralysed backs to protect both our ribs in front and those fans around us – people who seemed to be falling, sinking beneath us. But it was hopeless. The swell would eddy and build and break, and as we moved in a lump of tangled, compacted limbs, someone else would cry out.

Behind me, Peter Carney was about to have a near-death experience. 'Whenever I see a fish come up to the surface, that's how I must have been,' he says. 'My head was tilted back, gasping for air. Then I lost consciousness.' Carney had an out-of-body experience: he recalls passing out, then travelling down an endless pipe, filled with clouds. 'It seemed to go on for ever.

Then I'm looking down on the terrace, on a perfect circle of people, and I'm in the middle, and my head's lower than their heads, and I'm going down.'

Carney was lucky: he collapsed to the deck in a pocket of air, perhaps beneath the forked legs of a crush barrier, protected from the feet of those around him. He would be picked up by fellow supporters once the crush abated and carried back up the tunnel, unconscious.

Over to my left, pushed up against the radial fence beside pen 4, Steve, a 19-year-old student from Merseyside, was literally fighting for his life. 'I knew I had to get to the front of the pen to climb over the fence, and I was throwing people aside,' he says. 'There was this lad, with long, lank hair – that's all I remember about him – and I was wrestling with him to get to the fence.' Steve, in his panic, punched the other man in the head. 'I've no idea whether he lived or died . . . I've had to live with this every day since. But it was literally me or him.'

Steve managed to climb the fence, and joined the rescue operation now under way on the pitch.

Around 12 feet from that fence, I was going nowhere. I was vaguely aware that the game had kicked off, and that people were dead on their feet: with no room in which to fall, they were carried in the fitful surges like shop dummies. In pockets, the air above pens 3 and 4 was now thick with the smell of excrement and urine as people, slowly being asphyxiated, lost control of their bodily functions.

I had no control or feeling in my body from the neck down. I was exhausted, and stiff with shock. Unable to move, too exhausted now to shout, I began to take in the final minutes of my life. In those moments, I thought about my family, my friends, and mostly about the girl I had started going out with four months earlier, and I realised how much I loved her.

Who had allowed this to happen? People had been screaming for their lives for ten or 15 minutes now. First, 'Help! Help us!' Then, 'Open the gate, there are people dying in here!' Now, 'Help! There are people dead in here!'

Three men directly in front of me were going – slowly turning blue, their faces changing from a ghostly pallor to a pale violet, their lips almost trembling with cold. Some people were covered in vomit. Some were weeping. Others were gibbering, trying to black out what was happening.

I was losing strength; I knew I couldn't survive much longer. My head was trapped in a channel, looking slightly to the left, to the North Stand, when into that channel walked a policeman. He stopped and looked into the terrace and straight into my eyes. I knew I had him, and I slowly, simply mouthed the words: 'Help. Help me. Help.' The police officer narrowed his eyes, looked at me keenly and paused for a few seconds. Then he screwed up his mouth and smiled, uncertainly, and he walked off.

In the next few moments, I knew that I was about to die. Some people around me had been dead for some time – ten minutes, perhaps. I had no strength left, and something like sleep was beckoning. Then, from the back of my mind came a voice I had never heard before and have never heard since: 'Fifty seconds,' it said, 'you've got 50 seconds left.' As those seconds began to tick down, I summoned up every last ounce of strength left in my body to shove people off me, lever myself onto their shoulders, climb up and escape. But as I heaved and pressed and heaved again, I didn't move an inch. Those pressed tight around me were heavy and wet, and some would never move again. My head sank forward, and I gave up.

As the seconds passed, I thought again of my girlfriend, my family and my mates. I knew that my brother would have to identify my body shortly, and I didn't want him to find me with a look of pain on my face.

In those last few minutes on the Leppings Lane, I was overcome with euphoria. In the final few moments before death, the brain can flood the body with endorphins to protect against pain. Now, I began to float away, taking in the end of my life. I looked up at that beautiful blue day, opened my mouth towards the sky and sucked what I could out of it. And then I closed my eyes.

A few moments later, they opened. The police had finally unlocked the gate in the perimeter fence and were swearing at us. And I had survived.

Out on the concourse, someone laid Peter Carney down with the others who had died and who had been brought out of the tunnel. A jumper was placed over his head. But then Carney woke up. 'I came to,' he remembers, 'and everything was brilliantly coloured. The pain in my legs was unbelievable. I just remember thinking: "I'm here, I'm here . . . I'm here on this earth."'

A few yards away, Mike Bracken was witnessing scenes that would haunt him for years. Bodies were being raced back up the tunnel from the pens. 'I watched fans reason calmly and logically with the police while their friends clung to life,' he wrote in the *Guardian*. 'Amazingly, several police officers denied people access to the bodies. I saw fans being pushed and blamed by police for the grotesque scene I was witnessing.

Several young men, little older than me, appealed for calm, aware that the police would welcome any excuse to blame fans. Their self-control was remarkable.'

Back in pen 3, the crush around me abated as the police came through the gate in the perimeter fence. A group of people in front of me – who had had their backs to me throughout the crush, and who I thought were alive – simply keeled over and hit the concrete. A heap of tangled corpses piled up off the ground, three feet high. After a few seconds, I saw a limb move and realised someone was alive in there. One police officer who came through the gate said the scene 'was like Belsen'.

A few minutes later, Graham Kelly and Glen Kirton of the FA, accompanied by Graham Mackrell, secretary of Sheffield Wednesday, went to the police control room in the South Stand. There, they asked Chief Superintendent David Duckenfield a question that millions of people transfixed in front of *Grandstand* were now asking: what on earth is going on here?

Before the day was out, 94 people were dead. Two days later, a 14-year-old boy had his life-support machine switched off. The death toll would remain at 95 until 1993, when – after four years in a persistent vegetative state – Tony Bland's life-prolonging treatment was withdrawn.

Mike Bracken, Peter Carney, Damian Kavanagh, Peter Rankin, Steve and I were severely traumatised, and experienced symptoms associated with post-traumatic stress disorder for many years. Today, Mike Bracken is chief digital officer for the Co-operative Group. Between 2010 and 2015 he was executive director of the Government Digital Service, and he was awarded a CBE in 2014 for his services to digital transformation and his work in developing youth football in Hackney. In 2012, Peter Carney stepped down from his job as a play-development worker, providing after-school and holiday activities for young adults; he now runs Soccer in the City, a minibus tour of Liverpool's football landscape. Damian Kavanagh has spent his career in insurance; today, he works as a pensions administrator. Dr Peter Rankin is a consultant paediatric neuropsychologist at Great Ormond Street Hospital for Children and chair of the British Psychological Society's Division of Neuropsychology. Steve joined one of Britain's biggest police forces in the early 1990s and became a detective. He has since left the police and is training to be a solicitor. These are the survivors I know. Football supporters were just like us in the 1980s.

But, in 1989, we were something else too. At Anfield's Shankly Gates stands a memorial to the people who died around us and beneath us. It is a list simply of names and ages; there is nothing to indicate what those 96 people gave to society, or what they might have gone on to do. On 15 April 1989, they went to a football match and were crushed to death. And in the weeks, months and 23 years that followed, the likes of Mike Bracken, Peter Carney, Damian Kavanagh, Peter Rankin, Steve and me would be held responsible for their deaths.

2 : A Cosy Stitch-up

Our car slipped out of Sheffield at around 5 p.m. that after-noon and onto the M1, heading south to Nottingham. It is doubtful whether one of the country's busiest motorways has ever been quieter. We passed thousands of cars, but few of the people inside them appeared to be talking. It wasn't only the 54,000 spectators who had witnessed the disaster unfold; much of the country was now tuning in to the BBC, and those who weren't at home in front of the TV were listening for the latest news on BBC Radio 2's *Sports Report*.

The programme featured the late football broadcaster Peter Jones, who had gone to Hillsborough to commentate live on an FA Cup semi-final and found himself witness to a tragedy that left him a broken man. At around 5 p.m. that day, Jones signed off with his final report from Hillsborough: it remains one of the most poignant pieces of commentary in broadcasting history. 'Well,' he said,

> I think the biggest irony is that the sun is shining now, and Hillsborough's quiet, and over there, to the left, the green Yorkshire hills . . . and who would've known that people would die here in the stadium this afternoon.
>
> I don't necessarily want to reflect on Heysel, but I was there that night, broadcasting with Emlyn Hughes, and he was sitting behind me this afternoon, and after half an

hour of watching stretchers going out and oxygen cylinders being brought in, and ambulance sirens screaming, he touched me on the shoulder and he said, 'I can't take any more,' and Emlyn Hughes left.

The gymnasium here, at Hillsborough, is being used as a mortuary for the dead, and at this moment stewards have got little paper bags, and they're gathering up the personal belongings of the spectators . . . and there are red and white scarves of Liverpool, and red and white bobble hats of Liverpool, and red and white rosettes of Liverpool, and nothing else.

And the sun shines now.

On 17 April 1989, the home secretary, Douglas Hurd, appointed Lord Taylor of Gosforth to 'inquire into the events at Sheffield Wednesday football ground on 15 April 1989, and to make recommendations about the needs of crowd control and safety at sports events'.

Remarkably, Lord Justice Taylor – a regular at St James' Park in his younger days – was tasked with presenting an interim report in time for the start of the next football season, barely four months hence. If it was unseemly that the inquiry into the deaths of 95 people should present its key findings in time for the new season, it was as nothing compared with the response of the South Yorkshire Police.

On the morning of 16 April, Margaret Thatcher flew into Sheffield to inspect the Leppings Lane. The dated news footage of the PM picking her way through the wreckage looks grainy, almost spectral now, but it is not difficult to make out her escorts: there is Douglas Hurd, her home secretary; there is

Graham Mackrell, the secretary and safety officer of Sheffield Wednesday, a club without a valid safety certificate to stage the semi-final; there is her press secretary, Bernard Ingham, with South Yorkshire's Chief Constable Peter Wright and Chief Superintendent Duckenfield; Irvine Patnick, Conservative MP for Sheffield Hallam, is with them. There were no survivors to be heard on the Leppings Lane that day.

What followed remains one of the great unknowns about Hillsborough, even in the wake of the Hillsborough Independent Panel's exhaustive research. Many of the families of those who died are convinced that a secret meeting took place, soon afterwards, between the prime minister's party and South Yorkshire Police's top brass. Secret, because no minutes have ever been discovered and no one has ever confirmed what was discussed, or whether a meeting even took place. And yet it doesn't take a rabid conspiracy theorist to guess at what might have happened that morning, away from the cameras – not when Bernard Ingham would later insist: 'I know what I learnt on the spot. There would have been no Hillsborough if a mob, who were clearly tanked up, had not tried to force their way into the ground. To blame the police is a cop-out.'

So were the government and the police speaking as one? As they escorted the prime minister around Hillsborough that lunchtime, the South Yorkshire Police could reasonably claim that they had only done the PM's bidding – they had been asked to contain 'an enemy within', and they had done so. Moreover, their tactics, enshrined in the Operational Order, were broadly consistent with those deployed by police forces up and down the country every Saturday afternoon.

Besides, this wasn't the first enemy within that the South

Yorkshire Police had been asked to contain by Mrs Thatcher. It is a recorded fact that, while much of the heavy-handed policing during the 1984–5 miners' strike was the work of the Metropolitan Police, a number of the officers on duty at Hillsborough had also fought the miners to a standstill at Orgreave. The running battle between miners and the police at the Orgreave coking plant in South Yorkshire, in June 1984, would prove the defining moment in the year-long strike, and was confirmation, if it were needed, that the police had been deployed by the government to break an industrial dispute.

In 1985, 71 miners were charged with rioting at Orgreave, an offence that carried a potential sentence of life imprisonment. The charges were pressed at the behest of South Yorkshire's chief constable, Peter Wright, but the trial collapsed in 1985, when – after 48 days of police evidence – the prosecution real-ised it could no longer sustain a case.

Each of the miners wrongfully accused received a few thou-sand pounds in compensation, but not a single police officer was called to account for a systemic attempt to fabricate evi-dence. Dozens of police statements – submitted by officers from four forces on duty, detailing the miners' alleged offences – contained uncannily similar phrases, descriptions and accusa-tions. Mark George QC, a barrister who had access to 40 of the statements, later wrote: 'This was wholesale collusion . . . What the police achieved by this device was control of the media.'

As Michael Mansfield QC, who defended three of the acquit-ted miners, said: 'South Yorkshire Police operated a culture of fabricating evidence with impunity.'

Clearly, there was little political will to censure Peter Wright's force: as late as the early 1990s, Margaret Thatcher was still paying tribute to the South Yorkshire Police for facing down what she described in her memoirs as 'a mob' at Orgreave. And, on 16 April 1989, Thatcher flew into Sheffield to hear their account of what happened at Hillsborough.

Douglas Hurd's diary offers a brief but revealing insight: 'To Sheffield, miserably, in cold helicopter with MT. Earpads, so no speech. Briefing with chief constable, who is pale and inarticulate . . . In intensive care, youngsters fight against death or brain damage. Relations sit around. Clearly, there is one, perhaps two, police blunders.'

That wasn't how the police saw it. At 9 a.m. that day, a few hours before he met the prime minister, Peter Wright chaired a meeting of his senior officers on duty the previous day. The minutes record that the first to offer Wright his perspective on the disaster was Chief Superintendent Duckenfield.

'I looked out at 2.30 p.m.,' Duckenfield said. 'The Nottingham fans had got into the Spion Kop and as far as I was concerned it was pretty full; they were in the other areas on the South Stand and it was remarkable as far as I was concerned that the North Stand was almost empty, and also the Leppings Lane stand, particularly on the terracing.'

This is a remarkable statement, given the situation developing in pens 3 and 4 by 2.30 p.m. Nonetheless, Peter Wright asked his officers: 'Can anyone give an explanation as to why they [the Liverpool fans] weren't there?'

Superintendent Marshall replied: 'Because they were drinking outside off-licences.'

It was a view repeatedly put to Wright by some of the officers assembled, who ranged from constables and sergeants to inspectors and chief superintendents. 'So,' Wright said, 'there is no evidence whatsoever of the delay in transit of the fans. The fans arrived at the ground vicinity early enough to go in the ground but instead went drinking.'

A note in the minutes of the meeting reads, in capitals: 'THIS WAS AGREED.' Which makes it appear somewhat odd that no arrests were made – none, according to the minutes. For Inspector Sykes, that would have been 'Virtually impossible, the people who were arriving had been drinking and the sheer mass of numbers of people with drink and . . .'

Chief Constable: 'And if we'd started making arrests we would have . . . Tell me about the radio.'

The meeting continued in this vein: helter-skelter allegations with little supporting evidence – arrest rates, for instance – and Chief Constable Wright completing sentences started by his junior officers, before sliding off on another tangent. When one inspector told the meeting, 'I think that we must make the point that drink played a big part,' Wright replied: 'If drink played a big part, that will emerge. When the police actions were central to an issue like this the last thing we want to be seen to be doing is trying to blame someone else, and I think let other people find that out. I accept that completely. Everybody's saying it and it's true but it is really a question of how that's used.'

Before he drew the meeting to a close, Wright told his men: 'If it is that the drunken, marauding fans – and I thought of this last night – contributed to this, let somebody else say that . . . I don't think that we would be right now to be talking about the animalistic behaviour of fans, the level of drink. Whoever is looking at it overall will find that without any problem.'

Two days later, the *Sheffield Star* reported that 'ticketless thugs staged crush to gain entry, attacked an ambulanceman, threatened firemen, and punched and urinated on policemen as they gave the kiss of life to stricken victims'. Its source? Unnamed officers in the local constabulary.

Next up was Paul Middup, a spokesman for the Police Federation. 'I am sick of hearing how good the crowd were,' he told the *Daily Mail*. 'Just because they weren't tearing each other's throats out doesn't mean they were well-behaved. They were arriving tanked up on drink, and the situation faced by officers trying to control them was quite simply terrifying.' The fans, he said, 'were diving under the bellies of the horses and between their legs, and the only people who do that are either mental or have been drinking very heavily'.

Then, on Wednesday 19 April, Kelvin MacKenzie – who later claimed he was egged on by an MP and a policeman he didn't name – took up the *Sheffield Star*'s headlines, adding his own inimitable gloss. Liverpool fans, his newspaper reported, had offered to sexually abuse a dead girl.

'The Truth' was out.

The media had been frothing at the mouth for a month before Lord Justice Taylor got to work. Over 31 days, between 15 May and 29 June, he heard evidence in Sheffield from 174 witnesses and took a considerable number of written statements. He inspected the stadium, convened a Health and Safety committee, and pored over Sheffield Wednesday's accounts. The FA was summoned, along with Sheffield City Council and the South Yorkshire Police. The West Midlands Police, appointed to assist the inquiry, took 3,776 witness statements, and selected those suitable to go forward to the judge.

Either by accident or by design, key witness statements never found their way to Taylor's desk. A number of doctors at the hospitals in Sheffield joined thousands of witnesses from the Leppings Lane who went unheard. Arguably the most significant omission, however, was Tony Edwards. Edwards was the ambulance attendant whose lonely vehicle was seen by millions of people on *Grandstand*, weaving its way along the pitch almost half an hour after the match was abandoned. His was the only professional ambulance crew to reach the centre of the disaster, after two St John ambulances had been overwhelmed: it's thought the police had prevented 40 other ambulances entering the stadium behind him, after telling those crews that 'the fans are fighting'. They certainly told Edwards this, but he was ordered onto the pitch by a senior ambulance officer.

'There was no fighting!' Edwards told me in 2009, when I reported on Hillsborough for the *Observer*. 'The survivors were deciding who we should deal with. The police weren't. We weren't.'

Edwards suspected that the prompt response of those 40 ambulance crews might have saved many lives. But despite taking his witness statement, the West Midlands Police did not put him forward to Lord Justice Taylor. In fact, said Edwards, 'Taylor was told I didn't exist. The police denied that my ambulance ever made it onto the pitch. But it's there, in their own CCTV footage.' But then, as he told me: 'All these questions Taylor would have had to ask me were key to the mismanagement of Hillsborough. My testimony would have been disastrous for the South Yorkshire Police and ambulance services.'

39

Taylor acknowledged that 'the number of witnesses called were only a small fraction of those from whom statements were or could have been taken'. Nonetheless, he was satisfied that they were 'sufficient in number and reliability'.

As spring rolled on towards summer, the government made polite noises about awaiting the findings of Taylor's inquiry before pressing on with its plans to introduce ID cards for football fans, via the Football Spectators Bill. In private, the Tories were satisfied that they had been dealt a good hand at Hillsborough. John Carlisle MP, one of the chief cheerleaders for ID cards, told the *Daily Mail* on 17 April that the disaster should make 'a dramatic difference' to the government's chances of getting the controversial bill through Parliament.

The Tories could afford to be relaxed: the black-propaganda campaign emanating from South Yorkshire had persuaded much of the country that, sadly, Liverpool fans had killed their own. A tanked-up mob had forced open a gate.

Clearly, the time for pussyfooting around with football fans was over. On 21 April, Colin Welch, parliamentary sketch writer for the *Daily Mail*, summed up Thatcher's position: 'The [Football Spectators] Bill will be there waiting, so to speak, a "vehicle" ready for Taylor to board with his luggage. Whoever opposes it will bear, in her view, a heavy responsibility.'

On 4 August 1989, Lord Justice Taylor published his interim report, into the causes of the Hillsborough disaster. His conclusions were astonishing. The cause of the disaster was overcrowding, and the main reason was 'the failure of police control'. The presence of drunken fans was dismissed as a minor aggravating factor; they were not a cause. If the Leppings Lane's capacity of

10,100 had been exceeded, then it was by no more than 24 – the police allegation of ticketless fans was unfounded. The layout of the turnstiles had created problems the police had failed to anticipate. Crucially, Liverpool fans had not forced open a gate: this was revealed to be a lie on the part of Chief Superintendent Duckenfield – one repeated around the world within the hour. Duckenfield's decision to open exit gate C and not seal off the tunnel that led to the central pens was described by Taylor as 'a blunder of the first magnitude'.

Taylor praised the actions of a number of police officers on duty, who did their best 'in ghastly circumstances'. He also described the reaction of the Liverpool supporters to the chaos that engulfed them as 'magnificent'. However, Taylor found that senior officers on duty had made 'defensive or evasive witnesses' and that 'neither their handling of problems on the day nor their account of it in evidence showed the qualities of leadership to be expected of their rank'. He also found that the quality of evidence given was in 'inverse proportion' to the rank of those police witnesses.

Taylor ruled that the FA had failed to consider in any depth whether the stadium was suitable for the game and that they had neither made an inspection themselves nor consulted either Sheffield City Council or Sheffield Wednesday. Sheffield City Council was lambasted for its failures over the safety certificate: 'The attention given to this licensing function was woefully inadequate,' Taylor said.

And it was now that the real horror of the Leppings Lane was revealed. At around 2.53 p.m. on 15 April, the sudden influx of fans down the tunnel led to pens 3 and 4 bursting with almost 40 per cent more people than they were expected to hold. And yet their capacity had been overestimated in the first place.

In 1985, a drawing from Eastwood & Partners, Sheffield Wednesday's structural engineers, detailed that a safe capacity for pen 3 was 1,200, and for pen 4, 1,000. But as the Health and Safety Executive reported to Taylor, these figures would only have been safe had the strength and spacing of the crush barriers (which helped to regulate the flow of the crowd) complied with the recommendations of the *Green Guide*. They did not. In pen 3, four out of five gaps between the barriers did not conform to recommendations. In pen 4, nine out of ten failed to comply. Ten of the 14 barriers in these pens were also below the recommended height, which not only left many fans bent over them by the weight of people behind, it should also have reduced the calculations of capacity. Taylor reported that, taking into account all of these factors, the safe capacity for pen 3 should have been 822, and for pen 4, 871 – a total of 1,693 people.

However, in his research for the Hillsborough Independent Panel, Professor Phil Scraton found that the HSE had, in fact, reached a far more damning conclusion, one which Taylor overlooked. The HSE recorded that 'if only those barriers which meet the *Green Guide* recommendations were used in the calculation of safe capacity, the allowable numbers of persons able to use the central terraces [pens 3 and 4] would drop to 389 and 540.' The HSE estimated that at the height of the crush, there were over 3,000 people in pens 3 and 4.

In their submission to the Taylor inquiry, the South Yorkshire Police argued that the disaster could be blamed not on their mismanagement but on a defective barrier giving way at the front of pen 3, leading to supporters losing their footing – and to the stack of bodies Peter Carney saw. Taylor would not hear of it. 'Such an unrealistic approach gives cause for anxiety as to whether lessons have been learnt,' he concluded. 'It would have been more seemly and encouraging for the future if responsibility had been faced.'

Lord Justice Taylor had delivered a bombshell: hooliganism was not the cause of the Hillsborough disaster. It was a hammer blow not only to the South Yorkshire Police, but also to the government's policy on football fans.

In the *Guardian*, David Lacey wrote: 'Taylor's findings confirm one's own immediate impressions of a botched police operation born of ignorance, complacency and bad management.' While Chief Constable Peter Wright said he was 'surprised that the inquiry had seen things in a different light from the impression originally given [to him] by officers at the match', a *Guardian* editorial declared: 'The South Yorkshire Police performance, at the highest levels, was abysmal.'

Wright offered to resign, but the police authority refused to accept his notice. Sufficiently buoyed, he now made utterances to the effect that the inquests into the deaths of the 95 Liverpool supporters would exonerate his force. However, as the Hillsborough Independent Panel has revealed, two days before Taylor's interim report was published, the prime minister was briefed that 'little or no blame is attached to the Liverpool fans'. Instead, it was Wright's force that bore the brunt of the criticism: 'reference is made to poor operational orders [and] lack of leadership', she was informed, while Duckenfield's allegation that Liverpool fans had stormed an exit gate 'was not only untruthful . . . it caused grave offence and distress'.

In a further briefing, Thatcher learnt that 'senior officers involved sought to duck all responsibility when giving evidence to the inquiry', and that the home secretary believed Peter Wright 'will have to resign', as the 'enormity of the disaster, and the extent to which the inquiry blames the police, demand this'. The briefing also stated that 'the defensive – and at times close to deceitful – behaviour by the senior officers in South Yorkshire sounds depressingly familiar'.

The home secretary informed the PM that his own statement would 'welcome unreservedly the broad thrust of the report'. On a note she received requesting her agreement of Douglas Hurd's proposed statement, Thatcher replied: 'What do we mean by "welcoming the broad thrust of the report"? The broad thrust is devastating criticism of the police. Is that for us to welcome? . . . Surely we welcome the thoroughness of the report and its recommendations – MT.'

As the Hillsborough Independent Panel reported: 'This change was conveyed to the home secretary and adopted in his statement.' On publication of the report, Douglas Hurd was not reported as attaching most of the blame to the police; he praised Wright's 'typically dignified and honourable' offer of resignation, and stated that Taylor had revealed major deficiencies in the layout and organisation of Hillsborough.

By 6 August, two days after Taylor's interim report appeared, the *Sunday Telegraph* was indignant. Its Comment pages stated that 'It would be outrageous if any Sheffield policeman were to be made to stand trial.' Instead, it argued that those now gathering behind Lord Justice Taylor had overlooked 'the violent, unruly and uneducated' football supporter and, more specifically, 'a rabble' from Liverpool.

Across the country, the full force of Taylor's findings was felt immediately. There was a palpable sense of surprise, mixed with relief, that hooliganism was not to blame. The public, and football fans in particular, now looked to the government for a response. But there was none. Taylor's report was published on 4 August, during Parliament's annual summer recess. The law lord's findings into the causes of the biggest disaster in British sport were never debated in Parliament. MPs had gone on holiday.

One can only speculate over the Tories' motivation for giving Taylor an August deadline to report into the causes of Hillsborough. One can only guess, too, at the anger on the Conservative benches as they returned from recess to learn that the police were largely to blame. Moreover, the demonisation of football supporters had itself contributed to the disaster – Taylor ruling that the preoccupation with hooliganism within Duckenfield's force had exerted an unhelpful influence on its operation.

As the judge retreated to chambers to start work on the second part of his inquiry, the Tories were stumped. But Taylor was about to deliver them an unexpected present.

Margaret Thatcher's memoirs give no clue as to her feelings about football as the 1980s came to a close. Communism was crumbling across eastern Europe; the net was closing in on the Lockerbie bombers (Iran, Syria and the Popular Front for the Liberation of Palestine – General Command were in the frame); and satellite television was set to revolutionise the British media. Most pressing, perhaps, was the Poll Tax – due to be rolled out across England and Wales in 1990. Football would have been little more than an irritating blip on the government radar. Nonetheless, it is curious that the prime minister makes no reference to Hillsborough in her memoirs, *The Downing Street Years*. Her only allusion to the national sport is framed within the context of hooliganism – Heysel makes an entry. If Margaret Thatcher truly believed that hooligans were responsible for Hillsborough, she would surely have written as much in her memoirs. She did not.

And yet, in the autumn of 1989, football was undoubtedly a problem for the Tories. One of the country's major police forces had been implicated in the deaths of nearly a hundred people. Now, before the leaves were off the trees, word reached Number 10 that Lord Justice Taylor looked set to sink the Football Spectators Bill – legislation into which Mrs Thatcher had invested enormous personal effort. ID cards looked set to go too: Taylor was convinced they would have done nothing to prevent the crush at Hillsborough.

In November 1989, 'a well-publicised altercation' took place between Taylor and John Carlisle MP at the Home Office. Carlisle told Taylor he should not concern himself with the bill's proposals for issuing ID cards – effectively revoking assurances the judge had been given on his appointment in the spring. 'The clash', reported the *Guardian*, 'is said to have toughened the judge's determination not to be bullied.'

But Taylor was now on a collision course with Thatcher. According to former sports minister Richard Tracey, Thatcher and Colin Moynihan, her minister for sport, were now at the point of 'total frustration and anger' with the state of football. So, in December 1989, with the judge signalling the death knell for the Football Spectators Bill, the government asked Systems Reliability, one of the companies tendering to provide ID cards, to 'accelerate' its research into the scheme.

As New Year's Day dawned, Britain emerged into the 1990s. Few could have anticipated that the year ahead would see the end of Margaret Thatcher, or of football as Britain had known it for over a century.

On 29 January 1990, Lord Justice Taylor's final report on Hillsborough was presented to both Houses of Parliament. The debate in the Lords over Taylor's blueprint for reform had scarcely got under way before Lord Harris of Greenwich complained of leaks in the press that week, in which, he said, the government had carried out 'a series of quite deplorable attacks' on Taylor. He pointed a finger at *The Times*, in which John Carlisle MP had accused Taylor of being 'prejudiced' against ID cards. In a leader, *The Times* also argued that opponents of ID cards – whose ranks Taylor had joined – were 'myopic'. The bill, it argued, was 'one of the sharpest knives' in the government's armoury for dealing with hooligans. Lord Harris complained that Taylor had been the victim of 'an act of gross discourtesy' on the part of the government.

Over in the Commons, David Waddington, Douglas Hurd's successor as home secretary, was about to give a masterclass in elision: while citing overcrowding as the cause of the disaster, he either neglected or refused to acknowledge that the reason was the failure of police control. Instead, Waddington wasted no time in laying into hooliganism, excessive drinking, and poor leadership in the game. He made an early diversion, referring curiously to spectators as 'customers'. Then he confirmed what the public had known for a few days: the Football Spectators Bill, and ID cards, would be put on ice. Despite briefing bitterly against Taylor in the media, the government had no option but to accept that he had found their ID proposals wanting. And yet: 'Let no one imagine that this means there will be any let-up in the fight against hooliganism,' Waddington warned. 'Those who, unlike the government, have for so long shrugged off their responsibilities will now have to face up to them.' Ominously, the home secretary warned that those who opposed the ID cards scheme 'may not be quite so happy today', because Taylor's proposals for reforming football 'will undoubtedly be extremely costly'.

Over in the Lords, there was consternation. Repeating the home secretary's speech, Conservative peer Earl Ferrers introduced Taylor's report with Waddington's repeated references to hooliganism. He also broke off to contend that had the ID cards scheme been in place, football might not be in the mess it was in. The Lords grew increasingly restive.

Back in the Commons, the home secretary turned his attention to the police, paying tribute to 'the way they carry out the difficult, thankless and often unthanked tasks which are thrust upon them'. Waddington's speech left no one in any doubt that, in the government's eyes, responsibility for the safety of football supporters should lie not with the police but with football clubs: 'I can only repeat that those who invite people to a sporting occasion as a commercial venture have a duty to ensure that the ground is safe for those people,' he said. 'It is their responsibility and no other person's.'

The government's stance could be said to have been selective, at best. The home secretary – himself a QC – had taken a distinctly black-and-white reading of a crucial part of Taylor's final report, one which the judge had reiterated was a grey area. 'Which functions should be discharged by the police and which by the club's stewards is one of the most vexed questions,' Taylor wrote.

Taylor had grappled with the equivocations of Lord Justice Popplewell, who – in his inquiry into the Valley Parade disaster in 1985 – eventually settled on the finding that a club must bear ultimate responsibility for supporters' safety. Taylor noted: 'It is undisputed that the club, as a matter of law, has a duty to take reasonable care for the safety of the spectators invited to its premises. There have, however, been two practical difficulties about the club, rather than the police, being de facto in charge.'

The first was the inadequacy of club stewards, who, Taylor wrote, 'I have frequently been told are of limited capacity and reliability'. The second came in the form of a submission to Taylor from the Association of Chief Police Officers, which stated: 'Dual responsibility for safety is a recipe for confusion . . . the police must accept a leading role and, despite the requirements and civil liabilities of football clubs, themselves take on supervision of the overall conduct of events wherever crowd safety is an issue.'

In 1986, the South Yorkshire Police had taken Sheffield Utd to court, to press for payment for 'special' police services provided at Bramall Lane. Then, the judge agreed with Peter Wright's force that they had taken responsibility for the safety of the crowd, and that this was a 'special' service, one which merited payment. Lord Justice Taylor only reinforced this interpretation of the law when he ruled that at Hillsborough the South Yorkshire Police had de facto taken responsibility for the safety of supporters in Sheffield Wednesday's stadium too.

Now, in clarifying the respective role of the police and clubs, Taylor settled on a Statement of Intent, in which he wrote:

'What the division of functions should be must be a matter for local decision and in the last resort for the Police Commander to determine.'

The home secretary adopted the more commercial position: responsibility for supporters' safety, he said, 'now rests on the [football] industry'.

Taylor may have dithered over the issue of responsibility for supporters' safety, but he pulled no punches in his blueprint for the refurbishment of our stadiums: every ground in England's top two divisions must be converted into an all-seater venue by the start of the 1994/5 season. It was a programme of reform that Graham Kelly believed was 'eminently achievable' if the government allocated proper funds.

How much was football asking for in 1990? Today, set against the colossal sums of money swimming around the Premiership, the bill for all-seater stadiums for England's clubs seems so trifling as to appear a misprint. It was £130 million, according to Arthur Sandford, chief executive of the Football League. (This is around £260 million in today's money – a sum that wouldn't cover the combined annual wage bill of Chelsea and Man Utd.) Surely the public coffers could find this? As Sandford told *The Times* on 1 February 1990, the chancellor was already raking in £250 million a year in tax from the football pools companies. Six months and a week of that would finance Taylor's blueprint.

The case was strong, and it was put forcefully. Joe Ashton MP asked why the government couldn't give a similar grant for football-ground improvements as Labour had done prior to the 1966 World Cup. His argument was echoed by John

Cartwright, MP for Woolwich, who pointed to the 'substantial public help to commercial undertakings in the arts'.

However, according to David Waddington, 'it would be irresponsible if . . . Opposition Members were to allow a message to go out to the football authorities to the effect that, once again, they can shirk their responsibilities because the Opposition, if the British people were ever to return them to power, would take all the responsibility off their shoulders and force the bill onto the taxpayer'.

David Lacey had predicted as much in the *Guardian*, a few days earlier: 'But for the deaths at Hillsborough, the government would be hell-bent on enforcing [the Football Spectators Bill] next season,' he wrote. 'Having lost the argument over ID cards, the government is even less likely to be moved by pleas for such financial help.'

From a purely financial perspective, the government's argument was not without merit: English football clubs were private companies, leaning on the public realm for policing and other services when it suited them. The Metropolitan Police's bill for policing football matches in London in 1988/9 was £10 million, only £1 million of which was recoverable from the clubs, which meant the taxpayer was subsidising the policing of football to the tune of £9 million a year in London alone.

Ultimately, however, the government would direct substantial funding from the public purse towards Taylor's reforms. Taylor recommended the tax on the football pools companies be reduced from 42.5 to 40 per cent, and that this saving should be directed towards ground improvements, via the Football Trust. In the budget of spring 1990, the Tory government acceded. However, by June 1990 the £130 million refurbishment bill was revised upwards, to around £500 million. (This would prove an accurate estimate.) MPs, led by Labour's Tom Pendry, now pushed for a further reduction in the pools levy, and in 1991 it was reduced again, to 38 per cent. This channelled some £18–20 million a year into stadium renovations.

Effectively, the public would end up paying twice for the refit of these privately owned football clubs' stadiums: through the hike in ticket prices in the refurbished grounds, and through playing the pools.

But, again, it was the tone that was crucial: in January 1990, the government declined to acknowledge that public money might update our football-ground stock, because this might require recognition that the game fulfilled a social purpose. Instead, here was an attempt to further relocate football from the public realm into the private sector: the game had made unacceptable demands on the police, and Margaret Thatcher had declared an enemy of those who followed the national sport. As Waddington told the Commons, 'An intolerable burden is placed on the entire community as a result of the way in which the game is conducted now.'

Fortunately, there was something in Taylor's recommendations that pleased the government greatly. On his tour of Britain's football stadiums, Taylor had been alerted to the vast, untapped commercial opportunities in football. He had been especially impressed by the acumen of St Johnstone FC, who had sold their historic city-centre ground in Perth to Asda, and with the proceeds built a new ground on the outskirts of town. In TV rights, too, Taylor had identified a substantial opportunity for clubs to generate new income, and he also advised a levy on transfer fees be directed towards the refurbishment of stadiums. While Taylor had ruled that 'the bulk of the finances for ground improvement must be raised by the clubs themselves', he was now pointing the way to their means of recouping that investment. 'I would expect the football authorities to extract the highest possible price for TV rights,' he wrote.

In late January 1990, there were other influential voices urging a new, naked commercialism. Logan Gourley, a member of a consortium that bought Wembley in 1984, urged the clubs to 'concentrate on developing every commercial possibility that is not illegal'.

But what about ticket prices at these shiny new all-seater stadiums? What about the fans? A survey commissioned by the Sir Norman Chester Centre for Football Research in November 1989 found that a majority of fans were opposed to all-seater stadiums, even in the wake of Hillsborough. However, as Taylor noted, 'when one introduces provisos on price' the majority backed the move. Again, Taylor found the answer in Scotland. 'As to cost,' he said, 'clubs may well wish to charge somewhat more for seats than for standing, but it should be possible to plan a price structure which suits the cheapest seats to the pockets of those presently paying to stand. At Ibrox, for example, seating is £6, standing £4 – not a prohibitive price or differential.'

His naivety is striking: 'Clubs may well wish to charge somewhat more . . .' In January 1990, Lord Justice Taylor had Britain's football clubs at his mercy; his blueprint for the wholesale reform of our stadiums would be accepted in full by Parliament. And yet he neglected to put the brakes on the cost of ticket prices, which would inevitably rise as terraces gave way to seats. By stipulating that all first- and second-tier clubs in England and Wales must convert their grounds into all-seater stadiums by the start of the 1994/5 season, Taylor had ensured that ground improvements would be effected either in one fell swoop, or at the most over a period of four years. A substantial, yet finite, period of revenue-raising was required. And after that? Where was the consideration of how, and to what end, profits from football's new commercial opportunities might be directed, once the seats were bolted down and the leaking roofs fixed?

Taylor did not concern himself with such matters: shocked at the squalor of England's football grounds, he was unyielding in arguing now that safety concerns outweighed all other considerations. For their part, the Opposition believed the pools levy could foot the bill in just six months, and rein in football's more avaricious operators. But there was politics at play: the Tories could not allow Labour to set the agenda, and they were adamant that football must get its house in order. There was something else, too: in their determination to remove any stain from the police, the Tories laid ultimate responsibility for the safety of supporters on the clubs. In return, they dangled Taylor's golden carrot: clubs would be encouraged to exploit new commercial opportunities and negotiate more lucrative TV rights – 'to extract the highest possible price'.

Taylor had opened the door to TINA.

The Opposition were on to this. Roy Hughes, MP for Newport East, asked: 'Does the Home Secretary appreciate that getting rid of the terraces is likely to affect the price of tickets, and is he resigned to football's becoming a rich man's game?'

David Waddington replied: 'I can only repeat that those who

invite people to a sporting occasion as a commercial venture have a duty to ensure that the ground is safe for those people.'

Peter Snape, MP for West Bromwich East, was quick to retort: '. . . for millions of people in this country, watching their home-town football team is not a commercial proposition, as he so blithely puts it, but a long-standing commitment inherited from their parents'.

But the game was up. Taylor himself was sniffy about this romanticised idea of loyalty to a club passing through generations of families. And the Tories? As former sports minister Richard Tracey had said, they were at the point of 'total frustration and anger' with football. They could no longer trust the football authorities and neither understand nor control the supporters. The game would have to be left to the mercy of the market.

Two days earlier, the *Guardian*'s John Carver had signalled as much: the Tories, he wrote, 'believe Taylor's main criticism is of the football industry'. To most observers in 1990, that industry didn't exist. (According to Joe Ashton MP, 'Ninety-nine per cent of football clubs do not pay a dividend and do not make a profit.') Perhaps, to take issue with John Carver, it wasn't so much that the Tories had identified a failure in the football industry, but that it didn't exist in a functioning form; the creation of a flourishing football industry would surely fix a problem that was otherwise beyond their wit, just as the market would better manage all those utilities and industries the state had struggled to make profitable.

As the debate in the Commons wore on, the home secretary repeatedly referred to the clubs as commercial enterprises. Supporters were now making way for 'customers'.

*

It's tempting to imagine a partisan shoot-out in Parliament, on that cold night in January 1990, between a dogmatic Tory government and a Labour-led Opposition heroically refusing to abandon football. The truth is somewhat less clear-cut.

In April 2012, I went to the House of Lords to meet Peter Snape, the former MP for West Bromwich East, and now Lord Snape of Wednesbury. Over coffee, Snape – the chairman of Stockport County, and an engaging, pin-sharp, passionate football man – recalled the debate on Taylor 20 years earlier with ease. It was, he said, 'a cosy stitch-up'.

Representations had been made to the Tories by the Opposition, to press the case that Taylor's reforms could be funded by the public purse via the tax on the football pools. 'Pools promoters were doing very well out of football,' Snape recalled. 'We compared it to the horse-racing betting levy.' However, there was very little goodwill towards the game, and not just among Conservatives. 'Even then,' Snape said, 'the gentrification of the Labour Party was well under way. There was a comparative minority of us who were genuine football fans.' There was no inclination in either major political party to spend any of the £250 million tax take from pools companies on football. 'The view was that there were better things to spend it on,' he said. 'There wasn't a feeling that we could ever make it official Labour Party policy.'

Twenty years on, Snape remained visibly frustrated about the fact that the debate on Taylor was bogged down in minor detail. 'Denis Howell [shadow sports minister] was arguing that the booze ban, which applied to fans drinking in and around the ground, should be applied to the directors' box too. It was a kind of inverted snobbery. What we should have been debating was the big issue: that the game was about to be priced out of the reach of ordinary people.'

While Snape is dismissive of David Waddington – 'The most reactionary home secretary of my time; he knew absolutely nought about football' – he bears little animosity towards Thatcher over Taylor. 'It wasn't that she wasn't sympathetic,' Snape said. 'She was actually a good listener when you put your case. It just wasn't within her comprehension. She genuinely couldn't understand why people would watch football when they could spend their time shopping, or at home with the family.'

I was surprised to hear from Lord Snape that the final Taylor report and the future of football were settled not in the Commons, but in privy councils. Snape smiled, indulging me. 'Get a smaller group of people and you can get some degree of agreement about the way forward, away from the main debate, away from the press,' he explained. 'There were MPs saying, "We can talk to people in football, get them to get their house in order." It was an old boys' network, and Denis Howell was very much part of the old boy network; he was a kind of avuncular, cigar-smoking, "Leave it to me" guy. It's not a conspiracy, but people who are going to rock the boat don't get called [to take part] in the debate in the Commons.'

After that debate, on 29 January 1990, a Labour amendment urged the government to meet England's 92 league clubs, to discuss the financing of Taylor's stadium reforms through a pools levy. It was defeated by 277 votes to 210.

'It's not that the vote was fixed,' Lord Snape told me. 'But it represented a whipped vote along party lines. Had the Labour Party been in government, I suspect the outcome would have been the same.'

Was the future of football not worth greater consideration or debate, if not – perhaps – a free vote? What about the gravity of the issue? After all, this is the national sport we're talking about.

'It's a grave issue if you're interested in football,' Snape said. 'But football is a minority sport in the House of Commons.'

And to the Conservative government of 1990, it was no longer essentially a sport. On a date few English football fans can even vaguely remember, the Establishment washed its hands of the Hillsborough disaster and tossed football to the four winds.

The national sport was now the 'football industry'.

3 : Who Does Turandot Play for?

David Waddington was fishing in the dark beside the Thames. And yet the government was about to land a whopper. In January 1990, few MPs could have envisaged the atrophied national sport morphing into an entertainment industry in the near future. Yet, scarcely five months after the final Taylor Report was presented to Parliament, football took a leap forward so huge, so unexpected, it forced the sport's governing bodies and the clubs into a breathless game of catch-up. That giant leap was Italia '90.

In 2010, documentary-maker James Erskine explored this phenomenon in *One Night in Turin*. His film played to packed cinemas across England and became the fastest-selling British DVD documentary of the year. Erskine believes that his core cinema audience were in their twenties and early thirties; many were not old enough to have seen the 1990 World Cup or to remember much about it. What they grasped was the legend of Italia '90, in all its pathos.

The legend, of course, is Gazza and his tears. But the real story – if you think about it – is Stuart Pearce and his. Paul Gascoigne, it turns out, was always a hyperactive, unstable character, prone to volatile behaviour and to breakdowns. Not so the man we called Psycho. And yet it was the England left-back who prompted ITV commentator Brian Moore to make (albeit unwittingly) the most telling observation of England's epic World Cup semi-final against West Germany.

On 4 July 1990, after two hours of free-flowing football in Turin, England stood toe to toe with just about the best side in the world. And they stood on the verge of a World Cup final in Rome, against a mediocre Argentina – a team the whole of Italy wanted buried.

Paul Parker had given West Germany the lead with an outrageous deflection from Andy Brehme's free kick, the ball looping over Shilton's head as he stumbled back into his net. But England played their way back, calmly passing and moving, neutralising the likes of Matthäus, Berthold and Klinsmann. In the 80th minute, Parker made amends by hoisting a diagonal ball for Lineker to run on to and equalise with his left foot. From its four corners, England erupted.

Bobby Robson's men had chosen a game watched by a worldwide audience of 300 million people to deliver one of the best performances ever seen from an England side. Watch the match now and it isn't simply the drama that stands out, but the measured, tactical football. Possession was conceded where it wouldn't hurt; the English passed and moved fluently, and they played with their heads up. Bobby Robson, on the bench, looked as bemused as the rest of us. Seldom had an England side played so much chess. And as it went into extra time, they nearly won it – a shot from Waddle, driven across the box, hit the inside of the far post. In a pub in Stevenage, people around me screamed as a football bounced back across the grass and out of the penalty area.

When the referee blew the final whistle on the one-all draw, millions of people in England were standing on their feet – not just to applaud, but to watch something they had never seen before: England in a penalty shoot-out with the West Germans for a place in the World Cup final. And we were confident. England had finished the match the stronger side, and as the TV cameras panned across the faces of the players, they seemed unfazed out there in Turin. Who would Robson pick for penalties? Lineker, Beardsley and Platt were cool heads. Pearce was unstoppable from 12 yards. Wright and Gascoigne could both strike a ball, and Waddle had played a blinder.

This was our moment.

As first Lineker, Beardsley and then Platt struck the ball past Bodo Illgner, a roar threatened to punch a hole in the roof of the pub. It couldn't end here. No chance. And yet the Germans were matching us, penalty for penalty. Shilton couldn't lay a finger on Brehme, Matthäus or Riedle. Now it was Stuart Pearce's turn. If he could slot this, Germany were on the ropes.

As he bustled forward from the halfway line, Pearce didn't look right. He was sweating, and he walked a little too purposefully. His shorts had shrunk, and those solid oak legs seemed to wobble now, like inflatable bananas. By the time he got to the penalty area, people around me were growing edgy. Pearce planted the ball on the spot. He bent down to replace it, but thought better of it. He glanced at the ref, turned around towards the halfway line, stopped, turned again ('His tongue's hanging out . . .') and put his head down. It took Stuart Pearce six years to get over what happened next.

Now, little Olaf Thon, with his little flick moustache, shimmied forward for the chance to put West Germany 4–3 up, and into a decisive lead. I couldn't watch. I looked around the pub. Half the men in there were sat with their heads turned away or were watching through their hands. Women stood beside or over some of them, stroking their heads. The other lads were drilling their eyes into the screen. As Thon ran up to take his kick, a loud 'Aaaaahhhhh!' rose from the floor, but a groan told us he had scored – nonchalantly, as it turned out. 'Take Shilton off, for fuck's sake,' one of my mates shouted. But England had to score to stay alive.

Now, Chris Waddle, arguably our best player on the night, began to amble forward. For the first time in weeks, the pub fell silent, because as Waddle set off from the halfway line, his shoulders began to sag. It is difficult to think of anyone since Edmund Hillary who, single-handedly, has carried the hopes of so many Englishmen on his shoulders. No politician has done any such thing since Churchill. Neither pop stars nor actors nor royalty inspire hope like this. Cooper versus Ali, perhaps. Virginia Wade in 1977, or Daley Thompson at the LA Olympics. Bruno taking on Tyson . . . No, this was something way beyond. This really was England's Everest: a World Cup final on foreign soil.

1966 did not have tension or drama like this. Sir Alf Ramsey, famously, had promised that England would win the World Cup before the tournament started. Way before it started . . . like, in 1963. While the nation didn't exactly take Ramsey at his word, England's progress was at worst picaresque, and when a victorious Ramsey was pictured planting a kiss on the Jules Rimet trophy, the *Observer* ran the headline: 'Kiss Seals a Prophecy Fulfilled'.

Just as Ramsey was confident, so on 4 July 1990 were West Germany. They had destroyed Dragan Stojković's talented Yugoslavs in the group stages, and seen off the European Champions, Holland, in a spiteful second-round game. England could call on no such conviction. All we had left was hope, and our hopes rested on Chris Waddle, a man who had been ridiculed by England supporters for three or four seasons – for his indifferent displays, his stooping physique, for 'Diamond Lights', and that mullet. No one expected him to rescue England – least of all Waddle. His body language screamed it. Now, he set off on his long walk from the halfway line, without a sherpa to share his load. And as he put one foot in front of the other, his anguish became almost unbearable. Pearce, squatting on the halfway line, couldn't look. A towel over his shoulders, Pearce – like almost everyone in the pub now – had his hands over his eyes. Waddle planted the ball and turned around, with his back to Bodo Illgner. And as he turned again to launch into his run-up, I took my hands away from my eyes.

I had to watch this. For 15 months, my life had been a penalty shoot-out. I had watched people die within feet of me at Hillsborough, unable to save them. I had prepared myself to die, and I had lived. In the 15 months since, I had suffered blackouts and nightmares. I was head over heels in love too, because my girlfriend hadn't just made me laugh, she had kept me sane. Like many survivors, I was almost certainly suffering from post-traumatic stress disorder, and yet no one could tell me what it was. Life was just a sequence of extreme highs and lows. Life was this: a year earlier, football had nearly killed me. Now, if Chris Waddle could tuck this penalty away, we were back in with a chance of playing in the World Cup final against Argentina.

Waddle shimmied, like little Olaf Thon, and began to accelerate down the turf. What happened next was silence. Then the sound of a glass breaking, and someone screaming. And then

Brian Moore was all we could hear in the pub in that ordinary town, on that unforgettable night. 'Oh, oh . . . and he's in tears, Stuart Pearce,' Moore said. 'And I thought he was a really hard man . . .'

He was, Brian. He was.

Italia '90 . . . no World Cup, before or since, has been so synonymous with the host nation. The Italian public had boasted about the stadiums they would build, the pitches they would prepare, the cities, the food and the climate. Now, in the second week of June, the world could see that Italy had been as good as its word. In the most dramatic opening game in a World Cup that anyone could remember, Cameroon, the rank outsiders, had kicked glorious lumps out of Argentina, plunging the tournament into chaos on day one.

In the days that followed, TV viewers in Britain watched open-mouthed as the Italians unveiled one magnificent stadium after another. San Siro, Stadio delle Alpi, Stadio San Paolo . . . these were stadiums built on a cinematic scale. Even on TV, they soared. Footage of England fans arriving at the delle Alpi in Turin captured their awe on discovering a stadium that seemed to have landed from outer space.

On the field, Italy sent out Zenga, Maldini, Baresi, Donadoni, Giannini and Baggio – footballers who looked like gods. And if they couldn't play like gods, then here was the perfect Italian melodrama unfolding. The Azzurri inched their way through an easy group, moved up a gear to beat Uruguay in the second round, and overcame the Republic of Ireland in the quarter-finals with a solitary goal from Toto Schillaci. And yet, like the classical heroes they were held to be, Italy were plagued by their own familiar siren – *catenaccio*, which left them reluctant to launch their great attacking talent, Roberto Baggio. As the World Cup progressed, the adulation of the Italian public began to hang like beads of sweat from the Azzurri shirts.

Diego Maradona was at the heart of the drama. Still the world's greatest player, the Argentine had transformed Napoli from provincial no-hopers into Serie A champions for the first time. Something approaching a deity in Italy, Maradona now taunted his hosts, claiming that the draw for the finals had been fixed to ensure Italy's safe progress. Inevitably, when the first semi-final pitted the Azzurri against his reigning world champions in Naples, Maradona sought to drive a wedge down Italy's north–south fault line by urging the local crowd to support Argentina. 'The Neapolitans must remember one thing,' Maradona announced, a few days before the game: 'Italy makes Naples feel important one day of the year, but forgets about it the other 364.' A few hours before kick-off, the Neapolitans responded graciously, unfurling a huge banner in the Stadio San Paolo: 'Maradona, Naples loves you, but Italy is our homeland.'

No matter to Maradona. On a torturous night, a cynical Argentina progressed to their fourth World Cup final, after penalties. As the distinctly ungodly Aldo Serena missed Italy's crucial spot kick, Argentina launched into a pogo on the pitch that would have had the Sex Pistols gobbing their approval. Italy was convulsed with grief. The rest of the world didn't know whether to laugh or cry.

Who had seen this coming? Certainly not the English, for seldom has a country set off for a World Cup with such a poorly disguised sense of self-loathing.

That summer, the braying voices exhorting English football to take a good, hard look at itself had been at it again. Before the tournament kicked off, the FA informed Bobby Robson that it would not be renewing his contract, forcing Robson to announce that he would be joining PSV Eindhoven after the World Cup. The media were piling into Robson too. Bob Harris was sports editor of the *Sunday Mirror* during Italia '90; he remembers a friendly England played before the tournament, when one journalist 'stood up on this plane, drunk on the free booze, and told his press colleagues in a very loud voice: "We're here to bury Robson."'

They had already buried his squad: one tabloid waved England off to Italy with the headline 'World Cup Wallies'.

And as for the fans . . .

'Mrs Thatcher even had one or two senior journalists in Fleet Street telling her what a bad game it was, and how awful everyone involved in it was,' Harris recalls.

Little surprise, then, that the prime minister and Colin Moynihan, her 'Miniature of Sport', warned England supporters not to travel without tickets; now they urged the Italians to impose a 24-hour drinking ban either side of England games. The tabloids reported that even the Pope was on his guard as England prepared to slink into Italy quietly, and – the nation prayed – sneak out just as quietly, only more quickly.

England supporters who set off for Sardinia travelled light on optimism. Few were ignorant of the fact that it was 'their' hooligans who were responsible for England's effective quarantine on the island. Bobby Robson's squad had been seeded in Group F, ahead of European Champions Holland. If this was due reward for England's quarter-final place in the 1986 World

66

Cup in Mexico, when the Dutch were absent (as they were from Spain '82), Spain had a stronger claim to seeding than England: although the two nations had reached the same stage of the competition in 1986 and 1982, Spain – unlike England – had qualified for Argentina in 1978 and had finished top of their qualifying group for the 1990 finals. But FIFA encountered little opposition to their plan to seed England and assign them a billet in Cagliari – 'the animals' were now as far removed as possible from the grand stage of Italia '90.

England's group was hostile too: Holland boasted the great AC Milan trio of Van Basten, Gullit and Rijkaard; the Republic of Ireland were a dogged side intent on treating their clash with England as a derby; and Egypt, the expected whipping boys, were an unknown quantity, nonetheless.

While the Italians and the BBC were busy casting the World Cup as an opera, England began like the cast of *Oliver!* next door. On stormy Sardinia, Robson's side scraped a draw against Jack Charlton's Ireland (one Italian paper ran the clumsy headline 'No Football, Please, We're English'), had the best of the Dutch in a goalless draw, and overcame Egypt with a glancing header by Mark Wright. Thin pickings, but at least quarantine was over.

England headed now for the mainland, for a second-round knockout tie with Belgium in Bologna. The build-up to the game was overshadowed by the so-called Battle of Rimini, in which skirmishes outside the Rose and Crown pub in the seaside resort led to 246 people being deported back to England. A fans' World Cup diary made for the BBC by Kevin Allen (brother of the actor and 'World in Motion' co-writer Keith) remains an illuminating insight into what was going on behind the headlines. Allen reported that an aircraft was rumoured to have been chartered three days in advance of the trouble; conveniently, its 246 seats were filled by precisely 246 'hooligans' rounded up in Rimini and nearby towns. As Allen also found, some of those 'hooligans' weren't even there for the football, but were on a package holiday; two of them were South African tourists. The *carabinieri* and Colin Moynihan were engaged in a battle of political one-upmanship, and England's supporters – not all of them innocent, not all of them guilty – were caught in the crossfire. Such was his cynical performance in Italy, the squeaky-voiced minister for sport was christened Lord Haw-Haw by England supporters.

Back home, England's humdrum progress made little initial impact. Italia '90 was mood music to our ears, but no more. The early optimism engendered by Lord Justice Taylor's blueprint for reform had lasted barely three months. On 5 May 1990, on a blazing hot day on the south coast, around 3,000 Leeds Utd fans went on the rampage in Bournemouth. On the same day there was trouble, too, in Chesterfield, Aldershot, Sheffield, Birmingham, London, Leicester, Shrewsbury, Swansea and Cambridge. The violence in Sheffield took place at Hillsborough.

Football, for all its increased attendances that season, looked increasingly out of fashion. Who needed it, when clubs and pubs up and down the land were moving to the sound of Primal Scream, the Happy Mondays, the Charlatans and Soul II Soul? And something else too . . . a low, mysterious 'Mmm' sound. Ecstasy had moved from the obscurity of Shoom and the Haçienda and into the nation's bloodstream; now, it was forcing the tabloids to report that Britain's teenagers were no longer glassing each other in nightclubs, they were *hugging* each other.

If football was receding on the horizon, it was kicked to the outer edges of orbit on 27 May, when the Stone Roses played the defining gig of the 1990s. At Spike Island, the tribes of Liverpool and Manchester were joined, in baggy, amid the chemical-industrial landscape of Widnes, where they set about consuming industrial amounts of chemicals. As Mani, the Roses' bass player, said, it was a chance to 'get as many like minds in a field, get 'em off their tits, give 'em a bit of music and see what happens'.

In the summer of 1990, people in England were ready to see what happens. There was a palpable sense among the young working class that there was nothing left to lose. The riots in Trafalgar Square and at Strangeways, Hillsborough, the music, the drugs, the best summer since '76 . . . Something was falling apart, something was about to happen. And yet few expected it to happen in Italy – because football, like the Thatcher era, was dying on its feet. It had taken New Order to lend some credibility to the national team with 'World in Motion', the best football song ever written (perhaps the only good football song ever written). And yet that squad were no mugs. Shilton was still a commanding keeper. In front of him stood a back four of Paul Parker, Stuart Pearce, Des Walker and Terry Butcher, with Mark Wright emerging as a cultured *libero*. England took Bryan Robson and Steve McMahon as midfield enforcers. Up ahead, David Platt, Paul Gascoigne, Trevor Steven, John Barnes, Peter Beardsley, Chris Waddle and Gary Lineker were pushing for a place in the starting eleven. Paul Lake, regarded by many Man City fans as their best player since Colin Bell, didn't quite make the cut. This remains one of the best two England squads since

1970 – perhaps the best. That it should be waved off with two fingers was symptomatic of the treatment meted out to Bobby Robson by the media during his eight years in charge. But it was symptomatic of something else too.

'England was in a bad place before 1990,' says James Erskine, director of *One Night in Turin*. 'There was just a sense of "rubbish England". After the disasters of the '80s, you had all these amazing events happening around the world – from Mandela's release to the fall of the Berlin Wall. And what did we have? The most serious civil disturbances in 200 years.'

Erskine and I will have to disagree over the merits of the Poll Tax riots. But it is worth remembering Margaret Thatcher's response to the chaos in Trafalgar Square: she dismissed it as the work of 'the mob'. Would this be the same 'mob' who had been at Orgreave, and later arrived – tanked-up, allegedly – at Hillsborough? Probably. Now 'the mob' were setting off for the World Cup, and Thatcher and Moynihan seemed determined to put the wind up their reception committee.

Today, Anne-Marie Mockridge is a fans' ambassador at the Football Supporters' Federation; in 1990, a graduate trainee teacher, she arrived in southern Italy for her first World Cup to find the locals 'petrified' of the English. In Naples, when she tried to buy a packet of cigarettes in a newsagent's, the shopkeeper came around the counter, slung Mockridge over his shoulder and deposited her on the pavement outside. A few days later, a waiter spat at her when she asked for service in a restaurant. 'Why did you do that?' she asked. 'Because you're English,' he said.

In this context, it's not difficult to agree with Erskine when he likens England's journey at Italia '90 to nothing less than an

Arthurian legend. 'Everything was crap,' he says. 'England was crap. And then they set off, this band of disparate losers, led by Bobby Robson – this king in exile, almost – to win the golden cup in this foreign land. Robson's got his heroes, but what he needs is this magical element, his Merlin, and he found it in Paul Gascoigne.'

Gascoigne's performance at Italia '90 needs little rehearsing here. He flickered in Sardinia against Ireland and the Dutch; he swung in the cross for Wright's header against Egypt and provided a similar assist for David Platt's dramatic, 119th-minute winner against Belgium. As the tournament got tougher, Gazza got better: in the quarter-final in Naples, against Cameroon, he showed England how to play football by threading his way through the middle, and he matured before our eyes into one of the best players in the world.

This was a totemic moment for England. 'And Gascoigne, to play at the level he reached,' says Erskine, 'on the highest stage, in this wonderful setting . . . this is something *we* can't do. People sat there and watched it and they realised that this was something ordinary people can't do. There was something truly magical about it.'

Off the pitch, a different alchemy was taking place. Anne-Marie Mockridge has been to every World Cup with England since 1990, but, she says, nothing compares with what was going on in Italy: 'The dancing in the stadium in Naples, when we beat Cameroon . . . I've never seen anything like it. The government were hell-bent on putting football down, and the fans were determined to celebrate. There was a sense that "We're not the scum that people say we are."'

There were outbreaks of trouble involving England supporters in Sardinia, and in Rimini, and in Turin – where three-way battles were fought between Italian fans, England supporters and West Germans. But there was a growing recognition that this was far from an exclusively English problem.

Today, Rogan Taylor is director of the Football Industry Group at Liverpool University. Back in 1990, he was working for BBC2's *On the Line* show and for ITV when he travelled out to 'Prison Island', as the England fans had dubbed Sardinia. Taylor had been chairman of the Football Supporters' Association for five years and was widely recognised by England supporters. His job for BBC2 was to get among them and report their voices. And when England progressed to the second round, and the mainland, Taylor went with them. As he recalls, the editorial writers at the Italian papers had been prepared with material, ready to publish when the England hoolies kicked off. But the story blew up in their faces – in Milan, on the night West Germany played Yugoslavia. Taylor was there, and he witnessed 'one of the most serious outbreaks of football violence I have ever seen'.

The Berlin Wall had fallen six months earlier, and the East Germans, despite not having a team at Italia '90, were now emerging into the light of the West. And they were window-shopping in Milan. The West Germans were in town, with a sizeable hooligan presence. They weren't there for the shopping. Meanwhile, as Taylor told me: 'The Yugoslavs in Italy were the most frightening, well-organised fans I have ever seen in my life. They all seemed to be huge, powerful guys who knew what they were doing and acted together. Yugoslavia was two years shy of a brutal civil war and, as it turned out, some of these fans' groups were actively involved in ethnic cleansing when the time came. And, of course, the West German fans could do a bit themselves when they were provoked.'

On 10 June, the famous shopping thoroughfares of Milan turned into a battlefield.

'The West Germans and the Yugoslavs went toe to toe *for hours*,' Taylor says. 'It was like a medieval battle, with no side giving quarter. And while the *carabinieri* were being kept busy, the East Germans were systematically looting some of the most expensive shops in the world.'

And they had brought some transport with them: the trusty Trabant.

'It looked really weird,' Taylor recalls: 'cheap cars overflowing with Gucci and Versace stacked up to the roof.'

The Italian leader writers had to rewrite their editorials. Taylor could only admire their dexterity.

'Instead of saying, "What's wrong with the English? Here we go again . . . They can't handle their alcohol," it was now, "What's wrong with these northern Europeans?" And it was a fantastic analysis: effectively, it was, "They don't understand what alcohol is for: it's a complement to food. They don't get enough sex, and they have a dark Protestant God. It's dark and primitive up there, and they kill themselves on a regular basis because their life is pointlessly dull."'

In this pre-digital age, when fans travelled without mobiles, Facebook or satellite TV, England supporters in Italy were unaware of the frenzy building up there in northern Europe; unaware that people were no longer feeling gloomy about their football and were beginning to congregate in huge numbers in pubs to watch it on widescreen TVs. I remember how the biggest cheers at the bar were not when the camera panned across the England side, lined up for the national anthems, but when it cut to our supporters in the crowd: a roar took off in the pubs – people were applauding the England fans simply for being there. And they had found a fan of their own, in the *Sunday Mirror*'s Bob Harris. 'A lot of the England supporters out there were fabulous,' he says. 'Lovely people, very knowledgeable, and in love with the English game. There were also some heavy-duty villains.'

As England progressed, with Wright excelling in the Baresi role, Waddle and Lineker dovetailing, and Gascoigne playing Merlin, England fans began to head out to Italy in their thousands. Now, it dawned on the fans who had roughed it from Sardinia to Bologna, and down to Naples, that they were no longer lepers. 'When these guys came out for the quarter-final, there was a real solidarity,' says Anne-Marie Mockridge. 'And there had to be. There was a sense among our supporters that this time it had to be different.'

In July 1990, three average performances and two fairly good ones delivered something very different. Bobby Robson's wallies and the 'world's worst supporters' were heading for a World Cup semi-final against West Germany, in Turin – the home of Juventus, just five years after Heysel. Before it became a cliché, TV news images of England's towns and city centres showed squares, thoroughfares and shops deserted by 6 p.m. Trafalgar Square appeared to have been evacuated.

Just before eight o'clock, on 4 July 1990, 28 million people in England cheered their team onto the pitch at Stadio delle Alpi. We were about to watch the most nail-biting game of football England had ever played.

*

The statistics will tell you that Italia '90 was a dour, defensive tournament. It has the lowest goals-per-game average (2.21) in World Cup history. It set a new record of four penalty shoot-outs – two came in the semi-finals – and West Germany's victory over Argentina was described by Brian Glanville in his *History of the World Cup* as 'the worst, most tedious, bad-tempered final in history'. Afterwards, alarmed by the negativity, FIFA outlawed the back pass to the goalkeeper and introduced three points for a win.

And yet FIFA was looking the wrong way – because Italia '90 was most successful tournament ever. No other World Cup has seen such an explosion in TV viewing figures. Mexico '86 was watched by a worldwide audience of 13.5 billion viewers; Italia '90 was watched, worldwide, by 26.6 billion – nearly a 100 per cent increase. (By USA '94, the audience reached its highest-ever figure – 32.1 billion – but it fell away to 24.7 billion at France '98. Japan and South Korea, in 2002, recorded 28.8 billion viewers; Germany 2006 26.2 billion; and South Africa 2010 notched up 26.29 billion – and would surely have nudged the 30 billion mark without those fucking vuvuzelas.)

In one respect, then, Italia '90 was the first of the new World Cups – a tournament of unprecedented global reach. And yet its magic belonged to another age, one of scarcity and rarity. This was the last tournament before FIFA pimped the game around the New World, and it was the last before the arrival of the Champions League. In 1990, we caught a glimpse of the world's greatest players once every four years; by the time Diana Ross kicked off USA '94, they were on our TV screens every four weeks. In 1990, before the players' names appeared on their shirts, people in pubs would compete to identify these foreigners who played the game that we knew, only differently: 'Maldini . . . Careca . . . Ronald Koeman. No, that's Erwin Koeman, isn't it?'

Football hadn't changed over the course of four weeks in June and July 1990, but it had been transformed – from a sporting event into a spectacle of operatic dimensions. Everything from the kits (classic, silky) to the BBC's landmark opening credits and RAI TV's barcode screen graphics was a work of art. To English supporters reeling from Hillsborough, this was something new, something else. When an aria from *Turandot* played, pubs in England fell silent.*

And the football itself was epic drama – drama almost too big for the TV sets people were watching on. They made us sweat and scream and cheer, Robson's team – and ultimately, on that warm night in Turin, they made millions of people cry. And not all of them were men.

The national sport that Thatcher had grown to loathe blew everything else off the front page. Even *The Times* stuck its dainty toe in, with columnist Julie Welch declaring in September, two months after the tournament ended, that football was now a topic no self-respecting dinner party should go without.

As Alan Bairner, professor of sport and social theory at Loughborough University, says, 'Suddenly, football was a game that people with some interest in higher culture could take seriously, in a way that a sport like cricket had always been well served.' James Erskine agrees: 'It was the invention of the media circus,' he says. 'Because, suddenly, people realised: football has value.'

* The BBC's opening credits featured a ballerina – the sister of Peter Rankin, the Hillsborough survivor from Chapter 1.

Five years after the *Sunday Times* had pilloried the slum sport and its slum people, its sister paper was having them round for dinner. Where had the value come from? Perhaps, like Lord Justice Taylor's inspiration for all-seater stadiums, it came from Scotland. Because the Scots – whose triumphalism reached its hilarious nadir in 1978, with Ally MacLeod's tartan terrors – had long since grown accustomed to the truth of British football on the world stage. If the likes of Gemmill, Dalglish, Souness, Jordan and Masson were powerless to beat Peru or Iran in 1978, then the likes of Leighton and Aitken and Johnston could hardly be expected to escape a group at Italia '90 containing Brazil, Sweden and the might of Costa Rica.

No: the Scots had been quicker to forge an identity in defeat, and in doing so, to use football 'as an act of communing', as Richard Giulianotti, Norman Bonney and Mike Hepworth argue in *Football, Violence and Social Identity*. Now, unconsciously, the English followed suit, rediscovering their dignity in defeat. 'There's something about losing with dignity,' says Erskine. 'It says something about the English character. Italia '90 might not have had such a dramatic impact if we had actually won the World Cup. All that jingoism . . .'

Paul Gascoigne did many things for England, but he didn't lose with dignity – not in the way we understood it in 1990. Gazza's tears in Turin were born of unashamed self-pity, flushed out by a yellow card that ruled him out of the final. And in England, in 1990, we were so consumed with self-loathing we didn't dare entertain self-pity. That was a luxury the Italians could afford . . . the Italians, with their amazing cities and their wonderful food and their spaceship stadiums. We were English, we were rubbish, we were the sick man of Europe, and no one cried for us. So Gazza went it alone with his public breakdown in Turin. But try as they might, Pearce and Waddle couldn't help but break down too. Hands over their eyes, heads down, away from the cameras, they choked. And they choked for millions.

Let's forget about social commentators, and *The Times*, and people with an interest in higher culture. Because in the summer of 1990, nowhere was football's new currency more keenly valued than in the pub. Lord Justice Taylor's vision for the game was four years from fruition; his legacy could not be trusted, in the meantime, to Margaret Thatcher and Colin Moynihan – the people who had rubbished England's supporters from one end of Italy to another. The FA, tainted by Hillsborough, did not inspire faith among the fans (few could remember when it had). No, the pub was a safer, more manageable environment for football supporters to assemble in: a place where they could once again believe in their game; a place to commune. The view was in close-up, with replays and 'Nessun Dorma'. The beer and the toilets were on tap; the flags could be strung across the walls, and the squalor of the 1980s football ground locked outside.

'Going to the pub had always been a part of the match-day experience,' says Professor Bairner. 'Now, people realised that something had to give, and in the summer of 1990 they began to realise that what they could sacrifice was the match itself.'

Few of us gathered in the pubs that summer had grasped this: that we were about to become subscribers as well as supporters, and that the game in which we had invested so much time, and money, and risk was about to be transformed for our simple convenience. For those of us reeling from Turin, it was the message and not the medium that mattered: here was validation of our love for the game. For the broadcasters, another message: in June and July 1990, watching football had become the real event – not going to football. Not for the diehards, perhaps, but for an emerging market watching on television: 28 million people had tuned in to England's heartbreak in Turin.

It was the electricity grid that revealed the depth of their despair. The nation's power network always anticipates a major rush after national television events, because millions of kettles click on simultaneously as the English reach for a soothing cup of tea. The national grid later reported that the power surge following Chris Waddle's penalty was the highest ever recorded.

Italia '90 did this. It was beautiful, torrid, torturous and exhilarating. There has never been a tournament like it. It came at the right time, it came from the right country, and it signalled that a year after it fell to its knees, English football had got up again.

4 : Mr Murdoch for You, Prime Minister

In May 1992, I was revising for my English finals in Manchester. Revision was tough: sitting in bed for most of the day with a packet of Digestives on my knees, and a library copy of *One Flew Over the Cuckoo's Nest* or *Great Expectations*. Or *All Played Out*. It wasn't on the syllabus, strictly speaking, but I seemed to fit Ken Kesey or Dickens around Pete Davies's unforgettable account of Italia '90 – one of those books that immediately take you back to a summer, a World Cup, a song.

For many, Italia '90 was the beginning of something special; but as I devoured Davies's book, in the spring of '92, I had a sad sense that it was the end of something too. Euro '92, in utilitarian Sweden, with Graham Taylor's disjointed side, was already taking shape as a hangover I could live without. Gazza was injured; Carlton Palmer, David Batty and Alan Smith were in. And while Liverpool had just won the FA Cup, beating Sunderland in the final, our manager Graeme Souness – one of my childhood heroes – had chosen to talk about his recent heart problems in the *Sun*, of all papers, and in a story they ran on the third anniversary of Hillsborough.

The domestic game had fractured the previous summer, when the FA aided and abetted the First Division clubs to break away from the Football League and form the Premier League. Football seemed to be scheming in the shadow cast by the brilliance of Italia '90. What had seemed in Naples and

Turin like a turning point was already a wisp, luminescent but fragile. The future was already the past, and I didn't feel like getting out of bed.

So it barely registered when, on 18 May 1992, BSkyB secured exclusive rights to broadcast the newly formed Premier League's live football matches for the next five years. The negotiations were held at the Royal Lancaster Hotel, in London, and ITV had been confident of sealing the deal with a bid of £262 million. Until BSkyB received a rather handy tip-off . . .

Alan Sugar, the owner of Amstrad, was present at the meeting in his capacity as chairman of Spurs. It was reported that when Sugar, like the other chairmen, was handed an envelope containing ITV's bid, he phoned Sam Chisholm, BSkyB's chief executive, and told him to 'blow them out of the water'. Lord Sugar's role – albeit pre-ermine – appears questionable. As Barney Ronay wrote in *When Saturday Comes*: 'Amstrad, under his guidance, were the main suppliers of dishes to BSkyB.'

Chisholm duly provided his counter-bid – £304 million – and 'in a moment of laughable propriety', Ronay wrote, 'the Spurs chairman then offered not to vote on the deal, although it was subsequently agreed that he could do so. The Sky bid was accepted by 14 votes to six, Sugar's vote proving crucial in completing the [required] two-thirds majority . . . Amstrad's share price jumped by £7m on announcement of completion of the deal.'

It is worth repeating here that Sugar declared a conflict of interest. And it's worth qualifying too that while his vote tipped the balance decisively in BSkyB's favour, he did not deny ITV the prize. Sugar's vote increased the number of clubs in favour of striking a deal with BSkyB from 13 to 14; had Sugar voted for

ITV's bid, he would have increased their share from six votes to seven, but they would still have been seven votes short of the required majority.

Nonetheless, three years after it launched, Rupert Murdoch's satellite broadcaster had taken a huge punt on the national sport. When Sky arrived, in February 1989, Murdoch's gaze had been fixed firmly on Hollywood films; the broadcasting visionary announced that 'a small nominal charge – around 10p a week – might be made in three years' time for sport and news if income is below expectation'. But over the next two decades, football would be pivotal in the transformation of Rupert Murdoch from a media maverick into the most powerful broadcaster in Britain. It would also help to put him at the heart of one of the biggest political scandals since Watergate.

And the irony is, because it was football that did this, no one was watching.

In the spring of 2012, a shabby procession of media executives, politicians and police officers filed into the Royal Courts of Justice on the Strand to shed light on a bewildering nexus between Rupert Murdoch, the British government and London's Metropolitan Police.

The previous summer, David Cameron had bowed to public pressure and instructed Lord Justice Leveson to inquire into the culture, practice and ethics of the press, in the wake of revelations that Murdoch's *News of the World* newspaper had hacked into the mobile phones of dozens of innocent people, including murdered schoolgirl Milly Dowler, numerous celebrities and relatives of people killed in the 2005 London bombings.

As the public wondered why neither the police nor media

regulators had seen fit to intervene earlier, further allegations emerged – of Metropolitan Police officers taking payments from News International, Murdoch's UK newspaper hub. Meanwhile, in May 2012, with Leveson in the third of his three sittings – considering the relationship between the press and politicians – the former *News of the World* editor Andy Coulson was charged with committing perjury as a witness in a perjury trial . . . while employed as the prime minister's communications chief.

To the established facts of phone hacking at Britain's best-selling Sunday paper were added barely believable allegations surrounding the murder of a private investigator. In March 1987, Daniel Morgan was bludgeoned to death in the car park of a south London pub, an axe embedded so deep into his head that only the shaft remained visible. The killing was reputed to have taken place shortly after Morgan threatened to publicise links between corrupt officers at the Metropolitan Police and News International.

In March 2011, after no fewer than five Metropolitan Police investigations had failed to establish the truth of Morgan's murder, Detective Chief Superintendent Hamish Campbell, of the Met's Homicide and Serious Crime Command, admitted that 'the initial inquiry failed the family and wider public. It is quite apparent that police corruption was a debilitating factor in that investigation.'

One of the most serious allegations put to Lord Leveson came in the testimony of Jacqui Hames, a former detective turned presenter of the BBC's *Crimewatch*. Hames and her family had been put under surveillance by the *News of the World* after her husband, a detective called David Cook, appeared on *Crimewatch* appealing for information into Morgan's murder.

As reported in the *Guardian* on 28 February 2012, Hames told the Leveson inquiry that Rebekah Brooks had explained to the Metropolitan Police's head of PR that her tabloid had targeted Hames and Cook because the paper suspected Hames was having an affair. Hames told Leveson that she considered Brooks's explanation 'unconvincing', adding: 'I believe that the real reason for the *News of the World* placing us under surveillance was that suspects in the Daniel Morgan murder inquiry were using their association with a powerful and well-resourced newspaper to try to intimidate us, and so attempt to subvert the investigation.'

According to the *Guardian*, Hames 'told the inquiry that it was impossible not to conclude that there had been "collusion between people at the *News of the World* and people who were suspected of killing Daniel Morgan"'.

Here was a tangled web of epic proportions. And as it unravelled in 2011, the public became increasingly unsettled at the idea that the owner of the *News of the World* now looked set to buy the remaining 61 per cent stake of BSkyB* that he didn't already own.

Sky is the monopoly satellite broadcaster in Britain, and in 2011 its largest shareholder, with a 39 per cent stake, was Rupert Murdoch's global parent company, News Corp. In 2009–10, as Murdoch prepared to buy the company outright, BSkyB was generating revenues of £5.9 billion – over £1 billion more than the BBC and in excess of £4 billion more than ITV.

The public were furious at the idea that Murdoch stood poised to accumulate even greater influence. There were dire warnings too – from Channel 4, the BBC, the *Guardian* and

* BSkyB was rebranded Sky – its original name – in 2014.

the *Daily Telegraph*, among others – that the takeover would destroy the plurality of Britain's media, by handing a disproportionate level of market share to News Corp. As Stewart Purvis, the former head of Ofcom, said: 'The deal would have created the biggest media player in Europe.'

The widespread sense that the hacking scandal was the result of too much power vested in Murdoch's hands received short shrift in Parliament. On 1 July 2011, Jeremy Hunt, the secretary of state for culture, media and sport, provisionally approved News Corp.'s bid to buy BSkyB outright. Despite the fact that he was accused in Parliament of lying to MPs about his contact with Murdoch while he was weighing up the deal, Hunt had set the date on his rubber stamp to 19 July. Hunt's conscience was clear: as he told the House of Commons, 'With great respect to your office, Mr Speaker, I think that there is a huge difference between misleading Parliament inadvertently and lying.'

Three days later, the *Guardian* unearthed Murdoch's kryptonite. On 4 July 2011, Nick Davies reported that Milly Dowler's phone had been hacked during her disappearance in 2002. Davies initially reported that voicemails on her mobile had been deleted by private investigators working for the *News of the World*. Having gained the PIN number to Dowler's phone, they would then delete old messages to make room for new ones, which they would listen in to in order to lead the story of her disappearance in the press. This had given Dowler's parents false hope that their 13-year-old daughter – who was missing, feared abducted – was deleting the messages herself, and was therefore still alive.

The *Guardian* later acknowledged that it was unlikely the *News of the World* was responsible for the deletions, but the paper had certainly hacked Dowler's phone. As public revulsion erupted, the government appeared paralysed – either unwilling or unable to rein in the journalists or executives at News International who were thought to be responsible. While Ed Miliband realised that the Labour Party had finally to disown its relationship with News International, in the 48 hours after Nick Davies's scoop neither the secretary of state for culture, media and sport nor the prime minister acknowledged that the Dowler revelations might cast doubt on Rupert Murdoch's suitability to own outright the country's most profitable broadcaster – you know, the one that would enable him to flatten most of his rivals in the British media. It fell to Ofcom, the broadcasting standards watchdog, to intervene, raising concerns that BSkyB, if fully owned by News Corp., might not meet the criteria of a 'fit and proper' broadcaster.

On 13 July 2011, News Corp. bowed to public pressure and withdrew its bid for BSkyB. The public were incensed at the naked truth that morality was being bent to power. What few were prepared to acknowledge is that this was football-fuelled power.

It is worth emphasising here that BSkyB was entirely blameless in the hacking scandal. It did not hack Milly Dowler's phone. It was not accused of paying the Metropolitan Police for information, or spying on celebrities, the families of soldiers killed in Afghanistan or those bereaved on 7/7. It is a television broadcaster that – at the time of Hackgate – existed alongside Murdoch's News International papers within News Corp., but there was no allegation of contamination between the two companies. However, until June 2013 (when News

Corp. was restructured in the wake of Hackgate and Leveson) it was BSkyB that powered News Corp. in Britain.

Murdoch stepped up his bid for BSkyB in 2010. The previous year's accounts would have made plain the size of the prize. In 2009, News Corp.'s UK operations comprised BSkyB and News International, which was formed of two subsidiaries: Times Newspapers (*The Times* and *Sunday Times*) and News Group Newspapers (the *Sun* and *News of the World*). While News Group posted profits of £40.3 million in 2009, these were dwarfed by losses of £87.7 million at Times Newspapers – leaving the Murdoch papers £47 million in the red.

There would seem to be little incentive for a newspaper proprietor to sustain annual losses of almost £50 million – unless, of course, those newspapers brought him influence in political circles, and their losses could be underwritten. Fortunately, in 2009–10, BSkyB was posting profits in excess of £1 billion. It had 10 million subscribers, paying an average of £492 a year, and was valued at £8 billion.

Few at BSkyB have ever been under any illusions where that value comes from. Murdoch himself has described football as 'the battering ram' that drove BSkyB into an unassailable position in satellite TV by the mid-1990s. David Hill, the company's former director of sport, has said that 'football is first, second and third' in the appeal of satellite TV. In 2011–12, it was estimated that football delivered £3 billion a year into the BSkyB coffers – half of all its revenues. Accordingly, in May 2012, Kelvin MacKenzie wrote in the *Daily Telegraph* that if the company lost the rights to televise the Premier League, its share price would halve – and that, according to many analysts, was a conservative estimate.

So vital is football to BSkyB/Sky that in June 2012 it paid the Premier League £2.3 billion for 116 live matches in each of the seasons 2013–16. At a time when the company's majority shareholder was enmeshed in a scandal that cast the future of its broadcasting licence in doubt, it was still prepared to bid over 20 per cent of its market capitalisation on English football.

There is a delicious irony here: football, the game once pilloried by the *Sunday Times* as 'a slum sport watched by slum people', now subsidises the *Sunday Times*. But there is a darker truth: by 2010–11, a 20-year monopoly of televised football had given Murdoch so much power he was on the verge of wiping out his rivals in the British media. The threat to 'media plurality' may have seemed a rather technical issue set against the lurid headlines of Hackgate, but the ramifications of Murdoch's taking full control of BSkyB were staggering. The controversy is worth revisiting, because in 2016 the threat this eventuality poses to the rest of the UK media remains – indeed, if anything, it is even greater now.

The danger was spelt out in September 2010, when the media analysts Enders Analysis sent a memorandum to Vince Cable, the coalition business secretary, who was monitoring News Corp.'s bid for BSkyB. The most alarming argument in Enders's report was that if News Corp. acquired BSkyB it would be able to put together a multimedia bundle that could cripple its competitors – not only on television, but in print and online too. The bundle would comprise the Wapping papers, online content and BSkyB.

As Enders warned Cable, 'BSkyB's huge financial clout means that it can buy up popular TV programmes from the US, placing them behind a paywall in the UK . . . Such packages would be impossible for other newspapers to emulate . . . BSkyB and News International are already the largest companies in their respective sectors, and following the merger, the combined group will have annual revenues of £7 billion . . . If this happens, long-held reader loyalty to titles such as *The Mirror*, *The Daily Telegraph* and even *The Daily Mail* could be severely tested.'

Murdoch was already in control of 37 per cent of the country's national newspapers; now, he was on the verge of claiming nearly half of its TV revenues. The significance was clear: as Polly Toynbee wrote in the *Guardian*, other news providers would be reduced to 'a husk'. And Murdoch's influence over government of either stripe would be guaranteed in perpetuity.

In November 2010, when Vince Cable ordered Ofcom to review the takeover bid on the grounds of 'media plurality', James Murdoch played his ace: were concerns over media plurality really worth 'jeopardising an £8 billion investment in the UK', he asked?

And this was the crux: as Jeremy Hunt would freely admit to Lord Leveson, BSkyB was an £8 billion piece of business the country could ill afford to lose in these straitened times. Even as Murdoch's *News of the World* ran amok, the government felt powerless to rein in a mogul with an £8 billion business he could relocate if his nose were put out of joint. Football had given Murdoch his immunity.

The hacking scandal passed, of course, and the *News of the World* is no more. Murdoch's empire was restructured in 2013, with his print business retained under News Corp. and his TV interests assigned to 21st Century Fox. But the threat to his rivals remains. BSkyB is now Sky again, but it is no longer worth £8 billion. It now has 12 million customers in the UK and Ireland, and profits of £1.3 billion. It is currently worth £11.3 billion.

In October 2015, James Murdoch, the chief executive of 21st Century Fox, signalled the family would move again for Sky. 'The company has grown enormously,' he told the *Hollywood Reporter*. 'We've also been clear that, over time, having 40% of an unconsolidated asset is not an end state that is natural for us.'

In February 2016, he was reappointed chairman of Sky – a sign, many analysts believe, that the family is edging closer to a fresh takeover bid. Should Fox finally gobble up Sky, the British media landscape would appear to be Murdoch's to settle, once more. Football remains his battering ram. But as Peter Snape has explained, politicians don't grasp the real power of our national sport: consumed with focus groups and opinion polls, they are suckered into the historic conceit that control of news is the key to power, and that football is an irrelevance.

Our media laws only reinforce this. In October 2011, Jeremy Hunt wrote to Ofcom to request clarification on issues relating to media plurality in the event of a major takeover bid. Ofcom replied: 'In terms of scope, a review of plurality should be limited to news and current affairs.'

In short, in Britain concerns over media plurality are concerns about the provision of news – there must be a range of voices. History tells us that a state monopoly news broadcaster is inimical to democracy, while it is self-evident that politically biased broadcasters (such as Fox News, for example) are prone to propaganda; a balance in news provision therefore remains a foundation of a healthy democracy. It simply didn't matter to politicians that BSkyB had a monopoly on football for the two decades leading up to the Leveson inquiry, because football is a minority sport in the House of Commons. It is only a game.

But as 12 million subscribers to the rebranded Sky will tell you, no one coughs up £500 a year to watch the news.

Historic scepticism about the intrinsic value of football accounts for much of the myth-making around Rupert Murdoch, football saviour: surely only a genius could transform a game as worthless as this? Indeed, there are few ironies more bitter than the fact that the man ultimately responsible for the *Sun*'s Hillsborough calumny should be the man to profit most from the game that rose from the Taylor Report. Politicians might shrug: who cares? It's only football, and these were only football fans.

They should have taken more interest back in 1989. For in the *Sun*'s scandalous reporting of Hillsborough, Rupert Murdoch's newspapers were confirmed in their impunity. And just as the power he derived from football would ultimately help to bring Murdoch before Leveson, so it was football that encouraged a contempt for the dead that would resurface in the Dowler affair.

There is no one in politics better placed to argue this than Steve Rotheram, the Labour MP for Liverpool Walton and a member of the Commons select committee that investigated the hacking scandal in 2011–12. In the week I went to meet Rotheram at the House of Commons, in July 2012, he had just won an award for the year's best speech in the House – an accolade voted for by MPs of all parties. His moment came in October 2011, when he opened the historic parliamentary debate on Hillsborough – a full 22 years and six months late.

Rotheram is a Liverpool supporter; he was at Hillsborough, where he watched the disaster unfold from the stands. And his speech in the Commons was remarkable, not least for the fact that (as he cheerily admitted to me) he was still writing it as he got to his feet.

Steve Rotheram became the first MP ever to read aloud the names of the 96 in Parliament, and he corrected many other injustices and untruths. In fact, forget untruths: the debate was impressive for the way it dispensed with parliamentary protocol, for seldom can the words 'lies' and 'lied' have echoed around the chamber as they did that night.

Shortly afterwards, Rotheram was appointed to the House of Commons select committee that investigated the hacking scandal. Some observers criticised Rotheram for raising the *Sun*'s coverage of Hillsborough with James Murdoch, complaining that a Liverpool MP was 'shoehorning Hillsborough' into the hacking debate. But as Rotheram told me at the Commons, the hacking scandal might have been seeded by Hillsborough.

'Had the *Sun* (ergo Murdoch) been reined in over "The Truth",' he said, 'it is my contention that News International would have had to have been more circumspect with their reporting on other major issues. In 1989, besides a loss of circulation on Merseyside, the *Sun* got away with that outrage scot-free.'

And this was outrage on an historic scale: according to Rotheram, 'Kelvin MacKenzie committed one of the most shameful examples of duplicitous journalism since the *Daily Mail* published the Zinoviev letter.'

In 1924, four days before a general election, the *Daily Mail* 'leaked' a letter purporting to be from the chairman of the Soviet Comintern, Grigory Zinoviev, which urged British communists to mobilise within and around the Labour Party and promote revolution in Britain. Labour lost the election by a landslide. The letter was later revealed to be a forgery, probably written by Sidney Reilly ('ace of spies') and almost certainly circulated by MI6.

Rotheram believes the *Sun* was licensed to pursue an anti-Liverpool agenda that was fashionable in Tory circles in the 1980s. 'The Toxteth riots of the early '80s, the Militant Liverpool City Council of the mid-'80s and the Heysel disaster in 1985 all tarnished the city's reputation,' he said.

Rotheram has not overstated his case: cabinet papers released in December 2011 revealed that in the wake of Toxteth, in 1981, the government was drawing up plans to 'manage the decline' of Liverpool; there was even talk of evacuating the city. The chancellor, Geoffrey Howe, told the PM: 'I cannot help feeling that the option of managed decline is one which we should not forget altogether. We must not expend all our limited resources in trying to make water flow uphill.'

Not until 2004 would the *Sun* finally apologise for 'the most terrible mistake in our history'. But this was no mistake. As Peter Chippindale and Chris Horrie reported in *Stick It Up Your Punter*, their celebrated history of the *Sun*:

> As MacKenzie's layout was seen by more and more people, a collective shudder ran through the office, [but] MacKenzie's dominance was so total there was nobody left in the organisation who could rein him in except Murdoch. [Everyone] seemed paralysed, 'looking like rabbits in the

headlights', as one hack described them. The error staring them in the face was too glaring. It obviously wasn't a silly mistake; nor was it a simple oversight . . . It was a 'classic smear'.

Kelvin MacKenzie's Hillsborough coverage appears to mark the point at which the link between News International, the police and a Thatcher government – first explored between the miners' strike of 1984–5 and the Wapping print dispute of 1987 – was confirmed, over the deaths of 96 football supporters. As MacKenzie told a Commons select committee as long ago as 1994: 'I regret Hillsborough. It was a fundamental mistake. The mistake was I believed what an MP said. It was a Tory MP. If he had not said it and the chief superintendent had not agreed with it, we would not have gone with it.' Two years later, MacKenzie's account took another twist, when he told Radio 4 that in its coverage of Hillsborough, the *Sun* 'was a vehicle for others'.

In 2012, the Hillsborough Independent Panel revealed that the source of 'The Truth' was White's, a Sheffield news agency, which obtained the lurid allegations about drunken, marauding Liverpool fans from four South Yorkshire Police officers and Irvine Patnick, Conservative MP for Sheffield Hallam.

In April 1989, with football in ruins, the British government turned a blind eye to one of the most outrageous acts of defamation ever printed in a British newspaper – because it served their anti-football agenda. Remember Lord Onslow vowing, in March 1989, that the government was 'determined to get to grips with the members of the yob class' who attended football matches? Football was asking for it, and in 1989, the *Sun*

– selling 4.3 million copies a day – genuinely set the terms of the national debate around the tragedy. If proof were needed, it came in 2010, when Jeremy Hunt blithely trotted out the myth that Hillsborough was the work of hooligans. That Britain's secretary of state for culture, media and sport could be of this opinion as recently as 2010 beggars belief, but in the 20 intervening years the political will to tame the excesses of the Murdoch papers, or even to acknowledge their malpractice, had simply not existed.

As Steve Rotheram says, 'Perhaps if there were a proper regulatory body at the time which took decisive action against that sort of immoral reporting on Hillsborough, newspapers in general, but specifically the Murdoch media, may have been less likely to have plunged the depths with all that went on with Hackgate.'

Lord Justice Leveson published the conclusions to his inquiry in November 2012. He found no widespread corruption of the police by the press. He cleared Jeremy Hunt and David Cameron of being too close to the Murdoch empire. He ruled that there had been a failure of systems of management and compliance at the *News of the World*, and a general lack of respect for individual privacy and dignity at the paper. Leveson was not moved to comment on the role that football has played in the fortunes of Rupert Murdoch.

Many supporters who bristle at Murdoch's influence over the national game would no doubt have told Leveson (had he enquired) that Murdoch owes everything to football – that it saved him from bankruptcy. It is not a theory that would stand up in court.

In November 1990, Murdoch's Sky TV merged with its satellite rival, British Satellite Broadcasting, to form BSkyB. While Murdoch would later claim the merger represented his 'outstanding achievement as a journalist', his victory was somewhat pyrrhic. In the autumn of 1990 he was in debt to the tune of $8.7 billion – or, as the *Guardian* helpfully pointed out, 'roughly half the foreign debt of Colombia'. It would be 18 months before that first deal to televise Premier League football was signed. And it was in this interim period that Rupert Murdoch pulled News Corp. back from the brink.

So desperate was his plight in 1990–1 that Murdoch embarked on what is thought to be the biggest restructuring of debt ever seen outside a bankruptcy court. As the website Funding Universe outlines in a report titled *The History of News Corporation*, 'Project Dolphin' required Rupert Murdoch to repay $7.6 billion of debt by 1994. Murdoch agreed to sell off $800 million worth of business, and 55 per cent of News Corp.'s Australian printing and magazine businesses. Meanwhile, between 1989 and 1990 the percentage of News Corp.'s profits attributed to companies in tax havens rose from 25 per cent to 54.5 per cent, and by 1990, as the report outlines, 'News Corp.'s effective tax rate [in the US, where it is based] was 1.76 per cent, rather than the statutory 39 per cent'.

At the same time, Sam Chisholm, the first CEO of BSkyB, embarked on a ruthless period of crisis management, and by the summer of 1991 he had reduced the company's losses to £1.6 million a week. In renegotiating the exorbitant film rights signed by BSB and Sky with the Hollywood studios, Chisholm saved BSkyB £100 million a year with one deal. By the end of 1991, the banks were sufficiently reassured to allow Murdoch to defer the repayment of $3 billion of debt from February 1994 until 1997. Meanwhile, BSkyB was showing its first operating profits – £100,000 per week – two years ahead of schedule.

Murdoch had saved News Corp. before the Premier League even kicked off. And in 1992, the security of that first, five-year rights deal to football gave BSkyB a monopoly on satellite TV in Britain. By January 1995 it had almost 4 million subscribers, and the company was valued at £4 billion in a stock flotation that reduced Murdoch's holding to 39 per cent, where it stands at the time of writing. By 1996, BSkyB was posting profits of £257 million, and it has never looked back.

And yet, for all the brilliance of Project Dolphin, Murdoch had been afforded critical breathing space in November 1990 – because Sky's takeover of BSB was the deal that saved his empire. How the deal was ever permitted to take place, and how it would transform English football, was a prologue to much of what played out before Lord Leveson. And it was a hugely controversial backdrop to Margaret Thatcher's last stand.

On 18 October 1990, the Football League published its response to the Taylor Report. *One Game, One Team, One Voice: Managing Football's Future* was an attempt to build bridges with the FA, fundamentally; to deliver agreement on how best to maximise TV and sponsorship revenues; and to resolve the historic tensions arising whenever the League clubs' players were picked to play for a national team that, essentially, was the FA's greatest asset (alongside the FA Cup). The League's olive branch would be snapped in half the following year by the FA, whose own manifesto, *The Blueprint for the Future of Football*, was the approval the top clubs were seeking to break away to form the Premier League. However, the FA and Football League were united over the key argument: as *One Game, One Team, One Voice* noted, 'With respect to television, English football is about to enter an era of unprecedented opportunity.' That opportunity came in the form of satellite television.

Satellite TV's compelling commercial and technological value put it at the centre of the Broadcasting Act, one of the key pieces of legislation in Margaret Thatcher's final term. The Act (which would be passed in her final month as PM, November 1990) was designed to introduce more competition to television, and this was competition with a distinctly political imperative: the BBC and ITV had become a major irritation in Downing Street, and the arrival of satellite TV, with its proliferation of channels, would reduce their audience share.

Thatcher's antipathy towards the BBC had peaked in the early years of her reign: over its coverage of the Falklands war in 1982, and in particular the sinking of the Argentine warship *General Belgrano*. But tensions remained throughout her decade in power, and in 1987 Alasdair Milne was forced to resign as BBC director-general by the chairman, Marmaduke Hussey, who was appointed by Thatcher to bring the BBC into line, following controversy over its coverage of the miners' strike and the US air strikes on Libya in 1986. Milne had also refused to pull the *Real Lives* documentary, which included an interview with Sinn Fein's Martin McGuinness, and in January 1987 he was replaced by a technocrat, Michael Checkland.

Checkland took a more conciliatory approach before government, and towards the late 1980s it was ITV that proved the greater thorn in Thatcher's side. Granada's hard-hitting documentary series *World in Action* was a habitual troublemaker, but tension between ITV and Number 10 rose to boiling point in 1988, when Thames TV's *This Week* series exposed the SAS's controversial killing of three IRA agents in Gibraltar that March. Its programme, *Death on the Rock*, has entered broadcasting legend; it caused so much political damage that three years after it was broadcast, and at the first opportunity, Thames TV lost its London ITV franchise to Carlton.

According to Mark Wheeler, professor of political communications at London Metropolitan University, 'By the middle of the 1980s the British broadcasting elite and political elite were probably about as distant from one another as they have been in the last 30 years. Historically, there was always a close affiliation between the heads of the BBC and ITV with those in political power, but there wasn't that affiliation between the Thatcherites and the broadcasting elites.'

At the same time, England's biggest football clubs were also casting around for a hammer to break the dominance of terrestrial television. In 1988, the last TV rights before the Premier League was formed were sold to ITV, in a four-year deal worth £44 million. A pittance – and confirmation, the clubs have argued, that the BBC and ITV were operating a cartel to drive down the price for football. It is not a view shared by Jonathan Martin, who ran BBC Sport from 1981 to 1998.

'I would deny that idea emphatically,' Martin told me. 'It's rubbish. The idea that the BBC and ITV ever sat down in a room and said, "OK, you have the rugby, we'll have the cricket," is complete and utter nonsense. I spent my whole time competing with ITV, and they spent their whole time competing with the BBC. And Sky moved in on the football.'

Cartel or not, when it came to their football coverage, the terrestrial TV channels were on borrowed time. In 1987, Granada – a shareholder in British Satellite Broadcasting – approached the Football League with a view to striking a deal with the First Division clubs. Then, in March 1988, BSB met the Football League again, this time to discuss a ten-year deal worth £6.3 million a year, index-linked. However, the League got cold feet at the prospect of being locked into such a long contract. That same year, Sky TV offered £47 million for the rights to First Division matches.

ITV took fright. Now, its head of sport, Greg Dyke, offered £1 million each to Liverpool, Man Utd, Arsenal, Spurs and Everton for the rights to televise their matches; Dyke was content to leave the rest of the First Division clubs to broker their own deals with rival television networks. This breakaway was only thwarted when Philip Carter, the chairman of Everton, was ousted as president of the Football League in 1988, and replaced by Bill Fox of Blackburn Rovers.*

But the writing was on the wall: satellite TV promised a new revenue stream unlike anything football had seen before. And while the BBC had orchestrated football's renaissance at Italia '90, they never stood a chance. As Jonathan Martin explains: 'The thinking was: we are the least funded of the three players, so we are least likely to win a bidding war. We had nowhere else to go, so we looked for a partner. ITV wanted to go it alone and try to kill BSkyB at birth. That seemed unlikely. We went with BSkyB. There were some people inside the BBC who said: "We've given up. We've become the minor player." But

* Joe Lovejoy's *Glory, Goals and Greed: Twenty Years of the Premier League* offers an excellent insight into these negotiations.

we didn't, for a long, long while, because [by acting as junior partner in the 1992 TV deal] we were getting most of the audience and Sky were paying most of the money. That was a good deal. It was short-termist, but if you look around Europe, most of the national broadcasters have faced the same competition from satellite. The core thing is,' he says, 'you can never turn technology back. It's happened since: first we had satellite TV, now we have social media. Content is important, but technology leads the way.'

And in the autumn of 1990, the technology that was set to revolutionise football was in the possession of British Satellite Broadcasting. And then it wasn't.

It had never been Margaret Thatcher's intention to hand Rupert Murdoch 'the most important single advance since Caxton invented the printing press' (© R. Murdoch, pre-internet). The first broadcaster in Britain to get a run at satellite TV was in fact the BBC, which was awarded a licence for two satellite channels in 1982. However, by 1983, concerned at the rising cost of the project, the BBC invited co-operation from the independent television networks, and by 1985, unable to invest the huge sums required, the BBC left the field altogether. So it was that in December 1986, when a conglomerate called British Satellite Broadcasting won the tender to become Britain's first satellite station, it was formed initially of Anglia TV and Granada TV, along with Pearson, Virgin and Amstrad.

And this is what they won: as the only authorised Direct Broadcast by Satellite (DBS) provider, BSB was given sole legal rights to 'uplink' satellite television from British soil. It was an effective monopoly, one regulated by the Independent

Broadcasting Authority (IBA) until it would be enshrined in the Broadcasting Act of 1989/90.

Murdoch's News International bid for the licence in 1986, and was beaten fairly and squarely. But Murdoch simply refused to accept defeat. In 1988, his satellite company, Sky TV, struck a 'carriage deal' with SES (the Luxembourg-based operator of the Astra telecommunications satellite) to beam in a signal to Sky viewers in the UK from Europe. By using a telecommunications rather than a television satellite, and by beaming in images from Luxembourg rather than uplinking on British soil, Murdoch had stuck not one but two fingers up to the IBA.

Thus began a competition for Britain's fledgling satellite TV market where none should have existed. In February 1989, Murdoch switched on Sky TV from a muddy industrial estate in Osterley, west London, and beat BSB to launch by a year. The morning after the station appeared, a headline in *The Times* declared: 'Monopoly Over, Says Murdoch'. BSB were furious, complaining that 'Mr Murdoch has a position of unique power in British life that no other western country would permit a foreigner to hold.' But if the regulators appeared powerless to reel Murdoch in, it was partly because they couldn't fully comprehend the change that was heading their way. According to Professor Mark Wheeler, 'Murdoch baffled the authorities with technology, by using the telecommunications-based Astra satellite to broadcast television services, and put his trust in a sympathetic government to stay hands off.'

Hands off is one thing, but there was a giant handicap in this two-horse race, and it was carried by BSB. Because BSB was operating as a de facto national satellite broadcaster, it was charged with breaking new technological ground by introducing the D-Mac, an embryonic, high-definition TV system. This demanded huge investment: between late 1989 and January 1990, BSB's two Marco Polo satellites were launched from Cape Canaveral in Florida, at a cost of £500 million each. BSB had sunk £1 billion into its launch; Sky just £25 million into its Astra satellite.

Moreover, BSB was saddled with a requirement to maintain certain standards of content. Sky, on the other hand, was free to broadcast pretty much anything it liked. It seemed to have forgotten about football: now it preferred *Tony Blackburn's Sky by Day*, *The All-New Sale of the Century* and Derek Jameson, garrulous scourge of 'those bloody sausage-eating Germans' and other funny foreigners.

When Murdoch launched Sky TV in February 1989, he was uncharacteristically circumspect: 'As to whether people will buy dishes,' he said, 'we are going on a hunch.' His hunch was that, ultimately, if anything would sell the dish it would be Hollywood movies. As Professor Wheeler explains: 'Satellite was a new form of television, funded through viewer subscription and directed by exclusivity of service, so it required a critical mass of viewers, and the idea was to then sell on layers of product. And Hollywood movies were the gateway.'

So, throughout much of 1989 and 1990, BSB and Sky battered each other to a standstill in Hollywood: here were two British networks, barely up and running, offering the major studios two or three times the rate for movies that Hollywood was fetching from the US domestic market. While BSB won the rights to films from Columbia, MGM/United Artists, Paramount and Universal, at a cost of £400 million, Sky could bank on exclusive access to 20th Century Fox – because

Murdoch had bought the studio in 1985 (it was in pursuit of Fox that Murdoch became a naturalised American).

However, the cost of films, reported the *Guardian*, 'was higher possibly than even [Murdoch] had imagined'. Aside from Fox, he had committed £270 million for the rights to films from Disney, Orion, Touchstone, Warner and other independent studios. As Andrew Neil, chairman of Sky, told Richard Belfield, Christopher Hird and Sharon Kelly in *Murdoch: The Great Escape*: 'We had a simple choice. Either we matched these crazy sums [offered by BSB] or there was no point in going ahead at all.'

But as the unforgettable summer of 1990 bled into autumn, Arnie, Bruce and Demi weren't delivering. Now, BSB and Sky became locked in a death embrace. BSB's colossal outlay of £1 billion on its satellites alone had netted just 110,000 subscribers; its PR had become a disaster, and its hopeless square aerials (or Squarials) were widely reported to melt under a hot sun (nowhere more widely reported, presumably, than in the *Sun* and *News of the World*). Sky was streaking ahead, with 1.5 million viewers, but by September 1990 new installations of its dishes had flatlined, and by October, Rupert Murdoch was staring into the abyss – in debt to the tune of $8.7 billion.

As Belfield, Hird and Kelly report, in the 12 months to June 1990, Sky had lost £228 million. It owed News International £444 million and had a £33 million overdraft. In the next three months, it would lose another £59 million, and had committed £280 million to TV rights and capital expenditure. 'All this,' they wrote, 'in a company which was costing £6m a week to run, and only taking in £2m.'

It's worth re-reading those figures, for to realise how big

these losses were contemporaneously, in 1990, we must double them in today's money. In other words, News Corp. was the equivalent of $17.4 billion in debt – to 146 banks. Sky's losses were running at £456 million, and the debts/commitments at £1.5 billion, in a company costing £12 million a week to run and taking in just £4 million. Perhaps more significantly, these were debts that Sky needed to pay off not in the global, multimedia market of 2016, but in the struggling British satellite market of 1990 – a market in which BSB held the only licence.

Rupert Murdoch was finished. And then he wasn't.

In the last week of October 1990, BSB's four remaining shareholders – Reed, Pearson, Granada and Chargeurs, a French company – realised they had little chance of increasing their subscriber numbers from 110,000 to the required target of 400,000 by the year's end. Now, in a stunning piece of blindsiding, they decided to divest their licence as Britain's sole DBS provider and merge with Sky. BSkyB was born, and with it the 'unprecedented opportunity' for football.

The merger took place in the first week of November 1990 at the Lucknam Park hotel, near Bath. By this stage, the two companies had incurred a joint cost of £1.25 billion, over £1 billion of which was borne by BSB. The company had become synonymous with corporate extravagance, and it looked cumbersome and dull-witted alongside the more nimble Sky. But if the cost of bearing its technological remit wasn't enough, its audience had been swept up by a company operating if not strictly in breach of British media regulations then at least against the spirit of them for nearly two years. Now, the farcical irony was that because Sky was coming to the table in better health (i.e. it had more subscribers and much lower overheads), News International was required under the merger to commit a further £30 million, whereas BSB had to stump up £70 million. And News International would take 80 per cent of the first £400 million profit, despite the fact that BSB's was the better technology. This was nothing less than an extraordinary coup for Murdoch: as the *New York Times* wrote, it was 'a deal that probably has saved the empire'.*

Earlier that week, on 1 November 1990, the long-awaited Broadcasting Act had been passed. This should have disqualified Murdoch from owning a DBS licence and rendered the merger invalid. Firstly, Murdoch was a US citizen, and the Broadcasting Act forbade foreigners from owning a controlling share in a British DBS contract. Ownership of the Wapping newspapers meant that he should also have been restricted to a 20 per cent stake in a satellite broadcaster, and yet he had contrived to walk away with 48 per cent of the new BSkyB. When Sky announced the merger, they breached yet another regulation, as the power to dispose of the sole franchise was not within BSB's licence. However, neither BSB nor Sky had seen fit to report the deal to the minister in charge of broadcasting, Peter Lloyd. The IBA (which had the authority to revoke BSB's licence, thus rendering Sky's takeover pointless) only learnt of the merger an hour before it was finalised – too late to mount a barrier. Unimpressed, but impotent, it declared the deal 'a serious breach of BSB's contract', but decided that terminating the licence would not be in the interests of viewers.

Murdoch had crept in on the blindside. No one in

* See *Murdoch* by William Shawcross (1993).

government or among the broadcasting regulators had seen this extraordinary 'merger' coming. No one, that is, except the prime minister.

On 29 October, three days before the Broadcasting Bill became law, and with Sky on the brink of collapse, Rupert Murdoch arrived at Downing Street. Thatcher was in discussion with a foreign visitor, and as Murdoch told Mathew Horsman in *Sky High*, she turned to her visitor and said: 'Here is Mr Murdoch, who gives us Sky News, the only unbiased news in the UK.' To which Murdoch replied, 'Well, you know it is costing us a lot, and we are going to have to do a merger.' As Horsman reports, the PM nodded. According to Peter Chippindale, Suzanne Franks and Roma Felstein in *Dished: Rise and Fall of British Satellite Broadcasting*, 'Mrs Thatcher made a note but said nothing, and Murdoch left the room.'

That the conversation between the two should extend to no more than one sentence apiece is unlikely . . . but what happened to that note? Certainly, it appears the PM failed to pass it on to either Peter Lloyd or the IBA in time for them to block the 'merger'.

By 12 November, an earthquake was shaking Westminster. After 11 years in power, Margaret Thatcher was finally deserted by her most senior allies, aghast at her increasingly confrontational and isolationist stance with Europe and with her own cabinet. Despite the magnitude of Thatcher's increasingly inevitable departure, the BSkyB merger was itself causing uproar in the Commons. The home secretary, David Waddington, insisted that Thatcher had not been in dereliction of duty by failing to give the IBA or the House notice of a private conversation she had had with Rupert Murdoch on 29 October.

'It certainly was no business of the prime minister to go phoning around the place to all and sundry, and me included, saying that she had been told by Mr Murdoch what everybody already knew,' he said. 'The possibility of such a merger has been knocked around in the trade press for months and months. During the meeting with my right honourable friend the prime minister, Mr Murdoch mentioned the possibility of a merger, but only in the most general terms.'

The *Independent on Sunday* had predicted as much the previous day: 'The fact is that Mr Murdoch employs his media power in the direct service of a political party, which now turns a blind eye to what it has itself depicted in Parliament as a breach of the law in which Mr Murdoch is involved. So much for Mrs Thatcher's lectures on media bias.'

David Waddington rejected Roy Hattersley's demand that the deal be referred to the Monopolies and Mergers Commission. He told MPs: 'The [Broadcasting] Act is designed to open up new opportunities. It is for entrepreneurs to take up those opportunities and for viewers to decide whether they are to succeed. It is no part of the government's duty to prop up and subsidise these entrepreneurs.'

The hypocrisy was breathtaking: without Thatcher's decision to keep the merger under wraps, away from the IBA, the House of Commons and the minister Peter Lloyd, no one – least of all his 146 creditors – would have seen any reason to prop up Rupert Murdoch any longer. As a *Guardian* leader outlined: 'Mr Murdoch's successes are not built on the raw logic of the market alone. They often depend, from the start, on the tacit favours that politicians extend. He acquired that great cash cow, the *Sunday Times*, because Whitehall deemed it in loss, and thus beyond the Monopolies and Mergers Commission . . . there are dodgy, unsettling questions here.'

Indeed. Lord Snape regards David Waddington as 'the most reactionary home secretary of my time', but in one sense he was quite the revolutionary. For between January and November 1990, football and TV were remade for one another, on Waddington's watch. The season after he rebranded the national game a football industry that had now to exploit new TV revenues, it wasn't the home secretary's place to go phoning around all and sundry to alert the regulators to 'what every-body already knew' – the fact that a US citizen could be about to break, well, just a hatful of laws and walk off with the only licensed satellite TV broadcaster in Britain. Was it?

In a sense, the British public was signed up to the political movement that transformed football in 1990: sufficient num-bers voted for the laissez-faire policies the Conservative gov-ernment had promoted throughout the 1980s, and which had seen them win three elections back to back. But did they really understand the ramifications? Anthony Simonds-Gooding did. In the week following the BSB–Sky 'merger', the former chief executive of British Satellite Broadcasting recalled his fruitless battle to persuade Thatcher to subject Murdoch's ownership of Sky to cross-media regulations. 'The government must answer for this,' he said. 'They turned a blind eye . . . This is going to be a fearfully powerful company.'

The inevitability of BSkyB's power grab in Britain was sealed by the cynical disposal of England's national sport by the Tories, the FA and the top clubs. Not until 1998 would a government wake up to the danger inherent in a monopoly of football on TV.

In the autumn of that year, BSkyB made a move to buy Man Utd. Urged on by outraged United fans, by Tony Lloyd, a minister in the Foreign Office, and Stan Orme, a Labour MP for Salford, Stephen Byers, the trade and industry secretary, referred the deal to the Monopolies and Mergers Commission, which blocked it in April 1999.

Ownership of Man Utd would have given Murdoch the most influential voice when it came to the Premier League's negotiations with BSkyB over TV rights deals – the significance and absurdity of which are obvious. There was another, more serious concern.

In his office at the Commons, I spoke to Chris Bryant, the Labour MP for Rhondda, and erstwhile member of the Culture, Media and Sport Select Committee. Bryant has an intricate knowledge of broadcasting technology, and he explained how close Rupert Murdoch came to total domination of English football through the Man Utd bid.

'That deal would have been the golden ticket,' Bryant explained, 'because Murdoch would have had the value chain locked up. In broadcasting, the value chain consists of the performer, the production company, the channel that commissions the production, the broadcaster that hosts the channel, and the platform it goes out on. If all that is in one private hand, with no public interest, there is a danger.'

Labour broke the chain by withholding from Murdoch the star performer, Man Utd. But as I put it to Bryant, the clubs are still overly reliant on BSkyB money – or, once again, Sky's.

'Exactly,' he said.

So Sky effectively owns the product, regardless of losing one link in the value chain.

'Yes, exactly. They tried to own the product directly, and now they effectively own it indirectly. And that's, I think, a massive problem for the sport.'

The massive problem is that many Premier League clubs are dependent on Sky's money.

One of the more bewildering statistics to emerge from the 2013–16 TV deal is that the 71 per cent increase in the price of domestic rights resulted from sealed bids. This is remarkable when you consider that BT had only tentatively joined the fray, and that, as Enders Analysis reported to Vince Cable in 2010, 'There no longer exists any serious rival to [Sky] in terms of bidding for live televised Premier League matches . . .'

So why was Sky pouring £2.3 billion into a game it has enjoyed a monopoly on for two decades, and upping its tender by 71 per cent? According to the *Guardian's* Owen Gibson, it's a simple equation: 'The money [Sky] pours in is no longer dictated by what it must pay to outbid its rivals but by what it feels must be invested to maintain the quality,' he wrote. 'In other words, it pours billions into Premier League football in order that its clubs can continue to compete for the best players in a global market.'

English football is awash with Murdoch's money, because this is Murdoch's product. And the product requires the biggest stars in order that Sky can sell its dishes. For their part, the clubs have to spend Murdoch's money on these stars in order to stay in the money league, which means, as Enders Analysis reported, Sky's position 'is further strengthened by the poor financial state of many of the Premier League clubs, which makes them increasingly dependent on its willingness to back them'.

*

In the two decades since the Premier League arrived, governments have pursued a consistent line of thinking with regard to football and broadcasting: it is not in the national interest to regulate – competition remains the best form of regulation. But it's clear that the market did not allow for genuine competition to Murdoch from 1992 until as recently as 2013, when BT first entered the fray. And even as BT has grown into a genuine rival to Sky, in 2016, there is scant evidence that this delivers a better deal for subscribers.

In February 2015, the rights to televise live Premier League matches from 2016–19 were sold for £5.14 billion. BT secured 42 games a season; Sky, 126 games a season. Most analysts believe that once the overseas TV rights are factored in, the total income for the Premier League will be £8.2 billion. This marks the second consecutive 70 per cent price rise on the previous deal.

One of the more striking features of the auction was noted by Swissramble, as good a blogger as you'll find on football finance. In *The Premier League TV Deal: Master and Servant*, he wrote: 'Sky in particular have had to shell out a lot more for their share of the rights, with their cost per game rising 69%, from £6.6 million to £11 million. In contrast, BT's cost per game has only increased by 18%, from £6.5 million to £7.6 million.'

If it seems unfair that BSkyB/Sky's 20-year largesse has not resulted in cheaper per-match rights than those picked up by the newcomer BT, it's clear who will ultimately pick up the tab.

Paul Smith is a senior lecturer in media communications at De Montfort University, Leicester. In May 2014, he wrote a paper on broadcasting price structures for the London School of Economics, titled 'A Market in Two Halves: Why Ofcom

Should Still Make BSkyB Offer Sports to Its Competitors'. Smith noted that 'Over the last 10 years, [Ofcom has found that] competition has "underpinned declines in real prices", particularly for broadband access. Pay-TV, however, was deemed an exceptional case. According to Ofcom, subscribers to BSkyB's sports channels have seen "real terms price increases" of over 10 per cent since 2004, and subscribers to Sky Sports channels via Virgin Media have had to stomach even steeper price rises. Paradoxically then, the emergence of increased competition for BSkyB . . . in the shape of Setanta, ESPN and latterly BT has been accompanied by rising costs for consumers.'

Nor does the Premier League's increasing global appeal offer a saving to British viewers. The 70 per cent price increase in the latest TV package was driven in part by interest from overseas broadcasters. Discovery (which owns Eurosport) and beIN, the Qatari sports network, both expressed an interest in the 2015 rights, thereby helping to inflate the auction price. British viewers, it appears, are paying more to watch their national game on TV thanks to the historic mission of BSkyB/Sky and the Premier League to sell English football to emerging markets.

This is something we should all take pride in, according to the Premier League's chief executive, Richard Scudamore. 'Things like the Premier League, the BBC and the Queen are things that people feel are good about the UK,' he said, on completion of the deal. 'Ultimately, we're a success story. As are the people who have bought our broadcast rights.'

5 : Turning Rebellion into Money

It's a Tuesday night in September 2012. The season is slowly hitting its stride, and I'm talking football with a Geordie in a pub in London. Simon Donald is a Newcastle fan, and a stand-up comedian. He's probably best known, though, as a cult cartoonist. In 1979, Simon, his brother Chris and their friend Jim Brownlow launched *Viz*, the comic that brought us some of the most outrageous, foul-mouthed, horizontal characters in British cartoon history. But Simon doesn't want to talk about Student Grant or Biffa Bacon – or Papiss Cissé, now, for that matter. He wants to talk about the London Olympics.

'I haven't met anyone yet who didn't like the opening ceremony,' he says, in that gently arresting Geordie accent. 'It was brilliant. And I was a sceptic right up until kick-off.'

You, me and half the nation, Simon. As the Olympic Stadium was unveiled in the mizzle of a Friday evening in July 2012, it looked for all the world as if the Teletubbies had captured Stratford. Over the next two hours, Danny Boyle, Frank Cottrell Boyce and Akram Khan conjured up an epic piece of television. Simon shakes his head: 'The NHS thing was brilliant, the kids jumping up and down on their beds . . . The bikes coming out as doves, that was fucking incredible!' Yeah. And Mr Bean. And the Queen with James Bond. And the 7/7 tribute. And, well . . . everything.

A global TV audience of 900 million people was transfixed

(and occasionally baffled) by Danny Boyle's story of Britishness. As Sarah Lyall, a correspondent for the *New York Times*, wrote: 'Britain presented itself to the world as something it has often struggled to express even to itself: a nation secure in its own post-empire identity, whatever that actually is.'

Simon still doesn't want to talk about *Viz* or Newcastle Utd. 'And the *Windrush*,' he says, 'that was just . . . I can't imagine any other country doing that.'

It is two months before the England Under-21s' match in Serbia descended into a punch-up, after our black players were subjected to persistent monkey noises. Now Simon leans forward in his seat. 'Multiculturalism is something we don't know we're really good at,' he says. 'And you go to other countries that are so nearby, and they are so fucking racist it's unbelievable.' His voice rises into that Geordie drum roll. 'I've always thought this, but I've never seen it celebrated to such a degree before that ceremony . . . what we do so well is embrace everything, but quietly. That is British culture.'

Simon has been one of the more influential voices in British culture over the past 30 years. By 1990, *Viz* – led by Finbarr Saunders and his Double Entendres, Sid the Sexist and Roger Mellie, the Man on the Telly – was selling 1.2 million copies per issue. In what was still a thriving British magazine market, only the *TV Times* and *Radio Times* sold more. *Cosmopolitan*? Left for dead by the Fat Slags.

Post-London 2012, what has so enthused this cult cartoonist is that the Olympics had drawn the national character into focus. 'That ceremony showed that our generation have finally taken over,' he says, 'despite having to exist alongside some of the old wank we would rather have thrown out.'

Pretty much what the *New York Times* said.

In the summer of 2012, sport reminded us of its ability to unite where politics has failed. Two months after one of the best Olympics in history, Britain's three major political parties – the old wank – gathered for their annual conferences, unable to summon a single coherent narrative of the country they aspire to lead. While the left-wing motifs in Boyle's extravaganza were seized upon by Labour MPs as a rebuke to the coalition's austerity politics (and who didn't see David Cameron's face in the giant Voldemort, terrorising the children of Great Ormond Street Hospital?), Boyle appeared to stand aside from politics in order to celebrate Britain's liberal and progressive instincts over conservative values with a small 'c'. His message was ambient, and so intuitively could it be picked up that in November 2012 the *Independent on Sunday* reported that 'Britain is now the most powerful nation on earth, according to a new survey, when it comes to "soft power"'. 'Soft power' describes the global influence a nation enjoys through the promotion of its culture. And it was Danny Boyle, Jessica Ennis and Mo Farah who put Britain before America in this race, for the first time in my lifetime.

Why couldn't football do this? Is our national sport not meant to define us? Far from it, it seems: indeed, in the afterglow of London 2012 it wasn't enough simply to celebrate the Olympics – here was another opportunity for the media to attack football. In November 2012, in *When Saturday Comes*, Seb Patrick contrasted the reception afforded the likes of Farah, Wiggins and Ennis with the declining status of our footballers. 'While Roy Race's* principles of sportsmanship and loyalty

* The hero of *Roy of the Rovers*.

may have seemed quaint and old-fashioned around the time his comic was last cancelled,' Patrick wrote, 'they are exactly the sort of traits current footballers are being routinely decried for not having in this post-London 2012 landscape.'

Much of the enduring criticism of footballers is that they are poor role models for children – and here a collection of rowers, jumpers and judoka arrived to offer relief from the antics of what Seb Patrick described as 'the ready-made, moustache-twirling villains of the Premier League'. But as we shall see in Chapter 6, the notion that athletes in any sport are significant role models for children is misguided: an authoritative line of research suggests that kids seldom look to celebrities, in sporting or other fields, for inspiration or guidance. The role-model argument is a feint, a pious piece of hand-wringing, one which disguises the fact that much of the media vitriol is driven by a historic scepticism that football might possibly have merit as a culture.

If there is grudging respect for the game today, it is for a business that can no longer be gainsaid. In 2014, Brand Finance calculated that the total value of the 18 Premier League clubs stood at £3.79 billion, greater than that of the Bundesliga and Spain's La Liga combined. As far as much of the British media are concerned, if there is value in English football, then it is here.

As Rogan Taylor says: 'Today, the value of football lies in monetising the relationships between those who watch and those who play – the more people are watching, the greater those values. And so you end up with the Premier League being watched by 800 million people and hustling its arse for £5 billion. And people say, "Well, what's changed? It's just a fucking game." Well, it's the numbers, man . . . it's the numbers that change stuff!'

And those numbers come in the shape of television audience figures. Until the 1980s, match-going fans were the source of almost 100 per cent of a top-flight club's income; today, they contribute just 30 per cent, which means that subscribers – and not supporters – are the clubs' priority. This goes to the heart of much of the unease among football fans: how much do our clubs really need us any more, when the loyalty that once made us invaluable can be replaced by someone else's subscription? And how does the recasting of supporters into subscribers diminish our identity as fans?

Satellite TV didn't start this debate. To see how our identity as supporters began to change, we need to revisit the late 20th century, and the transformation of the English football fan – from scum to stakeholder.

In the weeks and months following the London 2012 Olympics the media were grappling with a historic conundrum: in England, football is the national sport that has seldom been permitted to speak for the nation.

English football kicked off in the afternoon of empire – between the formation of Sheffield FC (the world's oldest football club) in 1857, the FA in 1863 and the Football League in 1888. By the turn of the 20th century, those who kept Victoria's engine room running were heading to football in their millions. But theirs was not a sport fit for export: our governors and viceroys took rugby and cricket to the colonies, the games of the public schools whence they came.

Cricket, in particular, helped settle the new world: its

evocation of green grass and tea sustained our empire-builders on the plains and in the bush, and in its rhythms and rules it was something to set before the natives – here we are, a fair-minded breed of conqueror. So it was that cricket came to frame the English in their pomp, and decline, inspiring literary lions such as Neville Cardus and C. L. R. James.

And its potent imagery endures . . . When Geoffrey Howe plunged the dagger into Thatcher's back with his resignation speech in November 1990, he compared his hopeless position as her chief envoy to Brussels to that of a cricketer who goes out to the wicket only to find that the captain has broken his bat. And in June 2013, a Major Richard Streatfeild appeared on Radio 4's *Today* programme to put the war in Afghanistan into a test-match perspective. 'We put the Taliban in to bat in 2001 and took a flurry of early wickets,' he said. 'Now, with half an hour to play, we find ourselves some runs short, with our last recognised batsmen at the crease.'

Boxing, too, has a fine critical tradition, inspiring American literary giants such as Norman Mailer and George Plimpton, and in Britain, Hugh McIlvanney. As Spurs fan and *Observer* columnist Barbara Ellen says: 'Yes, people beating the shit out of each other – that was written about in hallowed tones. There were great writers writing about "the noble art", and cinema greats went to make documentaries about the Rumble in the Jungle. Football never had that.'

As secretary of the FA, Stanley Rous was alert to this cultural deficit when Muhammad Ali was still Cassius Clay. 'In the 1950s, Stanley Rous was trying to modernise the FA, and create a broader appreciation of the game,' says Alex Jackson, a collections officer at the National Football Museum. 'In 1953, he staged an FA art competition, and it was won by Lowry, with his *Going to the Match* painting. It was Rous's attempt to bring a touch of culture to football.'

There was Percy Young too.

'He was a musicologist,' says Jackson, 'and while he wrote some very good texts on classical composers, he also wrote about listening to Wolves vs Honved on the radio in the 1950s, and then going to watch his local village football team. That was an attempt to bring a touch of Neville Cardus into football.'

Young was followed in the 1960s and '70s by Arthur Hopcraft (*The Football Man*), Hunter Davies (*The Glory Game*) and essayists such as Roy Hattersley and Peter Cook. But this was a small – if undoubtedly deep – pool. Not until the 1990s, when Pete Davies wrote *All Played Out* and Nick Hornby opened the door to a generation of terrace diarists, did football possess a compelling critical voice.

Perhaps the reason our national game was shunned by literature is because it isn't as technical a sport as cricket or baseball (which has inspired many great American sports books), or as physically arresting as boxing. Or perhaps it's because until the late 20th century the people who went to football matches didn't write books, and the people who wrote books didn't go to football matches. As Geoff McDonald lamented in *Foul*, 'football's alternative paper', in October 1976: 'The atmosphere of football has never communicated itself to me through any novel, poem or television documentary, nor would I expect it to when these are produced by men whose understanding of the game is no more profound than mine or any other spectator's.'

Britain's narrative since the Second World War has often been one of frustration at our fading influence on the world stage. When this spirit of 'declinism' erupted in the 1960s, music, theatre, film and comedy were entitled to expose the unpalatable truth because these were recognised cultural forms. But football was a culture adrift. In one sense, it was simply a game in which two sides competed to outscore each other and win points. But as Chris Lightbown, a writer on *Foul*, told *The Face* in 1987: 'Football had simply not assimilated any of the social or cultural changes of the 1960s; it was in a complete timewarp.'

The media only colluded in football's exclusion from mainstream culture. As James Brown, a former editor of *GQ* and the man who launched *Loaded*, told me: 'It was bonkers, but football had never been a mainstay of men's magazines before *Loaded*. If you looked at *For Him*, *GQ*, *Arena* or *Man About Town* in the '60s, they just didn't have football, despite the fact it was such a staple of men's lives. They saw it as a bit grubby.'

Not surprisingly, those who could write about it, and those who aspired to write about it, began to look elsewhere.

'I loved English football as a kid,' says David Winner, author of *Those Feet: An Intimate History of English Football*. 'Although I had my nose broken by Norwich fans in the '70s. Every time you hear, "Oh, aren't they lovable, Norwich?" No, not really . . . In 1985, I went to a game and the bus driver was nearly stabbed. I thought, "I don't need this any more."'

In the 1970s, Winner had immersed himself in the great Ajax and Holland sides, and Holland's victory at Euro '88 inspired *Brilliant Orange*, his outstanding book about Dutch football. But each generation needs its inspiration, and the man who paved the way for Nick Hornby and David Winner was Brian Glanville, football correspondent of the *Sunday Times*.

'He was my hero,' Winner says. 'When you saw the Dutch play, and read his stuff about their football, you thought, "Wow, there's something fantastic going on here."'

The other great football writer in the 1970s was the *Observer*'s Hugh McIlvanney. 'He was the stylist,' says Winner. 'Some of his stuff was jaw-droppingly brilliant: these amazing 80-word sentences, so elegantly constructed. But Glanville knew more, and his observations were more interesting. His whole career was spent trying to alert the English to the richness of football elsewhere.'

Certainly, there were riches elsewhere, but neither Holland nor Italy, two of the richest European football cultures, boasts a great tradition of football writing. So if they saw little need to commit their glories to print, why, then, did the likes of Brian Glanville? It wasn't simply that football lacked cultural merit in England in the 1970s; Glanville had ambitions to be a novelist – and it would be difficult to win acceptance in literary circles if he were too close to English football.

The cultural cold shoulder was felt north of the border too, as Loughborough University's Alan Bairner recalls: 'There was this fantastic thing a writer called Archie McGregor did in the 1980s, in a Scottish fanzine called *The Absolute Game*. It was called "Bruno Glanvilla writes", and it was very much a skit of Glanville boasting, "I was in Italy last week, in *bella Italia*, and I was with Graeme Souness, and . . . oh, what a handsome man he is." Glanville was about showing off,' insists Bairner, gently, though his frustration is audible. 'It was all about the fine meal he enjoyed, and the wine he drank, and the people he met.'

In a word, culture. And by the 1970s, the English football fan had set about trashing if not the citadels of European culture, then at least the idea of them. In the early part of the decade, football emerged as an alternative means of social mobility, and this proved a challenge to much of the media. The idea of full employment may have been receding, but through Leeds Utd, Spurs or Liverpool the working class would no longer be confined to their own postcodes. As Mike Shallcross, deputy editor of *Men's Health*, says: 'Football fans were now heading to the great cities of Italy, Spain and France, previously frequented only by middle-class gastronomes and art aficionados. Football now provided a window onto sophistication for the working class. I think this was part of the horror of hooliganism, and why it was overstated. Remember,' he says, 'when Liverpool fans went to Rome for the 1977 European Cup final, this was less than 20 years after the *Lady Chatterley* trial. "Is this a book you would like your servants to read?" became "Is this a place you would like your plumber to go on holiday?"'

For their part, football supporters only conspired in their exclusion from the debate. They ignored a critical analysis of the game as early as October 1972, in the guise of *Foul*. 'Football's alternative paper' was launched by Steve Tongue, until recently the football correspondent of the *Independent on Sunday*; Harry Harris, who went on to the *Mail*; and future scriptwriters Andrew Nickolds and Stan Hey (the latter notable for *Auf Wiedersehen, Pet*). Published monthly, *Foul* also drew on the talents of occasional contributors such as Eamon Dunphy, Derek Dougan, Bill Tidy and Tony Wilson.

Foul was knocked up in Cambridge between 1972 and 1976 with an electric typewriter, a few sheets of Letraset and a tube of cow gum. Here, finally, was a football paper that lambasted the lack of critical thinking and writing around the game, ridiculed the FA's resistance to overseas coaches and players, and ran two hard-hitting investigative pieces into the 1971 Ibrox disaster, in which 66 people were crushed to death on a stairway exit. One of those reports, 'Falling Masonry', bravely picks apart the club's negligence in the decade prior to the tragedy, and exposes the cover-up that, it alleges, took place in its wake: 'Freemasonry is a strand that is woven so deeply into the history of the Rangers that the two are inseparable,' wrote Alan Stewart.*

Steve Tongue is modest about *Foul*'s impact. 'I don't think we'd want to make too many grand claims about its lasting influence,' he says. 'There was probably only one issue that made a profit.' Nonetheless, he remains proud of the fact that 'When the Trident Fair Play League started, we suggested the winners should be given a place in Europe. The replies from the FA and Football League were particularly scathing. Some 30-odd years later, UEFA introduced it.'

Foul was years ahead of its time, then, and neither the game's governing bodies nor supporters were buying it. In October 1976, Steve Tongue, Harry Harris and Stan Hey packed away the Letraset and cow gum.

'There was never sufficient advertising to make any money,' Tongue recalls, 'despite the fact that no contributors or editors were ever paid, and even though we were underwritten by Tim Rice. At one point we used a professional advertising salesman, who found it an impossible field to work in – the concepts of "alternative" and "football" not working for potential advertisers.'

In the 1970s, advertisers knew there was simply no alternative

* Stewart later became a TV producer, and was killed in 1985, when his car hit a landmine in Sudan.

to *Shoot!*. Britain's best-selling weekly football magazine deco-rated the bedroom walls of millions of teenage boys and girls, and its soft-focus format seldom wavered. Why bother with all that nasty business of hooliganism and racism when there was an interview with Derek Footballer?

Q: What's your favourite car, Derek?

A: Ford Capri.

Q: Favourite TV show?

A: *The Sweeney*.

Q: Favourite food?

A: Chicken and baked beans.

They never did speak for us, did they? As every child of the 1970s knows, the only food tastier than Spam was Spam fritters.

Similarly, there was only one national voice in support-ers' organisations in the 1970s – the National Federation of Football Supporters' Clubs. And the 'Nat Fed', as it liked to be known, displayed something of a cultural cringe: its motto was 'To Help and Not to Hinder', and as Rogan Taylor explains, it was made up of supporters' clubs that were often driven by a constituency not unlike the local Conservative Association.

'They would run lotteries for the clubs, basically,' Taylor says. 'The clubs couldn't do this within the laws governing gambling and gaming because they were corporate companies, so the Nat Fed Member Associations ran them instead. What was remarkable about the relationship was that the Nat Fed members raised money for clubs and handed it over out of blind loyalty, then they bent over and got screwed on a regular basis. They never had the political nous to say, "Hang on, what will these clubs do for us in return? What representation will we get?" The money they raised was often more than directors had contributed – but no one demanded a seat on the board. They functioned as a megaphone from the clubs to the fans, not the other way round.'

In this critical and cultural void, football supporters would travel the length of the country to pay for the privilege of standing on a terrace up to their toes in piss, when it was raining rubble and darts. Without a voice to catch the ear of the game's authorities, they tore into each other instead. By the early 1980s, as Taylor recalls, 'We were getting hoolie stories in the media every week, but you never saw a spokesperson from the Nat Fed on telly. They had hundreds of supporters' clubs, but 90 per cent of them were either at amateur clubs or semi-pro. They didn't have representation at all the big clubs either . . . far from it.'

Bereft of a critical voice, and friends, and excluded from 'respectable' culture, football came perilously close to extinction. From the vantage point of 2016, the prospect seems absurd; but as Martin Lacey, author of *The Dawn of Dissent*, a trilogy of books on fanzines, recalls: 'Every mention of football was as a problem in the early to mid-1980s. There was a feeling among football fans – and it may have been paranoia – that the government was effectively trying to abolish football.'

Halfway through the Thatcher decade, the most far-sighted football supporters grasped that if their game were to survive, they would have to move with the society in flux around them – a society that was becoming a market society, enticing football clubs onto the stock market. In 1983, Spurs became the first top-flight English club to announce plans to float. Under chairman Irving Scholar, they formed a holding company to circumvent the FA's restrictions on dividends and directors' salaries. These restrictions, under FA Rule 34, had prevented directors of football clubs drawing their main income from their ownership of a club, and they stipulated that dividends paid on shares in football clubs could not be more than 5 per cent of their face value. When the FA allowed Spurs to ignore Rule 34, the long-held implicit bargain in football – that clubs could operate as limited companies, but must be protected against asset-strippers in order to maintain their value to the local community – was broken. The 'holding company model' pioneered at White Hart Lane allowed football clubs to be owned by companies rather than individuals.

The clubs were moving for a piece of the market revolution. It was futile manning the barricades: obtaining a stake might be the only way for supporters to have a voice. But first the fans had to grasp their own value. They took their time getting there. And they started with punk.

Punk exploded in London in 1976, inspired a generation of great bands and terrible haircuts, and died of a heart attack less than three years later. And according to some critics, it changed nothing but the width of a generation's jeans. Certainly, punk failed in its mission – to subvert a music industry grown bloated on prog rock and the decadence of rock stars relegating the art of making music below that of making swimming pools in the shape of their instruments. Essentially, punk failed because, as Herbert Marcuse observed, whatever you throw at capitalism, it will absorb and sell back to you.

But even if the last word in rebellion had become just another commodity, punk remains our last word in rebellion. No other movement – not mods, not acid house – has so mortified the

Establishment over the past 50 years. That Danny Boyle should infuse his Olympic opener with the Clash and the Pistols and the giant pogoing mannequins suggests that punk was more than a bit of tight tailoring; that it is, if anything, fitted snugly within our cultural genes. And it was influential in putting football back on its feet.

Punks invented the modern fanzine. Between 1975 and '77, *Kill Your Pet Puppy*, *Ripped and Torn* and *Sniffin' Glue* (which employed the talents of a young Millwall fan called Danny Baker) spread the punk gospel, with band and singles reviews, club listings and general musings on the sterility of the pre-punk generation. These scratchy, handmade fanzines were different to *Foul*: they were home-made, stapled sheets of A4, handwritten in black ink, or stencilled, and they were sold hand to hand outside gigs to fund their publishers' next ticket to see the Damned, the Lurkers or the Pistols.

Punk fanzines changed the way music was written about: journalists such as James Brown, Tony Parsons, Julie Burchill, Danny Baker and Danny Kelly would reinvigorate the music press in the 1980s, and they were inspired by the punk gospel splashed across the likes of *Ripped and Torn* and *Sniffin' Glue*: 'Stop consuming the culture that is made for you. Make your own culture.'

'The 1960s bores the shit out of me,' says Barbara Ellen, a former writer on the *NME*. 'It was just a load of hippies sitting around talking about themselves; they had nothing to say about society. But in the late '70s, punk appealed to people who find it very stifling being told what to think and do, and say and feel, and where to get our enjoyment. Punk was all about people making a noise and a mess, and about chaos.'

In the 1970s, football had chaos, but *Shoot!* could hardly be expected to make sense of it, and *Foul* struggled to reach the working-class lads at the sharp end. Punk not only made sense of chaos, it celebrated it, and football fans were listening. And in Newcastle and Liverpool, a handful went out and launched two of the most important 'zines of the 1980s.

Viz and *The End* made only a passing nod to football, and as football fanzine expert Martin Lacey argues, they were not widely recognised as 'fanzines' either. But they were the first 'zines to talk football through the street language of working-class culture. More significantly, they were the bridge between the scattergun fury of punk and the polished indignation of *When Saturday Comes* and *Off the Ball*, the two national fanzines around which football supporters would mobilise to save the game in 1986.

Curiously, Andy Lyons, the editor and co-founder of *When Saturday Comes*, insists that neither *Viz* nor *The End* had any influence on his fanzine. He and Mike Ticher were working in a record shop when they launched *When Saturday Comes* in early 1986. 'Music had become a bit bland again by the mid-'80s,' Lyons says, 'and there was almost a "ten years on from punk" idea. We were caught up in that. We were also inspired by music 'zines such as *Slow Dazzle* and [James Brown's] *Attack on Bzag!*'

However, the influence was there – perhaps not in content, but in tone and style. As James Brown says: 'I remember looking at *When Saturday Comes* and *Off the Ball* and thinking they were copies of *The End*, in the way they looked.' Similarly, Simon Donald told me: 'The guys at *When Saturday Comes* told us that *Viz* was a big influence on them.'

Certainly, *The End* and *Viz* were crucial to the fanzine culture, because they were the living – literally surviving, thriving – embodiment of an oral, working-class culture in the dark days of the early 1980s, when Thatcher's was the only voice in politics. Violent, angry, witty and satirical, *Viz* and *The End* didn't just mint a new language, they put it into print for the first time. It was funny, sharp and subversive. It was the language of the street. And this was where the voice of football was hiding all along.

Viz came first, although Simon Donald, Chris Donald and Jim Brownlow never set out to change the language. A few years before *Viz* launched, in December 1979, the three were confirmed . . . 'Well, I suppose today you would call us nerds. We were trainspotters,' says Simon Donald, over that pint. 'We used to go to Gateshead to look at the trains in the sheds. And in 1975, Chris started a magazine aimed specifically at children who lived in our street and who were interested in trainspotting: literally, it was six kids, and it was called the *Lily Crescent Locomotive Times*.'

It took punk to shunt that into the sidings. 'Punk was just so well-placed, time-wise,' says Donald. 'I think there was a tangible feeling in the late '70s that Britain's leaders – in all fields – needed to be replaced by younger and more open-minded people. Punk thrived on that need, and that anger.'

And Donald was angry. He spent five years signing on. None of his family had access to university, despite the brothers' talent. 'I was bitter about that, and I think Chris was too.' There were problems at home. 'Our mam had multiple sclerosis, and although our eldest brother was a hugely talented artist and engineer, he had Asperger's syndrome, which made him very difficult socially. We faced a lot of challenges,' Donald says, the passion still simmering nearly four decades later. 'Our mission in *Viz* was just to laugh at everything, because it helped us cope.'

Viz barged its way onto newsagents' shelves packed with *The Dandy*, *Beano*, *Topper* and *Whizzer*. As Donald points out: 'These titles are all traditional English words for "good".' And life in inner-city England in the early '80s wasn't so good: Donald's dad was made redundant in 1980 and never worked again. The language of Roger the Dodger and Dennis the Menace didn't really cover everything the family wanted to say, so as Donald recalls, 'Me, Chris and Jim took the friendly, clean and slightly bizarre world in which these characters lived, and added simple touches of the gritty world around us. We celebrated the culture we saw around us in Newcastle by pillorying its traditions and violent, dark side. Then the new world of the late '70s came into that: the music, the street language, the football. It was all in there.'

Donald was no fan of punk 'zines. 'I didn't have a love for them, but they were a great vehicle for freedom of expression.' And Donald needed that, badly: he was resentful that his education was cut short. What he didn't realise at the time was that he's dyslexic.

So, too, is Phil Jones, one of the driving forces behind *The End*. A blend of music, fashion, politics and terrace culture, *The End* was launched in 1981 by Peter Hooton, who would later find fame as lead singer of the Farm. Hooton poached Phil Jones from *Time for Action*, a mod 'zine he launched in 1979 with none other than Steve Rotheram, now the Labour MP for Liverpool Walton. At *The End*, Jones joined Hooton, the cartoonist Mick Potter and Kevin Sampson, who would later become a novelist (*Powder, Awaydays, The Killing Pool*).

The End was pitched at football supporters across the city of Liverpool, mostly aged between the mid-teens and twenties. An average edition sold around 3,000 copies, but they often shifted 5,000, 'and during *Boys from the Blackstuff* we did 8,000 copies, when we had Bernard Hill [Yosser] in it'.

Seriously, not bad.

'Yeah,' Jones says, 'considering we didn't have a clue. We were the crappiest businessmen you've ever met. But it was the DIY ethic we got from punk.'

According to Phil Jones, 'it was the Jam and the Clash that really brought us together'. And just as these Scousers were inspired by the music coming out of Woking and west London, so they took an early fashion cue from Cockneys.

'West Ham were the first crowd I remember coming to Anfield not wearing their colours,' says Jones. 'We thought it was a bit cowardly at first, but it was actually the opposite – it was so they could try and get in the Kop, or the Paddock, without being spotted. Then they would start singing their songs, and all hell would break out.'

The idea the Hammers fans brought to town was to look as unhooligan-like as you could, to dress down but smarten up in order to blend in. This clobber wasn't designed with bovver in mind. Well, not entirely: while some infiltrated the Kop, many West Ham fans simply wanted to break out of police frog marches from station to stadium in away towns and feel like free men again, over a pint in a pub near the ground. The culture wasn't born at Upton Park, but it was from undercover operations like the Hammers' that the casuals emerged.

The casuals of the late 1970s and '80s were a fiercely fashion-conscious tribe of football supporters, famed for returning from foreign aways with trainers and raincoats that few in England had seen before. (And all with receipts, of course.) They wore Tacchini and Ellesse with style, even in the thick of the fighting. But they were just one fashion-conscious football tribe, as Phil Jones explains: 'There was a transition from mods to casuals at the turn of the '80s. Elsewhere you had punks and skins too, but in Liverpool you had lads with flicks and wedges. Then the tweed jackets came along, and the deerstalker hats.'

Today, the term 'casual' is still used ambivalently. Phil Jones insists the word never appeared in *The End* – at least, not consciously – but with supporters weary of being vilified in print, those who dared to tout fanzines outside the ground had to acknowledge the casuals and other elements. Jones recalls how 'we did a definition of "scallywag", and we drew diagrams of the archetypal scally: the tweed jacket, the too-tight cords with desert boots. Joe Wagg was our archetypal scally. We made it fictional, rather than say, "This person got up to this."'

Joe Wagg trod a fine line, but as Barbara Ellen recalls, 'People were a lot more fearless in the '80s. Today, you can sit down at a computer and type out "wanker". But if you wanted to say something in the '80s, you had to take a fanzine out to the ground and sell it hand to hand, and you might have got beaten up for it. Some of the blokes did, at music gigs.'

And in its fearlessness, *The End* had thrown the disenfranchised a lifeline. For as Dave Boyle, a former chief executive of Supporters Direct, points out: 'The National Federation of Football Supporters' Clubs tried to distance themselves from the troublemakers. So you had another school who tried to argue that this wasn't simple delinquency; that there are issues about the conditions we're in, the way the police treat us, the way you criminalise us, and actually, the easy solutions aren't going to work. The response among fans, essentially, is: "We're not going to demonise our own fans. While we don't want anything to do with the violence, we would have no credibility if we are seen as people who are doing the bidding of the police. Because we see the reality on a weekly basis."'

It was a point Peter Hooton made in *Four Four Two* in December 2011:

> Having requested and received a copy of *The End*, [Mike Ticher, co-founder of *When Saturday Comes*] replied to say he was under the impression we were a football fanzine, but was unimpressed by our lack of analysis and our obsession with terrace fashion and trouble at matches. We were unimpressed by his reply, as he'd obviously missed the point of our magazine completely: we were just reflecting what young, other match-going football fans were interested in.

While Phil Jones and Kevin Sampson disagree on much of the purpose and merit of *The End*, they agree on one key issue: 'For me,' says Jones, '*The End* was a tool to write about anything I wanted in the Liverpool vernacular.' For Sampson, 'it wasn't a studied or deliberate policy to write in the vernacular, though contributors did – and were encouraged to – write in their own "voice".'

So seductive was the Scouse that, Sampson says, 'I'd argue that quite a few popular expressions we take for granted today – "No Mates", for example [as in 'Billy No Mates'], "give it toes" and "Ted", as in "Acid Ted" – made their way into every-day usage from the pages of *The End.*'

Impressive, not least because, as Sampson stresses, no attempt was made to be more widely understood. '*The End* took a view that most readers would understand what was meant by, say, "zapping a dog", and those who didn't could make an educated guess.'

This emergence of a working-class vernacular was essential to fixing the credibility of 'zines such as *Viz* and *The End* beyond their own cities. The language of *The End* – trabs and trainees, wools and beauts – wasn't a tool simply to distinguish Liverpudlians from the rest of the country; for just as *Viz* was parodying the dark side of Newcastle, *The End* was having a crack at middle-class Scousers.

'One of the joys for me was attacking the Liverpool old guard,' says Phil Jones. 'We hated Jimmy Tarbuck and Cilla Black and Billy Butler. Whenever anything would happen about Liverpool, the press would go to those three – even Arthur Askey. Some of them didn't even live here. So we really went after them. They weren't gonna speak on my behalf – don't be talking about poverty when you're millionaires.'

Here, then, was a working-class subculture operating outside of 'respectable society'. And the vernacular was crucial. *Viz* made the leap to national distribution in 1985, when Virgin began to distribute it through their nationwide chain of record shops. But Simon, Chris and Jim had to fight hard to retain their Geordie currency.

'The first real criticism we had was from [the publisher] John Brown,' Donald says. 'He was still at Virgin publishing, and they started taking an interest in *Viz* in 1983–4. John said to us, "It's very good, it's very funny, but you must stop being so Geordie. People won't understand the dialect." We were selling around 7,000 copies, and we just ignored all that advice. We were sick of the BBC, and all the media in their wake – ever since the 1920s they had an attitude that "We've got to speak the Queen's English." Well, what fucking purpose did that serve?

'I said to John Brown, "You're not gonna change what I do. I'm gonna do what I wanna do, and if you wanna sell it, you fucking sell it."'

The Geordie fuelled *Viz* with an authenticity that defied all of Virgin's commercial expertise. 'We overtook *Punch*, then *Private Eye*, and we were selling double what they were selling. From the mid-'80s, once we got national distribution, our sales basically doubled every issue, up until about 1990. At our peak, we were selling 1.2 million copies.'

The vernacular of *The End* and *Viz* was first and foremost about celebrating working-class culture, when Thatcher was razing much of it to the ground. As Martin Lacey says of the fanzines that followed *Viz* and *The End*: 'They were a response to a very British situation. In the first half of the 1980s you had a Conservative government that was trying to dismantle the building blocks of British working-class life, one by one: the unions, the nationalised industries, neglecting education, the health service . . . and football was part of that.'

Football fans in Britain today should give thanks that those fanzine pioneers stuck around long enough to foment the sub-culture of writing outside the mainstream – post-*Foul*, post-punk, and before the emergence, in 1982–84, of prototype football fanzines such as *Terrace Talk* and *The City Gent* – not least because the 'zine culture demanded incredible dedication. As

James Brown remembers: 'To get people to read *Attack on Bzag!* I had to lay it out, I had to take it to the printers, I had to carry the fucking pieces of paper home, I had to fold them, I had to staple them and put them in piles, I had to find gigs being played by the bands I was writing about . . . it would take, like, three or four months to get rid of a thousand mags.'

The subculture survived for two other reasons: the first is that whereas punk 'zines could thrive only as long as the mainstream media declined to talk to Rotten and Strummer and Scabies (not long), football-related fanzines faced no such threat. In fact, as the 1980s progressed, Fleet Street didn't merely marginalise football fans, it began to delight in demonising the game, as Bob Harris has said. Fertile ground, then, for fanzines.

The second reason that leap was made is the more substantive: *Viz* and *The End* sprung from the peculiar resilience of English in the vernacular. Put into print for the first time, it connected working-class lads around the country. 'Funnily enough,' says Phil Jones, 'the people who really cottoned on to what we were doing at *The End* were Aberdeen fans – we got loads of letters from Aberdeen – and elements of Cardiff City and Leeds.'

The English, Scots and Welsh united.

As Dave Boyle says, 'There was a discovery through the 'zines of a truth that is now generally accepted: essentially, what was special about Liverpool, for example, wasn't in the end the players, it was the community of Liverpoolness. Up to that point it had been an oral tradition, but the 'zines captured that tradition and turned it into a written one. The proper football fanzines took up the baton; they became intrinsic to that prideful sense of self-recognition and identification.'

It's a point echoed by Kevin Sampson. His formative years at *The End* coincided with the peak of Bob Paisley's glittering reign, when the likes of Souness, Dalglish and Rush carted off silverware from every port of call. Remarkably, he says, 'I don't think there was a single footballer we identified with, and I can't think of one footballer we even tried to interview.'

If *Viz*, meanwhile, had little to no influence over the content of football fanzines, it was a huge shout out to the fanzine culture: its extraordinary sales confirmed that an unashamed working-class voice could be as influential as glossy magazines and newspapers. And that the spirit of punk was still intact.

'Our business model – such as it was – wasn't based on listening to blokes in suits telling us that art's a fucking science, which it clearly isn't,' says Simon Donald. 'Our business model – as such – was that we wanted to amuse one another, and if other people were interested, that was OK with us. And that is the only way genuinely artistic things can ever succeed. If you are creating something for a particular audience, then you're not necessarily creating it for yourself; the only way to really believe in something is to do it for yourself.'

This wasn't culture. This was subculture. These were people revelling in their outlaw status and celebrating the vitality of a lifestyle under threat. As Barbara Ellen says: 'People who went to football in the '80s were seen as scum. People were warned off going. But despite great pressure, they never gave up on this thing that they loved; it just refused to die, and I thought that was absolutely fascinating. I liked the stubbornness, the proleness of it: the masses were not letting themselves be diluted or beaten down. They were honouring their own class.'

And honouring, too, a classically British sense of humour:

this wasn't just the dawn of the fanzines, it was the era of inflat-able bananas (or inflatable haddock, if you were at Grimsby). As Dave Boyle says: 'You don't have to be Dick Hebdige to say, "This screams subculture!"'

And crucially, as Boyle argues, like Ellen: 'This wasn't inclu-sive, in an "Aren't we funky at football – come and watch it" kind of way; it was a way of saying, "We are different, we have our own cultural norms."'

What football supporters were saying – through *Viz*, through *The End*, through haddock – was: 'There is some-thing vibrant and positive in football, and in working-class culture, and it is us.'

In 2004, the *Observer*'s Euan Ferguson reviewed a TV docu-mentary about the Brighton bombing. The review, rather than the programme itself, sticks in the mind a decade later.

The documentary-maker, Peter Taylor, had interviewed the survivors and the bomber, Patrick Magee, who recalled the night he tried to assassinate Margaret Thatcher at the Grand Hotel in Brighton in October 1984. Taylor's film was a wasted opportu-nity, Ferguson wrote, not least because he repeatedly interrupted Magee, 'a quiet and obviously fiercely intelligent man doing his best to explain, slowly, why he thought for so many years that he had to murder people'. As Ferguson explained:

Younger viewers, sadly, will have been left with little or
no understanding of the political context of the attacks:
this retrospective accorded the high Tories, presiding at
the height of the Troubles, the same bewildered-innocent
status of the victims of, say, the Twin Towers. It was, surely,

necessary to touch on the depths to which that party was so reviled by so much of the country at that time, five turbulent years into the Thatcher experiment; in 1984, it wasn't just paid-up members of the Provisionals who were sketching quiet smiles at the footage. Grim this may sound but that doesn't make it any the less true: I was in a pub in Dundee the evening after the bomb, and knew lawyers and bandits and councillors and coppers who were punching the air that night as they watched the television; with glee, and with a mild disappointment at the body count.

Such was our prime minister and her party in the 1980s: loathed – bitterly – by millions. Whichever side we were on (and there were few neutrals left in Britain by 1984), few of us remained to be convinced of Thatcher's implacability. The working class might have ingrained a spirit of rebellion in football – Martin Lacey's dawn of dissent – but Thatcher would not be moved, and Britain would be remade. Football now had to move with the society around it: and it was, increasingly, an upwardly mobile society.

As Professor Alan Bairner argues: 'There was always an affection for football at all levels of society. However, the middle class was historically small, so it wasn't easy to identify them in football back in, say, the 1950s. But around 1990, the middle class was growing, in the sense of more people sitting at computers rather than digging coal or building ships. In fact, by the 1980s and 1990s, it actually became less easy to identify the traditional working class. Much of the working class moved on and up, and politically, it may have been that what is horribly described as "an underclass" developed. They weren't encouraged to go to the game – or to do anything at all, for that matter.'

A TUC report, *Life in the Middle* (2009), records how in 1965 the working class (skilled and unskilled combined) accounted for 69.1 per cent of the UK population outside of the upper class, with the middle class accounting for the remaining 30.9 per cent. By 1993, the working class accounted for 41 per cent of the population outside of the upper class, and the lower middle, middle and upper middle class were now in a majority, at 46.5 per cent.* Some 12.6 per cent of those who would previously have been categorised as working class were now 'residual' – casual or low-grade workers, pensioners, and others dependent on state benefits.

At the same time, the percentage of working-class kids educated at university had been rising since the early 1960s. The football fanzines that emerged in the wake of *Viz* and *The End* in the early '80s had increasingly to find room for town and gown. Now the spirit of dissent shifted towards one of engagement.

As Professor Bairner points out, 'There was an element of not-very-well-veiled intellectualism on the part of some fanzine editors. That fanzines had room for people discussing accusations of racism levelled at their club and supporters . . . there hadn't really been a forum for this before, and I think it can only have been inspired by people who are not anti-intellectual as such, but who were trying to hide their education – to keep it under cover, in order that this debate could reach a wider audience.'

* By 2007, the middle class accounted for 51.5 per cent of the UK population outside of the upper class.

Just as *The End* rubbed shoulders with the edgier elements of Liverpool and Everton supporters in order to engage with the subculture and articulate its grievances, now the 'better educated' fans had similarly to inveigle themselves into the centre of the terrace, behind the goal, in order to speak out for another significant element of the crowd. As Professor Bairner says: 'The tone of the fanzines, across the country, was, "We're light-hearted, like you lads"; but the writers were different from most fans because they wanted to raise these issues around racism and hooliganism. And with the humour and irony and self-reflection that they were able to get into many of the fanzines, these fans managed to carry serious political messages.'

Football fanzines began in earnest in 1982, when York City supporters sought to subsidise coach travel to away games by selling a new football publication, *Terrace Talk*. As early as September 1983, *Terrace Talk* offered an alternative view on hooliganism: 'The fine win at Stockport was marred by violence on the terraces,' it reported. 'From the moment we arrived we were threatened and assaulted, and this carried on throughout the game. Stockport supporters? No, this was the local police.'

Terrace Talk was joined by West Brom's *The Fingerpost*, which – alongside debating whether Leeds fans should be banned from away grounds, a topic generating widespread media coverage in the mid-1980s – also found room for the *Shoot!*-style player interview. One evening in 1987, *The Fingerpost* quizzed West Brom defender Martyn Bennett on the toughest opponents he'd faced.

'The first player to frighten me was Joe Jordan,' he said. 'Ally Rob warned me, "Jordan will kick you and spit at you, and that's just during the warm-up." During the game Jordan hit my nose with his elbow,' Bennett complained. 'Once he hit me so hard that I couldn't see. John Wile was running by and he shouted, "You're doing great," and I couldn't see a thing.'

Bring this man some chicken and beans!

Another subculture was emerging in these early fanzines, but it was markedly different from that delivered by *Viz* and *The End*: the language of *Terrace Talk* and *The Fingerpost* is largely devoid of a Yorkshire or West Midlands dialect, because fanzines were now taking on the media at their own game – in order to grasp the nettles the mainstream press were unwilling to touch. Another early issue of *Terrace Talk* described a play by a writer called Richard Ireson. The star player in *Just a Kick in the Grass* is black, and he delivers this soliloquy to the audience: 'Commentators on the box call us "black footballers", not just "footballers". Action replay of me over "that old black magic". Condescending bastards.'

The fanzine movement took another leap forward a little further west, in November 1984, when Bradford City fans became so disillusioned with the club's match-day programme that they launched *The City Gent*. Viewed in the imposing reading room of the British Library, the first edition of what is now the longest-running club fanzine in England is endearingly fragile. The A5 pamphlet carries on its cover the club mascot – a smiling, dapper chap wearing a Bradford shirt and bowler hat, touting a cane and briefcase – and, inside, some great jokes. After Bradford fans had returned from a particularly chilly afternoon at Boundary Park, with its plastic pitch, *The City Gent* reflected: 'As you freeze at Oldham, you become as anaesthetised as the football. The thought comes to mind of why Oldham should bother having a green pitch when plastic comes in any colour?'

In the same issue, a column called 'Look to the Future' appears – at 30 years' distance – eerily prescient.

> Bradford council has committed itself to a substantial investment at Odsal stadium, in the attempt at putting Bradford back on the sporting map. [Bradford] Northern will now become the envy of the other Rugby League clubs. The question in many people's minds has been whether City might not be better at Odsal as well, and although the question is purely hypothetical it is nevertheless interesting to gauge opinion on the idea of a move across town. Eleven years ago, City had the opportunity of moving to Park Avenue . . . but homage to tradition left City at Valley Parade. An opportunity to develop a new super stadium was missed, and by 1983 the new regime at City had inherited the years of neglect – crumbling terraces, a leaky roof, and inadequate supporters' facilities.

On the final day of the 1984/5 season, 56 people died at Valley Parade, after a discarded cigarette ignited rubbish under a stand and set its wooden structure ablaze. An empty packet of peanuts found in the charred remains carried the price stamp '6d' – the stadium hadn't been properly cleaned since decimalisation was introduced in 1971.

Eighteen days later, 39 people were killed before the European Cup final in Brussels, after fighting broke out in the shambolic stadium between Juventus and Liverpool fans. As a 15-year-old Liverpool supporter, the only saving grace I could find in Heysel was that it took place during half-term: I would not have to go to school the next day and hang my head in shame.

Eventually, 27 supporters would be extradited from Britain on manslaughter charges relating to Heysel – 60 per cent of those came from the Liverpool area. Fourteen were handed a three-year sentence for involuntary manslaughter (they would each serve about a year). UEFA general secretary Hans Bangerter was threatened with jail, but eventually received a conditional discharge. The former head of the Belgian FA, Albert Roosens, was given a six-month suspended sentence for 'regrettable negligence' with regard to ticketing arrangements. Captain Johan Mahieu of the Belgian police was given a suspended sentence of six months.

Long before justice had taken its course, the prime minister had set hers. 'We have to get the game cleaned up from this hooliganism at home and then perhaps we shall be able to go overseas again,' Thatcher said, in the days following the disaster.

The FA responded by withdrawing English clubs from European competition. Its secretary, Ted Croker, stood outside Number 10 and said, 'It is now up to English football to put its house in order.' The Football League was not consulted on the ban, which it opposed – as did Neil Kinnock, the leader of the Labour Party.

In the week following Heysel, Rogan Taylor, a writer and broadcaster, called for a ceasefire between those who ran and those who watched the game, in a missive to the *Guardian*.

'I said, "What Heysel tells us is that there are dead pilgrims in the temple. And if you unpack that, what it points to is the corruption of all these relationships, and it's about time these relationships were sorted out."'

According to Taylor, the relationship between the clubs and football authorities on the one side, and supporters on the other, was akin to that between a drug pusher and his junkies. 'They knew we would crawl through the sewers to get our fix,' he says. 'And we did. It was a criminal relationship, when you think about it. But there was no use pointing the finger of blame at the police, or the stadium, or the FA – that was just a domestic. The major dysfunction was that those people who paid for football had absolutely no part in the dialogue.'

And just as the authorities had to listen, so the fans had to vary their tone. In the 1970s, football fans neither had a commanding voice nor sought one. In the '80s, they found two, through the complementary subcultures of the 'zines and fanzines. But still the government and the game's authorities weren't listening. So, in the spring of 1985, in the aftermath of Heysel, Rogan Taylor and a small group of fellow Scousers came up with the idea of a national football supporters' representative body, the Football Supporters' Association. And they made a far-sighted decision in naming their new organisation.

'Pete Garrett was the driving force in the foundation of the FSA,' Taylor recalls. 'He said, "Right, we've got to have a union: the Football Supporters' Union." But there was a whole bunch of legislation out there that Mrs T had just passed, which would have made life impossible for a registered union.'

So out went the language of trade unionism; in came that of the stakeholder. As Taylor says: 'It was no good talking about the flat-capped hordes; we had to speak in the language that was current. If you're going to have something, have an association, because in 1985, if you're an association of people who pay money, that's what talks. Because in those days, supporters paid everybody's wages in football – not a third of it, as you might have now. We paid *all* of it. So what we had to do was press the clubs to ask us, "What would make it worthwhile for you to come and pay to be entertained at our commercial institution? What would be a better experience? And what would make you want to bring your kids, and others who haven't been before? How can we make it easier for you to travel to the stadium, and into the stadium? How can we improve the policing and stewarding? Does a 3 p.m. kick-off actually suit you?"

'Nobody had made that argument before, and that was the argument that won.'

What the FSA and others had grasped was that language was more important than numbers. In 1953, the National Federation of Football Supporters' Clubs claimed to have 500,000 members. But what had they achieved? Certainly not a profile: when the Football Supporters' Association launched in 1985, it was shocked to discover that a national fans' organisation was already in place – and had been since 1926. And although the FSA only managed to recruit around 5,000 members at its peak, in 1988/9, it can point to a significant victory nonetheless – in changing the terms of the debate around football.

It was the FSA who campaigned to derail the Football Spectators Bill (receiving a crucial helping hand from Lord Justice Taylor). They would be vindicated in arguing that the move to all-seater stadiums would price out working-class people without the imposition of strict ticket-pricing guidelines. (No helping hand from Taylor there.) And through shaping the stakeholder debate, the FSA were on message with the incoming New Labour government in 1997, who put the stakeholder at the centre of their Third Way philosophy. This would prove to be a significant meeting of minds. In 1998, New Labour set up the Football Task Force (which will be considered in Chapter 8). Dr Adam Brown, a Man Utd supporter and member of the Task Force working party, later wrote that this 'represented the most far-reaching consultation with football people and organisations ever undertaken in this country (or any other country that I can think of)'. And according to Rogan Taylor, 'The FSA were everywhere in the Task Force. And a lot of people in football were blooded into the game by the Task Force, who have since been able to exert some influence over the way the media thinks about the game, and who they think the relevant voices are.'

In late 1991, after the First Division clubs had broken away from the Football League to form the Premier League, Rogan Taylor approached Rick Parry, who was shortly to be appointed chief executive of the Premier League. Now, the FSA tilted the language of the game a notch further towards the high street.

'My argument to Parry was, "Listen: if Tesco are prepared to spend £10 million in research trying to find out whether I want the sliced bread on the top shelf or the bottom shelf, why don't we have consumer councils in football? You can sell that idea, because that's *now*. And make sure there's an older bloke on the council; there's a woman; there's someone who takes kids; there's a black guy, an Asian supporter; there's even a hoolie."'

The FSA had grasped the inexorable journey of the British in the 1980s – from citizens to stakeholders. It was a far cry from the Nat Fed, whose idea of giving women a platform was to stage a Miss Federation contest until the early 1980s.

However, there is a flipside. It is reasonable to argue that a stakeholder has a stake only proportionate to the money he or she puts in. The inevitable consequence here is that the more you pay, the greater your stake. Money becomes the ultimate measure of your value to the game. And as Rogan Taylor has said, the value in football now lies in monetising the relationships between those who watch and those who play.

In 1992, BSkyB had to begin recouping £304 million from a game screened free to air just a few years earlier. Initially, it sought to create a new product, a 'whole new ball game'. But cheerleaders wouldn't catch on. A ball could not grow more round. Astroturf had been and gone. And despite dark warnings before USA '94, the 90 minutes would not be carved into quarters, rather than halves, to accommodate more commercial breaks. No, the game could not be remade. Fortunately, it didn't need to be, for as Jonathan Martin, the former head of BBC Sport, argues: 'Content is important, but technology leads the way.'

Satellite TV required a new form of viewer – a subscriber. And football supporters were perfect, because they had a loyalty hitherto untapped by television. From 1992, satellite TV struck a new formula: turn football supporters into subscribers, then sell their loyalty back to them.

Primarily, this sales pitch takes the form of saturation TV coverage. Few supporters born since 1985 will remember a time when we didn't consume our football via 24-hour news channels, through hours of pre- and post-match analysis, through the language of drop zones and Super Sundays, and Breaking News that appears to have been broken longer than Britain itself. In the summer of 2013, satellite television found a new

line: with BT threatening to eat into BSkyB's football dominance, Sky Sports News began trailing 2013/14 as 'the biggest
season' we had ever seen. How so? The Premier League had not
been enlarged from 20 teams to 21 or 22. The number of fixtures remained the same. What had changed, what was bigger,
was the number of games to be broadcast on satellite television.
The game grows according to the profile television bestows.

At the same time, on 24-hour sports channels, injury updates
and transfer rumours are headline news. This is news as product, to sit alongside football as product: for if 'Vardy weighs
in with wonder strike' is top of the hour on TV, then it must
surely be important – ergo our subscriptions must be money
well spent. The stake is validated.

However, the need to reaffirm the value of our stake leads to
a news agenda that is increasingly rehashed, until it is no longer
news. On a Thursday night in July 2013, I turned on Sky Sports
News to see the banner flash: 'Breaking News – Liverpool bid
in excess of £20m for Diego Costa'. I went to bed. I got up the
following morning at 11 and switched on Sky Sports News to
see the banner flash: 'Breaking News – Liverpool bid in excess
of £20m for Diego Costa'. I wondered if I had even slept at all.

This saturation coverage is a form of triangulation: it takes
away the genuine supporter's voice, in order to empower the
subscriber. Authentic fandom was never merely a case of swivel-
eyed devotion: it was vested in the ability to talk about football with authority. This was hard won; before 1992, it required
supporters to travel long distances, often midweek, in terrible
conditions. They came back with anecdotes, wisdom and the
occasional scar – the traditional colours of the respected elder.
Now, with 24-hour sports-news channels, radio phone-ins and

online forums, there is no room for these fans to talk about the game with authority any more: the media do that instead, and we are expected to buy their voice. Just as Sky works tirelessly to assure us there is no history of football before 1992, today there is no truth other than that which is captured on television. The fan who was once able to say 'I was there' is now mute. We are all there now, and if we can't make it for kick-off, then we'll be there on Sky Plus.

The dish salesmen will argue that this saturation coverage is simply the response to an inexhaustible passion among English supporters. Evidence points to the contrary.

Forget the international superstars, forget the production values, forget the high-scoring entertainment . . . it is a little-known fact that the genuine passion of English supporters is the most valuable commodity in the Premier League brand. It sells the game in emerging markets. The soccer mom, crucial to the US soccer scene, has been tempted into the grounds by the raucous atmosphere – inspired by the English fans seen on TV, and notoriously absent in every other major American sport. 'EPL' fans in Asia? Gripped by the tribal tensions of the English crowds. However, while satellite TV roams ever further in pursuit of new markets, this passion – its most marketable commodity – is finite. And this is why, when genuine passion is temporarily spent, satellite TV will work feverishly to fabricate it.

The following is a genuine quote from a spokesperson at a prominent football supporters' organisation, who asked to remain anonymous.

'The Premier League are constantly surprised at how much money they get from the sale of overseas TV rights, compared with the German, Spanish and Italian leagues,' said my source.

'They've done quite a lot of research into why they get so much more. Now, the idea of the football being better in England doesn't stand up to scrutiny, when you look at the Champions League results. What makes their product more sellable is the atmosphere. Or rather, the perceived atmosphere: while the atmosphere in the Bundesliga is better than that in England, it doesn't come across as well on TV.'

The key phrase here is 'perceived atmosphere'. As long ago as 2001, the Premier League's own fan survey found that over 50 per cent of supporters at 13 of the 20 Premier League clubs felt that the atmosphere at their ground had deteriorated. At Old Trafford, 82 per cent of supporters complained that the prawn-sandwich brigade had taken the bite out of the match-day experience. Today, 'EPL' fans in emerging markets such as Indonesia, South Korea and the US might not fully appreciate that English crowds are no longer as raucous as they once were. But why would they – when satellite TV works harder to disguise the fact? So here comes the stadium announcer, whipping up a frenzy, here come the crying-for-the-camera fans, the rent-a-mob shirt burners and the purveyors of wanker banter.

The irony here is that the passion of English supporters is being repackaged to sell to overseas TV viewers, whose subscriptions increasingly render English match-goers an irrelevance. And, as with any valuable product in finite supply, salesmen will inevitably reach for counterfeit goods. Our passion is being faked to sell their dish.

Sky, of course, is loath to reveal its secret magic ingredient. For two decades it has sold us the line that we are lucky to have the game that Murdoch made. But with profits from football

TV rights deals in decline, they need us – and never more so than in 2016, with BT bagging the Champions League.

So, in late 2015, Sky invited us to take a share of the spoils. After Raheem Sterling scored a hat-trick for Manchester City against Bournemouth, a Sky Sports presenter announced that Sterling's treble 'underlined his status as the most expensive English footballer in Premier League history'. Here was confirmation that a price tag is now a status in itself. This goes to the heart of our connection to the game: it is a prescription now. Money is our way of understanding the sport, our means of appreciating the talent on display, of valuing the product we subscribe to.

Over the past two decades, satellite TV has sought to recast fans for television, and with considerable effect: we are confused now, caught somewhere between supporter and subscriber. As Andy Lyons, editor of *When Saturday Comes*, explains: 'It used to be the case that the football fan was a participant in football, but increasingly it's the case that they're more of a consumer. The crowd used to play a more dynamic role, but there's a general trend now, in the way the clubs present matches, to expect fans to applaud when they're told to applaud. People who are sat at the stadium are expected to behave more like somebody who is sat in front of the television; while on TV you have these studio audiences comprised of the ultra-loyal fan who wears a shirt. It's an archetype, and it's one that has been created for television.'

And part of the motive to remake the football fan for television is to sell the idea that we can all be fans, in the comfort of our own homes; that this is a safe, aspirant, convenient interest, and no longer the preserve of volatile fanatics. Television has made football a far more inclusive sport. The problem is, not everyone asked for that. The readiness with which many fans reject the modern breed of supporter reflects the sense that the game was never meant to belong to everyone. Not *everyone*. There is a sense of possessiveness that runs deep among football fans, and it accounts for much of the backlash against the other great narrative of modern football.

Fever Pitch is the most successful football book in Britain. First published in 1992, Nick Hornby's account of life on the North Bank at Highbury has sold over a million copies and has been translated into 26 languages. Here was a true fan's voice, and it appeared to tip the balance in favour of the argument that football writing could offer a literate critique of English life. However, as David Winner recalls, 'The response from many football supporters was, "Oh, those middle-class wankers have taken the game." There was a good deal of lingering resentment.'

As there no doubt was on the part of Hornby himself. As he wrote in the 20th-anniversary edition of the book: 'I have read, more than once, [that] my book sold the game to the middle classes, who then became the only people who could afford to watch it. I'd love to claim some credit for significant social and cultural change, however regrettable, but I can't . . .' *Fever Pitch*, he wrote, 'got credit it didn't earn and, sometimes, blame it didn't deserve'.

Hornby's fortune, and his misfortune, was that he was just too good: *Fever Pitch* invented a literary genre, and no one does that without being claimed by the intelligentsia. Now, his Cambridge degree was wheeled out as Exhibit A for the prosecution: the bastard must be middle class. And he was – by his own admission, 'first-generation middle class'.

But this isn't about class, it's about inclusiveness – or rather, exclusiveness. *Fever Pitch* and satellite TV have democratised football. In its inevitable reach for new markets, satellite TV must relentlessly broaden the appeal of the game. Hornby followed suit in print, inadvertently – and alienated many working-class supporters. For democracy was designed to redistribute the crumbs down the table, and here was a *Rough Guide to Football* for the ingénues of Islington. Didn't the middle class have enough already?

Today, there are millions of football supporters who reject one or both of these defining narratives, because there is a resentment that just as media coverage of the game has gone too far, so has its appeal. Note how the fanzines that channelled the dawn of dissent have retreated up the hill – or, as James Brown argues, 'They have become a bit spoddy, the badge of the real-ale-style football fan.' Perhaps their writers and readers would counter that fanzines represent the last refuge for those who object to their passion being counterfeited and sold overseas.

If the changing language of football tells us anything, it is that over the past 30 years the game has been coaxed into the light. The relationship between pusher and junkie has been decriminalised; the drug has become respectable. But if football supporters have won a stake in their game, they have paid a price – today, they are consumers as much as supporters. Those fans who hanker for a time when the game was less preoccupied with families, and the affluent middle class, and tourists, and other 'outsiders' are routinely portrayed as bigots, flat-earth dwellers – hooligan apologists. However, for many of us who sustained the game in its darkest days, football was a sport on the margins of society. Here was outlaw status; here were rebellion, satire and tribalism. There was nothing manufactured about our passion, or the adrenaline of a Saturday afternoon deep into injun country. And in our exclusion from the mainstream we found a bond of commonality. We had an identity. We were supporters and not subscribers. And we were not the unhappy band of losers that the Year Zero historians of satellite TV would have you believe.

6 : Go on, Son ... Give Us a Kick

Bobby Stokes. There you go. Not one of the greats, not one of my heroes, not even one of my team. But he was the first player I saw score a goal live on television. The magic of that goal was that it ever crept in at all: a diagonal bobbler from 20 yards that ambled past Alex Stepney in the Man Utd goal and gave Second Division Southampton victory in the 1976 FA Cup final. It was a revelatory moment for a six-year-old, for now I realised that anyone could do that; anyone could win the FA Cup, if Southampton, and Bobby Stokes, and that goal could. So, at around 5.15 p.m. on a May day in 1976, doors in our street were thrown open, and my best mate and I, and our two big brothers, and the big lad from a few doors down ran out onto the green in front of our houses and started winning FA Cups for our own teams, for our mums and dads, and for the glory.

I might be making this up, actually . . . because I can't really remember what I was doing at around 5.15 p.m. on 1 May 1976, after Peter Rodrigues, with his salt-and-pepper hair, had led Mick Channon, Bobby Stokes, David Peach and the rest up the famous old steps at Wembley. If I like to think I ran out of the front door and recreated Stokes's moment, this is because for me – for millions of men in Britain – the best of our childhood is refracted through football. Football is more than a means for boys to grow into an adult world, and to earn the respect of our dads or grudging older brothers; it is a way of writing our identities as we grow.

And I'm not making this up: 1976 was the year the green outside our house baked and cracked open. It was the year that the water stopped running from the kitchen taps. And it was the year that I started playing football for real – every day, every hour when the light shone, in the year it shone longer than in any other. My abiding memory of my mum in the 1970s is of a woman with a Purdey haircut standing at the door of a pebble-dashed house, jabbing her watch while I blipped around in the dusk like a firefly behind a ball.

John would be there. One of my best mates at primary school, he was an orthodox right-midfielder, long-running and honest in the English style, though susceptible to a nutmeg. We weren't half bad; we could trap and flick and volley, and pull off stunning saves, and we wore genuine Sondico goalie gloves.

A football doesn't have contours, but to a six-year-old boy it was a means of mapping the world. It was a football that first took me off the green in front of our house and to the neighbourhood beyond. I could blame the fact that I had strayed from the safety of our road on a football innocently rolling away, bouncing off a kerb and over a road, or blown half a street in the breeze. And following that ball I'd find streets I'd never seen before, and an adventure playground in the woods. I learnt to read traffic, stop that ball rolling, and ask strangers politely for my ball back, please.

By 1977, sloppy ball control was life's first lesson that pleasure might come at a cost. At 75p from the corner shop, a football was equivalent to five weeks' pocket money. Fights would break out – genuine fist fights – if bigger lads tried to walk off with our Bay City Rollers football. And we learnt that power wasn't everything, that sometimes it was better to pass the ball into the goal, rather than blast it between two jumpers and into a hedge. Because burst balls would sit in a hedge for weeks – like traitors' heads, they served as a grisly reminder of the cost of screwing up. And by 1977, the Bay City Rollers had screwed up – impaled on Mr Seymour's hedge.

By June 1978, Mr Callaghan and Mr Healey had come to the rescue, and with my inflation-linked pocket money I'd got my hands on a real beauty, a plastic World Cup ball, panelled in black and silver hexagons bearing the names of Peru, Iran, Holland, Scotland, Argentina, Brazil, Italy . . . Each thorny scratch on that ball became an insult to the brilliance of Cubillas, Antognoni or Johnny Rep. I would nurse that ball down sloping streets, bounce it up kerbs to set up headers, chip it across roads between the traffic (always a Datsun or Capri, in those days, or a Kawasaki 125). Running with a football, aged seven or eight, made teammates of passing strangers: grown men, on their way home from work, were cut down to my size – unable to resist the temptation to say, 'Go on, son, give us a kick.' To millions of boys growing up in the 1970s there was no such thing as a paedophile, only an old geezer who couldn't pass for toffee.

And yet I'm painting a rose-tinted spectacle. I must be, for it is now a truth rarely questioned in Britain that the 1970s were a disaster. It is one of the axioms of our age. The decade is rolled out like a stick to beat into people that while the banks, the press, the economy and the politicians may be rotten in 2016, we must never forget that where we came from was so much worse – and where we came from was the '70s. It was the decade when everything changed, and it had to, because ours was a country paralysed by the unions, powered by candles and drowning in rubbish. While strikes left the dead unburied in the streets, we were stuffing our mouths with Black Forest gateau and Hemeling. Documentaries now will paint us as a people too gauche even to realise that we were growing fat and stupid on clichés, forgetting of course that we were actually laughing at this stuff as we ate it. No, the historians insist: by the mid-1970s, things were so dire that was it any wonder the likes of General Sir Walter Walker and other old soldiers were ready to step in and shore up a country unable to fuel its schools, homes and factories for more than three days a week?

So how is it that in 2004 the New Economics Foundation reported that 1976 was the happiest year in Britain since the Second World War? Part of the reason for my contented generation is that we had something approaching full employment in Britain until the early 1970s, which meant there was relatively little need for people to uproot and look for work elsewhere. Which meant that communities remained intact, and neighbours had names and became part of the team.

And part of the reason is that the sunniest year in living memory was also the point at which inequality in Britain was at its lowest since the Second World War. If the likes of me and John are part of a happy generation, perhaps it's because we grew up in a decade when most of us were happy to be normal – to be equal and unremarkable. And in the year Peter Rodrigues became the most exotic-sounding footballer in Britain, nothing was more normal than a boy trundling along the street with a plastic football at his feet, lost in his own world and finding his way in it at the same time.

*

Where are those boys now? I look out of the window of my flat in north London and I don't see kids playing in the street, or walking home with steam on their shoulders and scabs on their knees, hotly contesting a goal that never was. I see them ferried instead between 'play dates' in 4x4s, faces so blurred behind the windows they could be faces drawn on balloons. And when I do see children playing out on the streets, occasionally, I don't see a childhood I recognise.

I don't have children, but many of my friends who do have kids admit to feeling uneasy that their sons don't look at football, or play the game, with the same passion or expression as we once did. Is this the yearning of a middle-aged generation for a mythical golden age? The evidence suggests not: as we shall see in this chapter, children today watch top-flight football and play the game in environments unrecognisable from those in which their parents grew up. Experts believe that children's access to top-flight football has changed so profoundly over the past 30 years that what is sold by the Premier League as a form of family entertainment may well be eroding family bonds. More alarmingly, football on a recreational level – the jumpers-for-goalposts culture threaded through my own childhood – is in serious decline, the result of a loss of childhood freedom that is leading to deep anxiety and even depression among adolescents.

In the Premier League era, the safety-first approach demanded by Lord Justice Taylor remains an outstanding legacy. A survey by Populus in 2008/9 found that, from a sample of 13,000 adults, 97 per cent who attended Premier League football with children felt safe inside and outside the ground. By 2014/15, stadium occupancy rates in the top flight had reached 95 per cent, with more than 58,000 junior season tickets sold (up from 46,000 in 2004/5).

But the price to be paid for all-seater stadiums is that young adults are disappearing from the match. For years, this has been due mostly to ticket-price inflation. In August 2011, in the *Guardian*, David Conn reported that the average age of a season-ticket holder in the Premier League was 41. While inflation in the UK between 1990 and 2011 stood at 77 per cent, Conn reported, tickets to watch category-A matches at Arsenal had risen by 920 per cent over the same period, while the price of the cheapest season tickets at Anfield and Old Trafford had increased by 1,108 per cent and 454 per cent respectively. This has impacted on one match-going demographic above all others. 'Premier League surveys for years show a consistent reduction in the proportion of young people, who pay full price from 16,' Conn wrote.

He pointed to research at First Division Coventry City in 1983 by the Sir Norman Chester Centre at Leicester University: then, 22 per cent of supporters at Coventry were aged 16–20. 'At Aston Villa in 1992,' Conn wrote, '25 per cent of the crowd was 16–20; at Arsenal, 17 per cent . . . By 2006–07, the proportion of fans in the Premier League aged 16–24 was 9 per cent. In 2007–08, the figure was 11 per cent. Last season [2010–11] it bounced back to 19 per cent, which the Premier League said was due to improvements in the way its survey was carried out.' That's some bounce.

More eye-catching research came from Old Trafford: in 1968, the average age of supporters on the Stretford End was 17; by 2008, it was over 40. Similarly, the average age of Newcastle supporters at St James' Park in 2002 was 35; by 2012, that had risen to 45. These are the same Geordies, simply a decade older.

So where do the teenage adults go? There is a widely held suspicion within the game that kids are welcome in their primary- and junior-school years not because they are worth cultivating as the next generation of supporters, but because they deliver family groups – including mum and dad, with their higher spending patterns. As a spokesperson at the Football Supporters' Federation told me: 'Anecdotally, we're hearing that even teenagers who do have [adult] season tickets are feeling disillusioned, because they pay all that money and turn up to see all these initiatives for families. They feel so unwanted.'

What kind of business model is this? As John Williams, a sports sociologist at the University of Leicester, says: 'I think the Premier League imagines that some teenage fans may dip in their attendance but return later, when they're affluent and at work. It is a kind of NFL model of fandom.'

It's certainly a risk, as Peter Daykin, a member of the Football Supporters' Federation board, has seen at first hand. Daykin is a Sunderland fan, and tells me that in 2015, people in Sunderland had on average the sixth-lowest income in the country, putting even the concessionary match tickets (£17–20) at the Stadium of Light beyond the reach of many over-16s. And as Daykin says, 'These kids are going to Sunderland with their parents until they are 15 or 16, then they outgrow that and simply stop going.'

And as they drift away, the continuity between childhood, adolescence and adulthood is at risk of being broken, and with it club loyalties passed down through families for generations.

In 2013, research conducted by ICM for Capital One, sponsors of the League Cup, found that 48 per cent of fans watched their first live game with their father, but only one in five went on to support the same team as their dads. The survey also found that only 39 per cent of supporters chose their local side. The internet and satellite TV offer children a choice now between traditional communities of domicile and communities of interest, which extend on a global scale. And this is causing a rupture between clubs and their traditional communities.

According to Daykin: 'You go around Sunderland on a match day, whether we're home or away, and you can walk up to pretty much any pub and there'll be a foreign satellite feed showing the Sunderland game. You can watch it for the price of a few pints, you can stand and have a sing-song, and you can go home. But these kids in the pub won't just watch Sunderland,' Daykin says, 'they'll watch Villarreal, or Real Sociedad too, because the choice is there and they want to be trendy.'

The Stadium of Light is just down the road, then, but the kids are in the pub watching Spanish football.

In the past couple of seasons, Premier League clubs have responded: today, most offer concessionary season-ticket prices for adults aged 16–21. But, in 2014/15, the Premier League revealed that the average age of a match-going fan was still 41.

This is no longer simply an issue of cost. There is a risk in our all-seater stadiums, after all – that young adults, as Daykin says, outgrow the experience of going with their parents, and 'when kids drift away from the stadium at 17 or 18, their match-day experience becomes imbued with the pub atmosphere. And when they come back to the game, in their late 20s, they don't like it any more.'

In 2015, MUST – the independent Manchester United Supporters Trust – conducted its first ever comprehensive survey of supporters' views and ideas. 'United Voice 2015' found that 'The biggest driver of the match-day experience, twice that of any other, was the atmosphere at Old Trafford.' However, only four in 10 of those aged under 35 were satisfied with the atmosphere, compared with 67 per cent of those aged 65 and over. When all age groups were asked 'What other things would enhance the match-day experience for you?', the most popular answer, by a clear margin? Safe-standing areas.

The contrast with Germany is stark. At the likes of Schalke, Dortmund and Bayern Munich, standing areas enable adult tickets to be sold for €16. But there is a positive age-discrimination policy at work too. When I visited Hamburg SV, I was alarmed to discover that within the HSV Supporters' Club (which has over 65,000 members), fans over 35 are required to join the Seniors Department. At 46, I am an old man in Germany, and that's official. Similarly, for years, the Supporters' Club has forbidden HSV to sell more than 50 per cent of its tickets as season tickets, because 'too many season tickets will cause an older fan scene in the future'. It's a strategy ignored by the Premier League, which boasts that 66 per cent of all match-goers in 2014/15 were season-ticket holders, but it seems to be working in Germany: the most recent nationwide research (conducted by the German Home Office in 2002) found that the average age of a member of a German supporters' club was 20.2. More recent research, in 2011, put the average age at 21–30, which means it's feasible that German fans were half the age of their English counterparts. At the very least, they were over a decade younger on average.

The Germans have a name for the younger generation: they call them *Fan-Nachwuchs* ('fan offspring'), and they trust them in safe-standing areas. These are seen as crucial to the continued attendance of young supporters once they reach adulthood. In 2007, Hamburg newspaper *Hamburger Abendblatt* asked HSV fans what motivated them to go to the match: 53.3 per cent cited the atmosphere in the stadium; only 22.6 per cent said they came primarily to watch their team.

Much of this reflects the value the Germans place on integrating young people and adults at football matches. In 1993, the German FA considered the introduction of all-seater stadiums, in light of their long-standing problems with crowd disorder and violence. They rejected the idea on the grounds of cost, declaring: 'Football, being a people's sport, should not banish the socially disadvantaged from its stadiums, and it should not place its social function in doubt.'

The idea of football providing a social function is now in considerable doubt in England. One such function it used to provide was what sociologists call 'socialisation': the modification by children of their behaviour as they mature, and their assimilation into an adult world through an introduction to customs, rituals and mores. It is not difficult to see how football used to serve such a purpose in England: the learning of songs, of standards, fashions and rituals was a key ingredient of going to the game. Today, as Chris Platts, lecturer in sport development at Sheffield Hallam University, says: 'Football still enables children's socialisation, because socialisation never ceases – children will always learn from the behaviour of adults, and they will adapt to a changing environment.' However, the range of adult behaviours to which children are exposed at football has narrowed significantly in the Premier League era. Sharply rising ticket prices, and the planning required to obtain a seat next to friends and family, have transformed English football from a social process, driven by men in crowds, to a form of entertainment – one in which people are repeatedly warned not to stand up, but to sit down where they are directed. This increasingly passive environment has impacted on the bond between fathers and their children, and the effect was noticeable from the moment the Premier League was formed.

Consider that by 1992 the traditional football heartlands of northern England and the Midlands had already suffered over a decade of economic decline. Now, the Premier League arrived, with ticket prices – in the words of Rogan Taylor – 'effectively moving out of the ambit of the working man'. Just seven years earlier, when the game was in the gutter thanks to Valley Parade and Heysel, and with league and FA Cup attendances at their lowest in post-war history (16.5 million in the mid-1980s, compared with a record 71 million in 1948), who remained the most loyal fans in crowds up and down the country? The working-class man. But by 1992, as Taylor says, 'He was finding himself on a variety of scrap heaps. And the exclusion of supporters, caused by rising ticket prices, was highly damaging to two demographics in particular: the middle-aged working man and his children.'

The impact on this family dynamic, Taylor argues, 'was almost instantaneous with the arrival of the Premier League'. And it has never let up. In 2007/8, a Premier League fan survey found that the national average income of match-going supporters was £38,000, down from £40,000 in the previous survey. (Season-ticket holders still earned an average of £40,000.) Inevitably, this figure accompanied a marked decline in the working-class supporter: in 2002/3, the percentage of supporters at a Premier League crowd from the DE (working-class/subsistence) group stood at 11 per cent, and from the C2 (skilled working) group at 20 per cent. By 2007/8, those figures had fallen to 9 per cent and 16 per cent respectively. Meanwhile, the C1 category (lower middle class) rose from 23 per cent in 2002/3 to 32 per cent in 2007/8.

Cost, clearly, has exerted severe pressure on the working man wanting to take himself and his children to the game. And many dads have lost the opportunity to pass on to their kids the values and rituals of football handed down through families for generations. 'I stood on the Kop continuously from 1973 onwards,' says Taylor. 'I had three daughters, all of whom would take it in turns to come to the game with me. I never felt any concern: they'd stand on the Kop with me because I could sit them on a crush barrier, surrounded by people I knew very well because I'd been going to the game with them for years. And if my daughter fell off the crush barrier, someone would catch her. I was never for a moment worried. Now, unless John Williams, who sits next to me, says he's not going to the game and gives me his ticket, I can't go with my daughter any more.'

At the same time as middle-aged men lost the ability to take their children to football, so they lost a degree of authority within the family. Those of us who remember Italia '90, and the best summer since 1976, will recall how the pub had become a viable alternative to going to the match, and a place to commune. However, as Taylor points out: 'People were saying, "Oh, watch it on the telly then, or down the pub, if you can't afford to be there." What's missed in that argument is the fact that going to the match – the *being there* – was a core element of the social activity of older men. It's not just about being exiled from the 90 minutes: there's a much more profound hinterland – it's about going to the pub beforehand; it's mixing with that group of people whose names you don't even know, but you've seen them every week for 30 years. And more importantly, it's talking with authority on the Monday morning: "I was there." Older men tend not to have the network of relationships that older women have,' Taylor says, 'and now this one was lost too.'

And as older men lost access to the game, or began to alternate with their sons, the lads lost the chance to watch their dads operate in a social environment.

Peter Daykin is the co-ordinator of the campaign for safe standing at the Football Supporters' Federation. He is also a parent. 'I've got a six-year-old and an eight-year-old,' he says, 'and at some stage I want to take them to football. I don't want to take them to the football we had when I was a kid, because a lot of that wasn't great. But although football is much safer today, it's a far less attractive thing for kids to do now, and they'll enjoy it less today.' According to Daykin, this is because children are now deprived of the chance to socialise with adults in a spontaneous environment. 'I fell in love with football because it was about going to Roker Park and seeing for the first time adults behaving in a completely different way to how they normally did,' he says. 'Particularly here in the north-east of England, where men didn't really share their emotions and were quite cold . . . you could go to the match and all of a sudden you've got guys shouting and screaming and hugging one another. You could understand things about humanity at football that you didn't see anywhere else.'

In England, as we have lost terraces, and younger crowds have lost the chance to mix freely with older men, so we have lost a means to navigate our way from boyhood to manhood.

'It's the good and bad,' says Daykin. 'It wasn't all good, and we're not trying to airbrush society; but those experiences we had as kids on the terraces were *real*.'

Daykin happily admits that the quality of football is much better now – 'I don't have to watch Tommy Hauser shinning the ball into the Roker End three times in a game and then falling over' – but, he says, 'it was never about the football; it was a social process. When I went to Sunderland from 1987, I started standing at the front of the Fulwell End; then as I got a bit bigger I'd move to the back, where there was an area known as the Cage, where all the bad lads went. When you were 16, 17 and you thought you were somebody, you'd stand in the Cage, and you thought, "This is great!" By the time you were 19, 20 you were too cool for the Cage, so you'd go to the Paddock, or stand a little bit away from the away fans, and be cynical and ironic. There was a natural progression.'

I used football to plot a similar route through my adolescence. As a 16-year-old, I spent weekends following Liverpool around the country, while other lads in the sixth form were slaying dragons in dungeons, headbanging to Anthrax or – later – starting to experiment with heroin. I was, it turns out, better off running the gauntlet of the ICF at Upton Park and the Headhunters at Chelsea after all . . . and moving into my own profound hinterland.

As a teenager in the 1980s, it was football that gave me an identity. I grew up in Stevenage, a new town born in 1946 and still devoid of history or culture. When my parents arrived in the town in the 1960s, they did so with identities fully formed: they were Londoners. I was a new-town boy, beaten up on more than one occasion as a teenager not for who I was, but for who my assailants were not: they grew up in a London satellite town but were not Londoners, and they spent their teens beating the shit out of strangers in order to prove they were harder than the people their families had left behind. I sought my identity not in heroin or fighting, but in football. And I had grasped its potential aged six, in 1976, when *Match of the Day* brought the Kop, a pulsating mass of Liverpudlian culture, into my life. I sat on the living-room floor, looked through my bowl haircut, and thought: 'I want to be part of that when I grow up.'

Peter Daykin found something similar. 'My parents weren't from the north-east,' he says, 'so I spoke with a different accent to everyone else in Sunderland – so everybody thought I was posh, or foreign! In the playground, I never felt part of things, but when I stood on the Fulwell End at Roker Park, I was exactly the same as everybody else. And when a goal went in, strangers would jump around and hug you. It was really important for me in terms of feeling comfortable, geographically, and in terms of my own cultural identity – football was vital to that. I kind of fell in love with the region, and after I moved away to university, I moved back here. I've set up businesses here. Football grounded me in the region, and in who I was and how I feel about who I am. And I want my kids to have that.'

And why can't they?

'Because the difference between seats and terraces is the difference between a form of entertainment and a form of culture . . . We've lost the culture.'

In 2015, at the time of writing, the demand for standing areas appears to be rising among young English supporters. Perhaps they have learnt something from their dads after all – that there is terrace culture, but there is no such thing as seat culture.

The clubs are listening too. In February 2013, 21 of the 22 clubs in the Championship approved a motion 'to encourage and support the instigation of a rail seat/safe standing trial period at any league club'. The only club to oppose the motion was Middlesbrough. In February 2014, the Football League agreed to lobby the government for safe standing; at the time of writing, the Premier League remains opposed. However, the business case is compelling: with rail standing – the safe-standing model common in Germany – clubs can accommodate 1.8 fans standing for every one sitting, so they have an opportunity to lower ticket prices but increase revenues through extra incidental spend. And as Peter Daykin explains: 'Because the prices come down, and those rail-standing areas are inherently attractive to children, you're going to get far more younger people through the door.'

Opponents of safe standing do not cite a potential risk to children standing on terraces; they claim that there is simply no demand for it among young fans. And yet data the Football Supporters' Federation has obtained from the Championship suggests otherwise: when Cardiff City began to get rid of standing at Ninian Park in 2007, they discovered that 45 per cent of the standing area was taken up by women and 35 per cent by under-16s. Similarly, research across the top four divisions in England consistently shows that 80–90 per cent of fans want standing areas, even if they might not want to stand themselves. The FSF has yet to see any rigorous research into the idea of restoring standing areas that has elicited a negative response. But, I put it to Peter Daykin, kids who have grown up in the Premier League era have never known what it's like to stand.

What evidence is there that they really want it, or understand what it's like to be part of the crowd?

'Just look at all the ultras movements springing up across Britain,' he says.

There are the Toon Ultras at Newcastle, Holmesdale Fanatics (Crystal Palace), Stanley Ultras (Accrington Stanley), Red Faction (Middlesbrough), Fosse Boys (Leicester City), Forza Eastend (Bristol City), Ultra Whites (Leeds Utd) and a dozen others. Rejecting politics and commercialism in football, these young British ultras appear, in their embryonic years, happiest simply to spice up one particular stand of their clubs with colour and noise. (Holmesdale are so fanatic that Crystal Palace have even featured them in the club's promotional literature.) And the ultras have swung behind the Stand Up Sit Down campaign to restore terraces to the top two divisions. The irony here is that these cocky young fans are replicating the terrace culture of Germany, mostly. And where does that originate? In the terrace culture of England in the 1960s and '70s.

As one ultra from the Holmesdale Fanatics was quoted in issue 24 of *The Football Supporter* (the official magazine of the FSF): 'Stadia are generally overpriced, over-policed and soulless: I feel sorry for the average young fan growing up in this climate.'

Perhaps we would all benefit if the climate were a little less temperate.

Tim Gill is a former adviser to the British government and the London mayor on children's play. He is the man behind the Rethinking Childhood website and blog, and his advice on increasing the fun in children's play and leisure time is in considerable demand in Britain and Australia. Essentially, all of Gill's work goes towards making the case for expanding children's horizons. When I put it to him that football has ceased to fully function as an environment in which children and young adults can socialise – or rather, experience socialisation – he cites the work of an American writer called Jane Jacobs.

'In her book *The Death and Life of Great American Cities*, there's a chapter called "The Uses of Sidewalks: Assimilating Children",' Gill says. 'She asks the question: how can people hope to grow up to be responsible adults in big cities, where you can't possibly know everybody you're going to meet, but you have to care about them a bit because you have to get along? Jacobs's argument is you learn that as a child by growing up in a place where there are adults who care about you, and look out for you, even if they're not your parents or your teachers.'

As a New Yorker, Jane Jacobs considered the sidewalks of Manhattan to be that environment. In *The Death and Life of Great American Cities*, written in 1961, she described how her children knew the shopkeepers, the business people, the deliverymen . . . As Tim Gill says: 'For Jacobs, that was the paradigm of where you get inducted into being a socially responsible citizen.' He ponders for a moment. 'Where does that happen today, in our society?'

It used to happen in football. Not always successfully, of course, and not without difficulties. But for millions of men, football was a place to initiate their sons and daughters into an adult environment, to pass on norms and rituals and standards, and to reveal a side of themselves they would seldom share elsewhere. For boys, especially, it was a rite of passage, with risk and reward, with kudos and boundaries – a social progression.

Today, football is entertainment, just as David Waddington imagined. And this, as much as anything, appears to unnerve the dads I know, because they realise they can't bequeath much of themselves through entertainment – their kids can order and buy their own, as they choose. And as the research by Capital One found, they are doing just that – and choosing other clubs to support. Culture, on the other hand . . . this is something we can pass on, something precious, something of us, our pride and our prejudice, the fallible and the hopelessly romantic, the irrational and occasionally hysterical, the *real* – if only a glimpse.

Today, English football has never been safer, better televised or more entertaining. And arguably, it has never been less about the culture of the people who shaped our football clubs.

I've no idea what happened to Cubillas, the Peruvian who first opened my eyes to the idea of bending a free kick around a wall with the outside of your foot. Or Antognoni. Or Peter Rodrigues, for that matter. I have it on good authority, sadly, that Johnny Rep has fallen on hard times, and the bottle. It must be desperately tough being Johnny Rep, or Johan Neeskens, or Ruud Krol: a majestic player in one of the world's greatest-ever sides, but never a World Cup winner, and never a Cruyff.

As a kid I never asked anything of Johnny Rep; only that he never tuck his shirt in, or retire, or change his name to John. But trawl through the papers on any given weekend in Britain today and you'll see constant demands made on footballers. One of the more curious is that they should be better role models for children.

The Premier League fan survey of 2007 found that 93 per cent of adults believe footballers have an important example to set as role models. Perhaps the idea is a reaction among my generation to the grim days of the 1970s and '80s, when players punched each other on the pitch, or kicked lumps out of opponents in the name of tough tackling, while we stood on the terraces and cheered. I can see their point. Alternatively, it might be that as football stadiums in Britain have moved from being arenas of socialisation towards theatres of entertainment, the older supporter has become a passive spectator, and as his traditional function as a role model for the next generation has been relinquished, he has passed on that responsibility to the footballers themselves. This leads us back to Rogan Taylor's point: that older men have lost a measure of authority. However, there is an implicit bargain at work here: if working men are stretched to their limit to attend the match, and stretched even further to bring their children too, they may well be tempted to expect more than entertainment from players earning upwards of £100,000 a week. Rising prices and the removal of standing areas have distorted the dynamic of the football crowd: as supporters have become something less than supporters, players have become more than mere players.

And yet research suggests that footballers have always occupied a limited, if special, place in the minds of children. The 2007 Premier League fan survey found that demand for players to act as role models was greatest among the oldest group of fans (aged 65 and over), those who have vacated the role; and demand was lowest among the youngest supporters (16–24). The Premier League did not ask any children who they looked to as a role model. Dr Simon Brownhill did, and in 2011 his findings went viral around the world.

Dr Brownhill is an education specialist, now based at the

University of Cambridge, where he works as a senior teaching associate. Between 2005 and 2011, while a senior lecturer at the University of Derby, Brownhill explored the idea of a male role model in the minds of children under eight.* The *Guardian* reported his findings under the headline 'Being Like Beckham Is Not What Kids Aspire To'. But it wasn't just footballers who were out of favour among kids. As Brownhill told me: 'I don't know if there is really this need among children for role models. There isn't one way of being a role model, just like there isn't one way of being a teacher, or a man.'

According to Brownhill, kids take qualities from different people and build up a composite. 'Take a footballer,' he says: 'is everything about that footballer what you aspire to? Very unlikely. What makes us human is that we're all flawed in one shape or form. You take influences from your dad, your step-brother, your sister, someone you see at the shops, and you become an amalgamation of that.'

Brownhill's research was inspired by a woman who told him (while he was working as a reception-class teacher) that he was 'the perfect role model for my child'. When Brownhill asked her what she meant by that, the mother couldn't answer. 'I was fascinated by the idea that someone could label me with this entity, without being able to describe or define it,' he says. 'So I began to look at it from the perspective of men who work in education [with kids up to eight], to see whether they saw themselves as role models.'

Research from the National Union of Teachers in 2002 found that teachers were annoyed at being expected to be role models

* See 'The Brave Man in the Early Years (0–8): The Ambiguities of Being a Role Model' (Simon Brownhill, 2015, LAP Lambert Academic Publishing).

as well as teachers. 'So,' says Dr Brownhill, 'how can a footballer – expected to perform, to do a job in front of 60,000 people – be expected to be a role model at the same time?' Not least when one considers that, according to Brownhill's research, 'no one knows how you earn this role-model status. There's no job description for a role model. What we have is a situation where footballers suffer the imposition of having an enforced role-model status.'

Simon Brownhill, with the rigour of all good academics, traces a consistent line of credible investigation into the role-model argument, and in particular cites research by Barbara Walker in 2007, which argues that for role models to be of value to children they need to be 'geographically, generationally and experientially close to their own lives'. Walker found that Hollywood icons were 'too glossily distant' to be useful as role models. According to Walker, 'The more famous a male celebrity becomes, and the more that is known about his glamorous private life, the less similarity his life bears to that of an ordinary boy, and the less point there is to try to emulate him.' Brownhill's research suggests boys aged up to eight are more likely to value their grandfathers or firemen than footballers.

And when they reach junior-school age, are children more impressionable? Again, the evidence suggests not. In 2009, the National Literacy Trust explored the concept of role models in a survey of 2,176 seven- to 15-year-olds. The Trust found that 78 per cent of children had a role model, and that 'these come predominantly from within the immediate family'. Although footballers were the role models cited most outside of the immediate family environment, the most prominent sporting role model, Cristiano Ronaldo, was named by just 2.7 per cent of the children who mentioned a specific person. Steven

Gerrard came next, with 1.4 per cent of the vote. This was in keeping with previous research carried out in 2003 by Alison Bryant and Marc Zimmerman, and it found that the qualities children aged seven to 15 still prized above all others were an appetite for hard work, honesty, and that people were kind and caring. Only a quarter of children believe that a role model needs to be famous, or make lots of money.

When one considers a previous large-scale survey of children and their evaluation of footballers, distinct patterns are confirmed. In 2004, BBC1's *Newsround* canvassed more than 10,000 children under 13, and found that eight out of ten thought footballers were bad role models who got into trouble; the same number thought they were paid too much. Only 9 per cent of kids said that footballers inspired them to try to be professional players.

Now, taken in the round, we can reasonably infer here that kids aged up to eight are not especially vulnerable to the influence of professional footballers. And that by the time they approach adolescence, and are more aware of famous people, children have developed their priorities and are able to identify the traits they admire in people in general. It appears that footballers are either making a negligible impression on kids, or that kids are able to filter out the worst excesses of footballers and reject them. In this regard, as in so many others historically, children have sought to take their football cues from male figures much closer to home, notably their fathers.

It was my dad who gave me a new perspective on the legendary Liverpool defender Ron Yeats. A few years ago, I went to an evening with Ron Yeats at a club off Scotland Road in

Liverpool. Even in his 70s, Yeats remained a bear of a man. He must have terrified his own mum in his prime. The audience was suitably reverential, but when one man asked, 'Who was the hardest player you ever faced?' I almost put my hand up and answered the question on Yeats's behalf. Because the night before, when I told my dad I was off to an evening with Ron Yeats, he said, with a chuckle, 'Ask him about Joe Baker.'

My dad grew up in Holloway and Highbury. A lifelong Arsenal fan, he recounted an afternoon on the North Bank in 1964, watching an FA Cup tie against Liverpool. The game is still remembered for a running battle between Yeats and his fellow Scotland international, Joe Baker, a nugget of barbed wire who played up front for Arsenal and stood the best part of a foot shorter than Yeats. 'Liverpool were attacking in front of the North Bank,' Dad said, 'and we were watching that when all of a sudden there was this huge roar from the halfway line. I looked down the pitch and there was Yeats, flat out on his back, with Baker standing over him, growling. He must have planted one on him.'

Now, in the club off Scotland Road, I wait for Yeats to recall the incident. 'Ron, who was the hardest player you ever faced?' Yeats grimaces, as he casts his mind back over his playing career. No, no . . . it's gone. He can't think of anyone particularly troublesome. Fair enough; even in his dotage, Ron Yeats has an aura to protect, a legend to live off, alongside his modest pension.

But I know about Joe Baker, Ron, because my dad was there.

There is no compelling evidence that the watching of elite sport has an impact on participation at grass-roots level.

However, just as the spectator's experience of top-flight football in England today is predicated on safety, so is the manner in which kids now play the game. And both are a legacy of the political climate of the 1980s and early '90s.

The selling off of school playing fields remains controversial in Britain (check the Fields in Trust website for the current figures), but experts I spoke to believe the issue has a far higher political profile than it deserves. I tend to agree: just think where you used to play football as a kid, in the 1950s, '60s or '70s – for most of us it was against a wall, on a scrap of land, down the park or outside our house, not on a school playing field. Instead, it appears to be another change at school that has had the greater impact on recreational football.

In the mid-1980s, the National Union of Miners was not the only union in conflict with Thatcher: tension between teachers' unions and the government saw many classroom staff withdraw as volunteers for after-school activities; no longer were they prepared to pick and coach the school netball and football sides, and drive the muddy minibus across the county. Now, the English Schools' Football Association (ESFA) – which had been highly influential in children's football since the 1950s – came to be sidelined. According to Andy Pitchford, a football researcher at Gloucestershire University, 'The FA was largely caught cold when the schools stepped away, and this created a vacuum, into which stepped the voluntary sector.'

Much of the voluntary sector took off in Britain in the 1950s, and until the 1980s it had focused, in football, on kids of junior-school age and teenagers. But in the mid-'80s, as the schools stood to one side, the voluntary sector 'exploded', in Pitchford's phrase, and began to reach down to all age groups

– as young as primary and even nursery school. The voluntary sector offered a more structured and supervised environment, in which parents were happy to leave their children in the care of vetted football coaches.

This more structured form of play coincided with a rapid commercialisation of football. The Bobby Charlton Soccer Schools were in the vanguard: these were modelled on American summer camps, and as Britain's first commercial football schools they proved a big hit with parents and kids. Elsewhere, children were getting their hands on new bits of kit: it took satellite technology to revolutionise top-flight football, but park football was transformed by something altogether more humble: new forms of plastic. 'You had plastic goals, cheaper shin pads, more kits,' says Andy Pitchford. 'Suddenly, kids could play on marked-out pitches, with cut grass and plastic corner flags. This was everything we would have aspired to when we were kids; we would have dreamed of playing football like this. But', he says, 'the game became commoditised.'

This commercialisation was soon followed by a new results culture in education, with SATS introduced in England in 1991 and school league tables the following year. Gradually, from primary to secondary school, the focus on play as a part of children's education gave way to a focus on winning.

Today, around 2 million people in England play football regularly. There are some excellent initiatives in kids' football: the FA's mini-soccer programme, introduced in 1995/6, won many admirers for the flexibility it brought to matches. The game is sustained every weekend by hundreds of thousands of volunteers, and the number of small-sided teams in England (which increase the emphasis on skill by allowing more time on the ball for each player) rose by 1,000 between 2006–11. There is also the FA's Full-Time . . . 'Oh,' says Pitchford, in raptures, 'it's their league-results database; it has hundreds of leagues on there, and it's fantastic! With smartphones, when you finish your kids' football game at half ten on a Saturday morning, you can text your result through and it'll be on the Full-Time database within 20 minutes. As the results come through, the league tables are adjusted. It's like having Final Score or Frank Bough's teleprinter on your phone!'

Kids sitting in changing rooms up and down the land are excited, engaged, debating the ramifications of that last-minute winner they've just slotted home, and how it's lifted them three places in the table. However, according to Andy Pitchford, take away the technology and the impact of Full-Time is felt a little less positively.

In his research, Pitchford has spoken to around 500 young people, to numerous parents and coaches, and he has also conducted research within the FA, all to gain an extensive insight into how children's football operates, who benefits from it, and what kids think about the game. And what he's discovered is that 'Children have a particular psychology: it's not output-driven, it's about what they're doing in the moment. They talk about the facets of the game – about sliding tackles, hitting the bar, hitting the ball over the bar, running down the wing. They don't talk about league positions, or beating their local rivals 17–0. They talk about the intrinsic value of football, rather than the extrinsic; they talk about the processes of the game, not the outcomes.'

Kids value the fun, the mud and the physicality. They live in the moment. However, those moments are few and far between, according to one of the most influential kids' coaches in Britain. Few people have studied the impact of the changing nature of children's football as closely as Paul Cooper. Cooper was a youth-team football coach in Cirencester when he co-founded Give Us Back Our Game, a programme designed to revive the spirit of street football, in 2006. 'It started with a post on an online forum and it mushroomed overnight,' he says. 'The reaction was incredible.'

Give Us Back Our Game grew into a campaign to persuade the FA to make football more child-focused, and to recognise the philosophy of football as a social game. Cooper was inspired by the realisation that when kids play football with no adults present, they immediately revert to behaving like kids again, with the emphasis not on results, but on playing.

Cooper had seen at first hand the impact on kids of playing club football from the age of five. Here, they came under the influence of adults whose obsession with results was creating an aggressive parenting culture on the sidelines. Simultaneously, Cooper believes, the greater uptake of club football, in the wake of the decline in the schools game, led to more FA committees, who – with customary self-importance – were eager to make more rules: about how many players a team should field, the type of pitches they could play on, and the required coaching styles. 'It became so much more structured, so you had adults imposing their will on kids' football,' he says. 'Now, it's horrendous: they're ruining the creativity.'

Give Us Back Our Game provoked a massive reaction in the press, and Cooper was duly recruited to an FA working committee. His ideas – emphasising light-touch, non-prescriptive coaching, encouraging kids to take risks and make mistakes, and the emphasis on small-sided games – were adopted in full. Today, the scheme has folded, but its impact should not be underestimated.

'Paul Cooper doesn't realise what a fantastic job he's done, how far he's helped to move the FA,' says Andy Pitchford. 'I can say this because I'm independent of either . . . and I can say that Paul has moved a mountain. Nick Levett, head of youth football at the FA, shares a lot with Paul in terms of putting kids at the top of the agenda.'

Levett also devised the FA's Youth Development Review, which was fairly radical – with plans to free up the structures within leagues, and to outlaw league tables for nine- and ten-year-olds. According to Pitchford, 'Nick's a very good, very brave guy, because he's leading major change in an old, established body that doesn't always appreciate new ideas.'

Levett might be wise to keep Paul Cooper on speed dial, for he remains an astute reader of trends in park football and of the impact of competitive parenting. Sadly, Cooper is unequivocal that the essence of children's football is in jeopardy: 'There's very little recreational football now,' he says.

The irony is that parents are probably investing more time and interest in their children's play and leisure activities than any generation of parents before them. However, this is precisely the problem: when adults invest, they usually want a stake in the outcome.

Most children's football in England is played in junior clubs: leagues start at under-seven, but they become competitive at under-nine level – and at this early age, many kids find themselves standing on the touchline, unwanted. A survey in one junior league in Essex found that only 54 per cent of children at clubs got a game every week. According to Cooper, a high proportion of the 46 per cent on the touchline will have committed the sin of being born between May and August: many parents and coaches are so fixated with winning that they favour the bigger, stronger lads, born earlier in the year group. As Malcolm Gladwell observed in *Outliers: The Story of Success*, children born in the autumn, at the start of the academic year, are more likely to flourish in sport. Remarkably, this pattern is sustained through the age groups in English football, and is even evident at football academies within the top four professional divisions, where over 50 per cent of players were born between September and December and fewer than 10 per cent between May and August. 'The minute adults are involved in kids' football, the bias kicks in,' Cooper says.

A competitive parenting culture has also triggered a shift in football from a recreational game to an aspirational pursuit. 'I work in an affluent town,' Cooper says, 'but there are some very poor parts of it, with some badly neglected kids. And what we've seen is that this "working-class sport" has become very middle class, because the fees are very expensive, and so is the kit.' (It is not unusual for parents to fork out £100 simply to register their child at a club and pay for his or her kit.)

Cooper tells me of a conversation he had a few years back with an academy director at a Premier League club on the south coast. 'He told me there was a massive council estate nearby, but there was just one kid from that estate at the academy – often, the poorer kids are not so well nourished, they don't have the parental support and they can't afford the fees.'

I heard the same from a former member of Sheffield Utd's academy. 'It's now so expensive to enrol kids at academies,' he said, 'that it's become an aspirational thing for parents. You'd look in the car park at the academy when the kids were here and it was all 4x4s. In Sheffield!'

Even more surprising is the age at which children are being enrolled in soccer schools: 'You can buy the commercialised football experience for kids as young as two or three now,' says Andy Pitchford. 'Soccer Tots is a franchise based in the Midlands, and they offer soft-play football coaching to kids at that age.'

Presumably the nappies are plastic too?

Paul Cooper didn't put fun at the heart of his football coaching for sentimental reasons: he is adamant that it underpins the success of footballers in their development, and into adulthood. But just as football supporters in the Premier League drift away in their mid- to late teens, England also has the highest drop-out rate in Europe of footballers in their mid-teens. 'People just don't get the connection between kids having fun and kids staying in football and succeeding,' Cooper says.

Insufficient numbers of football pitches are also a factor, especially in London, which has 16 per cent of England's population and only 3 per cent of its pitches. When the FA estimates that up to 1.5 million children and adults want to play football but do not have anywhere to go, it is easy to point the finger at the Premier League. Its sale of domestic TV rights for 2016–19 raised over £5 billion, yet it is set to contribute just £168 million to community facilities over that period. Admittedly, a fraction, but the Premier League contributes a significant amount to more pressing community causes, as we shall see in Chapter 8. Anyway, could I suggest something else . . . like finding a park or a patch of grass to play on, perhaps?

Or a wall? Why must we expect our national football authorities to invest millions of pounds to get our children outside,
playing?

The answer is that recreational football is in serious decline
because Britain has developed a risk-averse culture without
precedent in our modern history.

In 2007, research by the Children's Society found that the
median age at which parents thought it was safe for their children to play outside unsupervised was 14. (I had been playing
outside for almost a decade by the time I reached that age.) In the
same year, a report by UNICEF into childhood in the world's
21 richest nations ranked the UK as the worst place to grow up.
The report – which prompted considerable debate in government – was based on six criteria: material well-being; health and
safety; education; family and peer relationships; behaviour and
risks; and subjective well-being. In the furore that followed, a
survey by the National Trust found that 87 per cent of parents
wished that their children played out more; however, two years
later, in 2009, the charity Living Streets found that only half of
five- to ten-year-olds in the UK had played out on their street –
whereas 90 per cent of their grandparents had.

A sea change in parental attitudes appears to have taken hold
in Britain between 1970 and 1990: my generation have become
so wary of the world outside that we no longer trust children
to find their own way in it, to write their own identities as they
grow.

One of the best indicators of the changing nature of childhood freedoms comes from a survey first carried out in 1971,
then repeated in 1990 and again in 2012. These surveys were
conducted in schools by Mayer Hillman, John Adams and

John Whitelegg, and involved children aged seven to 11 and 11–15. As far as possible, the three surveys were carried out in the same schools over those four decades.

'These are the best numbers we have about children's everyday freedoms,' says Tim Gill, the former government adviser behind the Rethinking Childhood website. 'These were surveys of what you might call "children's licences": what kids are allowed to do at different ages. These covered things like going to the shops on their own, using public transport, crossing the road on their own and walking to school on their own. And what they show is a huge drop in children's everyday freedoms between 1970 and 1990.'

The publication of the second survey, in 1990, prompted a report called *One False Move*: this carried the headline statistic that in 1971, 80 per cent of eight-year-olds walked to school on their own, but by 1990 that had fallen to about 10 per cent. As Gill says: 'If you want to pick a litmus test for children's freedoms, the eight-year-old is a good one to pick. Now, since 1990 their freedom has fallen again, but only a bit – because there wasn't much scope for it to fall further.'

Again, Germany emerges as an interesting contrast, for in 1990, Hillman, Adams and Whitelegg also surveyed German children, and they did so again in 2012. And they found that German children have far more freedom than British kids: in fact, 'fan offspring' enjoyed the same kind of freedom in 1990 that British children last enjoyed in 1970. 'Since 1990, there's been a bit of a drop in the freedoms of German children, but not much,' says Gill. 'You would have to wait 60 years before German kids fall to the level British kids are at now.'

What accounts for this? No one really knows, but it appears

to be a combination of the environment, how we get around, and a change in attitudes. For Tim Gill, the single greatest factor is the increase in car use: 'A lot of people say it's technology – screens and screen games,' he says. 'But bear in mind that by far the biggest drop in children's freedoms took place between the 1970s and 1990s, and that can't have anything to do with screens, because children's use of technology hadn't changed that much in that period.' The greater change in screen use, he argues, has been seen since 1990. 'Screens are a symptom, not a cause,' Gill argues.

Gill traces a gradual shift in parenting patterns from the end of the Second World War. 'I don't find it very plausible that out of thin air, a generation of parents have become more paranoid,' he says. 'You could say that after the war, rich nations became more affluent societies, and we became less concerned about where we would get our next meal and whether we would have a roof over our heads, and more concerned with what we had to lose. It's what is called the "risk society". I think there is something in that.'

The rewards we once gained from dabbling in risk have been lost to the 'compensation culture' – reward-seeking from risk. However, this is a culture of fear: litigation rates in Britain are no higher today than they were ten years ago, but the fear of being sued is eroding our public-spiritedness. In 2008, Paul Cooper carried out a survey of a hundred schools, and found that 30 per cent had banned football in the playground because of health and safety fears: teachers were worried that kids might be hit by a ball. Meanwhile, out on the streets, the 4x4s are en route to play dates, each turn of the steering wheel describing a vicious circle: 90 per cent of eight-year-olds are now driven to and from school, leading many of those same parent drivers to stop their kids playing outside . . . for fear of cars. And if many neighbourhoods no longer feel safe, that is partly because people aren't walking around outside, and if parents look outside their houses and see fewer people walking around, they don't see a welcoming place. According to Tim Gill, 'The perceived threat from strangers becomes a shorthand for that fear, and it's a kind of bogeyman fear.'

In his book *No Fear: Growing Up in a Risk Averse Society* (2007), Gill argues that if we allow children to work out their own solutions to problems, to deal with arguments in their football games and other activities, and to develop confidence, those positive experiences build up to competence – or what sociologists call 'self-efficacy'. Conversely, if you have a child who is watched over all the time, who has parents stepping in to referee – call a halt to sliding tackles and the rough stuff – what children will develop is 'learned helplessness'.

Tim Gill, like Peter Daykin, like Rogan Taylor, like me – like millions of us – grew up with the freedom to play football and to watch top-flight football whenever he wanted. There was risk, but far greater reward. 'My childhood was incredibly free,' Gill recalls. 'When I was 11 we moved to a village outside Aylesbury, and I would go out with mates, cycling, and we'd ride 40, 50, 60 miles in a day. On a Saturday, I'd go out all day, and my parents wouldn't see me. I know,' he smiles, 'you can hear the nostalgia klaxons going off as we speak . . . But one thing I would do at 11, 12, I would go and see the Arsenal at Highbury. This was in 1976/7. I'd get the train, on my own, from Aylesbury, and get the Tube to Finsbury Park. *Fever Pitch* was like reading my own childhood. I would have been paying for the ticket out of my pocket money, and it wasn't a particular concern.'

Today, however, Gill can see a generation of young adults becoming teachers and parents themselves, but who have not faced the kinds of experiences that make them feel positive about challenge, adventure and freedom. He finds a significant echo in none other than Judith Hackitt, chair of the Health and Safety Executive, who has warned of the dangers of children growing up 'risk-naive'.

Is there no evidence that kids welcome more structured play, I ask Gill? 'No,' he says, 'quite the opposite. I carried out a survey of kids, commissioned by Dairylea. One question we asked was: what activity do you do the most? And the answer was: play on games consoles. We also asked them: what would you like to do more often? The most popular answer was: play on our bikes and scooters.'

There also appears to be a toxic thread running through the debate over kids in the UK: we increasingly distrust them, and we demonise them too. Experts believe the James Bulger killing had a part to play here, that it underscored a view of children as feral. This view certainly informed much of the coverage of the riots that broke out in London in the summer of 2011 and spread across England.

Equally, the problem is not just our children, but strange men, bogeymen . . . the paedo in the park. The Jimmy Savile scandal will have done nothing to alleviate this fear, of course, but there is no evidence that kids are any more at risk of stranger danger today than they were in the recent past. Home Office figures indicate that between 1990 and 2004 the number of murders of children by strangers hovered between zero and four a year.

'The occurrence is almost like lightning strikes coming down,' says Tim Gill, who obtained the figures. 'There's no evidence that there are more dangerous people out there today posing a significant threat to children than there were before.'

But as the survey by the Children's Society found, parents – on average – would like to keep their children indoors until they are 14. This fear, or loathing, of the outside world begins to affect the child's own mind: experts fear there is a generation of kids growing up who do not care about their environment, their neighbourhoods or their neighbours. And because these kids believe that the communities they're growing up in have no interest in them, they resort to leading isolated lives.

It is noticeable here that these patterns present most markedly in the English-speaking nations: in Australia, in the US, and in Britain. There is no discernible evidence that similar trends are occurring to the same degree in Scandinavia or Germany, for example. Perhaps there is something peculiarly British in our own situation. Since 1976, when I first chased a ball around the streets and fields near my council house in Stevenage, we have lost so many council houses – 900,000 were bought and sold into private ownership between 1981 and 1991 alone. Those bought and sold have become 'assets', with fences and gates and extensions. The private realm has expanded at the expense of public space. At the same time, as full employment becomes a distant dream, communities have become more transient, as people come and go in search of work. And the equality that reached a post-war peak in 1976 is long gone: in 1979, the Gini coefficient, the benchmark measure of levels of inequality, found that Britain was at .25, one of the most equal countries in the western world. (The lower the score, the more equal a society.)

In 2015, it was .404, meaning the UK is the most unequal country in the EU, and even more unequal than the US. People don't appear to value normality or equality as much as they have in previous generations. Exceptionalism and aspiration drive them into their 4x4s, into Soccer Tots and academies.

Since the 1970s, we have become an increasingly atomised country on so many levels. Is it any wonder that – withdrawn to their bedrooms and our cars – children are no longer trusted to go outside and play football by their parents? And is it any wonder that, in 2015, a quarter of 5–16-year-olds believe that playing video games is a form of exercise?* Increasingly inward looking, parents appear less willing to invest in their children the social or cultural norms and mores we were introduced to in the 1950s, 1960s or 1970s; rather, investment comes with a receipt, for classes and clubs, for private tuition, geared towards results – towards gaining an edge over the opponent, rather than levelling the playing field.

And as children no longer mix so freely and spontaneously with adults, their ability to learn responsible behaviour is curtailed. As Tim Gill says of our sanitised football stadiums: 'What do you get if there's nowhere for adults and kids to casually and spontaneously spend time around one another? One thing you get is adults who hate kids being around.'

Since the UNICEF report ranked Britain bottom of the premier league for children's happiness, there has been increasing optimism that people at all levels – parents, schools, local councillors, politicians – are heeding warnings from the HSE about our risk-naive society. Local authorities are funding more adventure playgrounds; there is a growing debate among parents about

* See 'The Class of 2035' (Youth Sport Trust, June 2015).

'free-range' as opposed to 'battery-reared' parenting; and there are local projects nationwide (inspired by parents in Bristol) that are closing streets to traffic once a week, so that kids can kick a ball around outside their houses. 'There is a pendulum change,' says Tim Gill. 'There's a much greater interest in children's play than 10 years ago, with some lively debates involving parents, educators and decision-makers about what needs to be done.'

In April 2013, the latest UNICEF table of children's well-being ranked the UK in 16th place out of 29 developed countries. Alongside a fall in young people who were overweight (from 15 per cent to 10 per cent), British children also reported an increase in their life satisfaction.

Similarly, there are some excellent people at the FA now, who have produced a document called *The Future Game*: on one level it's the FA's coaching philosophy; on the other a commentary on kids' football. And according to Andy Pitchford, 'It's the only coherent sports-coaching philosophy text I've ever seen.'

Meanwhile, up in Sunderland, Peter Daykin is seeing similarly positive signs that the pendulum is swinging his way, in the campaign for a return to safe-standing areas in our top two divisions. Maybe one day his kids will grow up to watch Sunderland while learning from the men around them – learn to move from the front of a terrace to the back, and integrate with the bad and not-so-bad lads. They might recognise humanity in a hug from a fellow Mackem, grasp irony and wit, and risk and reward. One day, they might learn to stand on their own two feet at football – and love Sunderland AFC, and invest in Sunderland, and lay down roots in Sunderland, and really love football, just like their dad.

7 : Next Stop, Milton Keynes

In March 2013, I went to meet the shadow health secretary, Andy Burnham, at his office in Westminster. Burnham was shortly to make a statement on the NHS in the Commons, but he was happy to talk football as he limbered up. In fact, he looked sorry to leave for the front benches: over the best part of an hour we talked about Hillsborough, Everton, Game 39, racism, the emasculated FA, and the influence the Premier League now has over government. And mostly, we talked about how English football clubs desperately needed to reconnect with their communities.

This sense of dislocation is eating away at football. It feeds off inconvenient kick-off times, designed to suit not local, match-going supporters, but overseas TV viewers, and which in 2013 led to rows of empty seats at the FA Cup final: that fans from Wigan and Manchester found it difficult to travel home from Wembley after a 5.15 p.m. kick-off was of little concern to the FA.

It feeds off the rebranding of clubs, such as Cardiff City, Chelsea and Wimbledon. It feeds off the foreign sensitivities of the boardroom. In August 2013, a Leeds Utd director suggested that alcohol should be banned from Elland Road, so that the club might respect the cultural beliefs of its owners – who hailed not from Yorkshire, but from Bahrain (via Dubai). It feeds off the language, too. A few weeks after we met, Burnham and I attended the service at Anfield to mark the 24th anniversary of Hillsborough. John W. Henry, Liverpool's principal owner, flew in from Boston by private jet to deliver a speech before the Kop, in which he conveyed his palpable sadness at the loss of 96 lives at somewhere called Hillsburrow.

Andy Burnham sensed this dislocation before the 1990s were out. Burnham was following Everton, home and away ('Joe Royle, dogs of war'), when he began working for Labour MP Tessa Jowell in 1994. In 1998, a year after Labour's landslide election victory, Burnham received a phone call from James Purnell, a special adviser at Number 10, offering him the chance to become administrator of a new body called the Football Task Force.

'For me, it was the best thing anyone had ever suggested,' Burnham says. 'There were some in government who didn't have much expectation of what it could do; but, being the kind of person I am, with the background in football that I have, I completely absorbed myself in it.'

One of the key publications to emerge from the Task Force (whose wider impact will be considered in the next chapter) was a report called *Investing in the Community*. In 1999, shortly before the report was finalised, Burnham left the Task Force to work for Chris Smith, the culture secretary, but he continued to steer the report from afar. 'I asked them to push for quite strong recommendations, one of which was to create a body to promote supporter ownership of clubs.'

The first English supporters to move into the boardroom were Northampton Town fans in 1992. Theirs was a response to the club's financial difficulties: the Cobblers were £1.6 million in debt, the equivalent of two years' turnover.

In 1997, Bournemouth became a community-owned club, and in 1999 the Labour Party conference pitched up in the seaside resort, determined to push ahead with a wider programme of social inclusion. Burnham now persuaded Chris Smith to pledge, in his speech to conference, that Labour would set up a body to support fan ownership of British clubs.

'Supporters Direct was born at that point,' Burnham says. 'At the time, a lot of people thought it was pie in the sky, but a pretty powerful seed was planted.'

Since 1992, over 120 supporters' trusts have taken a stake in their clubs. 'I think the idea is sitting there, building, building, building,' Burnham says, 'and I think there will come an opportunity to restructure a lot of clubs in the top flight.'

A few weeks later, on 19 April 2013, Portsmouth became the biggest English club to pass into the control of its supporters, after it finally emerged from administration. That the club avoided a worse fate – liquidation – was due to a salvage operation launched by a group of fans gathered under the umbrella of the Pompey Supporters' Trust. And it was they who walked out of the High Court with the keys to Fratton Park.

A few days later, I spoke to James Mathie, who co-ordinated Supporters Direct's assistance to the Trust.

'The achievement of the Pompey Supporters' Trust is the result of a monumental effort on the part of a monumental number of people,' he said. 'The community has come together, and now it deserves the opportunity to show the world how a club should be run. As the story of Pompey has unfolded in recent years, we've had more and more people ask us *how* they should take over their clubs, rather than *if* they should take over their clubs.'

Those fans now gathering around Supporters Direct would no doubt agree with Andy Burnham when he says that 'by the late 1990s, I felt that a few spivs had cashed in on clubs that had built their identities over decades. I was always clear that the best long-term solution for the game was to reconnect clubs with their identity.'

Today, Premier League owners are chiselling away at the foundations their clubs have been building since the late 19th century. If the Portsmouth saga was settled through a monumental effort by supporters, it began as a tale of how English fans are being forced to re-evaluate their relationship with the football clubs in their community.

Portsmouth FC have always done things their own way. They were the first club to host a league match under floodlights, in 1956; the first club south of London to win the FA Cup (they are still the only club south of London to win the top-flight league title), and the first to get rid of the youth and reserve teams, in the 1960s, to streamline the club. 'It didn't work out,' says Colin Farmery, a spokesperson for the Pompey Supporters' Trust, 'but we tried it. We've never been afraid to try something new.'

But they never wanted this: responsibility for the largest community-owned club in England. In fact, foreign ownership, under Russian-Israeli Sacha Gaydamak, was no problem for Pompey fans, as long as the club was performing.

'In 2007/8, Pompey were on the crest of a wave,' says Farmery. 'We were beating Man Utd at Old Trafford, en route to winning the FA Cup, and playing AC Milan in the UEFA Cup. And while this was happening, a guy called Barry Dewing from PISA

[Portsmouth Independent Supporters' Association] was ringing me up and saying, "We need to set up a supporters' trust."'

But as Farmery admits, 'Although a lot of fans were asking questions of the Gaydamak years, and what the implications would be if the taps were turned off, it's always difficult to sell the concept of an umbrella when the sun is out.'

However, by late 2009, Pompey fans had begun to listen to the likes of Barry Dewing, because Portsmouth had descended into what Farmery describes as 'the most chaotic state, I believe, that any English football club has ever been in, certainly in the Premier League'.

Farmery was involved with the steering committee that set up the Pompey Supporters' Trust. A fan since 1970, he is a teacher and writer, with several books on Pompey to his name. He once edited the club programme and has even painted the goalposts at Fratton Park (tip: start from the bottom and work your way up, if you want to avoid getting a large white stripe down the middle of your head). A month before the Trust finally bought the club, I met him at a rain-swept Fratton Park, where he described how the chaos first came to light.

'It was in August 2009,' he says, 'and the owner, Sacha Gaydamak, had apparently sold the club to an Abu Dhabi businessman called Sulaiman al Fahim. Nice guy though he was, Sulaiman proved to be the only Arab "sheikh" without a penny to his name, it seemed. He lasted six weeks, and then he sold the club to another Arab, called Ali al-Faraj. Al-Faraj was a Saudi Arabian hermit; no one ever saw him, no one ever heard from him, he never came to a game and he never arrived at the club in any meaningful sense or form. To this day, there are genuine concerns about whether he actually existed.'

Farmery's instinct is that Ali al-Faraj did exist, but that he never knew he owned a Premier League football club. 'I think he was a front, in effect, for a company called Portpin. I think that Portpin's was an asset-stripping exercise: I think that they wanted to suck some money out of the club because they thought they were owed it by the father of Sacha Gaydamak.'

So the club was being claimed as an IOU?

'Sacha Gaydamak, who I know reasonably well, is a nice enough guy, and he would always deny this,' says Farmery. 'Portpin, I expect, would equally deny this. But the facts stack up. And if it looks like a duck and quacks like a duck, it's likely to be a duck.'

Left to its own devices, or its owners' (whoever they were), Portsmouth's finances went into a tailspin. It didn't help that the man in charge of the club's finances at the time was a convicted fraudster, an Israeli called Daniel Azougy. Now, whichever way Portpin turned, Pompey fans smelt a rat. So, too, did the Premier League, and in January 2010 it began diverting TV payments away from Portsmouth and directly to clubs to whom they owed money, to prevent those funds being siphoned off.

In February 2010, after protests by Portsmouth supporters, the Premier League invited a delegation of Pompey fans to a meeting with its chief executive, Richard Scudamore. 'They laid on the table this matrix of ownership connections we had uncovered as fans,' says Farmery, 'and Scudamore sat there and said, "Yeah, I see your matrix, and . . . we've got one twice as big again."' But, as Farmery explains, 'Being the risk-averse organisation it was at the time, the Premier League weren't prepared to risk being sued by saying to Ali al-Faraj, "Well, actually, we don't think you are a fit and proper owner."'

That month, Portsmouth became the first Premier League club to go into administration. 'Pompey were becoming a rather smelly thing in this beautiful Premier League brand,' says Farmery. However, and no doubt to the relief of the Premier League and its broadcasting partners, Portsmouth were relegated three months later.

In August 2010, they began life in the Championship, shorn of the likes of Glen Johnson, Asmir Begović, Jermain Defoe, Sulley Muntari and Sol Campbell. It's not easy to establish what happened to the money the club received for these transfers, because prior to the Pompey Supporters' Trust takeover, Portsmouth last filed its annual accounts at Companies House in May 2008. Any fine the club faced for neglecting to file its accounts was a drop in the ocean of debt engulfing Pompey. So no one bothered.

The Pompey Supporters' Trust was formed in the early stages of the chaos, in November 2009, when it appeared that Portsmouth were unable to pay the players' salaries on time. However, by autumn 2010 – with the club now worth tens of millions less than it had been the previous season – the Trust was still in no position to consider a buyout. As Farmery explains: 'If you are setting up a trust in fair weather, it's a fairly arduous task: everything has to be open and transparent, with voting structures in place, otherwise you immediately lose credibility. And of course, we weren't setting things up in fair weather: we were trying to set things up at a club that was operating like the wild west.'

Portsmouth came out of administration in October 2010, and was sold back to Portpin. In March 2011, rumours began to emerge that Portpin had found a buyer for the club. Convers

Sports Initiatives (CSI) was led by Vladimir Antonov, a Russian banker, and it duly bought the club in June 2011. However, Portpin had retained – as security – a charge over Fratton Park, which represented the major part of its book valuation of the club, at around £17–18 million.

In November 2011, Antonov was arrested: the Lithuanian government sought to extradite him from London, on charges of fraud through a Lithuanian bank, Snoras, of which he was a director. Antonov denied the charges, and was bailed, but his assets were frozen. Because CSI owed Portpin money, which they were no longer able to pay, Portpin put CSI into administration. Portsmouth FC was not in administration itself, just CSI, its parent holding company; however, the financial plug had been pulled on the club, and Portsmouth went into administration for the second time in February 2012.

It was now that the Pompey Supporters' Trust decided to throw its hat into the ring. The Trust had been running for two years and, with the assistance of James Mathie at Supporters Direct, it was now a stable organisation. The Trust formed a small bid team of three from its executive board, two of whom were local businessmen, and in April 2012 it invited fans to pledge £100 that they could convert, in the future, into a £1,000 share. About 1,700–1,800 fans signed up, giving the Trust an assurance of £1.8 million.

In the summer of 2012, the Trust lodged a bid of around £2 million to buy the club. Few were surprised when it was rejected. However, the Trust had one unique advantage: the Portsmouth brand was now so toxic that, in Farmery's words, 'any credible buyer would have looked into the books and found a wriggling nest of vipers – these legacy issues – and thought it wasn't worth the trouble. At least we had some idea of the issues – we knew the snakes we had to kill.'

By August 2012, the Trust had its own share issue, and four or five key high-net-worth individuals, putting in around £1 million between them. With almost £3 million in pledges, they now brought on board a property partner, who would save the Trust the £2.5 million that they argued was the true value of Fratton Park by buying the ground and leasing it back at a preferential rate. With around £5 million worth of muscle, by early August 2012 the Pompey Supporters' Trust was a serious bidder. In early November 2012, the Trust launched a share issue. In effect, it was offering £2.5 million for the club, in order to satisfy the charge Portpin had on Fratton Park; they valued the remainder of the club at around £300,000. But Portpin were now demanding £9 million.

What the Trust was putting its store in was the prospect that the administrator, Trevor Birch, could persuade the High Court that the charge Portpin had levied on Fratton Park was simply unrealistic; knock that out and Birch could sell the club to the Trust for £2.5 million, hand that sum to Portpin, and effectively say, 'There you go, that's what I could get for it.'

On 19 April 2013, Trevor Birch came good: Portpin accepted a bid for the club of £3 million, with sweeteners should it win promotion within a fixed timetable. Portsmouth FC was reborn, after 125 years, as a fan-owned football club.

As the 2013/14 season got under way, Pompey were 58.5 per cent owned by the Trust and 41.5 per cent owned by their partners, 11 businessmen known as 'presidents'. According to Farmery, the Football League regarded Portsmouth as 'a good laboratory', an opportunity to establish whether a club of this size can succeed in the hands of a supporters' trust.

'It will be us, as fans, in control of our own destiny,' said Farmery. 'For the past 40-odd years, whatever has happened to Portsmouth FC has been done to us, for better or worse. Now, we're saying, "We want to take control."'

I caught up with Colin Farmery in November 2015, to see what that control looked like. Portsmouth are in League Two, and in the early stages of rebuilding, yet things are looking rosy. The club has paid off all its debts and loans. It has invested £1 million in the first training facilities Portsmouth have ever owned in the city, and it owns Fratton Park outright. It has outperformed its financial targets in the past two years, and has a turnover of £6–7 million.

Today, Portsmouth FC is 48 per cent owned by the Trust and 52 per cent owned by 16 presidents, who have invested between £50,000–600,000 each. A number of those presidents are also Trust members. This is a pragmatic model, as Farmery explains: 'We couldn't have raised the money we needed without those larger individual investments.'

The Trust is run on a one member, one vote basis. In the event of a takeover bid, the Trust casts one vote, as do each of the shareholders. The Trust's board comprises up to 12 people, elected on a rotating basis, with four places coming up for election every summer. The board elects three of its members to a seat on the club's own board. Three other places are taken by individual investors, and there is also a seat for someone with legal expertise.

So, what have the first two years taught you? I ask Farmery.

'Firstly, that it is eminently doable,' he says, 'even for a club the size of Portsmouth. We've increased our season-ticket holder base for two successive seasons, despite disappointing results on the pitch, and we've invested in our infrastructure in a way we weren't able to do even with Premier League money – most of that was spent on players and liabilities. Now, if someone were to want to buy Pompey, what they see is what they would get, and breaking once and for all the link with the opaque financial past of the club is the fundamental service the supporters have done Portsmouth FC. Ultimately,' he says, 'this isn't so much about ownership as custodianship.'

It's an interesting distinction. What responsibility do club owners have towards a club or its supporters? What responsibility does a community have towards a football club? And really, what does it matter who has custody of the bloody thing anyway?

If Portsmouth have settled one argument, it is that supporters will always care more for their club than any number of passing spivs. The Pompey chimes should be ringing all over the country: an English club might now be reduced to an IOU in a feud between foreign businessmen. And there are plenty of those in the boardrooms of English clubs.

In 2015/16, only seven clubs in the Premier League were entirely British owned; the other 13 were either part-foreign owned, majority controlled or owned outright by businessmen from Russia, New York, Florida, South Africa, Switzerland, Abu Dhabi, Boston, Bangkok and Missouri. The English game is now run by people from overseas, and increasingly for people overseas. In 2012,* the Premier League was watched by 102 million people every week, in 212 territories: British viewers accounted for just 16 per cent of the audience. Overseas TV-rights deals

* The most recent figures available at the time of writing.

increased in price from £650 million for the three seasons 2007–10 to £2.2 billion for 2013–16 – which means that foreign viewers stumped up 40 per cent of the total TV money flowing into the Premier League clubs. (Between 1992–97 the split was around 85/15 per cent domestic/foreign income.)

There is a clear imperative for clubs to chase overseas viewers ahead of their local fans. The 20 Premier League clubs' share of money from domestic rights deals is allocated in three tranches: 50 per cent of the pot is shared equally; 25 per cent according to how many times a club appears on TV, and 25 per cent according to a club's final league position. However, all of the overseas income is shared equally between the clubs, regardless of where they finish in the league – which makes it much more attractive than domestic income streams to the vast majority of clubs, who have no realistic chance of reaching the top four. We're unlikely to see the likes of Stoke or Sunderland objecting to those 5.30 p.m. kick-offs any time soon.

Few clubs sensed this shift in the wind as early as Man Utd. In 1996/7, the first Deloitte Football Money League reported that Man Utd generated €134 million in revenue, of which €19 million – 14 per cent – came from broadcasting. By 2011/12, the club's revenue had risen to almost three times this level, at €395 million, but its broadcasting revenue had risen almost sevenfold, to €128 million – 32 per cent of its entire income.

Unsurprisingly, Britain's biggest club lead the way in digital media. As Jonathan Dyson reported in the *Independent* in February 2013: 'The club have partnerships with mobile telecom providers in 42 countries and television providers in 54, while their website has attracted, on average, over 60 million page views a month over the past year.'

By May 2005, many United supporters had similarly sensed a shift in the wind, and left to set up FC United of Manchester. As the club's website states, the takeover of Man Utd by the Florida-based Glazers was 'the catalyst, the final straw, but not the sole reason. The material theft of a Manchester institution, forcibly taken from the people of Manchester, was the tip of a pyramid of destruction, with changing kick-off times for the benefit of television, soulless all-seater stadia full of "new" supporters intent to sit back and watch rather than partake in the occasion, heavy-handed stewarding and ridiculously priced tickets propping it all up.'

Today, the likes of FC United of Manchester, AFC Wimbledon and Enfield Town are a refuge for supporters who believe that football clubs should not only embody the identity of their communities, but be an integral part of the community too. However, communities are changing in football.

In October 2002, the Community and Education Panel at the Football Foundation (the UK's biggest sports charity) commissioned a team of five researchers from Manchester Metropolitan and Sheffield Hallam universities to 'provide the Panel and the wider football industry with a new vision and understanding of how to engage with "communities" of various types'.

Over the next three years, the researchers explored the relationship that three major clubs – Leeds Utd, Manchester City (each in the Premier League for at least one of those seasons) and Sheffield Utd – had with their local and wider communities. Their 80-page report found that

football supporters are rarely seen or described by clubs as a 'community' or 'communities'. Indeed, over the course of the past decade they have more commonly come to be identified as individual 'customers' . . . Where supporters are acknowledged as communities, it is usually only those particular groups such as current and potential supporters from black and minority ethnic 'communities', those with disabilities, and those from other 'disadvantaged' groups that are considered as such.

As the report makes clear:

This disadvantage/interest group approach establishes false distinctions within the fan base and undermines one of the principal characteristics of any club's support – that it is a communal expression of a strong attachment to the club from people with diverse social backgrounds.

On taking delivery of the report in 2005, the Football Foundation's Community and Education Panel shelved it, reputedly after pressure came from the Premier League. Here was a truth better kept under wraps: 'communities' are no longer regarded as proper communities in football, but as divisible markets of potential growth.

This has delivered some positive outcomes: women and black and minority ethnic supporters are the two fastest-growing supporter groups in the Premier League. That 13 per cent of match-going supporters in 2012 were black and minority ethnic (BME), when ethnic minorities accounted for 9 per cent of the population, is testament to the huge strides football has taken since the days when John Barnes was back-heeling bananas off the pitch. However, there is tangible growth potential in women and BME supporters. There can be no growth in the traditional white working-class communities who sustained football throughout its first hundred years.

This thinking was evident in an extraordinary statement by the Premier League chief executive Richard Scudamore, in 2011. 'Football is increasingly attractive to more sectors of society, which is fantastic,' he said, 'because it was only a generation ago that people used to look down their nose and see it as a rather narrow preserve for young white males.'

Even if Scudamore was guilty of being clumsy rather than offensive – even if his criticism was of those who looked down their noses, rather than those they saw over their noses – I'm not sure there's anything wrong with being a young white male. But you've only to throw in the prefix 'working-class' before 'white males' and you're looking at the mainstay of football crowds in England until the late 1980s. Had the mainstay been earmarked as the problem demographic?

As Rogan Taylor outlined in Chapter 6, the rise in ticket prices that accompanied the birth of the Premier League had an almost immediate impact on the demographic of football crowds, signalling a sharp decline in the presence of the middle-aged working man and his children. The trend has continued, with the percentage of seats at Premier League matches claimed by the lower middle class rising steadily during the first decade of this century: from 23 per cent in 2002/3 to 32 per cent in 2007/8.

If football clubs no longer cater primarily to their traditional male working-class communities, it is easy to argue that this is because club chairmen are – and have always been – irredeemably venal, and that the Premier League was their gilt-edged opportunity. It is also a left-wing canard. Football clubs have become dislocated from these communities because the

historic pact that bound clubs to their working-class supporters broke long before the Premier League arrived. And everyone – the FA, the clubs, the players and the supporters – must
take responsibility for that.

From the late nineteenth to the late 20th century, the relationship between football supporters and the local businessmen who (mostly) owned their clubs was one of detachment at
best, and at worst, of simmering contempt. If football was the
national game, so the relationship between those who owned
clubs and those who watched them was the weekend exten-
sion of a national malaise – boss and worker didn't talk to one
another. By the 1980s, this chronic lack of dialogue would break
down altogether, with catastrophic effect.

English football was designed for escapism. In the 1920s
and '30s, the terraces offered refuge from the hangover of the
Great War and the Depression. League and cup attendances
reached their post-war peak of 71 million in 1948, with the
public retreating from the Second World War and austerity.
In this release, terrace subcultures emerged. These were generated by homogeneous groups of people sharing a local dialect, humour and social mores. Before the culture of fan rivalry
emerged (with the arrival of away fans and segregation in the
'60s), working-class terrace humour was directed instead at the
nobs who sat in the directors' box. This was a form of power to
the people: witness the cheeky wag at the front of the terrace
– coat too long, but cap snug – cracking jokes at the distant
directors and furtively casting back for support, while a jolly
copper saunters by, truncheon dangling by his side. This was
the spirit of Andy Capp, and Andy Capp didn't talk to the boss.

In 1975, the historian Alan Bullock was commissioned by Labour prime minister Harold Wilson to find a solution to Britain's dire industrial relations. The Bullock Report was published in January 1977, and one of its key recommendations was that all firms with over 2,000 employees should give shop-floor staff a greater voice by appointing a worker to the board. Here was the bridge between the man and The Man, and it was the trade unions who sabotaged it – they feared the proposal would threaten their independence. As one shop steward said: 'It is not the job of unions to manage but to oppose management.'

Football supporters settled for a parallel form of exclusion. According to Dave Boyle, former chief executive of Supporters Direct, 'Football supporters, historically, might be hewn from the same rock as trade-union members and co-operatives – which were about working people getting off their arses and fighting for control of their own lives. But football fans spent Monday to Friday fighting for a bit of control, and I think they saw Saturday as their chance to take a day off and enjoy the game.'

Historically, it has fallen to supporters overseas to seek political engagement through football. When Spain, Italy, Germany and Argentina fell under totalitarian rule, football supporters had no option but to mobilise: they grasped that their societies were no longer functioning properly – were no longer able to host political discourse – so in Barcelona, Rome and Buenos Aires, football became one of the few places people could still do politics. Munich might have given Hitler his head, with the Beer Hall Putsch of 1923, but Bayern fought him all the way. Two of Bayern Munich's founding directors were Jews, and the club had several Jewish coaches prior to the Second World War.

Between 1933 and 1945, Bayern Munich players literally fought Nazis hand to hand; they also posed for pictures with Jesse Owens, and hid their silverware when other clubs were handing it over to be melted down for the war effort. In England, we did songs and fashions and tribal identities. We did not do politics.

And when we did, it was soon forgotten.

In 1919, 3,000 Huddersfield fans gathered at the club's ground to protest at its proposed merger with a new club to the west, Leeds Utd. The Football League had recently pulled the plug on Leeds City, after it was found guilty of making illegal payments to players; but a city like Leeds needed a football club. The Huddersfield Town chairman, a local mill owner called J. Hilton Crowther, had sunk considerable funds into the club over the previous decade, but he had grown exasperated at the meagre support – especially compared with the bumper crowds that turned out to watch Huddersfield Northern Rugby Union Club. As Crowther steered Huddersfield towards a merger with Leeds Utd, Town supporters formed a shareholders' association to buy their club. Pledges came in from MPs, clergy, factory workers, dignitaries, businessmen and the *Huddersfield Examiner* newspaper. Their victory was sealed in January 1920, when J. Hilton Crowther packed his bags for Leeds Utd.

Huddersfield not only survived without the mill owner, they would go on to appoint Herbert Chapman as manager in 1921. Chapman had first to be cleared of any wrongdoing himself at Leeds City: he had been manager of the tainted club, and was banned from football for life in 1919. In 1921, his ban was overturned, and Chapman went on to transform Huddersfield into one of the first great dynasties of English football, winning three league titles in the 1920s. However, the club's initial turn-around was born of a strike.

'Crowther was a local mill owner who was hated by the supporters,' says Dave Boyle, 'so thousands of Huddersfield fans rejected him – that's why the attendances were so low. The fans' response was, effectively, "If Huddersfield are going to become really good, then you're going to look really good, and we don't want that, because you're our boss. And besides, you will only be buying success with the pittance of money you pay us in wages, and which we give back to you at the turnstiles."'

This supporter boycott inspired the Huddersfield Town Shareholders' Association to publish a supporters' trust manifesto. This remains a little-known document, because no one picked up the baton.

Rogan Taylor's book *Football and Its Fans* (1992) remains the best account of supporter movements before the FSA. These were sporadic and only occasionally effective. There was an organised 'renegade' fans protest at Man United in 1930 led by George Greenough, a taxi driver, after a poor run of results. Greenough called for a boycott of the home game against Arsenal, with some success. And there was T. C. Newman, a supporter at Swindon Town, who in 1921 called for a new share issue in an attempt to get elected to the board. That Newman, and others, failed was largely due to the fact that English clubs were highly skilled at nullifying potential fan unrest. In *Red Men*, John Williams described how Liverpool's directors in the 1950s (mainly Freemasons and Tories) successfully stifled public debate at club AGMs when the club was playing especially poorly: meetings lasted less than an hour, complaints from the floor were shouted down or ignored, and potential new directors from 'outside' the cabal were effectively seen off. As Williams says today, 'Fans began to assume (as did directors) that nothing could change the status quo: you just had to wait until your club's fortunes changed "naturally".'

Since the end of the First World War, supporters had largely settled for an unspoken contract: if clubs provided a place for ordinary people to socialise, through cheap tickets, fans grudgingly accepted the most basic of stadiums, even while the disasters piled up.

In 1902, 25 spectators were killed at Ibrox Park, during a Scotland–England international, when a section of wooden terracing collapsed, causing people to fall 50 feet. In 1914, a wall collapsed at Hillsborough, injuring 75. The famous White Horse FA Cup final at Wembley in 1923 is routinely romanticised, but around a thousand supporters were estimated to have suffered injuries due to overcrowding. In 1934, a man named George Frederick Hill was crushed to death at Hillsborough, in a crowd of over 70,000. In 1946, 33 people were crushed to death at an FA Cup match at Burnden Park, in Bolton. Then Ibrox, again and again: in 1961, two people were killed and 44 injured on a stairway exit; in 1967, on the same stairway, 11 people were injured; in 1969, on the same stairway, 30 were seriously injured; then, in 1971, on the same stairway, 66 people were crushed to death.

There was little incentive to buy a season ticket to these uninspiring arenas. Similarly, the right to pay on the gate gave supporters sufficient power over the directors: just as the working men might withhold their labour through a strike, they could withhold their gate money if the team weren't performing. It was an uneasy, complacent dynamic, perhaps only partially illuminated by Bill Shankly, when he described the holy trinity at a football club: the players, the manager and the supporters. 'The directors don't come into it,' he said. 'They are only there to sign the cheques.'

Even today, at clubs run by supporters' trusts, there remains a gulf between those in the stands and those in the boardroom. As Dave Boyle explains: 'I've spoken to so many people who are involved in supporters' trusts and who (especially if they've been involved in ownership) don't go to see the game any more, because once they became directors they were accused of the lowest of ideals. There's this totemic idea that trust directors should pay for their own season tickets, which I completely understand; but there's an implicit idea here that regardless of the huge amount of effort and hours the director might be putting in to further the prospects of the club, if he or she doesn't pay £400 for a season ticket then they're clearly on the make!'

That friction persists, as Lord Snape – former chairman of Stockport County – found to his cost. 'Most County fans are wonderful people,' he told me in 2014, 'but I won't take my grandson with me to Stockport any more because of one or two supporters who make life difficult. I've lent the club £50,000, but I was at the match recently with my grandson and this fan in front was yelling at me, "Get your fucking hands in your pocket!" It's the same for one of our main investors,' Snape said. 'He's put £350,000 into the club, but he's scared of taking his nine-year-old son any more because he gets so much abuse from a couple of fans.'

Just as supporters have historically snubbed a dialogue with the directors, so they resisted the chance to talk to each other, or the game's administrators, before the 1980s. As recently as the 1970s, football fans rejected a critical analysis of the game – as advanced by the likes of Eamon Dunphy, Stan Hey and Steve Tongue in *Foul*. And they saw little need for a proper dialogue with the FA and Football League before the 1980s. What they demanded, in return for this exclusion, was that the owners stayed out of the fans' business – of creating their own cultures and identities on the terraces. The owners were only too happy to oblige: fan behaviour was alien, uncivilised, and frequently violent. Left alone, beyond the reach of the directors and the football authorities, supporters hatched the fashions and songs of their terrace tribes; they reserved the right to roar on their team while laughing at the owners – the brewers and car salesmen and purveyors of processed meat.

Meanwhile, in the boardrooms, a deadly form of dust was gathering.

In June 1966, the secretary of state for education and science appointed Norman Chester, CBE, to chair an inquiry 'into the state of Association Football at all levels, including the organisation, management, finance and administration, and the means by which the game may be developed for the public good'.

Even as Alf Ramsey was making good on his promise to put England on top of the world, doubts were growing about the health of the domestic game. Between 1956 and 1966, match receipts at Division One clubs had risen by 72 per cent, but overheads on players and ground expenses rose at more than double that rate – 157 per cent. This financial imbalance was tilted decisively in 1961, when Jimmy Hill led a successful players' campaign to abolish the maximum wage of £20 per week. Then, in 1963, former Newcastle United midfielder George

Eastham won his appeal against the right of a club to retain a player's registration even after his contract had expired and he was no longer their employee. The Football League had argued that their 'retain-and-transfer system' prevented the biggest clubs signing all the best players, but the judge, Mr Justice Wilberforce, ruled: 'The system is an employers' system, set up in an industry where the employers have succeeded in establishing a united monolithic front all over the world, and where it is clear that for the purpose of negotiation the employers are vastly more strongly organised than the employees.'

Eastham's victory meant that players' contracts would become a matter of free negotiation between the player and the club, and that once a contract expired, the club could only renew it on terms that were at least equal to the player's previous deal. The writing was on the wall: English clubs needed to move to a more commercial footing, to look beyond an inadequate income stream reliant on supporters who were increasingly unpredictable.

Hooliganism was now giving serious cause for concern. It had been an intermittent blight around football since the late 19th century, in the guise of proto-hooligans the 'roughs', who would not only set about rival supporters, but opposing players and the ref too. It began to pose a significant threat from the early 1960s; in the run-up to the World Cup, several British newspapers were warning that football violence would turn 1966 into a PR disaster for England.

The Chester Report sought to nudge the game forwards. Published in 1968, it recommended a restructuring of the FA, greater opportunities for former players to appear on committees, and a tighter committee for central policy making and planning. It also suggested the FA contribute more from its income to the county associations and towards coaching facilities. The FA was not impressed: 'It is not expected that a body of this kind [the Chester Committee] can fully understand the ramifications of the complex Football Association,' it declared. 'It is not surprising, therefore, that the FA does not accept some of the criticisms.'

Chester was followed, in 1968, by the Harrington Report, which made clear the link between the safety and comfort of supporters and their behaviour: 'We feel that improved ground facilities would not only help to deal with the hooligan problem, but do something towards its prevention,' it declared. 'Clubs often seem keener to spend money on the purchase of players than to undertake any major spending on ground improvement which would increase safety and make hooligan control easier.'

Harrington led to the establishment of a working party, chaired by Sir John Lang, which made 23 recommendations for the improvement of safety and comfort at football grounds. But none was binding in law. Lang's report was presented in November 1969, and in the introduction he wrote: 'The Working Party was dealing with a subject which has been discussed almost ad nauseam during recent years. Not unexpectedly, the Working Party has not found a single solution for a problem which is often due to a combination of factors . . .'

In the late 1960s, Chester and Harrington/Lang offered football the opportunity not only to address its growing financial difficulties, but to improve at the same time the safety and comfort of spectators. The Premier League might have started here, in 1969/70 – the parallels with the Taylor Report and the emergence of the whole new ball game are clear. However, the difference in 1969 was twofold: absent was the colossal alternative revenue stream of satellite TV; and the FA's Rule 34 was still intact, which meant that club chairmen were constrained, still, by a bond to the community. Increasingly frustrated, they reacted sluggishly to Chester and Harrington. Fourteen months after the Lang report was published, 66 people were crushed to death at Ibrox.

By the turn of the 1970s, the British ground stock was littered with deathtraps. The owners and chairmen now realised they were presiding over massive decline, and, in Dave Boyle's unerring phrase, 'you've got fans who'll be damned if they will carry the can for this shit'. Hooliganism became a proxy for the disconnect between boardroom and terrace. Fissures turned into ruptures. The violence that Spurs and Leeds fans exported to Rotterdam and Paris in 1974 and 1975 was now a common blight on English streets and trains, and at football grounds. The 1980s began bleakly, with England fans rioting at Euro '80 in Turin. The game was splintering from society, and the dynamic between supporters and their clubs was at breaking point. And according to Rogan Taylor, it snapped not in April 1989, but in May 1985.

'I teach my MBA students that the equation which describes the birth of modern-day football is Heysel plus Hillsborough over satellite TV,' says Taylor. 'But it was Heysel that birthed the Premier League, and most people don't realise that.'

In the spring of 1985, Taylor had helped to launch the Football Supporters' Association, and was already deeply engaged with the politics of football. 'Four months after Heysel,' he says, 'secret meetings were taking place between the so-called Big Five clubs, which were then Liverpool, Everton, Man Utd, Arsenal and Spurs. And you could feel for them: these guys were running a business. And they had gone to bed on a Tuesday night in May 1985 with a functioning business model, and they woke up on the Thursday morning and they didn't have a business model!'

As Taylor says, 'Liverpool were 20 years consecutively in Europe, and they wake up on the Thursday and they're not going to Europe for the foreseeable. But the club still had to honour all their players' contracts, and they would lose values on their sponsorship deals for not being in Europe. They would also lose the TV and gate money from home games in European competitions . . . I imagine within days of Heysel, phone calls were being made between the chairmen of some of those clubs, saying, "Right, guys, what the fuck do we do now? I don't know about you lot, but we've just lost about 20 per cent of our income, with no prospect of regaining it in the medium term."'

According to Taylor, 'The Premier League birth pangs started *then*, when the big clubs thought: "Hang on, what about keeping all the TV money to help compensate for our losses? It's not much but . . . they never show these minnow clubs on telly anyway, and we all know who the big draws are. What shall we do, then? Well, we either get an agreement with the Football League or we just fuck off." And in the end it was, "OK, let's fuck off."'

And when they fucked off, they left their traditional communities behind.

Lord Justice Taylor's reluctance to slam the brakes on rising ticket prices was an oversight that has only grown more acute since 1990. There are socio-economic factors in play too. The relative spending power of working men is in decline. As *The Spectator* reported in May 2010, among British workers aged 16–17, 'girls not only outnumber boys, they take home 12% more pay'. Meanwhile, the number of men who have primary responsibility for looking after the household has trebled since 1993, as women gain something approaching parity in the workplace. And as mass immigration becomes ingrained over a generation, it is those in the lowest-income groups who bear the brunt of wage depreciation.

What remains a matter of fierce debate is whether the FA, in its role as midwife to the Premier League, actively sought to drive a wedge between England's top clubs and their traditional working-class communities, or whether the increase in middle-class supporters was an unintended side effect of a game that had undergone a long-overdue transformation.

In 1990, the Henley Centre for Forecasting was commissioned to produce a report for the FA into the future of the game, post-Taylor. As Dave Boyle argues: 'Their report said, effectively, "The trouble with football is that it's too working class." It said that the key economic growth market in the late '80s was the affluent middle-class consumer with large disposable income. So you need to make yourself more attractive to the middle class, and you do this by charging more, in order to reposition the "product" as more upmarket, which has the benefit of changing the social mix of the crowd away from the core working-class fans, who were essentially seen as the problem demographic.'

In 1991, the FA responded to the Taylor Report, and the overtures of the First Division's big clubs, with its *Blueprint for the Future of Football*. It stated: 'the response of most sectors has been to move upmarket so as to follow the affluent middle-class consumer . . . in his or her pursuits or aspirations. We strongly suggest that there is a message in this for football.'

A significant contributor to the *Blueprint*? The Henley Centre for Forecasting, of course.

Boyle throws up his hands: 'You tell this to people, and they say, "Oh, this is conspiracy-theory nonsense." And you say, "No, it's called the *FA Blueprint for the Future of Football*, and it's there in black and white!"' Boyle pauses for a moment. 'I'll give credit to the FA for this: they actually delivered on something. This was not a happenstance chain of events.'

But what of the clubs? Kevin Miles, of the Football Supporters' Federation, says: 'I'm not aware of any evidence to suggest that ticket prices have increased as a means of conscious social engineering. The main driver of the increase in ticket prices has been market forces, which is a polite term for greed. To suggest that there has been social engineering would be to credit football clubs with perhaps even greater deviousness than even they are capable of.'

When I put Miles's argument to Dave Boyle, he doesn't miss a beat: 'The thing is, Kevin's right and I'm right. I don't believe the clubs ever sat in a boardroom in the late '80s and said, "Right, we're going to increase ticket prices to deliberately exclude a certain socio-economic group." But I think they got to the point where they simply didn't give a shit any more.'

'It's mind-boggling to get your head round what's happened in football, because it's happened so quickly. We want owners to respect our history and tradition, and it's not happening, is it?'

Words that could come from supporters at almost any club in the Premier League today, but these come with a Scouse accent, and from a man whom we shall call Paul. It is 'Paul' and his mates who are responsible for a banner on the Kop that has got right up the noses of rival supporters of late, and even offended some of Liverpool's own supporters. 'Scouse Not English' is a legend that first appeared at Anfield around 2006. Much like 'Against Modern Football', it appears to be an anti-ism, a form of distemper. So what does it mean to be Scouse Not English?

'It doesn't exist as a group or organisation,' Paul says. 'It's a notion, an idea of something. It's about recognising that we have a cultural identity that we should preserve.'

For decades, Liverpool Football Club was a vehicle for Scousers of the red persuasion to promote their cultural identity. Now, allegedly, the club poses a threat to their identity so grave that some of its supporters are turning their backs on the rest of the country, in order to safeguard their identity.

'I suspect that Scouse Not English was influenced by the increasing number of OOTs [out-of-towners] and out-of-country fans at Anfield,' Paul says. 'It wasn't a case of "We don't want them"; it was more a case of "Let's remember what we are."'

Paul acknowledges that 'the idea that Liverpool only ever had Scouse support is a myth. I also think it's a myth that we can survive without our wider support, not least because it's a clue that you're not very successful. But there is a noticeable change in our support. We need to keep a Scouse heartbeat: this is Liverpool Football Club and it *is* of this city, and that should never be forgotten.'

Everton are also of this city, but there is no blue branch of

Scouse Not English. This is an entirely red form of separatism, and it is not without merit: two years after the Scouse Not English banner first appeared, the Premier League fan survey of 2007/8 found that while Everton fans made an average journey of 44 miles to Goodison, the supporters who travelled furthest to home games were Liverpool fans, at an average of 82 miles. And that takes no account of the foreign fans. Walk around Anfield on match day and you'll need a squad of translators to talk to Liverpool's home crowd: the pubs, chippies and convenience stores are serving Norwegians, Icelanders, Danes, Dutch, Germans, South Africans, Americans and Canadians. Scouse Not English represent a tribe increasingly marginalised in their own city. Unlike Pompey fans, however, what they want is a stake not in the club's ownership, but in its culture.

'The club is beyond us,' Paul says. 'The only thing we can influence as supporters is our supporters.'

However, with England's top clubs increasingly turned towards the global market, some appear intent on reshaping the identity of their supporters too. In August 2013, on the eve of their return to the Premier League, Hull City's Egyptian-born owner Assem Allam announced that the club would be renamed Hull City Tigers; the AFC would be dropped from the club's name, after 109 years. 'Hull City is irrelevant,' Allam told the *Hull Daily Mail*. 'My dislike for the word "City" is because it is common. City is also associated with Leicester, Bristol, Manchester and many other clubs. I don't like being like everyone else. I want the club to be special. It is about identity. City is a lousy identity. Hull City Association Football Club is too long.'

Identity or branding? As Allam's son and vice-chairman,

Ehab Allam, said: 'We have dropped the AFC as it is something which has become redundant. The identity of the club is the Tigers, the stripes, and the colour scheme of amber and black, which remains. We just feel that, now being on the international stage, we need to strengthen the brand identity. AFC is redundant . . . we have dropped something that is of no value, and is of no use.'

When Hull fans took to the stands with banners proclaiming 'City Till We Die', Assem Allam responded: 'They can die as soon as they want, as long as they leave the club for the majority who just want to watch good football.' And the following month, he told the *Guardian*: 'If I were the owner of Manchester City I would change their name to "Manchester Hunter" – you need power.'

The tiger is certainly a potent symbol in Asia. So, too, are the dragon and the colour red – as Paul, at Scouse Not English, points out. 'Take Cardiff City: their Malaysian owner changed them from the bluebirds to the red dragons [a fans' campaign saw the club back in blue by January 2015]. And Roman Abramovich has created a whole new identity for Chelsea.'

Paul is not exaggerating. As Simon Kuper reported in the *Financial Times* in April 2012, a survey conducted by the Sport+Markt consultancy found that 90 per cent of English Chelsea fans in 2006 were not supporters of the club in 2003, prior to Roman Abramovich's arrival. There is huge value in recreating Chelsea: the club's sponsorship deal with Samsung delivered 15 million supporters in South Korea alone. And the club is making huge inroads in the US, where the bizarre approach Americans take to history is a major incentive for Chelsea to shed any lingering traces of the old Shed days.

'Football history means nothing to a certain type of American supporter,' says Dave Boyle. 'A club that talks about its history denotes that it has nothing to say about the present or future.'

Which means that Chelsea's image problems of the 1980s are no impediment when it comes to capturing swathes of the American market: you can dispose of history when you're reaching out to forward-thinking markets. At the same time, neither Chelsea's King's Road history – the glamour days of Osgood, Cooke and Hudson – nor its decent supporters (it was Chelsea fans who helped to see off the National Front at Stamford Bridge in the '80s) are of any value either. No, it is Chelsea's recent success on the pitch that is driving their expansion in the US, and – as Boyle argues – this is about branding: 'Chelsea's shtick in the emerging markets is fresh: it's "We've won trophies for as long as you've been here."' Man Utd offer permanent success: stick with us because we've always won trophies. Always, of course, since the Premier League arrived in 1992. Today, only Man Utd currently rival Chelsea in their claim on the American market: while Utd have a lead on the East Coast, Chelsea are making hay in the Midwest.

The likes of Arsenal, meanwhile, can trade on their metropolitan profile, but Liverpool have a weaker hand to play at the global table: they lack the recent history of Man Utd and the urbane cachet of the London clubs. Fenway Sports Group, the club's Boston-based owners, don't quite know where to pitch Liverpool abroad, and Scouse Not English are on to this.

'Ian Ayre [Liverpool's managing director] said a while back that he wanted supporters from around the world to be able to "taste the product" of Liverpool FC,' Paul says. 'So are we watching a sport that should be run as a business, or are we watching a business that just happens to be a sport? And that's where the issue of identity comes back in. What are we? Because if we are just consumers, then we don't have an identity.'

The paradox here is that identity remains crucial to football fans – and, therefore, to the appeal of football clubs. As Debbie Winardi, who manages international relations for Indonesia's official Liverpool supporters' club, told the *Independent* in February 2013: 'A contributor to the phenomenon of the Premier League in Indonesia has been the growth of Premier League communities. Indonesians like to gather and be involved in communities, and this makes them more passionate about their clubs.'

That's right: their clubs.

As the game becomes increasingly mobile – its roots substituted with a GM crop for the world to taste – supporters back in England draw to themselves the responsibility for protecting their culture.

'Look,' says Paul, 'I think there is some romanticism about the old days, but it's clear to see that supporters did shape Liverpool FC. This idea of the twelfth man, this idea of supporters travelling the length of Europe . . . this did happen. And remember the famous old footage of the BBC standing in front of the Kop, talking about the importance of the fans. But football has become a business. Liverpool believe that we are consumers, and they would probably alter their identity to appeal to new customers and everyone who wants to "taste the product". But we want it to be about sport, and your side, and the colours of your side, and your history and traditions. And if the owners won't respect that, then we'll do it ourselves.'

And in their response – in their 'Not' – Scouse Not English

are describing a fault line on the Kop. Paul is adamant that 'We don't need to skew the identity of our support that much, we just need to skew it a bit.'

Might Liverpool's fan scene be at risk of fracturing? While the club was primarily a Liverpool club and then an English club, it could hold together the Scousers and the OOTs. When I was following Liverpool as an OOT in the 1980s, I accepted my rank as an outsider – a guest, if you like; in fact, for many supporters like me, the Scouse culture was a crucial ingredient in the magic of the Kop. But increasingly, Liverpool fans feel detached from the rest of the country. The city has suffered massively at the hands of national government for three decades. The unwarranted vilification over Hillsborough still persists, in certain quarters, after two decades. And the idea that Liverpool is still an English club is increasingly a fiction; now, Liverpool FC – like Chelsea, like Man Utd – is a global product to taste. And in their exclusion from the club within their community, many Liverpool supporters appear to be trying to reclaim its identity by turning their backs on the rest of the country, and even their fellow supporters.

If any one party is making a mockery of the idea that clubs are rooted in their communities, it is the millionaire mercenaries who pitch up for a few years, kiss the badge and screw the clubs. Let's meet the players.

If the Premier League had been formed as early as 1968, then it would have been a reasonable response to the abolition of the maximum wage, and the Eastham ruling, and hooliganism. But club chairmen were men of comparatively limited vision in the 1960s. And that they were meat-packers and car salesmen and butchers with local businesses meant the historic settlement between clubs and their supporters would hold until the mid-'80s. Footballers played something of a responsible role in this compact: throughout the 1980s and until 1992, top-flight players' salaries were running at around 300 per cent of the national average wage. But in 1992, the Premier League and BSkyB created a narrative of newness, and in order to sell the whole new ball game to supporters who had previously watched it free to air, or cheaply in the stadium, they had to turn them into subscribers. Initially, Murdoch identified Hollywood movies as the inducement to his emerging subscribers; but by 1992, it was footballers who assumed the role of stars.

In its crucial early years, the Premier League was forced into playing a game of catch-up with Serie A. Italian football had been freshly anointed by the World Cup in 1990; it boasted the world's greatest players, and it was so flush with money in 1992 that long-forgotten players like Gianluigi Lentini were moving from Torino to AC Milan for £13 million. (Even the Vatican was moved to comment on the transfer fee, describing it as 'an offence against the dignity of work'.)

This hyper-inflation in transfer fees signalled a transfer of power to footballers that was accelerated by the Bosman ruling in 1995, which enabled players to run down their contracts in the hope of engineering a free transfer. At the same time, the Premier League joined an international market: previously, the likes of Liam Brady, Ian Rush and, as late as 1991, Paul Gascoigne had been unable to resist big-money overtures from Italy's wealthiest clubs. Now, to persuade their like to stay in England, and to attract the best foreign players too, the Premier League had to meet their soaring wage demands, commensurate with their international profile. In the long term, this has delivered cost-push inflation: ticket prices in the Premier League aren't rising in order that clubs' spending can be raised, they are rising in order to cover players' increasingly steep wages.

'The football labour market is an incredibly complex one, arguably unlike any other in any other industry,' says Simon Chadwick, professor of sports enterprise at Salford University. 'At one level, labour costs are an issue, because players possess a skill set that is in very limited supply. At the same time, given labour scarcity, the demand by clubs for talented players contributes to rising salaries and benefits. This means that in certain parts of the football labour market, we have witnessed hyper-wage inflation through a combination of high costs and excess labour demand.'

This doesn't sit comfortably with those on the left of the debate, because it pins the blame for exorbitant ticket prices not on the bosses (the club owners) but on the workers (the players). Many active campaigners in football are from left-of-centre politics: many are former trade unionists, and when people from the left are asked to side with either the boss who sets the ticket prices or the worker who causes the ticket prices to be set higher, the man on the left tends to side with the worker – or in football, the player whose wage demands cause ticket prices to be raised – and not the club chairmen.

This is head-in-the-sand thinking. It is the footballers who drive the numbers, and this is driving a wedge between club and community. Rising salaries for the top players continue to ratchet up average players' worth. And these wages are driven by rising TV deals. Between 1992 and 1997, the Premier League's total revenue from TV stood at £50.7 million per season. Between 2010 and 2013, it stood at £1.1 billion per season. Now look at players' salaries. In 2012, the High Pay Centre, an independent non-party think tank, published *Football Mad: Are We Paying More for Less?*. The report was written by Dave Boyle, and it revealed that by 2000/1, Premier League footballers' wages had risen to around 1,700 per cent of the national average; by 2009/10, they stood at around 3,500 per cent of the national average.

It's a problem exacerbated by the widening gulf between the Premier League and the Football League. As the Sporting Intelligence website revealed, in 2010/11 Blackburn Rovers drew 73 per cent of their income from the Premier League, whereas Man Utd took 18.2 per cent of theirs from the league. The likes of Blackburn are thus heavily dependent on remaining in the top flight, which exerts a back-breaking pressure on the club to attract the best players to Lancashire. This has created in England an international pay scale for regional clubs, and it means that a football club on Tyneside or in Lancashire no longer has a responsibility – if we can charge it with that – to reflect the economic realities of its community.

'Take Middlesbrough, for example,' says Boyle. 'Middlesbrough, as an area, is markedly less prosperous than Chelsea or Islington, but historically this wasn't so relevant: players weren't going to leave Teesside for Chelsea – with a national maximum wage of £20 a week there was no need. Now, clubs are increasingly dependent on foreign players, and if you're Ravanelli, Juninho or Mendieta, your next move is global . . . and if a club like Middlesbrough wants a seat at the global table, then it has to pay at the global level.'

But the people of Middlesbrough do not earn at the global

level. This not only leaves their supporters at a distance from the players, it leaves the clubs increasingly reliant on TV money. And this, again, ratchets up players' salaries. When the latest domestic TV rights deal was signed in February 2015, for £5.1 billion, Malcolm Clarke, chairman of the Football Supporters' Federation, said: '3% of the increase alone from the latest domestic Premier League deal would pay for a £20 away ticket cap, in line with the FSF's Twenty's Plenty campaign.'

But the clubs are still guided by players' wage demands. In recognition of this, in 2013 the Premier League restricted the amount that clubs could spend from the new TV deal on wages to £4 million per club. This immediately drove down the percentage spent on wages as part of clubs' expenditure – from 67 per cent in 2012/13 to 57.5 per cent in 2013/14. However, as David Conn noted in the *Guardian*, players' pay still increased by around 5.5 per cent. It was simply offset by the fact that the clubs' overall income rose by 22 per cent.

The players never lose out.

And it's match-going supporters who really pay the price for this. As Boyle also reported in *Football Mad*, between 1992 and 2010, the wages of footballers in the top flight rose by 1,508 per cent, but the national average wage had risen by just 186 per cent in the same period. Meanwhile, the increase in the cost of the cheapest tickets at Arsenal, Man Utd and Liverpool averaged out at a whisker under 900 per cent.

Liverpool FC has long since ceased to reflect the economic realities of its community. Anfield is situated in the borough of Walton, which is consistently ranked one of the most deprived areas in Britain. In 2015, Liverpool's most widely available season ticket was £869, the most expensive in the Premier League.

Scouse Not English are unlikely to find this product to their taste.

What the Hull City diehards were still wrestling with in 2015 (on behalf of millions of supporters) is the conundrum that also troubles their club's owners: football is a global business trading a local product – the regional identities of fiercely tribal football clubs. (This, more than anything, is what the Indonesians and Americans are subscribing to.) In this sense, clubs have always been brands, but the branding was regional and tribal. Today, this tribalism, this passion, is the most valuable commodity in English football. However, cost-push inflation erects an increasingly high barrier against local fans shouting on their teams, while soaring TV revenues render them increasingly incidental. If push comes to shove (and it invariably does when billions of pounds are floating around), then English clubs might one day be refashioned as a global 'product' that must be leveraged from the local community.

The issue came to the boil in 2008, with the arrival of Game 39. In February of that year, the Premier League's 20 clubs voted unanimously to consider the option of extending the season by one round of fixtures, to be staged at venues overseas. Ten extra games would be added to the season, in five stadiums around the world, with cities bidding for the right to host them. One idea was to pick the fixtures by a draw, similar to cup competitions; another was that the top five teams in the league would be seeded, to avoid playing each other.

In a statement from the Premier League, chief executive Richard Scudamore said: 'I think it's an idea whose time has come. It's an extra game, it's not taking anybody's game away, and it includes all 20 clubs, which is very important. All 20 clubs will benefit and there is a huge element of solidarity about it.'

Solidarity? How they have come for our language.

Ploughing on, Scudamore said: 'When the League does well, other people in the football family do well in terms of redistribution . . . You can't stand still, and if we don't do this then somebody else is going to do it, whether it be football or another sport.'

Now, with one ear cupped to the wind, Scudamore said: 'Every time there is an evolutionary step, the reaction of the fans is not always great, but I would ask them to take a step back and look at the positives.'

One fan was not prepared to take a step back, and he happened to be the secretary of state for culture, media and sport.

'I got a call from Number 10 about the idea,' Andy Burnham told me in April 2013, 'and they were saying, "Oh, the Premier League, fantastic, we'd better support this." I said, "No chance. There is no way I'm going out and supporting the thirty-ninth game." Number 10 were basically saying, "Oh, it's the Premier League; we don't want to fall out with them." I said, "I will never go out and publicly support an idea like that." It was a big call, but I went out in the media that day, without any cover from anyone else in government, and said, "There's no way we can support this; this is a disgrace. Who's the game for?"'

Burnham, not for the last time, had tapped into a well of discontent among football supporters. His courageous step ruffled feathers in Westminster and at the Premier League, and the massive public backlash carried him over the line and consigned Game 39 if not to history, then to the back burner – for now. According to Burnham, 'Game 39 was a sign that the game was losing its marbles; that it needed to get back to its roots, and understand its home supporters.'

Today, there is a widespread sense that many of our leading clubs neither understand their supporters nor care about them. Liverpool supporters stand increasingly divided on the Kop, splintering into factions as they stumble around in search of what remains of their identity. Thousands of Man Utd supporters have left, to set up FC United. The fans who gave England's two most successful clubs much of their identity in the 1960s and 1970s are now reduced to settling not for ownership, or any significant influence over the way these clubs are run, but for a notion of identity.

Perhaps that is what supporting your local club was always about, in England: a notion. And the lesson of the Pompey Supporters' Trust takeover is that the notion is loyalty. Whereas brands in almost any other market will live or die on their commercial viability, supporters are not consumers, as Scouse Not English protest. When Portsmouth were plunged into administration, twice, the likes of Colin Farmery weren't about to switch their loyalty to Southampton or Bournemouth. Equally, Farmery told me that he feels no more nor less a Pompey fan now he is a part-owner of the club: a financial stake in Portsmouth is immaterial – his is an investment that can't be measured in numbers.

So, what are our clubs in 2016: businesses or sporting institutions? Globalised commodity or community asset? Today, with Premier League clubs being pulled from all directions, they increasingly resemble a row of tents in a storm: their historic cultural identities increasingly flimsy pieces of fabric, with the locals – the pegs – straining to keep their place in the ground.

Nowhere was this storm more perfect than at Wimbledon. In 2002, Dons supporters mobilised to resist Pete Winkelman's plan to uproot their club and replant it in Milton Keynes as a new club, the MK Dons. Despite gathering huge support from the media and from fans across the country, Wimbledon supporters were undone by the FA, who ruled that their objections to the franchising of Wimbledon FC were 'not in the wider interests of football'.

Many regard the MK Dons as the first step towards the international franchising of our clubs, not least because the Norwegian businessmen who had bought Wimbledon prior to Pete Winkelman had done so with a view to relocating the club not to Milton Keynes, but to Dublin. As David Conn outlined in *The Beautiful Game?*: 'The Dublin move was approved by the Premier League clubs, which saw it as the opportunity to soak up the interest and money of the Irish . . .'

Crucially, it wasn't the English FA who blocked Wimbledon's move to Dublin, but the Irish FA.

Today, as the FA panel reminded Wimbledon fans, the wider interests of football appear to be located wherever a bigger market can be found. If the likes of Hull City can become a redundant identity and Liverpool a product to taste, then the mightiest of England's clubs might one day fall foul of the ultimate rule of a globalised market: if it is cheaper and more profitable to produce a product in China than in Liverpool, then the case for relocating the raw materials and labour to China becomes unanswerable. Football supporters will resist this, but the tension is mounting.

'It's clear to me', says Dave Boyle, 'that this is the battle line of the 21st century.'

8 : The University of Spurs

If the FA finally delivered on something with the Premier League in 1992, FIFA went for the jackpot with the World Cup of 1994. It would be the soccer moms who ultimately unlocked the world's greatest untapped football market, no doubt to the chagrin of Sepp Blatter. But there was a compelling logic here, after all: soccer was a far less physically dangerous game for American boys than gridiron. The atmosphere was irresistible too: as Dave Boyle says, 'If a basketball game is boring, how do you make your entertainment – go for some melted cheese?'

Perhaps, in this context, the 1994 World Cup in America wasn't such a gamble after all: it was perfectly located commercially, and the resurgent English game was expected to boost its profile on the world's biggest stage.

England, unfortunately, had the wrong coach. If Graham Taylor was an unlucky general – deprived of his two best players, Gascoigne and Shearer, at key moments – he was also a pragmatist, at odds with the glamour of the Premier League, and the football writers who trailed in its wake. In October 1993, after Holland beat England in the decisive qualifier for USA '94, the hacks got his head. Taylor was replaced by Terry Venables. Thus began the longest preparation for a party in 30 years.

Euro '96 was designed as the coronation of England's new game, and proof of its resilience. Football was coming home, 11 years on from Heysel – England was no longer the sick man of Europe. Our Victorian stadiums were dusted down; the Italians came to Anfield, the Romanians to St James', the Scots to Villa Park. Even the Belgians were impressed: one of the country's French-language papers reflected during the tournament that 'The English are sometimes bizarre, but definitely when it comes to football they don't cease to astonish us.'

By the time the tournament began, England had not played a competitive match in 30 months: the players, the press and the public were itching, much like the Italian public six years earlier, for their own party. Something approaching triumphalism was in the air.

In May 1996, a few weeks before their opener against Switzerland, Venables took his squad to Hong Kong for a couple of innocuous warm-up matches. There was little here for the press or watching England fans to get excited about – a scruffy 1–0 win over a Golden Select XI, led by an M. Duxbury and veteran Everton centre-half Dave Watson. The real action took place in a bar, when England players were photographed pouring spirits down each other's throats in a dentist's chair and wearing what appeared to be singlets.

We were meant to be outraged. And when we weren't, the media took offence on our behalf. On England's flight home from Hong Kong, in business class, the players smashed up two TV sets and a table. It made front-page news in *The Times*. One passenger on board the Cathay Pacific plane – clearly too traumatised to recall his own name – told the paper the business-class cabin 'looked like a bomb site'. The final three paragraphs of the story made for equally damning reading.

'The players would have had some of the very best service during their flight,' wrote the two *Times* journalists assigned to the story. 'The airline's Marco Polo business class section has won a number of awards recently, after it was relaunched two years ago.

'The England squad would have had generous amounts of leg room, and personal videos in English, Chinese, Japanese and Korean. Exotic dishes could have been washed down by copious amounts of champagne and wine.

'Cathay won the 1996 *Business Traveller Magazine* Award for the best business class airline to the east.'

And *The Times* should have been a shoo-in for most blatant advertorial of the year.

A few days later, John Carlisle MP remained outraged at the players' in-flight entertainment: 'This happens at a time when obviously we are worried about what is going to happen over the next few weeks,' he said. 'It sets a terrible example. The culprits should be identified, publicly exposed and thrown out of the squad at once. And if that includes Paul Gascoigne, so be it.'

There was little prospect of that. With impeccable timing, Gascoigne had re-emerged after the best part of six years in hiding: here was England's Norma Desmond, a little fuller of middle and leg since we had last glimpsed him; blond and perennially startled; pissed when he wasn't on screen. Captivating in his unstoppable decline.

And yet, for all that we searched for something new, there was an inescapable sense of knowingness about Euro '96. If Italia '90 was a rave, this was the hokey-cokey. Just as the media were assuming their role, on the Cathay Pacific flight home, so were the politicians and the players. And the fans followed suit: four years of BSkyB had bred an increasingly camera-conscious supporter. The dynamic between supporters and TV cameras during Italia '90 had been one of suspicion giving way to surprise: supporters were no longer being vilified by the media in Italy, and a new deal was emerging. By 1996, it was replaced by a wearying narcissism, as crowds gathered in public squares, faces half turned to the lens, ready for their own close-up. The dynamic between those who watched and those who played was subverted: we had begun to watch ourselves at play at Euro '96.

Occasionally, the football intruded: there was Gascoigne's twinkling humiliation of Colin Hendry and Andy Goram; Pearce's redemption after six years of torment, with that thumping penalty against Spain and that demented celebration; the emergence of Neville, McManaman, Redknapp and Anderton. And in the clinical demolition of the Dutch, Terry Venables dispensed with the failed long-ball orthodoxies of Graham Taylor and Charles Hughes. Ultimately, England were brave in defeat to Germany – a game they would have won had Gazza not contrived to miss a pass that came skating over the six-yard box, and over his toes, with the goal at his mercy.

You put your left leg in . . .

I watched the semi-final in a pub in Hammersmith. I got on the Tube back towards my flat in West Dulwich and woke up in Upminster at one o'clock in the morning. It was that kind of night: an inevitable sense of oblivion. Tony Adams was in similar mood as the Germans burst into a rendition of 'Football's Coming Home' on the hallowed turf. Adams decided to go on a bender; he would never be the same again.

Much else remained the same, though. English supporters rioted in London: 40 cars were damaged in the West End

– six overturned and two set alight. German cars, of course; not German-owned cars with German number plates, but German-made cars with British number plates. And 25 police officers and 23 members of the public were injured. In Bedford, 300 people went on the rampage; 60 kicked off in Newport, in Shropshire. And in Portslade, near Brighton, a 17-year-old Russian student was stabbed five times, as his attackers demanded to know if he was German. Meanwhile, German supporters left Wembley victorious, and incognito – wearing the Union Jack plastic bowler hats handed out by the *Sun*.

You put your left leg out . . .

Few of us really believed we would win the tournament. When the Germans swept on to the final against the Czech Republic, there was a mature shrug of the shoulders, at least among those of us not wielding bricks or scaffolding poles. I could only look on with admiration as Andy Möller pranced like a stag in front of England's outraged supporters, after thrashing his decisive penalty past David Seaman.

That's what it's all about . . .

If the Germans had discovered a sense of humour at Wembley in 1996, they were gracious too. So – excepting a few idiots – were we. In 1996, the national mood was not one of delivery, but deliverance – there was a sense that something bigger than football was coming home.

1996 was one long, happy wake for the Conservative era. Seventeen years had passed without respite, but by 1996, we had had enough, and so had they. As William Rees-Mogg, high Tory and former editor of *The Times*, wrote in the paper in May: 'There comes a time when nothing works for ministers.

They've used up the confidence of the people, they have used up most of their allies; they have exhausted their own energies; they have lost faith in themselves . . .'

Football was no longer our only hope: as the Tories grew old and tired, 1996 took shape as one spacious, very comfortable chill-out zone. Britain was about to shift on its axis, and those of us who had lived through a generation of Thatcher, and TINA, and John Carlisle were about to seize power – by proxy. We were a year out from a real game-changer, because no one expected anything other than a Labour government in 1997. As Rees-Mogg wrote, in the month before Euro '96 kicked off: 'In Britain, Tony Blair is already running for his second term.'

We were partying not so much in celebration as in antic- ipation. And the following year, Blair didn't so much win as collect: here was a nation that gave itself, ready to be trans- formed. We gave him, before we could rumble him, a majority of 179 – in other words, we gave him three election victories in one night. We were a giving kind of people in 1996. And we went out and partied all summer.

That August, long after the Germans had gone home with our trophy, 250,000 went to Oasis's party at Knebworth. Two million people had applied for a ticket. I was one of the unlucky ones: I got a ticket. Oasis were loose – Liam rambling, incoher- ent, irritable. But it really didn't matter: the Prodigy, all jubilant rage – the Sex Pistols on ecstasy – were the message, and the place was starting to jump. Even when Knebworth emptied and 13,000 people tried to board a single train at nearby Stevenage station, it really didn't matter.

Because New Labour were the next train into the station.

*

Three elections in one night. Count Blair's majority in 1997 – 179. It took until 2010 to fritter that away – on Iraq, the bankers and expense-fiddling MPs. They had the money and the mandate to remake Britain, and they blew it up the arse of Bush and the bankers.

Labour supporters might argue they were on a hiding to nothing in the first place. Not since Clement Attlee's in 1945 has a government been charged with the responsibility to change as much as Tony Blair's. Margaret Thatcher arrived in 1979 with a mandate to reform our industrial relations, and through those our economy; so drastic was her impact she would change Britain from a market economy into a market society. By 1997, we knew the price of everything, but had forgotten where we left our values. Labour were tasked with cleansing us of our own cynicism. At the same time, in the country at large, as in football, success was in – and the people wanted a share. It was a difficult circle to square.

Dan Corry served as a ministerial adviser to several Labour ministers between 1997 and 2007, among them Margaret Beckett, Stephen Byers, Ruth Kelly and Peter Mandelson. In 2007, he became Prime Minister Gordon Brown's senior economic adviser, and head of his policy unit. '1997 was tricky,' Corry tells me. 'We had a bloody pledge card which said very little, but people thought we were going to transform the world. And it was very hard. Why football got caught up in that mood . . . I'm not sure.'

Perhaps it was because in 1995, while in opposition, New Labour had promised substantive reform of the national game, via its Charter for Football. Drawn up by Tom Pendry, the shadow minister for sport, and Jack Cunningham, shadow trade and industry secretary, the Charter for Football was a response to mounting concerns over the direction the game was taking under the Premier League.

Just a year out from Euro '96, there were allegations of widespread corruption: John Fashanu, Bruce Grobbelaar and Hans Segers had been charged with match fixing (all would ultimately be acquitted). In February 1995, hooligans following England forced a friendly with the Republic of Ireland to be abandoned in Dublin. In April, Eric Cantona kung-fu kicked his way out of Selhurst Park. By May, Blackburn Rovers were proving that just three years into the Premier League, the title was there to be bought by a sugar daddy; while in January, Andy Cole's record transfer from Newcastle to Man Utd, for £6.25 million, had prompted Tony Blair to warn of the 'critical problems now associated with the game'.

Labour's Charter for Football was published in 1996. It recommended a restructuring of the FA; a review of the relationship between football and television, and of football's finances; and greater consideration of supporters' welfare abroad (notwithstanding Dublin, England's fans were vastly improved, but were still running the gauntlet of often brutal policing in Europe). Alongside the Charter there were law-and-order proposals for better policing, and ideas for improving the rights of minorities and for reviving the game at grass roots. Labour had also promised a new inquiry into Hillsborough if they were elected in 1997, following the furore caused by Jimmy McGovern's ITV docudrama in December 1996. They also acknowledged supporters' unease at clubs being floated on the stock market, and residual problems of violence and racism; while the co-operative model resurgent within the parliamentary Labour Party seemed a timely vehicle to promote football supporters' trusts.

On 1 May 1997 Labour won the largest majority in the Commons since Stanley Baldwin's in 1935. Few governments had ever been asked to change so much, and few had ever been given the tools: here was a huge mandate and a benign economy. Football, like the country, stood ready to be refashioned.

Within three months, Labour had established the Football Task Force. This marked a change from previous government attempts to tackle football's problems: historically, these had been carried on a law-and-order agenda, through individual pieces of legislation drafted in response to (usually disastrous) events. The Task Force was an advisory body, with a remit to recommend ways in which government might bring pressure to bear on the football authorities over their governance of the game. It was there to lead, not to react.

But supporters seeking a brake on the runaway commercialism of the Premier League looked askance at the composition of the Task Force. There was Keith Wiseman, chairman of the FA, who would later be replaced by Graham Kelly; Peter Leaver QC (chief executive of the Premier League); David Sheepshanks (chairman of the Football League); Gordon Taylor (Professional Footballers' Association); Sir Rodney Walker (Sport England); John Barnwell (League Managers' Association); David Phillips (Association of Premier and Football League Referees and Linesmen); Graham Bean (chairman of the Football Supporters' Association); Tony Kershaw (National Federation of Football Supporters' Clubs); Steve Hennigan (Disabled Supporters' Association); Chris Heinitz (the Local Government Association's chair of leisure and tourism); Sir Herman Ouseley (Commission for Racial Equality); and Rogan Taylor (Football Research Unit at Liverpool University).

Cumbersome? This was a walk-in wardrobe of suits, with one or two rolled-up sleeves showing. Critics were similarly unimpressed with its remit. The Task Force pledged to:

- eliminate racism in sport and encourage wider participation by ethnic minorities in both playing and spectating;

- improve disabled access to spectating facilities;

- encourage greater supporter involvement in the running of clubs;

- encourage ticketing and pricing policies that are geared to reflect the needs of all, on an equitable basis, including for cup and international matches;

- encourage merchandising policies that reflect the needs of supporters as well as commercial considerations;

- develop the opportunities for players to act as good role models in terms of behaviour and sportsmanship, and to become actively involved in community schemes;

- reconcile the potential conflict between the legitimate needs of shareholders, players and supporters where clubs have been floated on the Stock Exchange.

There doesn't appear much wrong with this, at first glance. But as Dr Adam Brown, a member of the Task Force working party, wrote in *A Game of Two Halves? The Business of Football* in 1999:

What is significant here is that these areas of remit bore only the most cursory resemblance to the declared aims of the Charter. Gone was a commitment to restructure the FA and the game's administration – the primary aim of the Charter; gone was the investigation into football's relationship with TV (the subject of two Department of Trade and Industry inquiries); gone were considerations of supporters' rights; and although commercial aspects of the game were included, it was much less wide ranging than the commitment to investigate football's finances in the Charter.

With even those appointed to the Task Force alert to its deficiencies – and Brown wasn't merely being wise after the event – Labour's football flagship needed a figurehead with credibility. It needed teeth. And it got them courtesy of a fight in a pub.

In the summer of 1998, Andy Burnham was appointed administrator on the Task Force. He had gone out to France for the World Cup, but had to come home for an operation.

'I'd had my nose broken campaigning for Labour in the South Staffordshire by-election in 1996, and finally I was getting it corrected.'

Heated debate, was it?

'Er, yeah . . . it was a bottle in a pub. I got it, basically, for being in a group of Labour people.'

Burnham went into hospital with a book called *The Football Business* by David Conn. Even today, 15 years on, he lights up as he recalls his epiphany.

'I read it, and . . . the scales fell from my eyes,' he says. 'I'd seen the gentrification of football happening, the commercialisation, but I hadn't fully understood the break that had come with the Premier League, the scrapping of the FA's Rule 34, and the rampant greed that was beginning to take hold. And I felt, "Right: we've got to do something about this." I had an instinct, but I hadn't had it laid out for me so clearly before I read that book.'

After leaving hospital with a new bluenose, Burnham got to work. As administrator of the Task Force, he reported to its chairman, David Mellor, the former Tory MP who had been routed from his safe seat in Putney at the 1997 election, and a Chelsea fan. They made an odd couple: Burnham wore a blue shirt following Joe Royle's dogs of war around the country; Mellor was reported to wear his to bed for toe-sucking sessions with Antonia de Sancha.

'I quite liked David, as a matter of fact,' Burnham recalls. 'We got on great.'

They surprised a few people too. First, the Task Force tackled racism. Previously, supporters could only be ejected from a stadium and/or charged with an offence of racist behaviour if the racism emanated from a group of fans. The Task Force insisted that individuals should be liable too, and the recommendation became law. They created Supporters Direct, an idea whose time has come, and will come again. Provisions for disabled supporters were improved, with better access to stadiums and better sightlines (although much of this was provided for by the Disability Discrimination Act of 1995). Then, in autumn 1998, came a genuinely big battle: as Burnham recalls, 'all hell broke loose in government' when BSkyB tried to buy Man Utd. 'I don't think people have given us enough credit for that,' Burnham says. 'We didn't roll over for Murdoch, and he was bringing massive pressure to bear.'

And yet, as Chris Bryant MP has said, Murdoch 'effectively owns the product, indirectly, and that, I think, is a massive problem for the sport'.

So, excepting Andy Burnham, in 2016 – with TV coverage attuned to foreign supporters, with the game increasingly reliant on foreign capital, with fans and owners at loggerheads over the identity of their clubs, and with the FA emasculated – the charge remains that not only did Labour fail to get to grips with the 'critical problems now associated with the game', but its light-touch regulation was an amber light for the Premier League and BSkyB to run amok.

Did Rupert Murdoch bend Tony Blair's ear between the seeds of the Charter for Football in 1995 and the arrival of the Task Force in 1997 – perhaps when Blair flew to Hayman Island in Australia, in June 1995, to plead for Murdoch's backing at the next general election? There might be a clue in the wonderfully indiscreet diaries of the late Tory peer Woodrow Wyatt.

In 1995, Wyatt was despairing at how Murdoch appeared to be tilting from the ailing government of John Major towards Tony Blair: '[Murdoch] doesn't seem to value what I did for him,' wrote Wyatt. 'I had all the rules bent for him over the *Sunday Times* and *The Times* when he bought them . . . Through Margaret I got it arranged that the deal didn't go to the Monopolies Commission, which almost certainly would have blocked it . . .'

That counted for little now, it seemed, for as Wyatt lamented: '[Murdoch] has got Blair not to mention the way he makes his money all over the world and pays a different tax rate . . . and not to mention the possible reference of BSkyB to the Monopolies Commission . . . That is a clear monopoly.'

There is certainly no monopoly view on New Labour's record on football. One of their old guard speaks for many football fans today, as he did on the Taylor Report in January 1990. 'Credit to the Task Force on racism,' says Peter Snape, 'things have improved there. But New Labour never had the guts, the ability or the inclination to tackle football at governance level.'

Lord Snape finds an echo in Dave Boyle, the former chief executive of Supporters Direct.

'New Labour's record was conflicted,' Boyle says. 'Their genuine fandom and greater affinity for football meant they were aware of the problems, and there was more investment in grass roots and more fan involvement at lower levels. But they were held back by ideological uncertainty: they never grasped the antipathy to the status quo, and being founded on pessimism about people's desire for change, they never had the confidence in building a coalition to challenge established power. That pessimism in the people was met with an un-realistic optimism in the power of markets, and the capacity of leaders to play nice, despite having no meaningful incentive to do so. Those whose behaviour it was trying to alter knew that the government neither had the appetite to act nor the stomach for the fight.'

It is a point borne out by Dr Adam Brown, now the research director at Substance, a social research co-operative working in the sport, community and youth sectors. 'Many of us on the Task Force proposed a regulatory body for football, along the lines of an Audit Commission,' he says. 'But the Premier League in particular, along with the FA and the Football League, fought tooth and nail to oppose it. By the autumn of 1999, many of us were not prepared to sign up to a Task Force report which was driven by the Premier League, and which was effectively saying, "There is no need for change."'

High among supporters' concerns were steeply rising ticket prices. The Task Force found that top-flight ticket prices had risen by 312 per cent between 1989 and 1999, while the retail price index had increased by just 54.8 per cent. John Williams, of Leicester University, found that 70 per cent of those who had stopped going to football cited rising ticket prices as the main cause (the figure rose to 80 per cent among the unemployed). And it was now that the FA revealed itself in all its impotence: Graham Kelly, David Davies or Nic Coward repeatedly insisted that clubs were private businesses and that the FA had no scope to compel them to set their prices at a reasonable level.

As Adam Brown noted back in 1999, 'Whereas fans' groups and others argued that it was the responsibility of the English game's governing body to rein in the commercial voraciousness of the club chairmen, and ensure that football remained a popularly accessible sport, football's authorities argued that they were either unable or unwilling to protect access to the game for all.'

Frustration at New Labour's timidity is compounded by the fact that the 1997–2010 Labour governments included a caucus of genuine football fans who wielded no little influence. Many of them played football together in Demon Eyes, a New Labour side that competed in London's Thames League and was named after the Tories' 1997 general-election poster campaign, which sought to demonise Tony Blair by warning of the danger lurking behind those twinkling pupils. As Demon Eyes stalwart Dan Corry says: 'We were serious about football, and we became advisers and ministers.'

In the 1980s, in the days before he headed up the prime minister's policy unit, Corry was a regular at Stamford Bridge, and he followed England to the World Cup in 1982 and 1986. Andy Burnham would sign up for Demon Eyes in the late 1990s. And 'I remember when I worked for Gordon, when he was prime minister,' says Corry, 'and he was picking his first Cabinet, and I had played football with five or six of these ministers.'

There was Ed Balls, who as an economics journalist had played for the *Financial Times* against Red Menace (Demon Eyes' first incarnation). 'Ed was good when he was young,' Corry recalls. 'David Miliband played centre-half for us because he's a big guy . . . not quite a footballer, but he was a good sportsman. There was Hilary Benn and James Purnell. Mick Fisher, who worked for Jack Cunningham, was a tough player, and very good. Phil Collins, who went on to become Blair's key speechwriter, was a fantastic player. And Ben Lucas and Ed Owen used to work for Jack Straw.'

If it is easy to sniff at the likes of David Miliband at centre-half, it's easy, too, to overlook the fact that by the time Labour took office, football had changed fundamentally – the opportunity for genuine reform of the game was beyond the likes of Demon Eyes. When I ask Andy Burnham if the chance was lost along with the 1992 general election, he is unequivocal. 'Absolutely,' he says. 'The real football fans around the 1997 government definitely felt that the horse had already bolted by the time we got in.'

If there was a game-changing election for football in the 1990s, it came not in 1997, then, but in 1992. John Major's surprise victory remains one of the great 'What if?' moments of modern politics. It certainly had a crucial bearing on the future of football.

In the run-up to the 1992 election, Neil Kinnock had promised to refer the issue of media ownership to the Monopolies and Mergers Commission if Labour were elected. His proposal cast doubt on Rupert Murdoch retaining a controlling share in both News International and BSkyB. In early 1992, Murdoch, a man with ink in his veins, might have looked at his satellite station – turning over a measly £5 million a year in profit, having helped to saddle News Corp. with losses of $8.7 billion in 1990 – and thought BSkyB a safe sell, especially with most pollsters putting Kinnock in Downing Street. Remember, too, that the new Premier League wasn't due to auction its first TV-rights package until May 1992, a month *after* the general election – and ITV were confident of sealing the deal. BSkyB was by no means the safe bet.

What happened next would colour the relationship between government and the media for a generation. On election day, 9 April 1992, Kelvin MacKenzie ran a picture of a light bulb on the front page of the *Sun*, with the Labour leader depicted inside, and the headline: 'If Kinnock Wins Today Will the Last Person to Leave Britain Please Turn Out the Lights'.

Later that day, John Major pulled off a shock victory. It wasn't just 'The Sun Wot Won It': a month later, with Kinnock's cross-media proposal consigned to history, Sam Chisholm walked into the Royal Lancaster Hotel in London and blew ITV out of the water. Football belonged to Murdoch now.

By the time Labour finally won power in 1997, the game had been transformed by five years of BSkyB's largesse – and with it the relationship between those in power and those with real power. As Peter Snape says: 'I get the sense that the 1997 Labour intake looked at football and thought, "We don't really understand the game, and it seems to be working just fine, so we might as well leave things as they are."'

Andy Burnham recalls that he was up against it from day one: 'Every day, every single day I ran into people who were saying, "Oh, let's just use football for a bit of PR here and there."'

If there was little appetite for change in Downing Street in 1997, there was scant encouragement from the media. As Burnham recalls: 'Football was officially bad news for the tabloids in the '80s, and in the '90s it was officially good news. It wasn't that simple, of course, but in the '90s they saw that it was working financially and thought it was great.'

Nor were influential think tanks much concerned with the national game. As Dan Corry recalls: 'There wasn't that much intellectual chat around football at the time. Rogan Taylor had started to write stuff, but he was probably the only person taking it seriously . . . But even as recently as 2004, think tanks were still devoting very little time to football.'

Corry certainly tried, to his credit. In 1994, he co-authored a pamphlet called *Game Without Vision: Crisis in English Football (Great Market Failure)*. 'It was sort of an attack on the creation of the Premier League,' he says. 'We were working at a centre-left think tank, and we were trying to say, "Overall, we can see the merits in competition and markets, but they do destroy things too. And where's the balance?"'

Certainly, by the final term of New Labour's period in office, Andy Burnham, as secretary of state for culture, media and sport, believed the balance had to be weighed by football's governing bodies: that it remains their responsibility – not government's – to safeguard football for the fans. In October 2008, Burnham threw down the gauntlet to the FA, the Premier League and the Football League. In a speech to a Supporters Direct conference in London, he declared that 'football needs to reassess its relationship with money'. And he asked the FA to consider whether:

- The rules governing finances can be made consistent between the leagues;

- There can be greater transparency and scrutiny of clubs' ownership, including the amount of debt used to finance a takeover and whether that debt is 'sustainable and in the wider interests of the game';

- The rules which penalise clubs falling into insolvency can be reviewed;

- The rule which requires insolvent clubs to pay football debts in full, unlike other debts, should be reviewed;

- The fit-and-proper-persons test for club directors and 30 per cent shareholders needs to be strengthened;

- 'Competitive balance' can be promoted, preventing the game becoming too predictable;

- Everything possible is being done to bolster the national side, and if there is a case for introducing a specified number of home-grown players into club sides.

As Burnham told me in April 2013, 'this was an attempt to give the FA a leg-up, a chance to reassert their authority, particularly over the Premier League. But their response was very revealing.'

Lord Triesman was chairman of the FA at the time, and he happily grasped the levers that Burnham extended.

'Triesman developed a very expansive paper on how the FA were going to respond to all these questions we had set them,' Burnham says, 'and I think this precipitated his departure from the FA. I don't know that for sure, but I think it did. Because the FA decided it was to issue a nil response. The FA then sent me a letter. It said, basically, "Thank you for your letter setting out seven areas of concern. We don't have a view on these and we refer you to the reply from the Premier League."'

As far as Burnham was concerned, 'This flushed out the issue that everyone had suspected: that the Premier League has basically taken over the running of the game. They've reduced the governing body of the game to such a degree of timidity that it didn't feel it could have a view on those issues. When the Premier League was created, the FA was still a bit of a power in the land,' he says, 'but within 20 years of the Premier League arriving they've kind of killed off the FA, almost. Its preserve is now the amateur game and the England team. Lord Triesman was an impressive figure, but what he found out – as had Adam Crozier before him – was that if you rattle the Premier League cage, they will close down the space in which you operate.'

In June 2009, shortly after receiving his letter from the FA, Burnham left the department of culture, media and sport. He had been due to speak to the Football League chairmen at their annual meeting. 'I was going to deliver a speech that said, "Look, we've finally come to this" . . .' But before he could blow the whistle, Burnham was moved in a reshuffle. His successor quietly dropped the matter.

The jury may be out on New Labour's record on football, but it was they who began to rebalance the scales of justice in the biggest football-related controversy of them all.

'Hillsborough was massive unfinished business,' Andy Burnham told me in April 2013. 'And we hadn't done enough early in the government. We'd had the Stuart-Smith scrutiny, in 1998, but that had been a stitch-up.'

Murray Stuart-Smith was a senior appeal court judge who had served as a commissioner for the security services, and later the intelligence services – his role was to provide independent judicial oversight of MI5 and SIS (the Secret Intelligence Service). In 1997, following the Jimmy McGovern docudrama, Stuart-Smith was appointed to lead a scrutiny of the Hillsborough evidence by the home secretary, Jack Straw, who took the curious step of setting Stuart-Smith on his way by explaining that there were insufficient grounds to merit a full inquiry, hence a scrutiny. Tony Blair's backing had amounted to five words scrawled on an internal memo: 'Why, what is the point?'

Suitably instructed, Stuart-Smith arrived in Liverpool on his first day at work to meet with several of the bereaved families, and loftily enquired of them: 'Are there a few more people here, or are they . . . it's not like Liverpool fans to turn up at the last minute.'

The judge concluded his scrutiny by ruling that the altering of South Yorkshire Police statements by senior officers did not amount to evidence of irregularity or malpractice. He also ruled that the removal of two CCTV videos from the police control room at Hillsborough on the evening of 15 April 1989 was not significant; this, despite the fact that he hadn't been able to view the tapes, and that the control room had been locked and alarmed, and there were no signs of forced entry that night.

In February 1998, Jack Straw accepted the noble lord's findings that there were no grounds for a new public inquiry. As Jenni Hicks, who lost both of her daughters in the disaster, told the BBC's *Panorama* in May 2013: 'That makes me so sad. Because it was another 14 years of my life that I have been made to look for the truth, when it was already there. I mean . . . that is a national disgrace.'

Hillsborough is now widely regarded as the largest cover-up in British legal history – at least, the largest ever exposed. Andy Burnham deserves great credit for setting up the Hillsborough Independent Panel, which finally unpacked those 23 years of lies. So, too, does Phil Scraton, professor in criminology at Queen's University, Belfast, and the panel's driving force. There is someone else, too, who deserves recognition, and who has steadfastly refused to take it.

'When I did reopen Hillsborough, Gordon Brown, to his great credit, accepted it,' says Burnham. 'I'll never forget the Cabinet meeting the day after the twentieth anniversary at Anfield. I said to Gordon, "We can't leave this as it is, and I need some support on this." And he gave me permission to add it to the Cabinet agenda, which is quite an issue – you can't always just bring along new issues. I spoke to the Cabinet and there was quite a discussion, but then Gordon said, "No, I think we're going to back Andy on this." And I just sat there and thought . . . that was the moment where it all changed.'

*

Just as truth changes lives, so another of New Labour's legacies to football has helped change lives – millions of them. At the same time, it has brought into focus the changing nature of the relationship between clubs and their communities.

Football community programmes began in the late 1980s as coaching schemes run by retired players. Today, they have evolved into sophisticated care programmes run by football clubs in the community, and they are delivering remarkable results in health, education and crime reduction. And they were given a crucial push during a stand-off between Mellor and Burnham and the Premier League.

'In the first 12 months of the Task Force, the football authorities had been opposing everything we did,' says Andy Burnham. 'And they hated David Mellor!'

But in 1998, the Premier League sought to enlist the support of the Task Force, after the Office of Fair Trading challenged the principle of collective selling of Premier League TV rights. The OFT argued that it might be in the public interest for Premier League clubs to sell their own TV rights to their matches individually, rather than appoint the Premier League to sell the games as one package. On the back foot, the Premier League came cap in hand to the Task Force. Andy Burnham could barely believe their nerve.

'I received a letter from the Premier League saying, "We're lining up witnesses to speak for football at the Restrictive Practices Court, and would David Mellor be prepared to come and speak for us?" I remember thinking, "Why would we go and back up this case?" The principle of collective selling is a good thing, as long as it works for the collective good, and not just for the good of a small number. So we came up with this argument that collective selling has to work for the whole of football, and therefore they had to reinvest funds from the Premier League down. And that's when we came up with [the report] *Investing in the Community*.'

The Premier League saw off the OFT. And in return for the support of the Task Force, it promised to divert 5 per cent of its revenue from domestic TV-rights deals to the lower-league clubs. At a stroke, £26.8 million was earmarked between 1998–2001. (The Premier League had just sold its latest rights package, for 1997–2001, for £670 million.)

The fund was to be distributed in three tranches: 75 per cent would be given via a new body, the Football Foundation, to grass-roots facility development – new pitches, changing rooms, floodlights, and so on; 12.5 per cent was set aside for the improvement of football-ground stock, primarily in the lower and non-leagues; and 12.5 per cent was reserved for community football and education projects. However, any community organisation could apply for funding from this final pot – not just football clubs. This was seed funding, designed to encourage local authorities, voluntary groups, charities and clubs to work together; and if football clubs' community programmes wanted to access these funds, they would have to deliver football and education projects that offered a benefit to the community.

The first attempts to force football clubs to address their social responsibilities came during the 1970s, as hooliganism became a frequent problem. However, it was not until the mid-'80s that the concept was properly explored, under the Professional Footballers' Association education programme. This developed partly as a second career for retired footballers, and funding came via the Manpower Services Commission.

The schemes were spurred on by the final Taylor Report in 1990, which explicitly linked football hooliganism to the clubs' lack of engagement with their communities. By the mid-'90s, all clubs in the four divisions were working to establish better links in their catchment areas. Three clubs in London led the way: Millwall, Brentford and Leyton Orient, the latter under the inspirational leadership of Neil Watson.

Today, Neil Watson – like Adam Brown – is a director at Substance. He is also a deputy chair of the national youth charity Ambition, and a trustee of Wallsend Boys Club. In 1989, he resigned as a teacher at a west London secondary school to manage the Os' community programme.

'In 1989, no one had heard of football in the community,' Watson says. 'I had a desk in the corner of the sponsors' lounge at Orient for three years, with people walking back and forth around me. If someone phoned the club to complain about racism on the terraces, the switchboard would think, "Oh, let's put it through to that guy in the lounge."'

The community was similarly nonplussed.

'During my first week at Orient, I walked up to Newport Primary school, near Brisbane Road, introduced myself and asked if I could teach the kids football skills during their PE lessons. The head said, "No! I don't want anybody from the football club in here. Football sets a bad example to young people!" That was in May 1989, just after Hillsborough . . . there was a sense that "We don't want anything to do with a football club."'

Over the next 13 years, Leyton Orient's community sports programme would win national recognition and a hatful of awards. It pioneered sport-based social-inclusion projects, taking football onto the estates of north-east London and working directly with youth-offending teams and drug services. In 2002, Watson became director of the Home Office Positive Futures programme, a national sport- and activity-based drug-prevention initiative, and between 2006–7 he worked as an assistant director at the Government Respect Task Force, leading on young people's issues.

'The football schemes were set up [mostly in the early 1990s] because there was a general feeling that football clubs had become so disconnected from their communities,' Watson says. 'Clubs were in the community only in the sense that they occupied a lot of its space, but they only opened their doors once a fortnight to let the people in. So the thinking was: why not start running some outreach programmes to engage with local people?'

Prior to the formation of the Premier League, each of the 92 Football League clubs received £6,000 in funding for their community work. Inevitably, much of this took the form of football coaching – partly because the PFA drove the funding, and partly because clubs had an eye to attracting new supporters while they polished their PR. In 1992, the Premier League and Football League clubs went their separate ways, and over the next 20 years so did their community schemes. Those at the top-flight clubs were able – at least potentially – to access greater funds; those at Football League clubs had to live off their wits, which meant for many a redefinition of their communities – and the clubs' relationship with them.

During the 1990s, English clubs began to reach out to five of the most under-represented groups within their stadiums: black and minority ethnic supporters; girls and women; people with disabilities; children; and the elderly. And through their community schemes they realised that football could unlock doors that were barred to the local authority. Social workers and council officers wore suits, didn't they? And they talked to the police. And if central or local government turned off their funding taps, they were here today, gone tomorrow. Football clubs were a constant in the community, and the appeal of the game bridged the multiple languages and ethnic divisions of England's inner cities.

Neil Watson saw this first-hand in the mid-1990s. Leyton Orient's community programme had just received funding from the Major government to run a drug-rehabilitation programme, so Watson took a team to the Shadwell estate in Tower Hamlets, east London. 'It was seen as a really challenging place to work,' he says, in his understated Geordie. 'So we didn't advertise it; we just turned up one day with a minibus, the first day of the school holidays, and about 20 or 30 kids appeared at the top of the tower block, and within ten minutes we had them playing football.'

At the time, Watson's department at Leyton Orient was turning over £60–70,000 a year, through funding from local authorities and the PFA. By the end of the 1990s, it was turning over £600,000–700,000 a year, through contracts with charitable foundations, housing associations and government-funded regeneration programmes. And this at a club whose football business was only turning over around £1.5 million. The programme now employed teachers, drug-prevention officers and community-development staff. 'We had programmes dealing with travellers, refugees, young offenders,' he says. 'We commissioned ARC Theatre Company to perform a play about challenging racism, and it performed over 600 times. For a year or two, our department probably had a higher profile than the club itself.'

By the early 2000s, dozens of English football clubs were running sophisticated sport-based youth work programmes. And when TV rights for the Premier League for the seasons 2001–4 were sold for £1.2 billion, community schemes had access (in theory) to 12.5 per cent of the 5 per cent won by Mellor and Burnham – or £7.5 million. With millions now pouring down to the clubs, in 2006 the Premier League decided to set up its own Charitable Fund, to distribute the monies for community and education programmes directly; the Football Foundation would now concentrate solely on facilities improvement.

'This was a key moment,' says Watson. 'The required skill set of people running community schemes changed: whereas two years previously you'd have gone to a meeting of scheme managers and they'd all be sitting there in tracksuits, now everyone's in a suit, and they look like they run a charity.'

Under the new funding structures put in place in 2006, 90 per cent of the 5 per cent of domestic TV-rights deals is shared between the Football Foundation, good causes around the world, and via national community schemes under the Creating Chances programme. (One such scheme is Kickz, which uses football to bring together youngsters and the police in some of England's most deprived neighbourhoods. To date, 19 police forces and 60 local authorities have signed up to the programme, and some schemes have contributed to a 60 per cent reduction in anti-social behaviour in the neighbourhood.) The Premier League clubs share the remaining 10 per cent (of the 5 per cent fund) to use at their discretion: in 2013–16, domestic TV revenues totalled £3.018 billion, which means that around an average of £250,000 a year should be available to each Premier League club's community schemes.

While this is not an insignificant amount, its real value is to underwrite the clubs' expansion into the services sector: because, after 17 years in the field, football community programmes are so adept at raising funds that the Premier League funding now accounts for just 10 per cent of many clubs' total budget for such programmes.

In recent years, few clubs have worked harder at making friends with their community than Spurs. It was a piece of bridge-building that was long overdue.

Since 1961, Spurs have won many friends among neutrals for their attacking, cup-friendly football. Their 1961 Double-winning side, led by Danny Blanchflower, was widely regarded as the most attractive English team between 1960 and the great Liverpool side of 1987/8. Even my dad, an Arsenal fan, will talk fondly of Cliff Jones and Bobby Smith. In April 2013, when I went to White Hart Lane to meet the team behind Spurs' community programme, the reception was dominated not by images of Gareth Bale or André Villas-Boas, but by a large photo of the Double side on an open-top bus tour through Tottenham. The bus is pretty as a picture, a vintage cream and green vehicle that you might see in *Foyle's War*. The hair on the top deck is Brylcreemed against the wind. The players wear suits borrowed from Butlin's. There is scarcely a black or Asian face in the adoring crowd – all of whom are middle-aged, including the children. And the vehicle bears the destination 'Private' – as if anyone were about to hail a bus carrying Bill Nicholson and Dave Mackay, and the League trophy and FA

Cup, and ask of the driver, 'You going to Tottenham Hale, mate?'

Off the pitch, however, Tottenham's image would pale over the next four decades; by the early 2000s, the club had an unenviable reputation in the community. Then, in 2006, Spurs' chairman Daniel Levy pledged a substantial sum to establish the Tottenham Hotspur Foundation and underwrite its community schemes for ten years.

In May 2007, Levy signed Grant Cornwell from Leyton Orient. Cornwell had quit the fire brigade to join Neil Watson's quiet revolution at Brisbane Road in 1990, and eventually became the Os' director of community programmes. Such was his impact that in 2005 he was awarded an MBE for services to young people. Cornwell arrived at the Tottenham Hotspur Foundation in 2007, with a brief to 'embed the club' in the boroughs in which it had an impact: Haringey, then Enfield, Barnet and Waltham Forest. He found Spurs stuck in the past.

'Spurs were running traditional community programmes, which revolved around charging kids for soccer schools. This didn't lend itself very well to the community,' he says. 'Tottenham is a very deprived area, so most of the people in its soccer schools tended to travel in from the more affluent parts of Essex and Hertfordshire.'

Cornwell spent his first three months in post asking community personalities and local authorities what they thought of the club. Their response was withering: 'Most of them said, "Spurs do nothing for the community."'

As far as Cornwell was concerned, this wasn't particularly accurate, 'but perhaps they hadn't seen any benefits directly'. 'Directly' is the key word: when Cornwell asked the community leaders what it was they wanted Spurs to do, 'it nearly always came back to the same thing: giving them money to run their own projects. I had to explain that we weren't a donation-making foundation.'

Cornwell decided to prioritise Spurs' existing involvement with children and young adults in care, through a mentoring programme called Ei8hteen. Ei8hteen is run in partnership with Virtual Schools, a department at the local authority that looks after the education of children in care, and it is a 'very discreet' programme. Many of the people involved have led chaotic lives. 'We had one girl stand up in front of a group of head teachers and say, "The local authority are my parents." That has a real impact on you,' Cornwell says. 'I can say, "I have a mum and dad." Hers are the local authority.'

The Tottenham Hotspur Foundation acts as something akin to a foster parent to children like this young girl. There are ten mentors at Ei8hteen and they work one-to-one with 160 young adults, who come through in cohorts of 20 at a time. The Foundation will bring them to the stadium and provide a quiet room in which they can share their concerns and aspirations.

Most community programmes run by professional clubs focus on helping disadvantaged people aged 14–25. The core years are 14–18, and because social services tend to write off their commitment to young adults at 18, Spurs' Ei8hteen project is aimed at 16- to 19-year-olds – enabling them to stay in education, employment or training for an extra year, which in turn ensures continued access to wider support.

At the time of my visit, Ei8hteen is managed by Alex White. White was a promising youth footballer (he had trials with Bright-on) before studying sports science at university and deciding on a career in the charitable sector. His scheme is a two-year pilot, and it has attracted the attention of the Premier League. West Brom have an impressive record working with children in care, but Spurs are the first to involve mentors on this basis.

'The players are also on hand to lend advice,' White explains, 'including Jermain Defoe. His cousin was stabbed to death in 2011, and he talks to them about the dangers of everyday life. They can also look at him as someone who has reached a goal that they might aspire to.'*

Music is Benoît Assou-Ekotto's passion, so before moving to QPR he offered to help out with an urban-arts programme. Prior to his transfer to Hull, Jake Livermore had expressed an interest in helping with a disability scheme.

How do you measure success in this scheme?

'There are different yardsticks,' says White. 'I took a young kid to the Kickz Awards this week: Edward was shortlisted for Outstanding Volunteer of the Year. He didn't win the award, but it was a real lift for him to be recognised among over 100 Kickz projects around the country. Edward has gone on to get a level-one football qualification, he's on our education programme . . . he's confident, and looks the part.'

That's Edward's story. Then there's Person X.

'When we first started working with X, they were in foster care and had never engaged in anything, ever – with anybody. They had suffered years of abuse, and wouldn't pick up the phone, wouldn't speak to a mentor. But after consistent approaches from our mentors, they began to engage, then they came to the training ground and met with Jermain. The

* Since Defoe's departure from Spurs, former captain Ledley King has taken on the role of ambassador.

council's social workers said that whereas they couldn't reach Person X, the club had opened the door. Something in the club has sparked an interest.'

As White explains, 'Some of these kids will never take the 18 hours of contact required for us to hit our targets, but this is where I have to make the case to the local authority: to see Person X finally make eye contact with a mentor, after suffering years of abuse . . . you can't overstate the impact of that.'

Initially, as Grant Cornwell explains, local people (and the local authority) were sceptical about the potential of his team. 'They said, "You're a football club, what can you do?" But we have an ability to attract and engage people like few other organisations. Kids just want to play football, and we bolt on services to that. We use the power of the game to do our work.'

Tottenham Hotspur has been in the community for over 130 years; it is a rare constant in the lives of people who otherwise lack foundations. And Cornwell acknowledges the value of Premier League funding: 'We said to potential partners, "We can bring £120,000 to the table; if you can bring £60,000, do you want to be a partner?" And they said, "Yeah, let's do it."'

The Tottenham Hotspur Foundation has also become an education provider, offering BTec Diplomas in Sport. Barnet and Southgate College or Waltham Forest College will deliver the educational component, and Spurs will deliver the football – and you can't do one without the other. As Cornwell says: 'These are kids who might not have gone on to college, but through football they can get an education.'

In fact, Spurs are now an accredited higher-education institution. The Foundation employs lecturers (from Middlesex

University) and offers two foundation degrees: applied football coaching and performance, and applied sport and community development, with the advantage that students are associated with a Premier League club. And, of course, they charge their own fees: £6,000 per annum over a two-year foundation course represents a saving for students of £6,000 in total, by comparison with most degree institutions. The Foundation runs its own student-loan schemes too; it aims to cover its costs, and no more. 'We have to pay lecturers,' says Alex White, 'but we can offset some of the cost of facilities because we'll use the club's.'

The Foundation also runs apprenticeships, and currently has 15 apprentices working in the City. This impressive range of services has created 2.4 million life-changing opportunities, according to PricewaterhouseCoopers, who conducted research at the Foundation pro bono; and it has attracted the attention of Number 10 – three prime ministers have visited the club in recent years. Today, the Tottenham Hotspur Foundation runs outreach programmes not just in Haringey, Waltham Forest and Enfield, but in Sri Lanka, China and South Africa. It has even been asked to set up a project in the favelas of Rio.

Spurs have come a long way in Tottenham.

Grant Cornwell has a plane to catch: he's going on holiday to Florida. He is excited about that, but not as excited as he was last week, when he met Johan Cruyff. His face lights up; he starts pirouetting in the office, attempting a Cruyff turn, but thinks better of it and retires gracefully with a cup of coffee. So Alex White walks me back through reception at White Hart Lane, past the 1961 Double winners and their charabanc, into the stadium and onto the pitch. As I crane my neck around the stands of one of the more atmospheric grounds in the Premier League, I spy the club logo high above. What does that mean, *Audere est Facere*?

'To dare is to do,' Alex says. 'We've adopted it for the Foundation. Our motto is: "To care is to do."'

Spurs are not alone. In 2013, south of the river, Charlton Athletic were running the entire programme of youth services for Greenwich Council.

'Charlton's community scheme was probably turning over almost as much as Charlton FC that year,' says Neil Watson. 'And I'm not exaggerating. Charlton were taking a £3–4 million contract there.'

For every £1 spent by the Tottenham Hotspur Foundation, £7 is saved on welfare costs. The Foundation has brought over £7 million of funding into Haringey since 2007, and it is now clinching £1 million-plus contracts. Today, all of the Premier League clubs run community schemes. Beyond the lure of football, what enables them to emerge as providers of social, health and educational programmes in the 21st century?

'We're not curtailed by the bureaucracy of local authorities,' says Grant Cornwell. 'Many youth centres would shut on Friday nights; well, what kind of a youth centre is any good only when kids are in school? We're flexible, we can offer weekend provision.'

Local authorities are also beset by image problems. Local-authority housing has become a byword for failure in our property-owning market society. Councils are the bane of local papers and council-tax payers; even the NHS is suffering a crisis of public confidence, despite Danny Boyle's Olympic tribute.

Football clubs aren't tarred with the same brush: just as the occasion of Sir Alex Ferguson's retirement in 2013 prompted some commentators to laud him as the most successful public figure in Britain over the past two decades, so vulnerable children and young adults will never have known a time when Premier League clubs were not rich with resources or associated with success.

Football is its own universal language too, which is useful in a place like Haringey, where 193 other languages are spoken. And men trust their football clubs: Premier League clubs are proving hugely successful in treating male health disorders, because men would rather go to a mobile clinic that rolls up at the Emirates or Goodison than go to their GP. Spurs have seen remarkable success in promoting awareness of bowel cancer (which affects men predominantly) and prostate cancer. Those robust outcomes-analysis teams found that in a three-month period in 2013, there were no bowel- or prostate-awareness campaigns in Haringey other than those run by Spurs, and in that period there was a huge spike in the number of men going to their GPs.

'The club's website also receives over a million hits a month,' Grant Cornwell says. 'And put guys and girls in Tottenham tracksuits on the street, and people are much more inclined to talk to them than someone wearing a bib, or a local authority who might put them on a database. It's sometimes as simple as that.'

After our meeting at White Hart Lane, Alex White takes me to Ferry Lane, a housing estate a short drive from Spurs. Around 95 per cent of the residents here are on benefits. The streets and houses appear tidy and stoic, and on a football pitch behind the estate, two of White's coaches, Courtney and Josh, are putting a group of 20 lads through a Kickz training session. The kids are aged 12–15, and are a familiar jumble of shapes and sizes. At the coaches' instruction, they run on the spot – 'Turn! Turn!' – then race in 30-yard bursts to either goal. There are cheats and playful scuffles, and some kids don't know their left from their right, like kids anywhere. But this isn't just anywhere. It was on the Ferry Lane estate in August 2011 that police shot dead a man called Mark Duggan, sparking a riot in Tottenham that would ignite widespread civil unrest across England over the next seven days.

This is an area with acute needs, and Johan Cruyff is delivering. The pitch the kids are playing on was developed in tandem with Haringey Council and the Cruyff Foundation, which aims to bring young people across Europe together, through football. The facilities here are so good that the children's ability has gone through the roof, and kids from surrounding housing estates are asking to play – breaking down the postcode tensions that often suffuse gang culture.

White's coaches provide 12 hours of free sports coaching a week and supervise three hours of free sessions for the kids. They are casual staff, paid an hourly rate, and they will have a minimum Level 2 FA coaching badge. They are also trained in conflict resolution, and in how to give advice on drugs and substance misuse, as well as sports leadership. As White says: 'These people are really worth investing in. Their ability to spot problems affecting the kids allows them to work on an informal level. One of the coaches lives on the estate . . . they know the kids, they know the signs.'

After the riots in 2011, the likes of Courtney and Josh sat down with the kids after every session and asked them what they thought of the unrest. What were the reasons behind it? Theirs was a slightly more thoughtful response than that of BBC Radio 4, who sent reporters to Spurs the next morning, asking whether the riots weren't proof that football community schemes are a waste of money.

Well, count this . . .

'When the riots were taking place,' says Grant Cornwell, 'we know that none of the [800-plus] kids on our programmes was implicated or arrested. One thing Alex and his team did that night was text these kids. We were saying, "Look, get yourself inside, don't be part of this; think of the implications, and the repercussions."'

As White and I drive away from Ferry Lane, I can't erase from my mind the image of the Spurs Double bus winding its way through the borough in 1961. The most romanticised of all Spurs sides, immortalised in a Kodak moment. Look at the players on the top deck, basking in the sunlight, heads in the sky; look at the people on the ground, in the shadow of the bus, casting up at their heroes. And now look around the bus: half hidden in the shade of the old vehicle is a phalanx of striding, buttoned-up coppers, there to make sure the people of Tottenham got nowhere near that team.

Fifty years on, the Tottenham Hotspur Foundation is turning on the lights behind the Ferry Lane estate, where Mark Duggan was killed. And on the night the biggest riots to hit Britain in a generation began, less than a mile from White Hart Lane, the Foundation was out on the streets, texting hundreds of vulnerable children and young adults and urging them to stay inside, out of trouble, and to think of their futures.

New Labour's Third Way has come a long way. So have football clubs. Today, many in the Premier League have largely ceased to function as a forum for socialisation. The people no longer have a claim on the clubs at the heart of their communities because they can no longer afford to support them. The clubs are making so much money from television they no longer need the community that built them into world-class brands; now, increasingly, the community needs them.

This is not what football clubs used to stand for. And yet who would deny that the likes of the Tottenham Hotspur Foundation have worked minor miracles in one of the country's most challenging neighbourhoods?

As Neil Watson says, 'There is a tension . . . if football clubs charge £65 a ticket and are 95 per cent full, they will think there's no reason to drop their ticket prices. So what they do instead is say, "We'll make sure the club is a major asset in the community." Football clubs have gone from being about social inclusion through sport to being community-development organisations.'

9 : Those Bloody Germans

Whenever I ride a tram, anywhere in the world, I'm reminded of how foreign they are, and how foreign I am. That beyond the windows is an unknown city of unknown people and customs, and a language I can't possibly hope to grasp inside a weekend. It could be Manchester, of course, but today it is Gelsenkirchen.

When I told friends I was visiting Germany for the first time, they presumed Berlin. No. Hamburg? Not yet. Munich? No, I am visiting Gelsenkirchen, a city few people ever visit for reasons other than family, friends or football. Today, Schalke 04, the pride of Gelsenkirchen, are at home to Eintracht Frankfurt, and while Frankfurt bring with them the most fearsome supporters in the Bundesliga, Schalke attract supporters from all over Europe. For this historic German club, built by miners, has become a beacon for football fans in Britain who believe their role is to be something more than passive spectators – that they can not only run their club, but use it to promote the values of the community.

Schalke's community is Gelsenkirchen. Home to around 250,000 people, Gelsenkirchen is in the Ruhr, in the far west of Germany, close to the Dutch border. This is Germany's former industrial heartland, and the target of intensive bombing during the Second World War. Three-quarters of Gelsenkirchen was destroyed by Allied air raids, which appear to have levelled not only the city, but the landscape itself. In the surrounding countryside there is barely a hillock or a mound; in truth, it is scarcely countryside, much less a landscape. The tram ride out from Gelsenkirchen Hauptbahnhof towards Schalke (the club takes its name from one of the city's neighbourhoods) is a familiar journey through the drab post-war apartment blocks that litter the neighbouring Low Countries.

Still, there is poetry in these parts. Gelsenkirchen is known as 'the city of a thousand fires', because it grew up around the coal mines that powered the Ruhr. This was once the most important mining hub in western Europe; now, only three pits remain open, and these will soon be gone. Today, Gelsenkirchen is luring investors with something more valuable than coal. When I spoke to prominent campaigners in football to ask which German club best embodies the spirit of supporter ownership, the response was emphatic: go to Schalke.

On a cold, dark afternoon in November 2012, I am at Schalke's Veltins-Arena to watch a team that fascinated me as a kid. On my seventh birthday, in March 1977 – on the legendary night that Liverpool played St Etienne at Anfield, in the European Cup – I was given a red transistor radio as a present. I still remember peeling away from my own birthday party, from pass the parcel or blind man's buff, to listen in on my transistor to the hurricane of noise that blew down from the Kop that night. Over the next couple of years, in bed, under the blankets, I would pass the needle on that radio like a steering wheel through foreign cities – Hilversum, Haarlem, Utrecht – to pick up the captivating voices of Bryon Butler and Peter Jones. On those first European aways, one foreign club stuck in the mind above all others. I never saw Eintracht Frankfurt play, much less knew their players, or even their kit. But, I got it . . . so many consonants, so guttural and foreign, a club to be roared on if ever there was one. I was not to know that *Eintracht* means 'harmony' in German. And it was probably for the best that I had never heard of Schalke.

Historically, Schalke occupy a place in German football not dissimilar to that of Arsenal in the eyes of the English. Following FC Nürnberg – who won five league titles in the 1920s – Schalke were the second great power in German football. In the 1930s they won five titles of their own, and invented a passing game called '*pektop*', so named because their teams moved the ball around the pitch like a child's spinning top, known in Germany as a *Pektop* (or a *Kreisel*). They even contrived to lose championship deciders because they were dedicated unflinchingly to the art of beautiful football. Today, despite the fact their last championship was won in 1958, Schalke remain the third-best-supported club in Germany, after Bayern and Dortmund. They have over four million supporters nationwide, and the club has more than 139,000 paid-up members.

But I came here in the 2012/13 season because Schalke are not Arsenal: they are not majority owned by a foreign investor. They do not charge exorbitant ticket prices. They are a club with an identity protected in a mission statement, which proclaims that 'the way we see ourselves is shaped by our local and regional roots in the Ruhr; therefore the club is and will remain based in Gelsenkirchen, the city of a thousand fires'. The significance will not be lost on the likes of AFC Wimbledon, or the last surviving fans of the Brooklyn Dodgers: Schalke are a club, and not a franchise, and the community has enshrined its claim to the club in its articles of association.

Moreover, it has protected the right of the working people who shaped the club to support it still. Clause 4 of the constitution states: 'FC Schalke 04 began as a colliers' and grafters' club. For this reason, our club shall, within the financial means at its disposal, enable its supporters from all social backgrounds to participate in the life of the club and attend matches.'

Football supporters are flocking here from Britain, drawn by the idea that Schalke not only draw their identity from the community, they also take their philosophy from their history. And they have managed to safeguard both in their statutes. Schalke's constitution states that 'Our future lies in our past.' Given that Gelsenkirchen's better days appear long gone, this might seem a reckless way of operating in a football market in 2012 in which the top 20 most successful clubs in Europe generated a combined turnover of €4.4 billion. However, Schalke were one of those 20 clubs: participation in the Champions League helped them to revenues of €202 million. This miners' club, in a city of mothballed pits, was the tenth most financially successful football club in Europe in 2011/12.

What Schalke have captured is a concept that appears increasingly fundamental, yet elusive, to many football supporters in England: the idea that success at a football club can be pursued without risk to its history, roots and culture. I'm particularly fond of Clause 6, which proclaims: 'Collective elation and collective pain are important and valuable parts of our identity.' (Ratified again at the AGM of June 2015.)

On a cold November Saturday, in the car park behind the Nordkurve of the Veltins-Arena, hundreds of supporters are huddling around the beer tents. There is Willi, a local lad in a mod parka stitched sparingly with Jam stickers. There is Markus, big and gentle, his ears ribbed with almost as many sleepers as the tram track out of town. There is a lad from Oldham, a ball of energy, tall and wiry. 'Why would I go to Boundary Park when I can come here?' he says, itching from one foot to another, itching for another pint, itching to get in there, on the terraces. There's Marko from Finland, and a family – mum, dad and two lads – from Gillingham. 'It's just as quick to drive out here as it is to drive to Manchester or Leeds,' they tell me, unfurling a Gillingham flag in what doubles, happily, for Schalke blue. This is not their first visit, and it won't be their last. 'We come over for about ten or 12 games every season,' they tell me. A Union Jack dyed entirely in blue disappears up the steps to the Nordkurve bearing the legend 'Schalke FanClub UK'. Someone wonders if Yorkshire Schalke are here today – or Sheep Schalke, as they are known affectionately in these parts.

There is an hour to go till kick-off, and we have no banners to lay out, and we are talking – my brother and I – about the first time we will have stood on a terrace in 20 years. For me, it is a moment of reckoning, and it feels good to face it here, abroad. It is 2 p.m., and in the gloom – the kind of light that draws only the homeless into sharper definition – blue and white scarves are tied gratefully around our shoulders.

'Blue just doesn't feel right as a football colour,' says my brother, quietly, and (even if we can't put to one side our tribal loyalties) he's right.

I scan the car parks and beer tents sprawling around the stadium for police, but see none. We had passed a few on the walk up to the stadium from the tram stop: they were lazing, bored and sullen, in their wagons. There is a barely concealed contempt between the fans and the police here: in the week I spend at three German clubs, talking to supporters, security officers, ultras, businessmen and directors, they are almost without exception contemptuous of the German police. Eintracht Frankfurt's reputation may have got here before them, but there is no sign of any trouble. And besides, we are Schalke 04 – and the '*null vier*' echoes boldly through the thin air like 'no fear'.

We, of course, are Liverpool fans, and Forest fans, and Oldham fans, and Gillingham fans. And we are not the only ones flocking to Schalke. The club has recently been talking to Leeds Utd, the French rugby federation, the US ice-hockey federation and the Dutch football federation, who are coming next week with representatives of all the Eredivisie clubs. Because this miners' club, in one of Germany's poorest cities, is increasingly held up as a model not only for football fans across Europe, but for sports clubs too.

Everything changed here in 1994, when Schalke effected a small but significant amendment to the historic membership structure that was still in place at nearly all Bundesliga clubs. Until 1998, the vast majority of football clubs in Germany's top two divisions were owned entirely by their members (the exceptions were Wolfsburg and Bayer Leverkusen, the works teams of Volkswagen and pharmaceutical giant Bayer respectively). These members were supporters, who voted for the club's board of directors on a one-member, one-vote basis. At most clubs, board members had been elected directly, at the annual meeting of members – and often, all it required was a tub-thumping speech to transform the board every 12 months. This was no longer adequate at Schalke – a club in dire need of stability. So, in 1994, Schalke became the first Bundesliga club to change its structure so that the managing board was no longer appointed directly by the members. The supporters demanded a new mechanism whereby members would elect a supervisory board, and this, in turn, would appoint the managing board. It was that simple, and on the face of it, quite unremarkable. But what Schalke did was combine accountability with continuity.

Since 1994, Schalke members have regularly elected six of their own to a supervisory board: these six are free to appoint a maximum of five other members to their board, and they also hire and fire the three members of the managing board, with whom they meet every three months. The fans' influence accrues because not all six elected members of the supervisory board are elected together: in one year, two are elected; the following year another two are elected; and in the third year the final pair – each for a three-year term. Rather than deliver one supervisory board elected en bloc for three years, rolling elections reduce the risk of complacency, or groupthink. Crucially, the fans can still influence the managing board on an annual basis, via their influence over the supervisory board; however, absent is the impetuous decision-making inspired at a frequently raucous AGM, and the power it delivered to just one or two elbows.

As Thomas Spiegel, Schalke's director of media communications, told me: 'History – especially at a very emotional club like Schalke – has shown that a swing of fortune or misfortune could turn around the whole structure of the board when you allowed members to elect the board directly. For example, former player Helmut Kremers won a seat in 1994 [before the constitutional change] because of one good line in his speech – it was a swipe against our arch-rivals, Borussia Dortmund: "In my time we didn't even need to change clothes to beat them," he said.'

Result: elected.

Then there was Günter Siebert, a member of the 1958 title-winning team, who was elected for three terms because, according to Spiegel, 'he was a very charismatic plebeian tribune, sensing the mood at every annual meeting. He used to threaten to quit, to sue all of his opponents, promising the best of futures, presenting himself as the only one really understanding the soul of the club, and offering free beer – in the very same speech. In my opinion, he wouldn't have returned if the board was picked under the model we have now.'

Schalke (known as the Royal Blues, or *Königsblaue*) were the first top-flight club in Germany to introduce the idea of a supervisory board, and it was a response to decades of executive failure. During the 1960s, '70s and '80s, Schalke were overhauled financially by other clubs, despite the fact that after relegation to the Second Division they still attracted the fifth-highest attendances in Germany. They had also been at the centre of the great Bundesliga match-fixing scandal of 1970/1. This deep-seated mismanagement was having a corrosive effect on the supporters: by 1990/1, the terraces at Schalke had become infested with racists. Now, the club moved to define its values, and reaffirm its identity with the people of Gelsenkirchen, a multicultural city.

On the day before the Frankfurt game, I visited the club offices, not far from the Veltins-Arena.

On a wet November Friday, the complex is barely ticking over, and the club's training pitches stand idle in the rain. The fan shop is selling everything from *königsblau* Babygros to coffee machines, but this isn't the Man Utd megastore. The cafe is doing a quiet but dutiful trade, and outside, two men are trying to brighten things up with Christmas lights – *königsblau*, of course. Inside, Thomas Spiegel, the smart and affable director of media communications, recalls the moment when Schalke fans moved to reform their battered club.

'In the late 1980s,' Spiegel tells me over coffee, 'Schalke 04 were playing in the Second Division against 1 FC Saarbrücken, who had an outstanding Ghanaian striker called Anthony Yeboah. He caused us a lot of problems. It was quite common at the time to hear supporters make a lot of monkey noises, and our supporters started making monkey noises at Yeboah. I was there in the Parkstadion [Schalke's old stadium], and I was extremely ashamed. It was the first time I felt happy for someone playing well against us. We lost 2–1. At least 15 to 20 per cent of the fans made monkey noises, and the others didn't say a word.'

A year later, Schalke were playing against a team led by a Nigerian forward, and the noise started again, this time in the North Stand. 'But this time,' Spiegel says, emphatically, 'more people felt like me. I could see fans in the stand saying, "Shut up, we don't want to hear this."'

Schalke fans responded with an initiative called Schalke Against Racism. The problem was not confined to their club; historically, Schalke hasn't had problems with racism. Conversely, nor is it a left-wing club, more readily inclined to take a stance on social or political issues within the stadium, in the manner of St Pauli or Union Berlin. No, according to Spiegel, if Schalke were to be found on the political spectrum historically, it was on the right of centre during the Weimar

Republic. Schalke supporters were simply responding to a problem rife in Germany by the early 1990s.

'There were some nasty things happening to people who were coming here looking for asylum,' says Spiegel. 'People were saying, "The boat is full."'

After the Berlin Wall came down in 1989, German reunification became a complicating factor. Spiegel recounts how, in the eastern city of Rostock, 'A big building full of foreign people was attacked for days by people trying to burn it down . . . they had to flee to the roof! It was lucky that no one died. But later on people did die: in the early 1990s,' he says, 'houses of Turkish people were burnt down, families burnt to death, and it was deliberately done by right-wing people. This was in two cities: in Solingen and in Mölln, in the north.'

Since the 1970s, Gelsenkirchen has had around twice the national average of non-German-born inhabitants (currently, at around 27 per cent locally, it is nearer three times the national average), most of them of Turkish or Lebanese origin, a pattern replicated across the Ruhr. In the early '90s, Schalke Against Racism gathered rapid momentum – and the support of several influential players, including Jens Lehmann, Andreas Müller and Mike Büskens. According to Spiegel, 'In no time at all it was accepted, and the racist chanting never happened again. Everyone had the feeling that, "OK, this is a good movement, and I'll join."'

Schalke were one of the first clubs in Germany, after St Pauli, to publicly and officially renounce racism. (In fact, they became the first to outlaw racist behaviour in their constitution, which enables the club to refuse membership to known Nazis or racists.) And it was this newfound unity that provided the impetus for a new, written constitution, which would evolve over the next three years and become officially ratified in December 1994. There was a hard-headed pragmatism at work here, as Spiegel explains with impressive candour. 'We just wanted the club to do well,' he says. And the club had not done well since *pektop*. In fact, by the 1970s, Schalke had become known throughout Germany as 'the scandal club'.

The Bundesliga was formed as recently as 1963. Prior to this, German football was amateur, and its players were semi-pro, their maximum wage capped at 320 marks a year. But Schalke were not short of brown envelopes. According to Thomas Spiegel, almost everyone was at it, but so fat were Schalke's bungs that in 1964 the club had run out of money. Now, they had no option but to sell their historic stadium, where they had won all their titles, back to the city of Gelsenkirchen.

Greater shame was to follow, when – in 1970/1 – the great German match-fixing scandal erupted. After relegation deciders were revealed to have been rigged, the Deutscher Fussball-Bund (the German FA) sanctioned 52 players, two coaches and six club managers. According to Spiegel, around a dozen clubs were implicated. Initially, the DFB assured players that if they admitted their guilt they would be treated leniently, but when Gerd Kentschke from MSV Duisburg became the first player to hold up his hand, he was slapped with a ten-year ban. The Schalke players took fright: many were in their early 20s, and saw in Kentschke's ban a career-ending suspension. So their lawyers persuaded them to lie under oath. 'No one really knows that other clubs were involved in this scandal,' Spiegel says, 'because only Schalke were stupid enough to lie under oath. In Germany we call this *Meineid*, and so Schalke became known as FC Meineid.'

And so they came to be vilified in Germany: other clubs blamed their own relegation on FC Perjury's match-fixing; others argued that Schalke subsequently retained their league licence purely because of their history and profile. Here, then, was a club with huge potential, but a scandal club. Even as they slowly shrugged off the notoriety, Schalke lurched from one mishap to another. Their great sides of the 1970s, led by the striker Klaus Fischer, won just a solitary cup, and in the 1980s Schalke spent five years in the Second Division. By the end of that decade they were in such dire straits they couldn't afford enough washing powder to wash the first-team's shirts.

When Schalke Against Racism emerged in late 1991/early '92, it energised the supporter base. Now, crucially, the supporters sought to change the club's structure as well as its constitution, and they had an influential ally on the board. Peter Peters became the general secretary of Schalke in 1993. 'He was very smart,' says Spiegel. 'He didn't come up with the new structure in his room, then come out and present it; he asked all the members to join him. He said, "Please bring your ideas, and tell us how we should change the constitution." At the first meeting there were a hundred members, and they could see they were genuinely being involved. Proposals were voted on. Then, three months later, there was a big general meeting of members, and people could see that we could change things.'

At the same time, Peters began to repair Schalke's lukewarm relationship with the Deutscher Fussball-Bund. 'Schalke players were often overlooked for the national team, and Peters tried to change this,' says Spiegel. 'At the time, the DFB were critical of our financial situation, so Peters said, "OK, please give us time to sort it out, and in return we will be a pilot club for the whole of the league." The DFB thought it would be better for all the clubs to have a more professional structure, and they certainly did support us: they gave us the space and time to develop the new structure.'

In December 1994, Schalke published their new, written constitution. Spiegel chuckles: 'It was adopted overwhelmingly – 99 per cent voted for it!' But this was no cosmetic make-over: according to Spiegel, it had a huge impact on Schalke's re-emergence as a football force. 'I certainly think that without the new structure we wouldn't be where we are today,' he says.

It may be difficult for an outsider to pinpoint precisely how a re-evaluation of the club's ethos, its constitution, can effect a rapid turnaround in its fortunes on and off the pitch, but since 1992, when the anti-racism initiative began, Schalke's member-ship has risen from 14,000 to 139,000. Spiegel attributes this to the constitution: 'It brought continuity and calmness to the club,' he says. 'People were no longer anxious as to how the club policy might change after every annual meeting.'

The impact was also clear to see on the pitch. According to Spiegel, 'You could see the success within two years, when we qualified for the European Cup for the first time in 19 years. It was celebrated like we had won the title. The feeling of the fans was, "Wow! We did it!"'

In 1997, Schalke won the UEFA Cup, beating Inter Milan on penalties at the San Siro. And in 2000/1, they were moments away from winning the league for the first time since 1958. Having won their final match of the season, the title was Schalke's – if Hamburg SV could beat Bayern Munich up in Hamburg. HSV were 1–0 up when, in the 93rd minute, referee Markus Merk controversially ruled that a ball picked up by the HSV keeper had been a back pass. He awarded Bayern an indirect free kick inside the box, from which Patrik Andersson scored, and Bayern were champions once more. Merk was never permitted to referee another game involving Schalke.

The chairman who oversaw Schalke's transformation in the mid-'90s was Gerhard Rehberg, a former coalminer. In Thomas Spiegel's words, 'He was Gelsenkirchen's answer to Zaphod Beeblebrox!'

Beeblebrox is a character from *The Hitchhiker's Guide to the Galaxy*: nominally the president of the galaxy, his job was to draw attention away from those who really ran the universe. As Spiegel says of Rehberg: 'He was maybe the most powerless president in the history of Schalke. But he was content to let the professionals do their job. He never talked about sport in great detail, but he had very good credibility because he was a former coalminer.'

Whereas Rehberg's predecessors had ruled much like Louis XV – in Spiegel's words, 'They had been great impresarios: "After me, the flood"' – Schalke finally had a president who took more rational, long-term decisions, and declined to throw money away.

In 2001, the Royal Blues decided to build themselves a new stadium. Currently named the Veltins-Arena, it is one of the best in Europe, with a capacity of 61,500 and a slide-out pitch that can be removed from the stadium to grow in normal atmospheric conditions – and be spared any damage when the arena hosts concerts. Its retractable roof also means the Veltins can function as both an indoor and outdoor arena. Schalke raised the money from banks, the city of Gelsenkirchen and private investors. However, eyebrows were raised in 2008, when it was reported that Schalke had run up debts of €248 million. It is an issue Spiegel doesn't duck: he tells me that by 2011, the debts had been reduced to €185 million. 'The debts are mainly due to the financing of the stadium – €128.8 million can be attributed to loans. Another €41.5 million relates to bond issues, €10.2 million is the silent partner's interest [the silent partner being the city of Gelsenkirchen] in connection with the stadium, and €4.6 million is accrued expenses.'*

Spiegel emphasises that Schalke took on these debts to secure long-term financial stability: they will be paid down by 2022, and the club will own the Veltins outright by 2018 (the stadium was built to such a high specification, and at such a low cost, that Schalke have sold the specs to construction companies in Chile and Russia). Equally impressive is the transparency here. I'm just a writer, and an English writer at that. It's difficult to imagine a Premier League club being as candid – especially with a German writer who might drop in one day asking for coffee and a look at the club accounts.

On the field, players of the calibre of Raúl have arrived from Real Madrid, and Klaas-Jan Huntelaar from AC Milan. And in 2011/12, Schalke 04 were the biggest climbers in the Deloitte Football Money League, which ranks clubs by revenue gen-erated by their football operations: between 2007 and 2011, Schalke's revenue grew by €88 million to €202 million, which saw them ranked among Europe's top ten wealthiest football clubs for the first time. By 2015, they were 13th in the rich list, with revenues of €219 million.

* By June 2015, the debts had been reduced to €154 million.

What began as an anti-racist initiative, driven by supporters, not only brought Schalke success at home and in Europe;
it allowed the supporters to protect their values, and those of
the local community, within the club's constitution – to give
their club a written and legally protected identity. The possibility of financial mismanagement is never far away at any
club, but the 139,000 members have the facility, every year, to
replace individual members of the supervisory board.

Schalke supporters had no need to turn to the German FA
for support, or UEFA, or either federal or national government:
their mobilisation had its roots in the local people.

After my meeting with Thomas Spiegel, I spend an hour
with Moritz Beckers Schwarz, the deputy general secretary of
Schalke 04. Over a coffee, and one of those miraculously twisty
German pastries, he tells me: 'It's not so much that the people
here have a history of organised labour, or militancy; it's more
that because the Ruhr was the industrial heartland of Germany,
the region of North Rhine-Westphalia was always one of the
biggest and most influential in the German federation. People
here know how to get things done.'

And because Schalke remains deeply committed to its roots,
and keeps ticket prices affordable to the local people, it was
able to call on the locals who understand the club, and who
understand this part of the world. It was they who took on
the racists, restructured the board and turned the scandal club
into a beacon for sports clubs and supporters across Europe
and North America. As Beckers Schwarz says: 'The miners are
not here any more, but the club still stands for their values:
working hard, traditions, family, standing together. And the
club still stands for these things in the community. And a lot of

people are finding these values again in the club, and they are investing in the club.'

The following day, I am investing quite substantially in Schalke 04. There is my brother, Martin; the lad from Oldham; Markus with the earrings; Marko from Finland, an Andy Möller look-alike; Willi in his parka; and the Gillingham crew. That's quite a big round, especially as Marko seems to drink two pints at a time. It's three o'clock, half an hour to go until kick-off, and it's time to head for the terraces. For me, it has been 20 years.

The first time I stood on a terrace following Hillsborough was in March 1990. And it would be the last time. In the 12 months following the disaster, I would often wake in a sweat that drenched the sheets. I would toss and turn so violently in my sleep I occasionally woke up with my feet on the pillow and my head hanging over the side of the bed. One summer's day, I woke up on the kitchen floor, after blacking out. After a year of this, in March 1990, I went back to Anfield for the first time: I needed to know if there was still a place for football in my life.

On that spring Saturday, Kenny Dalglish's Liverpool were grinding towards the club's 18th league title, while in London, a demonstration against the poll tax was turning into one of the biggest riots in British history. As I went through the turnstiles off Walton Breck Road at around 2 p.m. that day, I came in at the top of the Kop to find scarves still tied to the crush barriers in tribute to the dead. Names were written in black marker pen over the crush barriers and on the back wall: names I rec-ognised, names that might have gone with faces I couldn't get out of my mind, with voices still ringing in my ears. I knew, even as I set off for my usual spot on a terrace – just to the right of the right-hand goalpost, about halfway up – that this was a mistake.

My final memories of the old Kop are of an atmosphere that was strained and sullen. People were snapping at the players, and at each other. Crowd surges were awkward and muted. On the pitch, the players moved like empty bottles at sea. In the dugout, Kenny Dalglish was going through his own private torment. None of it made sense any more, and when I walked out of that stadium, I knew I had to walk away from football for ever.*

Today, in Gelsenkirchen, those 20 years away from the terraces certainly feel like for ever. So long, in fact, that back home the clamour for safe standing areas is gaining momentum, with Aston Villa declaring their intention of trialling a safe-standing area beside the Holte End. A debate among the Association of Chief Police Officers found some in favour, others against. Inevitably, the Hillsborough Family Support Group (HFSG) are an influential voice and their opposition to a return to standing areas is unwavering. While I understand their view, I disagree – primarily because their loved ones were not killed by terracing, and for the authorities to suggest that they were only allowed the real culprits to get away with the deaths of the 96. I have always suspected that the powers that be have thrown their weight behind all-seater stadiums to confirm the false impression the public had after Hillsborough – that the 96 were killed because football terraces were inherently unsafe. The truth, of course, is that terraces per se are not unsafe – the Leppings Lane was unsafe. The truth is that not all football grounds lacked a valid safety certificate in 1989, but

* I didn't go back to Anfield until April 2009, to a seat on the Kop this time.

Hillsborough did. And as many in the safe-standing campaign have long argued: why are terraces still permitted at rugby grounds, and at football grounds in the third and fourth tiers, if they are inherently dangerous?

Today, I am having a beer and I am going to stand on a terrace. In fact, I am taking that beer with me onto the terrace, and no one will stop me, because it is legal in Germany. And, to my brother's delight, it is legal to smoke in the stadium too. The previous night, Martin had been amazed to find bars in Düsseldorf's pub mile displaying cigarette symbols on their doors, to denote that they were 'smoking-friendly'. For all New Labour's Third Way politics, they were unable to find a compromise that allowed licensed premises to set their own guidelines on smoking. In Germany, there is everywhere the sense that people are trusted to make their own decisions. Much of this, in the bars and football stadiums, encourages a distinctly laddish environment that has been lost in England in recent years. In the stadium on that November afternoon, as Eintracht Frankfurt and Schalke played out an open 1–1 draw, I couldn't help but notice how many teenage lads filled the terraces. And I was reminded of a conversation I'd had with the journalist and Spurs fan Barbara Ellen a few months earlier.

'The laddish environment is not a bad thing, if it gives men somewhere to go on their own and have a laugh together with their own gender,' she said. 'Football is where men can relax and have fun, and nothing else is asked of them at that moment. If you can carve out niches like that, that's a very important part of life. Men need to do that . . . they need somewhere to go. You don't always need women diluting every fucking thing that happens in their world. Men need a psychological escape from family life, from women – and women do from men. What's wrong with that?'

As we took our place on the Nordkurve, I struggled to remember a time when I had been in a more laddish environment. Banks of lads, huge numbers of them teenagers, ranged as far as I could see. Some wore flat caps, others the old-style football sun hats I used to wear in the mid-'80s, with the back edge flipped up. People were smoking, shuffling from foot to foot, passing pints of beer over heads and along the terrace.

We stood aside from and above the bank of Schalke ultras behind the goal; down there, the capo went to work on his raised platform, inciting the ultra hordes. Giant flags billowed back and forth like fish flapping on a riverbank. From the far end the Frankfurt fans let out a chant that washed from one end of the stadium up towards the Schalke fans and seemed to pop beside my ear. The ultras on the Nordkurve below, in their royal-blue tracksuits, moved onto their toes and seemed to bite into the netting behind the goal (there to prevent missiles being lobbed onto the pitch). They leant forward, thousands of them, and roared back. They hissed and whipped their flags. Boom: the Frankfurt fans exploded in their V-shaped section at the far end, a phalanx of around 2,000 people who seemed to vibrate like a saw being played. Back and forth went the chants, and on they went throughout the match.

Much of this is orchestrated, of course: the ultra capos on their platforms are conductors here, and cynics might argue that the fans in Germany leave little to spontaneity. And there wasn't the intensity of the terraces of old: at no point was I lifted off my feet, or caught up in a crowd surge. Nor, for all the promise, was the noise quite up there with the likes of Besiktas. I remember a Saturday evening in Istanbul, in a taxi that stopped at traffic lights on the hill above Besiktas's stadium during a game. The home fans were so loud the windows of the taxi were vibrating. It reminded me of a night I played football in Regent's Park, beside London Zoo, and went to retrieve the ball near a fence beside the ostrich enclosure. It was unseen, behind the trees, but I could hear the ostrich somewhere; there was the accelerated thumping heart of an animal that's bigger than you.

The noise and intensity at the Veltins are magnificent, though. And there were thousands of young blokes on the terrace, looking happy with life. As Barbara Ellen had said to me: 'There's something rather beautiful about men walking to a game, just as there was with those images of thousands of people walking to work at the local factory. There's nothing frightening about a crowd of men just because football is happening at the same time.'

Indeed, because there are women and children here too. In front of me on the Nordkurve a woman in her 30s was stood with her little girl, perhaps eight or nine years old. People in front had stood apart slightly so the little girl could see. She was rapt in the game. Her mum was so engrossed she seemed to forget her daughter was behind her, for she scarcely looked round. And then it struck me: people on a terrace will take responsibility for each other in a way that you are not encouraged to do whilst sat in an individual seat. On a terrace, you are a crowd, and not an audience. And as Barbara Ellen says, there is nothing inherently wrong in being part of a crowd.

If the people of Gelsenkirchen are investing in Schalke, this is not only because it embodies their values, but because they can afford to. In a meeting that stretches for nearly an hour at the club offices the day before Frankfurt come to town, Moritz Beckers Schwarz proudly steers me through Schalke's values; but he remains proudest of one thing. 'We see at international club games now how high the ticket prices are in England. We would *never* make the prices so high. We could not even do it, because then we would have a revolution in the stadiums, with our supporters.'

Looking at this lot on the Nordkurve, I don't doubt it.

Schalke charge from €16 for a standing ticket to €52 for the best seats – with a €10 mark-up for matches against Borussia Dortmund and Bayern Munich. Gelsenkirchen doesn't wear the broken-toothed neglect of the worst hit of England's post-industrial north (I don't recall seeing a single closed shop in the city centre). Nonetheless, it has one of the highest rates of child poverty in Germany, and high unemployment. It is one of the poorest cities in the country – poorer, even, than much of the east. Mayors in the Ruhr have cause to complain about the taxes the *Wessis* (or Germans in the west) still pay to finance the re-juvenation of the east (where the *Ossis* live), protesting that the likes of Gelsenkirchen are in similar need of repair. However, as Beckers Schwarz explains, 'People here are still going regularly to the game. There is a lot of hope, and football gives them structure. It is not a religion, but there is faith.'

Thomas Spiegel touched on a similar point. 'Peter Peters once said that Schalke is more like a church, because people have come forward to us and said, "My husband has died, I have no money to raise my kids: Schalke, can you please help me?" People would rather come here than go to the state or the church, because they are Schalke fans.'

So integrated are these supporters with the club that it is not uncommon for local lads who get into trouble, fall behind on their mortgages or rent, or even fall out with their girlfriends or wives to go for advice not to a counsellor or social worker, but to the club's supporter-liaison officer.

'We are not a church, of course,' says Spiegel, 'but we believe we should be a foundation in the community and give something back. It also gets a message across to our fans: these are values that we stand for.'

Moritz Beckers Schwarz wears two hats: he is the deputy general secretary of Schalke and the general secretary of the Schalke foundation, Schalke Hilft! (Schalke Helps!), established in 2008. 'We were one of the first clubs to set up a foundation like this,' he explains. 'Bayern Munich do something similar, and Werder Bremen are very good.'

Schalke Hilft! directs much of its funding to local schools, with a particular emphasis on encouraging kids to learn German. With increasing immigration, children are finding it harder to learn the language. 'It's nothing racist,' says Beckers Schwarz. 'The kids need to learn it to go on to further education.' And because it's not in their nature to go to after-school classes, Schalke run them instead, with a simple deal: 'If they go to German language lessons, they can then come to football training with us.' The club also offers football training each week for disabled kids. The club coaches run the sessions and the under-17 players take part – to remind them that life isn't always so easy.

Merchandising suppliers are also vetted: 'We look at how sponsors are producing the little teddy bear for our shop,' says Beckers Schwarz. 'Are they using kids for labour? We send them our values, we have clear rules, but it is not always easy to keep track of production processes in Taiwan.'

There is, however, one major fly in the balm here. In late 2006, Schalke announced a five-year shirt sponsorship deal with Gazprom, worth €25 million a season – an even bigger deal than the one Bayern Munich struck with Deutsche Telekom. The deal was reported to have been brokered by former German chancellor Gerhard Schröder, who was by then in charge of a Gazprom subsidiary. This was the first time a Russian company had invested significantly in sports sponsorship outside Russia, and it threatened to bring if not scandal back to Schalke, then no little controversy.

Gazprom has long been linked to the Kremlin, and has been accused of cutting off gas supplies to neighbouring states that have fallen foul of Moscow, among them Georgia, Ukraine and Belarus. It is also a major shareholder in the Nord Stream project that delivers Russian gas to Europe, a pipeline that stands accused of impacting on the lives of nomads in northern Russia. The EU has also accused the company of anti-competitive pricing. Notwithstanding this, in May 2011, Schalke extended the shirt deal for another five years, at a reduced rate of €15 million a season. Just a week after my visit to the club, a report by RepRisk into the most controversial companies in the emerging BRIC economies (Brazil, Russia, India and China) rated Gazprom the most controversial in Russia.

'When we signed the contract, there was a lot of discussion,' Beckers Schwarz told me. 'But we have a lot of contacts in Russia and we were finding nothing negative about it. You can, of course, discuss political structures and democracy in Russia, but that is a political debate.'

It's certainly controversial, and some Schalke fans I spoke to were less than enamoured. However, perhaps there is logic in a city built on fuel attracting a successor to coal – and also in the fact that Gazprom now sits third behind German electricity giant E.ON among the major investors in Gelsenkirchen. Schalke itself is the second biggest source of revenue in the city – which indicates how great the financial onus is on a club like this, in a city like this. No one can brush Gazprom under the carpet, but few English clubs in similarly poor cities are required to be such a beacon of investment. Certainly, Beckers Schwarz is right when he says, 'We know that if you mention Gelsenkirchen to people around Europe, they will say "Schalke". The city knows what it has from Schalke, and Schalke knows what it has from the city. We are partners.'

At many clubs this corporate speak would come straight out of a manual, but the city once persuaded the club to change its name to Gelsenkirchen-Schalke, such is its pulling power. And today, 'When we play football, or we have a concert here, we do everything ourselves – catering, marketing, merchandising – so we are giving a lot of work to the city. We employ 300 people, but when we have a match or a concert, we have work for 2,500 people. This is not a common model in Europe.'

According to Beckers Schwarz, the reason Schalke is so rooted in the community is simple: 'We are still a club,' he says. 'We cannot be owned by just someone. If Mr Abramovich is coming here, he has one vote, like everyone else. We also discuss everything with our members, otherwise there would be a big, big gap between us and the supporters, like there is in England.'

Few Schalke fans are in a position to recognise that gap as

clearly as Stuart Dykes, my guide and translator in Gelsen-kirchen. Stuart is from Mansfield, but moved to Germany in 1987. Originally a Man Utd supporter, he bought his first season ticket at Schalke in 1989, and later became a founder member of FC United of Manchester. Today, he works as a consultant both to Supporters Direct and to Schalke on social-responsibility issues. Stuart had been at the Emirates not long before I went to Germany, to watch Schalke take on Arsenal in the Champions League. He grins broadly: 'The Schalke players came over to our fans after the game and shook hands with the entire front row of one section, and said, "Well done, lads." Can you imagine an English team doing that?'

No wonder they have come calling for advice from Leeds, and Holland, and the United States. According to Beckers Schwarz, 'We don't charge everyone for this advice: if companies come to us, they pay from the first minute. But not sports clubs: we know the need for clubs to have a longer-term view, and for supporters to participate. If you want to use our knowledge, you can have it for free.'

10 : The Good Ship St Pauli

Gelsenkirchen is not a seat of revolution. Supporters in Germany have owned giant clubs such as Schalke 04 and Stuttgart for over a century, thanks to a unique combination of social and political factors. And today, even as the financial pressure to compete with the Spanish giants and the Premier League clubs intensifies, it is these supporter-owners who decide how to adapt the clubs' business models.

Two days after watching Schalke vs Eintracht Frankfurt, I travelled north to Hamburg, to meet members of its two Bundesliga clubs, Hamburg SV and St Pauli. At the time of my visit, in November 2012, it was difficult to find a top-flight club in Europe in which supporters were so deeply integrated at every social and executive level as those at HSV. Much of this was provided for under the *Eingetragener Vereine* (EV) model of ownership, which we shall come to shortly. However, in the spring of 2014, HSV fans voted to abandon EV and move to the model increasingly dominant in the Bundesliga – the 50+1.

In the 2015/16 season, there are 18 clubs in Bundesliga 1, and they split into three models of ownership. Bayer Leverkusen are the works team of pharmaceutical giant Bayer, and Wolfsburg the works team of Volkswagen. This model is long accepted, but in recent years it has begun to stoke resentment. In the 2008/9 season, when Wolfsburg won the title, Volkswagen

paid their own team €62.5 million in sponsorship and advertising – three times the amount Bayern Munich were able to
raise.

Of the remaining 16 clubs in Bundesliga 1, four are traditional *Eingetragener Vereine*, or registered associations, in
which the football club is but one department (they often sit
alongside rugby departments, marathon departments, poker,
ice-hockey and darts departments). EVs are not-for-profit
organisations owned by their members, who elect representatives on a one-member, one-vote basis. The EVs are bound
by strict rules of transparency: all revenues they generate must
be reinvested in the club, and they are unable to draw on any
income that is not generated by football revenues or membership subscriptions. This historic model emerged in Germany
in the late 19th century, and in the 2015/16 season it is still in
operation in Bundesliga 1 at Darmstadt, Mainz 05, Schalke 04
and Stuttgart.

Until 1998, all Bundesliga clubs were formed on the EV
basis (with the exception of the works teams), but by the late
1990s German clubs were increasingly unnerved by the exodus
of their best players to La Liga or Serie A, and by the financial
might of England's Premier League. Now, the 36 clubs in the
two divisions of the Bundesliga broke away from the DFB,
partly in order to broker more commercial deals. New rules
were drawn up that permitted Bundesliga clubs to abandon
the EV model by separating the professional football department from the wider sporting club; in doing so, they could
operate as limited-liability companies, free to attract investment from beyond their traditional membership. However,
legislation remained to protect members' interests: today, at

all clubs other than the works teams, members must maintain a majority stake of at least 50 per cent plus one share. In 2015/16, the Bundesliga 1 clubs operating under the 50+1 model (and no longer EVs) are Augsburg, Bayern Munich, Borussia Dortmund, Borussia Mönchengladbach, Eintracht Frankfurt, Hamburg SV, Hannover 96, Hertha Berlin, Hoffenheim, Ingolstadt, FC Köln and Werder Bremen.

Inevitably, this makes for something less than a level playing field between the EVs and the 50+1 clubs who have sold off sizeable chunks of minority shares – let alone the likes of Wolfsburg and Bayer Leverkusen. At the start of the last decade, Bayern Munich cashed in on their long-standing links with Adidas to sell the sportswear giant 9 per cent of Bayern's shares, for €77 million; they sold another 9 per cent to Audi, for €90 million. The likes of Stuttgart, Schalke or Mainz 05 are unable to sell shares in this manner, because they belong entirely to their supporters on a one-member, one-vote basis.

Of course, as HSV have shown, EV clubs have only to change the constitution to embrace the 50+1 model; the power is in their hands. Much of this influence accrues from a near-universal demand among German supporters for something increasingly unfashionable in Britain: civic engagement.

On a wet Wednesday night in November 2012, Jens Wagner – a freelance illustrator and graphic designer, and HSV's unofficial 'minister for foreign affairs' – took me for a pint at the HSV Supporters' Club pub off Reeperbahn. Sportpub Tankstelle is on a road adjacent to a street that is barricaded at each end and hung with a sign: 'No women or men under-18 allowed.' Inside the pub – part grunge, part metal – stools are cut into the shape of punctured black-and-white footballs; various clubs' scarves, banners and pennants plaster the walls; while a TV shows the midweek live game from Bundesliga 2 – St Pauli, HSV's local rivals, are away to Eintracht Braunschweig.

Once a month, the Sportpub Tankstelle hosts a meeting of HSV supporters, who gather to discuss issues affecting the club, or their fan department, or wider football matters across Germany. Sometimes 50 people will turn up; on other nights, barely a handful. There are about 20 fans here tonight: a couple of middle-aged men in suits, a few lads in their mid-teens; most are in their twenties, and one is a member of HSV ultras The Chosen Few. A Werder Bremen fan has also turned up, in peace. Jens introduces me as a writer from England who is interested in the culture of German football. The supporters sit attentively, listening comfortably to Jens speak almost entirely in English, and they study me with polite curiosity. I have come to listen in, but have barely settled down with a beer when I realise I am in fact the star attraction.

The HSV fans here tonight talk affectionately of England as the 'mother country' of football, and drop easily the names of Nick Hornby, Pete Davies and, in particular, Kevin Sampson, whose book *Awaydays*, about the casuals culture of the late 1970s, appears to have lost nothing in translation. But across Germany, the anglophiles are in retreat. In Gelsenkirchen, Düsseldorf and Hamburg, I repeatedly hear warnings among fans that they must fight to protect their Fan Culture, or else 'we will end up with a situation like it is in England now'.

And this is what the HSV fans want to ask me about: why have English supporters surrendered their culture so meekly to the corporate creed of the Premier League? The idea is an affront to the Germans – not only because they defend their own Fan Culture so passionately, but because they have huge respect for what the English invented.

The previous night, Jens had taken me for a superb Thai curry at a restaurant in Hamburg harbour that seemed to be staffed entirely by ladyboys. 'In the 1970s and '80s,' he told me, over chicken pa-naeng, 'we had English football on TV, just one match a week, and it was really exciting. In Germany, you had all these stadiums with an athletics track around the pitch, so on TV all you could see was the pitch and the game, but there was no atmosphere. In the English matches, the fans were just one metre behind the goal, and you had all these faces you could see, and sometimes right at the front of the terrace, low down [he laughs], just a head in a hat looking out from behind the fence. We really loved it: you could see what clothes they were wearing, what songs they were singing, and when somebody shot at goal, you could see the crowd surging. This is why English football remains so popular in Germany today.'

Many of the impressive stadiums the Germans unveiled for the 2006 World Cup were inspired by English football: demand from supporters saw the old grounds replaced by more compact arenas, with roofs built low to amplify the acoustics, and supporters sat close to the touchlines. They took many of our songs too, and not just the football anthems. Just as I would move my transistor through Hilversum and Haarlem in the late '70s, Jens would move the radio antenna around his bedroom in the '80s to catch the latest John Peel. A big fan of the Undertones, the Specials and the Sex Pistols, he delights in telling me how he saw the legendary riot at a Clash gig in Hamburg, when Joe Strummer cracked a guitar over someone's head. But Jens, like many German supporters I meet, is disappointed with the decline in English Fan Culture – with the all-seater stadiums and passive spectators – and he is determined that Germany will not go down the same route.

Such is the concern here that Germany will follow England that in the week I visit, a fans' protest, 12:12, has spread across the country. Supporters nationwide have mobilised to resist a security paper circulated by the German football league and the 36 clubs in Bundesligen 1 and 2. The fans argue that the paper is a violation of their civil liberties and, more significantly, their Fan Culture. Proposals include the erection of tents outside stadiums to facilitate total strip searches, the banning of flares and the reduction in ticket allocations to away supporters. At every league match in the top two divisions for three consecutive fixtures, ending on 12 December, the fans would sit silently in the stadiums for the first 12 minutes and 12 seconds, to protest. The idea was to give the German football league (DFL) a taste of what the atmosphere at German football would become like if Fan Culture were put at risk. And they left no one in any doubt: what German football stadiums would begin to look and sound like is modern English stadiums.

Tonight, at the HSV pub, we discuss the renewed debate in England over terracing, ticket prices, hooliganism and gentrification. One of the supporters gathered in the bar is Ralph, a thoughtful, lugubrious fan in his late twenties who spent four years at university in the US before returning home to Hamburg. Ralph fears that German clubs may be only five or ten years away from 'going the same way as the English' and losing their vibrant atmosphere. Philipp Markhardt agrees: a charismatic spokesman for ProFans, Germany's nationwide ultras lobby, Philipp has a voice thick with nicotine, and a mischievous grin is never far from his lips. He is a member of Hamburg ultras The Chosen Few, a great student of English and German football, and co-author of a stunning 600-page book about the history of HSV supporters, *Kinder der Westkurve*. According to Philipp, German fans can locate the precise moment when something went wrong with the atmosphere in English grounds.

'Everyone in Hamburg was looking to English football culture until the mid-'90s,' he says, 'but then we could see it was getting worse, the focus was changing, from 1997/8. We're looking at England . . .' he nods. 'I went to Old Trafford at the end of March, to see Man Utd vs Fulham. We were sitting in the tourist area and thinking, "What the fuck are we doing here?" Outside the stadium it was only tourists, standing at the statues with the bobbies and taking pictures; I think if I had been standing at a wall with a friend of mine, the Asian tourists would have taken a picture of me too.'

Things did not improve inside.

'It was not really support,' he says, 'it was like a teeny-pop concert. The announcer said over the Tannoy: "Welcome to the Theatre of Dreams, the home of MANCHESTER UNITED!" The crowd went, "Hooray!" We thought, "This is sick."'

Tonight, the HSV fans appear genuinely pained at what they see as an abdication of responsibility on the part of the English. I talk them through Reclaim the Kop, the Liverpool fan movement that sought to discourage the jester-hat wearers and 'Who are ya?' merchants from Anfield, and the Spirit of Shankly, which fought to dislodge Tom Hicks and George Gillett. I mention the 3 p.m. movement at Old Trafford, and United's green-and-gold lobby. And as I am in Germany in the week the

Pompey Supporters' Trust signed a deal with administrators to buy their club, I refer them to Portsmouth, FC United, AFC Wimbledon and Swansea. One lad asks why more fans don't mobilise on a similar footing. I reply with a brief history of English clubs, and how, since 1888, when Small Heath (which later changed its name to Birmingham City) became the first, they have been free to form limited companies. The HSV fans look confused; I wonder if my English has not translated, and turn to Jens. No, he says, they understand perfectly what I said. They just don't get it.

The idea that football clubs might not be majority owned by supporters is not alien in Germany: they know the reality of football elsewhere. However, the notion remains an affront – not only to their idea of what sports clubs are meant to be, but also to the notion of citizenship.

Membership of football clubs is common because the Germans have a rare obsession with joining societies. As Jens tells me: 'We have clubs for everything: we start with stamp collectors' clubs, rabbit breeders' clubs, model-car clubs.' These hobby clubs are organised with no more or less rigour than a Bundesliga football club or a political party – and all are protected under German law. Jens explains how it works: 'You have to go to the tax authority and say, "I would like to run a club." The tax authority says, "What's the reason for the club? OK, you need a minimum of eight people, including a first director and a deputy director, and you must have statutes. So come back with the statutes."'

The statutes govern regulations concerning elections to the board, and require strict rules of transparency. 'You go back to the tax authority,' Jens says, 'they give you a tax number, and you go and set up a bank account and off you go.' Every club established in Germany must operate along these lines. 'Even churches – you have to be a member,' says Jens.

This communal spirit is informed by a historic mantra: *'Nur gemeinsam sind wir stark'* – 'Only together are we strong.' It denotes a fondness for consensus that runs through German society, as Simon Chadwick, professor of sports enterprise at Salford University, explains: 'German society is incredibly consensual. I see it myself in research centres where I work; in England, it's like herding cats, and in the end I often say, "Oh . . . OK, you do what you want to do then." But in Germany . . . I did some work at the University of Bayreuth, and when the research director tells his team, "OK, guys, this is what we're going to do," nobody questions it, nobody argues, they just do it. Similarly,' he says, 'Germany is very powerful economically, and there are lots of reasons why they would want to keep the EU intact; but again, it's in the German mentality to form a consensus and bring people together. They are predisposed towards consensus, rather than driving people apart – which is certainly what David Cameron is keen on doing.'

While Professor Chadwick freely acknowledges that this consensual streak might explain 'why it was relatively straight-forward for somebody like Hitler to get everyone behind him', since the end of the Second World War the consensus has worked the other way – to dilute the power of politicians, or other leaders. As Philipp Markhardt notes, wryly: 'Of course, we Germans also know our history. We know what happens when there is no democracy, but dictatorship. It is what is taught in school, very early.' As Markhardt argues, people in Germany are perhaps more readily inclined to intervene, to

influence, to vote and protest against abuses of power than –
for example – the English. Not for nothing is the country littered with political parties and its governments often formed
by a rainbow coalition. Germany is also a federal nation: each
state makes its own laws, so there is arguably a greater incentive
for people to influence matters at a local level.

However, this spirit of civic engagement predates both
Nazism and the nation state. 'I studied culture management,'
says Jens Wagner, 'and this kind of thing was always supported
by the emperors [in the 18th and 19th centuries], because they
thought it was better that people should share their hobbies
and join clubs than go on the streets and demonstrate.'

As I suggest to Professor Chadwick, the consensual society
was evident in Britain, too, was it not – perhaps as recently as
the early 1970s?

'Yes, I suppose so,' he said. 'Then Britain gave birth to the
Sex Pistols, and Germany didn't. What emerged in Britain
in the 1970s was much more of a kind of "Fuck you" society,
and when Thatcher got into power it was definitely a case of
"Fuck you, I'm going to look after myself." The Germans,' he
says, 'have been able to maintain a consensus in a way that the
British have not.'

And here we must come back to the war. Not the Second
World War, and the Nazis, but the First World War, and the
Kaiser's last stand. In Germany, as Jens Wagner explains, 'We
don't have this working-class culture, as you do in England. We
have a very wide middle class; many more workers belong to
the middle class than to the working class, in fact. And since
1918, we have had no monarchy, so the upper class are not existing any more. What we have is about culture, not about class.'

German football is innately more democratic for this – and it has saved the national sport from becoming a political football. In England, the game was at the forefront of working-class culture as recently as the late 1980s, when it stuck out its chin for a savage right hook. Not in Germany: the absence of a class system, allied to a consensual society, means that football has not been claimed as a class totem; it has remained a sport, one in which local people are free to invest in their clubs and manage them – in no small part because big business is not required or permitted to strike a blow for political purposes.

And yet there is something in German football that the likes of Thatcher would once have admired: an instinct for financial prudency. 'Notwithstanding all the things people might say about the Germans and what they did,' says Professor Chadwick, 'for a lot of German people the Second World War and its aftermath were desperate . . . really gruesome. They had very little money, or food. So, after the war, German consumers began to search out cheap food and clothing. Good value, and prudency, were born out of what happened to them during the war,' he says. 'This was their economic and social shock therapy.'

And according to Chadwick, it informs the economic thinking of German football fans today. Chadwick visits relatives in Dortmund three times a year, and drives across the country to his wife's family in Poland ('She's like Bergkamp on a plane'). He has also studied German retail patterns in depth. 'Aldi is not somewhere where the lower-income groups in Germany go to shop,' he says. '*Everybody* goes to have a look in Aldi. Alongside this, as the country began to rebuild after the war, and industry developed, and people became slightly more affluent, quality was also very important. Germans don't just want to buy cheap stuff; they want to buy quality products. So you have this price–quality–value proposition that they work towards, which I think pervades all elements of their society.'

The war also gave the Germans a deep aversion to debt: in fact, the German word for debt translates as 'guilt'. This stood them in good stead in 2007, when Germany escaped the financial crash triggered by the collapse of Lehman Brothers, and which deflated Britain's property-fuelled boom. As Jörg Asmussen, Germany's deputy minister of finance, told Michael Lewis in *Boomerang*, his book about the financial meltdown: 'There was no credit boom in Germany. Real estate prices were flat. There was no borrowing for consumption – this behaviour is totally unacceptable in Germany.'

So, financial prudency, allied to an aversion to debt and a keen sense of value. 'In football,' says Professor Chadwick, 'this means there's an implicit bargain that clubs need to keep their affairs in order.'

Now not even I would prefer the Nazis to Margaret Thatcher. But if Britain and Germany had their own, very different shock therapies in the 20th century, at least the Germans' was over by 1945. And its legacy is not entirely negative. Consensus, prudency, vigilance – all shaped by a visceral reaction to Hitler. For the British, no such nightmare: rather, decades of freedom – freedom to birth the Sex Pistols and Thatcherism, freedom to take a gamble, and to do away with consensus. Today, as Professor Chadwick notes, we have a government clearly intent on dividing the country still further, whereas in Germany, the post-war consensus survives.

It is a consensus very much delivered of the left. As Rogan

Taylor says: 'I was at a Dutch football federation conference in January 2013, and I said to them, "The Germans had the advantage of losing the Second World War." Because when the Allies started to put West Germany together as a democracy, who were the good Germans who were left? They were the old lefties and commies who'd been hiding in the woods or escaped before 1939; they were the only people the Allies could trust. So when they sat down with a blank sheet of paper in 1945, they could write things like, "German football belongs to the German people, and German clubs must be majority owned by local people."'

The consensus endures: in fact, we could be looking at one of the least divided countries in Europe. When the issue of the American ownership of Man Utd and Liverpool was raised by HSV fans at the Sportpub Tankstelle, I explained how elements of Liverpool's and Utd's support were thought to be considering starting a dialogue in 2010, with a view to staging a joint protest against Hicks, Gillett and the Glazers at a Liverpool vs United game. Of course, this never got over the line: tribal animosity would not be placated. The HSV fans are incredulous at this lack of solidarity, when so much lay at stake; so I explain to them the hatred that has grown between the two groups of supporters over the past three decades, and how some of this is rooted in a regional rivalry dating back to the 19th century. One suited supporter responds, in flawless English: 'There is very little regional rivalry in Germany, unlike in England, Italy or Spain. There are still traces of rivalry between *Ossis* and *Wessis*,' he says, 'and we occasionally make jokes about Bavarians, but we have a strong national feeling. It's strange,' he muses, 'because Germany hasn't existed for very long as one country.

Even smaller countries, like Belgium, are more divided than us. We feel as one country.'

Much of Germany shuts down on a Sunday. The only shops allowed to open are convenience stores. Families are encouraged to spend time together, rather than spend money. So, on the Sunday I am in Düsseldorf I take a tip from Moritz Beckers Schwarz, and head with my brother to Köln, and the cathedral.

Köln cathedral is located immediately outside the Hauptbahnhof, and it is an awful sight, in the medieval sense: how it must have terrified the emperors' rabbit breeders and stamp collectors. Inside, it is decorated with the most beautiful stained-glass windows. In the early afternoon, a weak winter sunlight coming through the glass was enough to cast a sherbety blur of colours across the nave, as if a giant hand were waving a tube of Refreshers at the Lord. The windows are decorated mostly with flags: what you see at Köln cathedral is a love of heraldry, and it endures today on the terraces of the Bundesliga.

German supporters love flags: they will fly their huge club banners for almost the entirety of a game. They are not universally popular, of course: the biggest banners can easily block the view for dozens of spectators – but some of these are the flags of the ultras, and they are invested with an almost medieval significance. So passionately do certain ultras revere their banners that if they are stolen by rivals, or lost, the ultras have no option but to disband.

The ultras of Germany are not to be confused with those elsewhere in Europe: they might attract the hardcore supporters, and often the hooligan fringe, but they actively seek out neither. And unlike their counterparts in Italy, they are not strictly informed by political sympathies. Italian ultras broadly divide along a right- or left-wing axis, and often at the extremes of the spectrum; while in certain former Balkan states, ultras are openly nationalist organisations. In Germany, they are primarily custodians of Fan Culture, and – broadly speaking – the clubs are appreciative of the fervour they bring to football. Much of the stadium choreography that underpins Europe's most vibrant support comes out of ultra culture. In Hamburg, in 2012, to mark the 125th anniversary of HSV, the HSV ultras recruited 700 volunteers for a display inside the stadium. They worked on the choreography for months, making double-stick flags in over a hundred designs, all spray-painted by hand. The resulting Flag Day saw 45,000 flags in the stadium, each an original drawing, and everyone got to take one home.

And yet there are traces of left- and right-wing elements in German football; indeed, the Bundesliga appears – at least from the outside – to accommodate one of the most dynamic political cultures in Europe.

No club has a manifesto to match that of St Pauli. Hamburg's second club was formed in 1910 in the eponymous inner-city district. Today, St Pauli (pronounced 'Zankt Powli') is in Bundesliga 2, and is very much a yo-yo club; but its identity and wide-ranging fan base are testament to the sense that something other than football is at work here.

On a chilly Tuesday lunchtime, I walk up to St Pauli's stadium from my hotel in Hamburg am Michel. The stadium is concealed behind the best fairground I've ever seen, with a big wheel only slightly smaller than the London Eye. Just as Schalke's Veltins-Arena emerges rather humbly from behind a flank of trees, so St Pauli fits in nicely with its environment, for the penny arcades and the ghost train and the haunted house of the fair give way to a clubhouse with a skull-and-crossbones emblem. St Pauli is a pirate club in Europe's wealthiest port city.

I head inside the clubhouse to grab a coffee while I wait for Daniella Wurbs, my contact and guide for the day, and am delighted to see a menu offering such delights as labskaus burger – good enough to warm the heart of any Liverpool fan. (And this one comes 'mit rollmops und spiegelei'!) As I wait for Dani, it strikes me that in the week I've been in Germany, my preconceptions have taken a bit of a dent: only two or three people out of a dozen have turned up on time to a meeting. And between Düsseldorf, Köln, Gelsenkirchen and Hamburg, only two or three trains out of 15 have arrived on time. Germany is not Switzerland. Switzerland does not have pirates.

St Pauli is not one of Germany's more historic clubs, but its unofficial motto – 'St Pauli: Not Established Since 1910' – says much about where it stands in the affections of football fans. The club is a renegade, anti-Establishment outfit. It has never won a major trophy, but when St Pauli play away, they usually attract more supporters from the opponent's catchment area than almost any other team in Germany. What they are drawn by is its left-wing identity.

'I am from a small village in southern Germany,' Dani Wurbs explains, as we set off around the stadium, 'and when I was younger I was hanging out with punks, and they wore the Jolly Roger. So I asked them what it was, and they said, "Oh, it's the emblem of St Pauli. They're fucking great, an anti-fascist club." And that's how I started getting interested in them.'

St Pauli certainly take the fight to the kind of neo-Nazism

that remains rife in Germany. Neo-Nazi parties (foremost among them the National Democratic Party, or NPD) are not illegal here, and in late 2012 a survey in *Der Spiegel* reported that around 9 per cent of the German people have far-right sympathies. Numerous Bundesliga clubs contain both extreme right- and left-wing elements in their fan bases, and many ultras groups are targeted by neo-Nazis. Which makes for some lively confrontation.

'It was NPD party policy to infiltrate the ultras at Dresden,' one contact told me, 'because they identify football fans and hooligans as a potential source of recruits. There was a group called Fist of the East, who were about 200 strong and hardcore right wing, and they were actively organising on the terraces at Dresden. But the ultras don't tolerate any other groups on their terrace. So the ultras said, "Look, we're not having this," and they agreed to meet the Nazis one morning in the woods somewhere. Basically, they said, "Whoever wins the fight has control of the terraces." The ultras gave the Nazis a pasting. It wasn't that the Dresden ultras were specifically anti-Nazi; it was about territory.'

The police raided Fist of the East, but as my contact chuckled: 'Dresden put out a press release saying, "The problem has been sorted out by the fans." And it had.'

Despite the residual tension between extreme right and left, it would be wrong to ascribe political identities to most German clubs. Admittedly, Union Berlin are renowned as left wing because of the presence of socialist intellectuals in their fan base, and because, remarkably, their supporters financed the rebuilding of the club's 19,000-capacity stadium. But if one club seems to consciously cultivate a political reputation, it is

St Pauli. And yet a closer look at the club reveals that their political identity is only 30 years old. More significantly, the spirit of St Pauli is inspired not by ideology or a manifesto, but by concerns peculiar to the St Pauli neighbourhood – about gentrification, commercialisation, and that poorer residents should eat well.

Dani Wurbs is 33, and a board member of the fans' department at FC St Pauli. She is also the co-ordinator of Football Supporters Europe (FSE), a European network of football supporters' organisations, of which Supporters Direct is a member. Dani spent 18 months living in Newcastle, and speaks fluent English, and she is about to take me on a fascinating walking tour of this inner-city district. It is a multicultural neighbourhood, and has long attracted the countercultural left – hippies, Greens, anti-war and anti-capitalist protesters, and squatters.

'There has been a certain alternative element within St Pauli football club for quite some time,' Dani explains, 'but the majority of the fan base wasn't really left wing before the 1980s. Then it became very visible, because a lot of things happened at the same time. There is a row of houses in the harbour street here, and the inhabitants were meant to be evicted, but huge riots broke out in protest. Some of the people from these houses were also St Pauli supporters, so they took their protests inside the ground. One of them brought the pirate flag into the ground, and his flag became the symbol for a new movement inside the stadium.'

Did this not bring problems for the club? Did the local authorities not say: 'Stay out of this, this is not a football club's issue'?

'I don't think they had much choice!' Dani says.

The squatters' riots became a national spectacle, as Jens Wagner recalls. 'When they occupied the houses in St Pauli, they were throwing all their piss and shit over the cops [who were trying to evict them]. After football matches, the hooligans tried to storm these houses to attack the squatters, and after a while the scene became so popular that people would come on tour buses from the south of Germany to look at it.'

Eventually, the city council gave way. As Dani explains: 'The inhabitants were fighting for months, if not years. They were finally allowed to stay, so they are now regular tenants and they pay just several euros a year in rent.'

Their cause became the birth of resistance to the gentrification of a working-class neighbourhood, and it was very much championed by the St Pauli supporters. 'I'm not aware that anything similar was happening at HSV,' Dani says. 'HSV had quite a far-right fan base in the 1980s, so St Pauli was a natural shift for everyone who thought differently. This used to be a very poor district, with a lot of students, and immigrants – partly because of the red-light district we have here. I know some people who were HSV fans in the 1980s, but they came here because they said: "I don't want to go to that stadium any more, with all those far-right dickheads. I don't want to stand next to a Nazi and support that team."'

Dani acknowledges that the fan base at HSV in the '80s was far more nuanced than some on the left would acknowledge, and that it has improved dramatically – no little thanks to Jens and his friends: 'Issues like far left and right are not an issue at HSV now,' Dani says. Nor was it entirely cut and dried at St Pauli. There is a striking photograph in *Kinder der Westkurve*, taken on the terraces of St Pauli in the 1980s, featuring a supporter wearing an iron cross.

Nonetheless, the overwhelming majority of St Pauli fans had mobilised behind the skull-and-crossbones and the squatters, and they weren't finished yet. Following the harbour-street riots, St Pauli unveiled plans to build a new stadium. 'It was a sports dome,' Dani says, 'with a supermarket inside, with hotels and whatnot.' (The Germans are very fond of the word 'whatnot'.) 'These were very weird plans, and the fan base opposed them: they used the dynamic that was already there. They mobilised big numbers inside the fan base and within the district, and the board backed off.' As Dani emphasises: 'A real spirit developed through these two events, and the fans found that we could achieve anything if we stick together. Only once these stadium plans were dropped did they really get organised to address football issues.'

St Pauli supporters had found a common purpose and spirit from the squatters' movement. In 1989, they founded the Fanladen – a contact point where supporters could meet, to organise activities. The Fanladen produced films, broadcast radio programmes for fans who couldn't be at the game, and began organising away travel for supporters. 'It was such a dynamic moment,' Dani says. 'Other clubs at our level weren't doing this. I haven't heard of a similar movement in Germany, and it came from that historic moment.'

Today, St Pauli retains the traditional multi-sports model of EV, and of supporter ownership. The professional football club exists alongside at least 15 other departments, offering everything from marathon running to cycling, chess and boxing. Both the supervisory and executive boards at the football club are directly elected at the AGM by the supporters.

'We have about 18,000 members,' Dani says, 'and the biggest

department by far is the fans' department, with 11,000 members. I pay about €15 a month adult membership.' In an echo of Professor Chadwick, she says: 'No one questions the price or the idea. There are discounts for students and the unemployed. In St Pauli, there is a huge spirit of solidarity among the people, so we all know that we do this together. Many activities, and the reputation of the club, rely mostly on input from the fans.'

Our walking tour had begun behind the clubhouse, on a building site – St Pauli's new, 27,000-capacity stadium is taking shape. Dani pauses behind the east stand, the spiritual home of the St Pauli supporters, and points to a shell in the building site. 'This will be Rooms for Fans,' she says. 'St Pauli fans from all over the country raised €400,000 to build their own premises inside the ground, and we're moving in in spring 2013.' And some will be staying over: close to the stadium is the main fan pub, the Jolly Roger, which is also run by fans. Above the bar is a hostel, where St Pauli fans who travel long distances to home games can book a bed for the night.

In 2009, St Pauli's fan base produced a document called *The Fundamental Principles of St Pauli*, which is now a part of the club's identity. It emerged from a fan congress, in which 250 people came to discuss issues such as advertising on match days; safety and security; racism and discrimination; employment contracts; sponsorship, and whatnot.

However, this constitution does not always ensure good governance, as Dani acknowledges. 'We have a huge problem at St Pauli with the fact that the identity of the club – which was created by the fan base and which makes the reputation of the club, and which accounts for much of the merchandise income – is more or less being sold out at the moment.'

A walk through the neighbourhood bears this out: shop windows are full of T-shirts, sports bags and other merchandise riffing off the Pistols: 'Never mind the Hamburg, here's St Pauli.' The Jolly Roger is now sold on everything from wristbands to handbags. 'We've got a management in place that is . . .' Dani pauses, '. . . struggling to understand that there is a limit to how much you can sell the reputation of the club while still allowing people to live it.'

I found this out to my own cost the following day, at the club shop, where beanies and T-shirts were selling for €19, and tracksuit tops for almost €70. According to Dani, 'It's a constant tension at St Pauli, because we are in the top ten of merchandise sales in the whole Bundesliga. The Jolly Roger was created by the fans, but it is now the second crest of the club, and it is now under copyright, so the fans can't use it.'

Even more alarming is the sense that the club is courting sponsors who violate the principles of the fan base. 'They put a table-dance bar in one of the VIP boxes in the ground,' Dani tells me. 'That's not too bad, because it's part of the district [Reeperbahn is a hundred yards away] and nobody would oppose that too much; but they put a pole in there, and when a goal was scored, the female dancers undressed!'

It gets worse.

'There was also a deal they did with a company called Kalte Muschi. "*Kalte*" means "cold", and "*Muschi*" is a . . . well, it's a typical pet name, but it's also a disrespectful word for the vagina. It is often a nickname for a cat, and' – Dani smiles, wryly – 'it plays with that analogy very deliberately. So when the advertising boards for Kalte Muschi appeared in the stadium for the first time, the fans were like: "What the fuck!"

We were up in protest, so the management board eventually tried to cancel the contract. Same with the striptease bar: they received a warning, but only because the fans protested; they only act if the fans protest.'

St Pauli even tried to introduce its own currency, the Millerntaler, which would have become the only usable tender within the stadium, and which would effectively have become an indirect loan to the caterer, because, as Dani explains, 'People don't usually cash in the credit they have left over after a match.' Within a week, there were three petitions by the fans. The caterer was called to meet them and eventually backed off.

It's far from perfect, the German model, isn't it.

'It is . . . it is,' she says. 'There is always a tension, but at least the fans are always aware; there is always suspicion of what the board does, and we know that we can always replace them if we need to. We can always put pressure on them: we know that there's gonna be another AGM, that there's gonna be another election.'

If the identities of German clubs today are less about politics and more about community interests, the fact remains that much of the energy at work in German football was fomented in the political turbulence of the 1980s. Some of the key instigators of the Schalke constitution and St Pauli's community initiatives grew up as part of an intensely politicised generation.

Once again, Germany in the 1980s makes for an interesting contrast with Britain: our political agitators were largely corralled within unions or industry, and/or along a binary axis – two big beasts, Labour and Conservative, going head to head in a fight for nothing less than the right to determine the social and political destiny of the next generation. No such war erupted in West Germany: this was a scene of almost perpetual minor skirmishes, involving players at every notch on the political spectrum, fighting for cumulative gains, points victories, tangible results. This was not a winner-takes-all confrontation, and because of that, the fight goes on.

Jens Wagner, 47, was in his late teens when the Nazis came to HSV in the early 1980s. 'We already had the right-wing tendencies in Germany, as you did in England with the National Front,' he says, 'but at school, all our teachers were old hippies from 1968, and kids began rebelling against this – because kids do. And so there were more right-wing tendencies: they weren't joining the Nazi parties, they were just rebelling against their teachers. I don't know how many times we were taught about the Nazi period – it was maybe three or four times at school in four years, and a lot of kids thought, "Oh, come on, we don't need to hear this any more."'

So it was that the stiff-arm salutes returned to the stadiums. And as they did, the left-wing elements responded.

Millions of German football supporters aren't especially interested in politics, however, because by the time they left school, they had had just about enough. The 1980s was not only the decade that pitted hard left against hard right; it was the era in which West Germany gave rise to the Green movement and the anti-nuclear lobby. German teenagers were thus assailed by political arguments from every direction. 'Other teachers would tell us the Soviet system was not too bad,' Jens recalls. 'It wasn't working, they'd say, but the people were not so bad. Others were always saying that the Soviets would throw the H-bomb at us, and that tanks were here and there . . . We were right in the middle of the cold war! We had British military bases here, American military bases there, and in East Germany, Russian bases. And we had all the statistics about how long we would survive when the war would start – three minutes!'

As Jens says: 'Kids are kids, and many rebelled.'

Jens's generation rebelled by immersing themselves in youth culture: in British punk, in particular, and in football. So it was that West Germany in the 1980s bred these football supporters: kids who grew up edgy, violent, rebellious, and caught in the crosshairs of the cold war like no other teenagers in Europe. This was an intensely fractious climate, and many simply switched off from their history lessons and sought sanctuary in football. Today, despite the 'left-wing' garlands strung around the likes of St Pauli, the reality is that while many of the supporters so influential at German clubs were indeed radicalised, they were not so much motivated by an interest in politics as by a desire to get away from them. What they had were the tools to get things done, and a readiness to fight for what they believed in. And their history has led them to believe, more than anything, in being engaged.

At St Pauli, the club's reputation as a left-wing hotbed obscures the fact that, more than anything, this is a community club with an eye on local issues. The main purpose of St Pauli Fanladen is not simply to represent the fans, but to support youth football in the city – for the benefit of the club and local lads. None of this will make headlines in the papers; much of it operates on a rather humble scale. Dani Wurbs is a fine ambassador for her club, and she is evidently most proud of a project the fans developed to offer free football training sessions for the kids from the district: if they turn up for coaching, they will get fruit and muesli bars. 'This might be the only fresh food they will eat all day,' she says, 'because there are still some very poor parts of the district.'

The coaching sessions demand no minimum standard of footballing ability; on a recent Friday afternoon there were up to 80 kids, aged between five and 18. They are given free match tickets in return for regular attendance and good discipline. As Dani says: 'It keeps them off the streets, and out of the red-light district. Every week we have a meeting at our Fanladen, where under-18s are encouraged to get involved in debating issues. They go together on away matches, on buses without alcohol and nicotine. We give them a structure to speak out.'

Among the fans' movement at St Pauli there is a growing feeling of responsibility for what happens in the district. On our walk around the neighbourhood, Dani explains how poorer residents are being forced out because they can no longer afford the rents; just as in Berlin, gentrification is causing considerable debate in Hamburg. What can the club's supporters do to resist this, I ask. She answers without hesitation, and matter-of-factly: 'You can use the stadium as a platform in order to voice your protest about what's going on.'

She points to a nearby wall. 'You see these posters? These are part of an anti-gentrification campaign. Our supporter-liaison officer is part of this poster campaign, to express that the club is part of this movement. People living in the district . . . some are normal workers and some are more well known.' She points to one poster with a distinct face and a signature: 'This woman owns that small hotel over the street, which is a punk hotel. This man produces theatre plays and he is also in a famous punk-rock band. They are making a statement on this poster, protesting against the development of the district.'

And at St Pauli, they continue to fly the skull-and-crossbones.

Perhaps it is our misfortune in Britain to be so politically disconnected, so signally failed by the monotone politics of our big three parties, that we feel cut adrift – and look, with envy, at Germany and imagine that we can see a thriving political energy among its football clubs. But as Stuart Dykes, a son of Mansfield, explained: 'I wouldn't say German fans are particularly political. Schalke range from the conservative CDU to the far left. The fans here are political with a small "p".'

The likes of Schalke and St Pauli aren't political clubs so much as clubs that take their place at the heart of communities – enabling people of all ages, ethnicities and economic backgrounds to participate in the social and civic life of their town or city. In England, our clubs – like so many of our national assets – have been wrenched from their communities and turned into global brands. Local people may engage with their clubs only if they can afford to; the relationship is reduced to a transaction.

Dani talks fondly of her time in Britain, of Newcastle and Lancashire, of the beautiful houses and 'lovely people'. But, she says, 'When I lived in Newcastle [which is twinned with Gelsenkirchen], I had a feeling that, "Oh, there are so many things you could do here, and there is so much going wrong, and all this CCTV surveillance . . . and nobody is doing anything." I spoke to people and they just said, "We've lost a lot of important battles since Thatcher destroyed the unions. And no one really thinks you can achieve anything any more."'

11 : Still in There, Fighting

German football is not without problems of its own. At the time of my visit, midway through the 2012/13 season, the Bundesliga is the scene of fierce conflict, with not one but two disputes pitting fans against the German football league, against the police, against their rivals, their own clubs and even, in the lower divisions, against their own fans.

The more urgent matter is the pressure on the football authorities to crack down on hooliganism – the more urgent, that is, on the part of the authorities. Among millions of German supporters, the greater threat is to the future of their historic supporter-owned clubs. Curiously, there are two proposed solutions to both problems: one is to be found in UEFA's Club Licensing and Financial Fair Play Regulations; the other is in the Premier League. This choice between two very different alternatives has called into question the essence of German football, with all its social and community identity. The fans, however, are standing firm: they will not go down the English route.

Firstly, let's consider the tension over club ownership. The inequalities in German football were brought into focus in the winter break during the 2011/12 season, when – with the threat of relegation looming – Wolfsburg splashed out €30 million of Volkswagen's money on new signings, and duly escaped the drop. A shrewd piece of business, but one beyond the likes of FC Köln, Stuttgart or Mainz 05. Now, the more money that washes in to

German football, and the greater the exposure to Europe's wealthiest clubs, the more EV clubs are facing an existential threat.

While no model of ownership guarantees success, it is nonetheless jarring for many Germans that VW – sorry, Wolfsburg – won the title in 2009. Bayern Munich may be 82 per cent owned by their member-supporters, but their historic success – and minority shareholders Adidas and Audi – make Bayern Germany's wealthiest club by far; little surprise they are perennial contenders. Conversely, the only time an EV club have won the Bundesliga since 1992 was Stuttgart, in 1992 and 2007.

Off the field, the EV model is being subjected to fierce scrutiny. In the Deloitte Football Money League 2011, HSV – then the biggest EV club in Germany – were ranked the second most successful club in the Bundesliga and 11th in the world, but the following year they tumbled to fourth in the domestic league and 18th globally – despite their revenue falling relatively modestly, from €146 million to €128 million. That Schalke outstripped HSV in 2012, rising to second in Germany and tenth worldwide, was the result of good governance under EV rules and Champions League qualification. But HSV lost huge ground to the 50+1 giants Bayern and Dortmund, and as we have seen, in spring 2014, after a century as an EV powerhouse, the club's 70,000 members voted to adopt the 50+1 model.

However, financial question marks hang over clubs owned under each of the three German models. Since the Bundesliga was formed in 1963, its clubs have been issued a licence to compete in the league on an annual basis, and while the licence is conditional on a club proving that it is solvent and has not run up excessive debts, this rule has not always been enforced with the utmost rigour.

In 2003, Borussia Dortmund (50+1) almost went bankrupt expanding their stadium. While they were struggling to pay their players, they were saved by a €2 million loan from Bayern Munich, who only admitted to their largesse several years later.

Hansa Rostock (EV) were only saved from relegation from Bundesliga 2 to the amateur leagues because the local council stepped in with an aid package. As Martin Samuel reported in the *Daily Mail* in May 2012, this included 'a partial waiver of tax debt, the purchase of property located in Hansa's training complex and a significant grant'. As for TSV Munich 1860, they were forced to sell their half of the Allianz Arena to Bayern Munich to stay afloat, while Kaiserslautern (50+1) 'were in such a mess', Samuel wrote, 'they mortgaged their star player, Miroslav Klose, to the state lottery'.

Then there are the 'works teams'. Why Volkswagen is allowed to own Wolfsburg and sponsor the German cup too certainly appears questionable. So does the fact that its subsidiary, Audi, bought a 9 per cent stake in Bayern Munich in 2009, for €90 million. And for all that the likes of Bayern complain about the obscene investment at Manchester City, their own dominance of German football is not without controversy. Bayern have a long-standing relationship with Adidas, who bought a 9 per cent stake in the club in 2001. In 2007, when the German FA were reported to be considering switching their shirt supplier for the national side from Adidas to Nike, Agence France-Press reported that 'Bayern Munich has "threatened to prevent its players" from playing for the national team.' The report quoted a Bayern spokesperson as saying 'it would be seen as a betrayal' for club players to wear Nike on their shirts. Bayern's Karl-Heinz Rummenigge was quoted: 'I just cannot imagine that a Bayern player would wear a German shirt with the Nike logo on it.' In 2011, the Adidas contract to supply shirts for Germany was extended, despite intense competition from Nike.

In the past three seasons, Alemannia Aachen have been in administration. MSV Duisburg, Hansa Rostock, Dynamo Dresden, VFL Osnabrück, 1860 Munich and Arminia Bielefeld have all faced serious financial problems, while Werder Bremen made a loss of nearly €40 million in 2010/11. And yet, in the 2012/13 season, the Bundesligen 1 and 2 posted a record turn-over for the ninth consecutive year. All but one of the 18 clubs in Bundesliga 1 were in profit.

However, many German fans fear that the licensing regulations addressing club ownership have invited a new threat, in the shape of clubs such as RB Leipzig and Hoffenheim.

In 2009, the energy-drinks brand Red Bull bought the DFL licence of Markranstadt, a club in the former East Germany, and sought to rebrand it Red Bull Leipzig. The DFB refused, so a compromise was struck: RB Leipzig took to the field of Division 5 at the start of the 2009 season. Initially, Red Bull were forbidden to use their logo on the club's shirts, but after the company threatened to withdraw from Leipzig, the local FA relented. Red Bull are still not permitted to call the club Red Bull Leipzig, but RB Leipzig is fine. Jens Wagner is extremely sceptical: 'This is a test-tube-baby club,' he says, 'and the DFB isn't doing anything about it.' Certainly, questions should be asked as to whether a conflict of interest arises in the fact that the second most important official at the DFB, general secretary Helmut Sandrock, is a former president of Red Bull Salzburg.

Many German fans have stopped asking questions, because

the answers are not forthcoming. So suspicion grows that Red Bull have taken a giant step towards the franchising of German football clubs. In Leipzig, one of Germany's poorer cities, the offer to build a new 42,000-capacity stadium, and pay for its naming rights for 20 years, must have been music to the ears of the local FA. But what came next appears cynical in the extreme. German law requires that each club must have at least eight members, so when Red Bull bought Markranstadt's licence, they started a new club with no members, and recruited eight – and, coincidentally, they are all people from Red Bull. According to Jens Wagner: 'It's a closed shop. This is a total disaster, in my opinion, and nobody is doing anything against this.'

There are similar concerns over the rise of Hoffenheim. Germany's mightiest mouse is bankrolled by software billionaire Dietmar Hopp, who bought a stake in the club in 2000/1. The exact date of his arrival remains unclear, as does the influence he exerts over a club still notionally operating under the 50+1 rule.

Since Hopp's arrival, Hoffenheim have risen from Germany's equivalent of the Conference North to the Bundesliga 1, and have signed players of the calibre of Ryan Babel and coaches such as Markus Babbel. Not bad, considering Hoffenheim's population is just over 3,200. The club's stadium, the Rhein-Neckar Arena, has a capacity which – at 21,000 – is six times the size of the village. Not for nothing are Hoffenheim dubbed 'the richest village football club in the world'. Hopp, at least, is a native of Hoffenheim, so there is merit in his investing in his home-town club. But concerns remain. 'Nothing against the club, or the fans,' says Jens Wagner, 'but it is not good, all this money coming so quickly into such a small club.'

Hoffenheim is so small, in fact, that inter-city trains can't even stop there, because the station platform isn't long enough. But it is sending a giant signal to other clubs in Germany, with businesses now looking to buy clubs in the Fourth Division to secure a football licence. As Jens says: 'When Wolfsburg won the league, many companies thought, "We don't need to be sponsors any more, we can just buy the clubs."'

The biggest complaint among German supporters, however, is that for all the influence members retain at their clubs, they have limited traction within the German FA. Partly, this is because the German FA is the largest in the world, with almost 26,000 registered clubs; and it's partly because the 36 Bundesliga clubs (in Bundesligen 1 and 2) have no more influence over their governing body than do the local teams from Dani Wurbs's village in southern Germany. The frustration among supporters was captured in a survey of football fans in eight countries in 2012, conducted by the social research co-operative Substance: when asked if they were happy with the way their clubs are organised, 80 per cent of fans in Germany said yes; however, they complained about the lack of dialogue between the clubs and the game's governing bodies.

'Our directors go to the football league meetings, and as long as the TV money is divided fairly they don't care about anything else, and they go home,' Jens Wagner tells me. 'Our football system is not run in a professional way, in my opinion. I wrote a paper raising issues about licensing, about the implications of clubs like Wolfsburg being backed by Volkswagen, and Volkswagen chairman Martin Winterkorn being on the supervisory board of Bayern Munich, and I was told by a club director: "Jens, this is very good, but this is too much for the club directors."' He shakes his head. 'There are people earning a few million euros each year to run our football clubs who don't understand issues like these. What does this say if Germany, Europe's shining example, is run like this?'

Not content with running their own clubs, Jens and a number of other football supporters decided they needed greater influence over the DFB. So, in 2005, he founded Unsere Kurve (Our End), to bring together football fans from rival clubs in a national lobby, with membership on an individual rather than club basis – similar to the Football Supporters' Association in England. Unsere Kurve started with six or seven organisations in 2005 and now has 15, from Divisions 1 to 3. And its rallying cry is simple: to retain the 50+1 rule, either with or without the EV foundations.

Unsere Kurve has its work cut out. In 2011, opponents of the historic model rallied around Martin Kind, president of Hannover 96, who argued that the 50+1 mechanism was holding clubs at a disadvantage to Bayer Leverkusen and Wolfsburg. 'He is totally right,' says Jens. 'They use financial doping.* But instead of getting rid of the 50+1 rule, we say we should strengthen the rule. There are gaps in it, and clubs like RB Leipzig and Hoffenheim are using these gaps.'

If 15 out of 18 clubs in Bundesliga 1 are majority owned by supporters, is there not the possibility that supporters could take their clubs out of the league and set up a new one? Jens draws a deep breath: 'It is possible, but we haven't had this discussion so far. If you have 60,000 members, you can't expect that they all feel the same. And we have people who say, "Oh,

---

* This is not Jens's own term; it was coined by a former CEO of UEFA, and not strictly with regard to Wolfsburg and Bayer Leverkusen.

I am embarrassed about all these discussions we have about how to run the club. I just want to watch good football."'

The fact is, however, that before 1998 there was no need for such a debate. The reason the rules were relaxed that year, to allow for the 50+1 model, is that the greatest pressure on German clubs to compete financially comes not from each other, but from the country the Germans have historically looked to for their footballing example. Real Madrid and Barcelona may be the world's richest clubs, but the Germans see through the Spanish model for the duopoly it is, and have little historical regard for Spanish football culture. England is their barometer, and the increasing financial might of the English game is putting a huge strain on the Bundesliga.

In February 2015, Bundesliga officials responded to the Premier League's latest TV bonanza by warning supporters that they may have to take drastic action to compete financially with the English clubs. The current TV deal with Sky Germany, which runs to 2016, nets the Bundesliga £465 million a season, compared with the Premier League's domestic rights deal of £1.7 billion a season from 2016. As the *Daily Mail* noted: 'As it stands, the club that finishes bottom of the Premier League can earn more than Bayern Munich in television money.'

While Bayern fans responded with banners proclaiming, 'This ain't no Premier League: no to the English model', Bundesliga CEO Christian Seifert asked: 'Are we ready to take unpopular measures to be able to keep the best players in the world in the Bundesliga?' Max Eberl, managing director of Borussia Mönchengladbach, was less circumspect: 'Traditions may have to be broken,' he said.

This break with tradition would see a far greater number

of matches screened live on TV. However, as Seifert himself pointed out, the economic model of the Bundesliga is better balanced than that of the Premier League, in part because it isn't overly reliant on TV money. Whereas over 50 per cent of the Premier League's revenues come from TV rights, in Germany media deals contribute 29 per cent of total revenues, which leaves the traditional 3.30 p.m. Saturday-afternoon fixture list largely intact. (A further 27 per cent of Bundesliga revenues come from advertising, 22 per cent from match revenues, and 22 per cent from a combination of transfer fees, merchandising and 'other' sources.) As Seifert said: 'The Bundesliga is succeeding in the split between top-level sports performance and economic rationality, especially compared to others in Europe.'

The fear among many German supporters is that the further the Bundesliga moves towards becoming a TV spectacle, the more its clubs will attract predatory foreign investors.

If neither Hamburg nor Gelsenkirchen is a seat of revolution, Leipzig just might be. 'It's starting,' said Ralph, one of the HSV fans I spoke to in the Sportpub Tankstelle. 'We are maybe five or ten years behind England, but I fear we will follow. I fear foreign investment in Germany.' So does Jens Wagner. 'We already have Red Bull, who are Austrian,' he says. 'And 1860 Munich is majority owned by a Jordanian.'

In Germany, supporter-owned clubs are banking on UEFA's Financial Fair Play regulations, which were implemented in 2015. Approved by UEFA in September 2009, they are designed to protect the long-term viability of clubs, and to encourage them to compete within their means. In September 2013, UEFA announced that in the financial year 2012/13, the 725 clubs in Europe's first divisions had lost €1.066 billion, compared with €1.7 billion the previous year. 'The clubs are getting the message,' said Gianni Infantino, UEFA's general secretary.

The irony, of course, is that Financial Fair Play was partly inspired by the German model of club licensing, which is far from unblemished – but the Germans are eager to see FFP rigorously enforced across the rest of Europe. According to Ralph: 'Much of German Fan Culture depends on this, because if UEFA don't see it through, then the pressure on German clubs to compete in Europe will intensify.'

Jens Wagner is hopeful. 'If we took this idea through Divisions 1 to 3, this would protect our system against companies or billionaires who are buying football clubs.'

Thomas Spiegel, Schalke's director of media communications, agrees: 'If the Financial Fair Play system is a success, then the one who will win is the one with the best football education system, not the one with the best oligarch, or the man from Qatar.'

Despite the licensing irregularities in the Bundesliga, most football supporters would surely see the merit in FFP succeeding, and in German supporters remaining in control of their clubs. Can UEFA make it work? 'They're determined to do it,' says Stuart Dykes.

And yet such is the latent profit in clubs such as Bayern and HSV and Schalke, and such is the threat from the man from Qatar. In January 2013, it was revealed that the Qatar Tourism Authority had agreed to sponsor Paris Saint-Germain (owned by the Qatari state) for €150–200 million a season. The deal doesn't even include shirt sponsorship.

*

Since 1992, English football has led the way in Europe in combating hooliganism. The violence that nearly destroyed the game in England as recently as the mid-1980s has largely dissipated. Ask the authorities, and they will point to a combination of intelligent policing, CCTV and the reach and influence of supporter organisations. In Germany, however, hooliganism remains a headline issue. Partly because, it has to be said, the Germans are quite fond of a punch-up.

There were football riots in Germany in the 1930s, '40s and '50s. Uwe Seeler was once forced to smuggle a rival team's player out of HSV's stadium under his coat, as Hamburg fans went on the rampage. This excitable behaviour wasn't confined to football: riots accompanied a Beatles gig in Hamburg in the 1960s, when 600 people set about the police. Similar trouble flared when the Rolling Stones came to town. However, a hooligan 'culture' only began to take root in Germany as recently as the 1980s, and at the time of my visit in 2012, according to the German police, it was on the rise again.

The 2011/12 season saw the highest rate of prosecutions for football-related disorder in Germany in 12 years, with the number of hooligan-related injuries among supporters almost doubling on the previous season. In October 2012, a month before I went to Schalke, 200 people were arrested in disturbances between Borussia Dortmund and Schalke fans before the Ruhr derby. In the week of my visit, 46 people were injured at a match between Hansa Rostock and RW Erfurt, another eastern German team. In total, 1,300 people were arrested in football-related trouble across the country in that week alone.

We shall come back to these figures later, for they became the focus of a fierce dispute between supporters, the media and the police. What isn't in dispute is that hooligans are still active in Germany.

'In the last year,' Thomas Spiegel told me in November 2012, 'there have been really ugly scenes across Germany. FC Köln fans attacked buses carrying Mönchengladbach fans, and they were trying to drop Gladbach supporters over the side of the motorway. The fans say there is no problem with fan violence in Germany, but they are wrong. The politicians exaggerate it,' Spiegel says, 'but the problem is there.'

On that Friday afternoon at Schalke, Spiegel was commendably candid throughout the hour we spoke about German football, English football and the man from Qatar. And no less so about crowd disorder in Germany.

'We had a discussion with our fans on recent security issues, and they were very angry with the club,' he says. 'They said, "You should have come out first and said we, as Schalke fans, did nothing wrong, and we are perfect." And we can't say that. Because when we played Man United recently [in the 2012 Champions League] at Old Trafford, the United stewards went into the Schalke end to stop them using flares and they were attacked by our fans, for no reason at all.' Spiegel looks genuinely pained. 'Our fans were in the upper tier at Old Trafford and they were even throwing things down on the United fans below. I've had complaints from people at Man United – they are really nice people – and they said, "Why did your fans do that? We always thought German fans were . . . we never expected that." It was pretty embarrassing, but our fans said, "We did nothing wrong. Oh, it was people from Macedonia, and how can we control them? And how did they get tickets?"'

Spiegel shakes his head. 'Our away tickets are controlled by our fans, to make sure the right people get tickets! Never do I hear fans say, "OK, we are at fault sometimes."'

Spiegel's is a nuanced voice in an increasingly polarised debate. In 2012, fears over football violence in Germany led to the drafting of a security paper by the German football league (DFL). Proposals included the erection of tents outside stadiums to facilitate total strip searches; the banning of flares (or 'pyrotechnics') inside the stadium; and a reduction in the number of tickets for away supporters from 10 per cent to 5 per cent of capacity. There were even dire warnings that the terraces might be replaced with seats: the German authorities pointed to the Premier League as evidence that all-seater stadiums were key to eradicating hooliganism in England.

Initially, the circulation of this security paper went largely unnoticed. The only opposition came from Union Berlin, the Bundesliga 2 club with a left-wing intellectual fan base. Gradually, other clubs began to cry foul, and as opposition spread, German supporters at the 36 clubs in the top two Bundesligen held debates on whether or not to accept the security paper, which they came to regard as a serious assault on Fan Culture. It appears that the DFL overplayed their hand: in raising the Premier League as a possible panacea, they succeeded only in raising the spectre of what Germans regard as listless football grounds and an over-sanitised match-day experience.

On 24 November 2012, I was invited to the debate convened for Schalke's supporters by their ultras, the Nordkurve. The ultras' pub, not far from the Veltins-Arena, is a long, low-ceilinged hall, thick with smoke. Inside, around 150 to 200 people are gathered; lads are carrying plates of chilli con carne back to the tables, and beer is selling for €1 a bottle. Around

90 per cent of those here are lads; many are ultras, standing slightly self-consciously in their baggy royal-blue tracksuits with 'Nordkurve' across the back. The tracksuits are winning, in a slightly disco style circa *The Warriors*, but the atmosphere is purposeful: when I ask Stuart Dykes, my translator, whether it would be OK to switch on my dictaphone, he looks at me like I've just admitted to whacking Princess Diana.

On a low stage, unseen to me – even Germans from poor cities tend to be tall – the ultras' spokesmen explain the situation regarding the security paper; how meetings will be taking place in dozens of towns and cities across Germany this weekend, and how the dialogue resisting the paper is taking shape. Now, only three Bundesliga clubs are not opposing it. The ultras explain that the security situation isn't being taken lightly, and that they appreciate there are valid concerns, but the Fan Culture in Germany must be protected. There was an own goal the previous night, when HSV played in Düsseldorf, and Hamburg ultras The Chosen Few only went and set light to their own banner with a flare. The Nordkurve spokesman says that this has already prompted a letter of complaint to HSV from Union Berlin. The Schalke ultras have little sympathy. (Such is the rivalry among ultras that when Schalke goalkeeper Manuel Neuer joined Bayern Munich, he was initially rejected by Bayern fans because he was a Schalke ultra himself.)

However, as the meeting progresses it becomes clear that German supporters are united nationwide in rejecting the security paper. Lads tilt their heads towards the floor (as people do, strangely) to hear more clearly. They glance up to check they have heard correctly, and then back to the floor. No one on the floor speaks, apart from Stuart, who is translating for me in a low voice. A protest has been agreed upon, and while it is not yet clear how many clubs will take part, for the three games following today's, supporters will protest against the security paper by refusing to create any atmosphere in the stadiums for the first 12 minutes and 12 seconds of the match. This will happen at three games leading up to 12 December, when the security paper is to be debated. The idea behind '12:12' is to show the German football authorities how valuable an atmosphere is within the ground, and how the paper will put Fan Culture at risk. Disparaging comparisons are made with the atmosphere in English Premier League stadiums.

There is quiet concern among the 200 people in the hall. Their mood is solemn, but steely. They will not tolerate strip searches, and the issue of pyrotechnics must be debated with supporters. Democratic niceties are observed: the issues are explained, carefully and rationally; the tone and language are moderate and calm; the stage is open to questions from the floor. When the debate is over, a vote is taken: a massive show of hands confirms that the security paper must be rejected.

And it is. Three days later, on 27 November 2012, the 12:12 protest spread across the country. 'Erupted' would be the wrong word: for the first 12 minutes and 12 seconds of every game in the top two divisions, supporters across Germany refused to sing, cheer or wave their flags; they simply stood around chatting, or sat and watched the game in silence. I was at HSV vs Schalke that night, and with all the meetings, the travelling, the beer, I'd forgotten about the protest. For the first ten minutes of the game, the atmosphere was indeed odd: just 57,000 fans talking in a low murmur. No goals were scored in the Volkspark, but attacks were left to play out in virtual silence.

In truth, it felt not unlike large periods of an average Premier League game. Then, after 12 minutes, the stadium began to boil, and boil, and then the lid blew off the Volkspark. At the far end, Schalke fans began to bounce and sing: 'German football league: you are shit!' The HSV fans echoed the sentiment. Back and forth it bounced, the delay of a couple of seconds creating a momentary silence, before the sonic boom erupted again at the far end of the stadium. 'German football league: you are shit!' The solidarity continued for a minute, before both sets of fans applauded each other, and the game could begin in earnest.

By 12 December, the fans called a halt to the protest, and met the football league to debate the paper. Stuart Dykes emailed me: 'I only know of one instance where the silent protest wasn't observed,' he said. 'Only Babelsberg in the third division did not participate: that was a far-left thing, because a couple of the ultras groups who are in favour of the protest have been infiltrated by the far right, so other fans were saying, "We're not going to sit down with the far right." Elsewhere, there were goals scored in that moment, and of course people cheered, but then there was no singing or chanting around it.' As Stuart said: 'It's a massive show of strength.'

While Fan Culture was at the heart of the protest, there is growing suspicion in Germany that just as the British police have trialled on football fans many tactics now in use at demonstrations, the German police are following suit. Philipp Markhardt, the HSV ultra, told me that the names of German football fans can now be entered on a database, even if they haven't committed a criminal offence. 'The fan will only know if he or she has been put on this database if they ask to know, otherwise this record is kept secret,' he said. 'When they go to travel abroad, fans can be checked at border control, who can refuse travel – the fans might not even know why they are refused. This has been trialled on football fans, and now the thinking is, "We can now do this on left-wing activists . . . we can do it on right-wing activists."'

I was shocked to learn, too, that before the 2006 World Cup, the police in Hamburg were considering deploying drones to monitor football supporters. 'You can't do this if you have a political demonstration,' Jens Wagner said. 'You could have the Taliban demonstrating in Hamburg and you couldn't do this.'

In Germany, however, football supporters have the law on their side – or rather, the constitution. Germany is a federal state, which means that Lower Saxony, North Rhine-Westphalia, Bavaria and elsewhere set their own police laws. Not only does this make it awkward for the government to effect one security law across the country, but, as Stuart Dykes says, 'because we're a federal country, there is apparently no legal basis for this security paper'.

And yet, for all that German supporters bemoan the lack of constructive dialogue with the football authorities, the latter are coming under huge pressure from politicians, as Stuart explains: 'It's always been the case, as long as I've been involved in supporter politics here, that German football authorities have regarded the fans as allies, not enemies. The common enemy is the politicians, the hardliners who don't understand football.'

Football: an easy target? Where have we heard that before? Only the political motivation differs from one country to another. And in Germany, in 2013, football was being lined up as a distraction from a shocking failure in state security.

On a Monday night in Hamburg, I was invited by Jens Wagner to TIDE TV studios, where HSV Supporters' Club are broadcasting a 45-minute debate to a potential audience of up to two million in the greater Hamburg area. Five members of HSV are here to discuss the security paper. It's a spirited debate, and one that becomes even more revealing once the cameras stop rolling. Off screen, Philipp Markhardt joins me, with another spokesman, whom I shall call Jürgen. Philipp begins by reiterating the fans' key concern: 'Politicians are to blame, mostly, for attacking Fan Culture in Germany. Many people who don't have a clue about it are writing about it, and politicians are seeing an opportunity before the general elections next year [2013]. Usually, it's the federal states in Germany who have to deal with what is happening in the stadiums,' he says, 'but at the moment the minister [Germany's home secretary] is talking about it as a problem, and this is not his field. But the minister is not really successful at the moment – the Nazi murders are bad press for him, and football is an easy target.'

The 'Nazi murders' involved a far-right cell who stand accused of the deaths of a policewoman and nine men of Turkish or Greek origin over the past decade.* The cell has also been linked to two bomb attacks and a number of bank robberies. While none of these crimes occurred on the current minister's watch, the issue is dogging the Merkel government just a year out from a general election.

Now Jürgen chips in: 'The constitutional secret service were using these Nazis as informants, but they didn't realise these guys were going round killing people. That is a big issue here.

* Two of the three suspects killed themselves in a suicide pact in 2011. The third, Beate Zschäpe, has been on trial since May 2013.

Can one say "Fuck-up"? It's a big fuck-up, and it's always the guy at the end holding the stick who has to take responsibility. So they're looking at somewhere to deflect media attention, and it's football fans they're looking at.'

To German supporters, this interference by political opportunists – combined with the clamour to open up ownership models along British lines – is an existential threat to their football culture. It's a point made by the supporter-liaison officer at St Pauli, who hosted Schalke fans at their clubhouse on the day they came to HSV. In a back room of the clubhouse, Stefan Schatz told me: 'Our big fear now is that if we don't come together – football fans and organised football clubs – and fight hand in hand, the politicians will bring strong pressure to end the terraces. I don't believe the pressure for seats is about money; it's about the culture, and fans want to keep it. In England, the Hillsborough Panel report has shown that the disaster wasn't about terraces, it was about police mistakes.'

What struck me about Schatz's argument is not the point about Hillsborough, but that the removal of terraces is an attack on football culture, rather than financially motivated. He is right about Hillsborough, of course, but when do the police ever hold up their hands? They are not in the habit in Germany, either. In fact, the police unions are using football for a recruitment drive, as Jens Wagner explains: 'There are two big police unions in Germany, and they are competing to attract more members, and the head of one of them is trying to prove that if they can be tough on football . . . Also, the press is printing what he's saying without trying to prove it or not. They are talking about possibly bringing in electronic tagging for fans . . . the police and press here have learnt nothing since Hillsborough.'

In January 2013, German supporters called off the 12:12 protest: after they were invited to talks with the DFL, the 36 clubs
from Bundesligen 1 and 2 agreed to tighter stadium checks, a
crackdown on pyrotechnics and smoke bombs, tougher sanc-
tions for offenders, video monitoring and better stadium staff.
On its website, the 12:12 movement said: 'We have received an
invitation from the Bundesliga for a first interview, so that a
dialogue can finally begin in earnest . . . It can be argued that
the protest helped to prevent more disproportionate measures.'

This is no mere propaganda. 'The security paper has been
watered down because of the supporters' demands,' confirms
Stuart Dykes. 'Even the police have got the message that this
isn't just the ultras protesting.' The hardliners' arguments simply didn't add up, he says. 'Politicians are using figures about
the number of arrests and injuries, but their own figures have
been shown to be meaningless. Even the media have cottoned
onto this now.'

The German fans, it appears, have settled a debate that was
increasingly hysterical and ill informed. 'There's been a complete turnaround in the media now,' Stuart says. 'Even the
media are saying, "This is ridiculous." And even the police are
coming out with statements they would not have made just a
few weeks ago [acknowledging as much].'

Stuart Dykes has seen it all in Germany, and at his first club,
Man Utd. He's a respected consultant to UEFA on supporter
issues, and has been around German football since the dark
days of the late 1980s. Now, he says, 'German supporters are
at a fork in the road. It will be interesting to see who wins the
debate among the fans – the hardliners or moderates.'

*

German supporters may be at a fork in the road, but at least they are driving the bus. On both of the key issues troubling their game, supporter-owned clubs can insist on exercising their rights and their responsibilities: their right to own their clubs, and the responsibility of tackling hooliganism.

The numb silence in the HSV fans' pub when I recounted how English clubs are businesses to be bought and sold was one to savour – born of a sense that clubs deserve protection from the global free market. It is an idea increasingly gaining traction in England. In January 2013, Will Hutton, writing in the *Observer*, considered the crisis at Birmingham City. 'Birmingham City FC fans are in revolt,' he wrote.

> Their once proud club has not been well managed – to put it mildly – by 'businessman' Carson Yeung, currently awaiting trial in his native Hong Kong, for an alleged £59m-worth of money laundering, and the process is not over yet. It is the degeneracy of British economy and society in a football microcosm – nothing to stop Cayman Island ownership, and lush, anonymous director fees.

Hutton thundered on:

> In Britain, there are no legal or governance structures that put football or the fans at the centre of a club owner's concerns. Rather, in keeping with the wider culture, football is 'open for business'. Market forces are deified as the only value worth celebrating, and a business – even a football club – is no more than its owner's private plaything. The result is a moral and economic disaster – in football as in the wider economy.

Hutton is no Trotskyite rabble-rouser, but principal of Hertford College, Oxford, and the former chief executive of The Work Foundation. His measured voice was joined a few weeks later by John Studzinski's, in the *Guardian*. Studzinski, a senior managing director and global head of business strategy advisers Blackstone Advisory Partners, made no specific mention of football, but the parallels were blindingly obvious when he considered why Germany's unemployment rate stood at a comparatively benign 6.9 per cent, when the average in the eurozone was 11.7 per cent.

'Germany's resilience', he wrote, 'springs from the strength of its medium-sized, often family-owned manufacturing companies, collectively known as the *Mittelstand*, which account for 60% of the workforce and 52% of Germany's GDP.'

According to Studzinski, the underlying ethos of the *Mittelstand* is 'that business is a constructive enterprise that aims to be socially useful. Making a profit is not an end in itself. Taking on debt is treated with suspicion.'

While Studzinski was adamant that the German model could work in Britain – 'The enduring success of the *Mittelstand* has been well documented but rarely emulated,' he wrote. 'The standard excuse is that it is rooted in German history and culture and therefore unexportable. This excuse is wearing thin' – Will Hutton was altogether more defeatist. 'Why worry about British society?' he wrote. 'We exist to be looted and privately mocked for our connivance in our own destruction.'

So why are the Germans getting so much right – or, at the very least, still in the fight? According to Simon Chadwick, professor of sports enterprise at Salford University, it's partly because the Germans retain a strong sense of national identity.

'The British whinge, "Oh, the Spanish own our banks, or the Chinese are doing this," but the reality is we sold our assets on the cheap,' he says. 'There isn't this passion to protect organisations or businesses from foreign ownership as there is in Germany. They are prepared to step in and prevent foreign ownership, because they see German business as important to German identity.'

It's a point raised unprompted by Thomas Spiegel, at Schalke, who insists that Financial Fair Play is not simply a means of curtailing excessive spending, but of preserving the identity of a German football team: 'The idea of bringing our own talent through the ranks is very popular. The fans know it's a cheaper way of building a team, but they also like to relate to the team. Eleven foreigners is a horror vision – not for a xenophobic reason, but because of the idea of identifying with the team.'

Professor Chadwick refers, intriguingly, to how the British are still regarded in Europe as a people who play by the rules. The problem here, I suggest, is that there are no rules any more – not in the free market in which our football and businesses operate. The British appear to have been suckered. 'The Germans also operate in this world, where rules are disappearing and boundaries are being blurred,' Chadwick points out. 'But because of their self-confidence, they are prepared to work at defining the rules themselves.'

Britain's plight is not simply the consequence of neoliberal economics. German businesses and football clubs both embrace the principle of co-determination – the practice of appointing workers/supporters to the board. The model was proposed in Britain in 1977 by the Bullock Report, and it wasn't the emerging Thatcherites who buried the idea. As Will Hutton noted in another article in the *Observer*, in January 2013: 'Those with long memories will recall the militant opposition of the British trade union movement to co-determination in the 1970s. Stupid.'

So it is that in Germany, football supporters with a strong national identity, and a law that encourages co-determination, are in there fighting to retain the ownership of their clubs.

At the same time, over the past two decades, they have taken a very different approach to hooliganism to that seen – to great effect, it must be argued – in England. In Germany, supporters have resisted price hikes, and have argued that cheaper tickets need not come at the expense of safety. Their approach is to balance social rights with responsibilities – in short, to empower supporters rather than defer to a law-and-order agenda.

In 2010, UEFA reported that since 1992, German football has seen a reduction in violence despite a threefold increase in attendances. Today, the Bundesliga has the highest average league attendance in Europe. And at the heart of the German solution to hooliganism is the supporter-liaison officer, or SLO – whose arrival, says UEFA, 'constitutes a new landmark in club–supporter relations'.

SLOs were introduced at Borussia Mönchengladbach in 1988, and subsequently rolled out across Germany. So successful have they proved that in 2010, UEFA stipulated that all clubs across Europe would be required to appoint an SLO before the 2012/13 season. The job of an SLO is not to act as a security officer, and not to intervene in violence or disorder, but to act as a bridge between supporters (ranging from the occasional visitor through to hardcore ultras) and their clubs. As Michel Platini wrote in UEFA's Club Licensing and Financial Fair

Play Regulations: 'The SLO requirement centres on improving communication and providing a focal point for supporters to organise themselves better, and make their voice heard.'

The SLO requirement (under Article 35 of UEFA's Licensing Regulations) resulted from close co-operation between UEFA and Supporters Direct. Today, it is Stuart Dykes's job to roll out the project across Europe. He works as a consultant to Supporters Direct, who report to the head of UEFA once a year. 'I break the SLO's job down into three areas,' Stuart says. 'Dialogue and communication; service – providing both fans and clubs a service; and prevention/security.'

Before he became a consultant to Supporters Direct, Stuart worked as a translator and interpreter, and translated FIFA's Technical Report for the 2006 World Cup; he has also worked as a consultant to Schalke on social-responsibility issues. Stuart has seen the SLO role develop over two decades, and tells me it took about ten years to make a significant impact.

'There's a fair bit of resistance to the SLOs across Europe,' he says. 'Basically, it means bringing a supporter inside the club, and clubs are wary of it. If you look at some countries in Europe, you'll find hardened criminals, fascists and neo-Nazis with influence in the fan base.'

Nazism will not go away in Germany. In football, it's often painted as a problem confined to the poorer east of the country, but this is misleading: neo-Nazis have a foothold in the west too, among the supporter base at Borussia Dortmund, Aachen, Braunschweig and MSV Duisburg. And in the trouble that marred the Schalke–Dortmund derby in the autumn of 2012, some of those arrested on the Dortmund side were NPD cadres – Nazi party officials. It is a problem the national media are slow to acknowledge, and not every club has moved as swiftly to root out the fascists as it might have done.

The city of Dortmund is a focal point for neo-Nazis in the Ruhr, and although it must be stressed that Borussia Dortmund are not renowned for having an extremist fan base, before the 2012/13 season was four months old there were three incidents of Dortmund supporters displaying far-right banners at matches. Both Thomas Spiegel and Stuart Dykes told me that part of the club's problem lay in their reluctance to empower their fans.

'They never did the supporter work that Schalke did,' says Dykes. 'They were the last Bundesliga club to even have an SLO: it took Dortmund 15 years to appoint one, even though they've got one of the biggest fan bases. They've got one of the best SLOs in the country now, but he only started in 2008.'

In Germany, the DFB prefers SLOs to have a social-science background, to have close contact with the fan scene, and to know the history of the club. In essence, they are there to put the supporters' concerns – on issues such as safety and violence, comfort and consultation – to the club, the police and the football authorities. This attempt to involve supporters in addressing issues that affect them more than anyone else is a form of delegating responsibility, and one that can only benefit the club itself. As UEFA states: 'Rather than being seen as potential trouble-makers, fans should be considered as people capable of making an active contribution to the wider agenda of their clubs.'

There is a sizeable rump of resistance to the idea in England. One well-placed source, who asked to remain anonymous, told me: 'The Premier League are incredibly short-sighted. They talk a good talk about liaison, but there's a prevailing attitude of keeping the fans at arm's length. They do what they have to do to tick boxes. Not all clubs in England are like that: Doncaster Rovers do very good work with their fans, and Crystal Palace are brilliant. But at most clubs there are so many pertinent issues the fans need to be involved with, and they're just not.'

Stuart Dykes acknowledges there are teething problems in England.

'Premier League clubs look at the SLO role from a customer-service perspective: that this should be a professional service person. The Premier League clubs have appointed someone from *within* the club as their SLO.'

At some clubs in England's top two divisions, the SLO happens to be the director of communications, or a marketing manager.

'There is nothing wrong with this per se,' says Dykes, 'and it is not in breach of Article 35 of UEFA's Licensing Regulations; but it would be nice to see an English club grasp the nettle and appoint a supporter. The English clubs are already doing excellent work in the area of fan engagement, but to me, supporter liaison is something different: it's about engaging with those supporters who don't see themselves as customers. The "Love United, Hate Glazer" types – who engages with them? Who talks to the 5 per cent of supporters who moan or whinge or criticise? It's about bringing them onside.'

It's a sentiment spelt out in black and white in the UEFA handbook: 'The SLO project acknowledges that supporters are not defined by their role as consumers in the professional football system . . .'

Perhaps the Premier League could take their cue from the Football League: they have instructed their clubs that the SLO and customer-care roles are separate, and that clubs should not appoint customer-care people to the SLO role.

Stuart Dykes's own club, Schalke, have three SLOs. On the Friday I spent at the club's headquarters in November 2012, I met one of them for what turned out to be one of the most illuminating interviews during my week in Germany.

Patrick Arnold is a full-time SLO at the club. After training as a social worker, Patrick was appointed by the local government to the Schalke fan project, where he took responsibility for category-C supporters. This broad category encompasses the high-risk supporters, ranging from ultras to hardcore hooligans. German spotters and other intelligence sources estimate that there are around 8,000 match-going hooligans in Germany within the category-C band.*

'I know every one of the category-C supporters at Schalke,' Patrick tells me, matter-of-factly. 'I am well-known to the category-C supporters; I am trusted. This makes it easier for them to come to the club with their problems.'

But surely this is the problem with hooligans in particular – that they bring their problems to the club? No problem here. Patrick reaches behind his desk and pulls out a photo of the night he took the German FA Cup to the Schalke hooligans' pub. I ask him if I could have a copy. He shakes his head.

'They have big problems with their photo appearing in a British book.'

They look a lively bunch, I say.

He nods. 'We have a lot of Turkish people in our fan scene, and in our hooligans. Really, really good guys.'

* The ABC categorisation is in the process of being replaced with 'risk' and 'non-risk' bands.

I'm trying not to smile, but it's not working. Patrick looks puzzled. So, I ask him, the club see value in engaging with problem supporters?

He nods, thoughtfully. 'Yes.'

They don't just wash their hands of them?

'No, no, no. When we play away – say, in London recently, at Arsenal – the club always say to the SLOs: "How many supporters are coming, from which categories?" And they say, "Patrick, make sure the guys have tickets. Even if they are not members of the club, make sure they have a ticket, because we would rather have them in the stadium than outside on the streets."'

In England, I venture, the police would tell the clubs that they cannot have these hooligans at the club, and that you should not engage with them.

'You have to,' Patrick insists. 'Look at this picture.'

He produces a cutting from what appears to be the *Daily Mail* – a half-page photo of Schalke fans amid a red mist at Old Trafford. 'When we played at Manchester United in the Champions League, one of our fans set off that flare. And directly after the game he went out of one exit, and police officers arrested him. I went up to the police, showed them my accreditation, and they said, "But he is a hooligan." And I said, "Yes, but no problem for the club. I want to know what has happened to him, to keep the other supporters quiet. If I have the information, everyone will be fine; if they don't know what has happened to their friend, then we may have trouble."'

The offender was taken to 'a quick court'. Patrick joined him, produced his accreditation as an SLO, and escorted him home to Germany. Patrick has no right to accompany arrested supporters inside a court, and he cannot act in their defence. 'I had to wait outside the court,' he says, 'but he had a translator inside. When he came out, I said to his friends, "I am with him."'

Schalke operate something akin to a courtesy coach for their category-C supporters in Europe: 'When one is arrested,' Patrick says, 'we take him back home in our plane.' The club have even been known to pick up fines levied on misbehaving supporters. 'When a guy was arrested and the court said he had to pay a penalty, I paid the penalty with the club's credit card. I told the guy: "You organise with your friends at your fan club to pay me back." I pay in advance and, no problem, we got the money back.'

The supporter's membership no doubt depended on it: but then, if you enrol supporters as members, this is a pretty effective sanction when you need one. In England, of course, few clubs have member-owners, so they rely on the law.

In 2012, Amanda Jacks, a case worker at the Football Supporters' Federation, took on 15 mostly low-level cases of supporters hit with stadium bans – for celebratory pitch encroachment, drunkenness on entering the stadium and section-five public-order offences. One man was arrested for taking a sip from a hip flask in view of the pitch.

'It's unusual for us to get violent-disorder cases,' Jacks tells me, 'although we have taken on a handful. But every single case that comes to my desk, regardless of the charge, the CPS will apply for a football banning order. Every single case. An example: we've had four cases of fans charged with pitch incursion recently. They've been at the front of the stand, their team has scored, they've jumped up and down celebrating and gone over the fence, accidentally. They've been hauled off by stewards, and the police have applied for a banning order. One of our solicitors said recently that when it comes to football, the justice system operates in a parallel universe.'

The pragmatism required here is all part of the job for an SLO. In their handbook, UEFA acknowledge that 'In liaising between the club on the one side and the fans on the other, the role of the SLO has been likened to trying to ride two horses at the same time.'

Patrick Arnold nods. 'I have to be a diplomat, always. There are some situations where it is difficult for me to hang around with the supporters; in other situations it is very useful for me to do that. In general, it is an honest dialogue; it is sometimes difficult, because the fans ask me sometimes for information from the club, and I don't want to share that. And sometimes the police try to ask me: "Where do the hooligans meet, and what do you know?" But it is not my duty to tell them, so they try to blame me for trouble sometimes, saying, "You were with him, what happened?"'

Is it true that German SLOs are big fans of the British police? 'Yes,' he says. 'When we are in Britain, we see the British police as being very highly accepted by English fans. If one bobby comes along and says, "Stop that!" everyone is quiet.'

So in Germany, if one policeman came along, the fans would not respect him?

'No! They would laugh at him! The relationship between German football fans and the police is the worst. It's worse than the relationship between rival fans.'

The situation began to deteriorate markedly at the end of the 1990s, with the rise of the ultra movement: the hooligans,

360

in Patrick's words, 'stopped doing business, they slowed down', and the ultra movement took off. While the ultras' priority is to support the club, the German police began to treat them as if they were the next generation of hooligans. 'I think the police were too heavy handed from the beginning,' Patrick says. 'The dialogue couldn't start.' And this is where an SLO comes in handy at a club like Schalke.

How will you prepare for tomorrow's game, given that Eintracht Frankfurt have the most feared supporters in Germany?

'One week before the game, [the SLOs at both clubs] start to exchange information. We ask each other: how many high-risk supporters are you bringing? Are there any choreographies your supporters do, or do they want to bring flags or megaphones to our stadium? Then we say, "This is allowed," or, "I'm sorry, this isn't allowed." Eintracht Frankfurt have been coming many times, so we have a good pattern with their SLOs. I start at 11 a.m. on home matches, then I go into the stadium and pick up my walkie-talkie, so my security officer can always contact me if there's any problem. I start working by walking around, looking, talking. I go to the pub of the hooligans.'

Patrick has to call time on our interview because he has an appointment at Borussia Dortmund – they are proposing a stadium ban on 150 Schalke supporters, following the recent trouble at the derby. 'And I said, as an SLO, "Come on, you can't treat everyone as one problem." There were children, there were women [caught up in the trouble], and the police arrested them as a whole group. And they want to give all of them a three-year stadium ban. And I said, "This is too much, because they weren't fighting."'

One of my favourite moments of the week had come an hour earlier, in the same offices at Schalke, when Thomas Spiegel touched on the club's mission statement, and its rejection of violence. 'Obviously,' he said, 'if our fans were to be attacked, they should have the right to protect themselves . . . our fans cannot be Mahatma Gandhi. But unless they have no other option, they should not be doing it.'

Now Patrick picks up the theme: 'Everyone who is considered for a stadium ban gets a letter from us, saying we have information that you were in a big scene, and you have one week to give us a call, to make an appointment, and we listen to everyone's story. Maybe the fan had a good reason for it.' As he acknowledges: 'This is a big problem for the police, because sometimes the supporters come back and say, "It was the fucking police." Sometimes I will give the fan a final warning, or the duty of helping fans in wheelchairs in the stadium for five games. And if there are videos where we have proof that you hit someone, or it was 100 per cent you, then you will be banned. But sometimes, if the police are saying this or that, but it turns out that the supporter was in there without any lawyer, then . . . no.'

If there is a dispute between an SLO at Schalke and the police, then the Schalke security officer settles the issue. 'It's our stadium!' Patrick insists. 'And the stadiums in the whole league belong to the clubs, not the government, so the clubs can decide who is enjoying our activities, not the police.'

Matters came to a head in March 2012, when for the first time the police in Germany (not the FA, not a club) issued a stadium ban, preventing Rostock fans from attending their match at St Pauli. Rostock supporters responded by travelling 100 miles to Hamburg by train, walking out of the station, staging a demonstration against the banning order, then head-ing back into the station to catch the train home. St Pauli's SLO, Stefan Schatz, told me that the club lost their first court case against the police action, but have appealed to a higher court. 'We want a decision in this case, because the police shouldn't be allowed to decide who should go to the stadium,' he said. 'We are a private club and it's our decision who we give our tickets to. OK, we have problems, but we want to keep football alive, and away supporters are part of football.'

The Germans have never had a Hillsborough, or a Heysel. They can talk freely about wanting to keep football alive because they have never been forced to confront the idea that it might be dying in front of their eyes, as the English had to in the 1980s. In the same way, the political dynamic of West Germany in that decade resulted in a climate of constant skirmishes rather than a bitter winner-takes-all battle, so their football has never required emergency resuscitation in the manner of the Taylor Report.

And yet, in 1992, in the year the Premier League arrived, the Germans were also at a critical moment in their football history. Stuart Dykes was part of the massed red ranks that followed Man Utd around the country in the 1970s, but when he arrived in Germany in 1987 he found the hooligan situation worse than it was in England. 'There were fights at every game – every game – in the late 1980s,' he says. 'And not just outside the stadium, but inside too.'

Confronted with this emergency, which erupted at the 1988 European Championships in West Germany, and with one eye also on the Taylor Report, the Germans set their own course. In 1992, consultation between football supporters, the governing bodies, politicians, social workers – 'anyone who was anyone', as Stuart Dykes puts it – led to the National Concept for Sport and Security. This process delivered six mechanisms to tackle hooliganism, one of which was the SLO. The following year, the DFB considered a seventh step: the introduction of all-seater stadiums. They rejected the idea on consideration of the price, declaring: 'Football, being a people's sport, should not banish the socially disadvantaged from its stadiums, and it should not place its social function in doubt.'

Two decades on from 1992, just as German supporters are in there fighting to retain custody of their clubs, they have seen off the latest attempt by police, media and political hard-liners to hoodwink the public into supporting a crackdown on football-fan culture and the introduction of all-seater stadiums. As Stefan Schatz, the SLO at St Pauli, said: 'This is not about money, it is about culture.' And he has the evidence on his side: research has found that the hooligans in Germany do not con-gregate mostly on the *Kurves* – on the terraces or safe-standing areas – but in the seats.

Schatz finds an ally in Thomas Spiegel: 'The politicians argue that terraces are the cause of the trouble, but we know that even at Hillsborough, terraces were not the cause of the disaster. But politicians say, "In England, they did it, and England is now the better place for it." But the atmosphere is the thing, and the safe-standing areas give people a chance to afford to come, and if you take these away it will be a disaster, really.'

Today, there is a sense abroad that the Germans – not the English – have been gradually winning the argument since 1992. As Will Hutton noted in the *Observer* in January 2013: 'In Britain, there are no legal or governance structures that put football or the fans at the centre of a club owner's concerns . . . Market forces are deified as the only value worth celebrating . . . The result is a moral and economic disaster – in football as in the wider economy.'

It is tempting to imagine that UEFA thinks so too: that European football's governing body thumbs its nose at the excesses of the Premier League by incorporating the bones of Germany's licensing model into its Financial Fair Play Regulations ('The idea of supporter ownership has very good support within UEFA,' says Stuart Dykes). UEFA has also embraced the German approach of integrating football supporters, via the SLOs, encouraging them to rise to their own responsibilities. 'The evidence shows that if fans have a say in the way they are treated, they will behave better,' UEFA wrote in their Club Licensing and Financial Fair Play Regulations, 'whereas exclusion and repression demonstrably do not work very well. Self-regulation by fans will always be the best form of prevention.'

Proof came during the 2006 World Cup in Germany: while the police in Hamburg toyed with deploying drones, the German supporters were fighting hard for fan zones and fan parks. UEFA came down resoundingly on the side of the supporters: 'Who can forget the scenes at the 2006 FIFA World Cup in Germany, or UEFA Euro 2008 in Austria and Switzerland, where fans mingled and celebrated together . . . All this was possible because the safety and security concepts introduced in Germany in 1992 with regard to fan liaison and support were integrated in the fan hosting and security concept for these major international competitions.'

*

In the week after I came back from Germany, I found it hard to relax at home. After any intense week abroad – meeting passionate people, digesting so many arguments, listening, often, to another language, travelling long distances to countless meetings, and drinking lots of beer – an inevitable fatigue sets in. But this was slightly different: I felt dislocated at home, and I wasn't alone. My brother texted: 'Finding it hard to readjust.' Partly, it was because his own club, Forest, were struggling under their new Kuwaiti owners (category-C sheikhs, as one HSV fan dubbed them). But it was more than that: we were already making plans to head back to the Bundesliga. It is one thing to be welcomed into the heart of a Champions League club, as I had been at Schalke, but Martin did not accompany me behind the scenes: he simply went to watch the Schalke–Frankfurt match, stood on a terrace with some football supporters and drank a few beers. His, if anything, was the more genuine football experience – and he felt more connected to football in one weekend in Gelsenkirchen than he had been in Nottingham for years.

As we stood on the Nordkurve at Schalke, beneath the low roof of the Veltins, holding a pint of Veltins, there was a connection I hadn't felt to the game for more than two decades. With thousands of lads screaming and shouting, and waving flags and drinking, and massing like an army on a terrace lit with flares, I had the sense, for the first time since I was a teenager, that nothing else really existed outside of the stadium.

12 : Truth and Reconciliation

It's a strange thing to be caught up in a major international story as it unfolds, minute by minute, and to have no idea how it is playing out in the public eye. For the second time in my life, Hillsborough put me at the centre of one of the biggest news events in modern times.

On 12 September 2012, I was one of 80 journalists who filed into the Chapel of Our Lady, in Liverpool's Anglican cathedral, to attend the press conference convened by the Hillsborough Independent Panel. After two years' analysis of the remaining documented evidence relating to the disaster, the nine-strong panel were ready, finally, to present the full, unvarnished truth about the biggest disaster in British sport.

This was the starting gun for the recent inquests, and I was present in the cathedral as part of the *Guardian*'s team, to record my emotions that day as a survivor. It was by turns an exhilarating and difficult afternoon. The Hillsborough Independent Panel had sifted through 450,000 documents relating to the tragedy. In Professor Phil Scraton, the principal author of its report, it possessed the world's leading authority on the disaster. And many of the other journalists gathered in the cathedral had been reporting on Hillsborough for years – had, in fact, been influential in driving the campaign for justice. However, to the best of my knowledge, only one other person in the chapel – a broadcaster at LFC TV – had been where I had been on 15 April 1989: on the Leppings Lane, behind the goal. My only fear, as the panel filed in, was that a *Guardian* journalist might break down in tears before the nation's TV cameras.

Over the course of the next hour, 23 years of lies were unpacked before the British public. Here was the largest report ever committed to digital archive anywhere in the world, and it exposed what was now, according to Michael Mansfield QC, 'the biggest cover-up in British history'.

To sit at the centre of this, as a survivor, was a bewildering experience. The world, finally, was waking up to the truth I had known for years. Elsewhere in the cathedral the families of the 96 were overwhelmed by the magnitude of the findings. When the panel reported its conclusions to the bereaved that morning, all but two of them burst into spontaneous applause; the other two fainted.

In the press conference that afternoon, there were moments of profound silence between the questions directed by the media first at the panel and then at the families' and survivors' groups. I nearly broke that silence with my own tears when it was revealed that 41 of the 96 who died might have been saved if the emergency response had been better co-ordinated.

That figure was subsequently revised upwards, to as high as 58. However, this initial panel finding alone was sufficient to expose as farcical the 3.15 cut-off, whereby the South Yorkshire coroner at the 1990–1 inquests ruled that there need be no investigation into the emergency services' response after 3.15 p.m. because all of the 96 had received fatal injuries that were irreversible by that stage.

It was also revealed that 164 police statements had been amended; in 116 of these, comments deemed to be unhelpful to the South Yorkshire Police's case had been removed or altered by senior officers. That figure was also subsequently revised upwards, to 238 amended statements. And the South Yorkshire Metropolitan Ambulance Service was also found to have amended statements made by its officers.

The panel also revealed the level at which members of the Tory party and the police were co-operating in preparing material to put before the coroner at the original inquests, in the interests of the South Yorkshire Police. Irvine Patnick, the Conservative MP for Sheffield Hallam in 1989, had not merely been instrumental in feeding the lies about supporters' behaviour to the press agency White's, he also liaised directly with the West Midlands Police officer who played a key role in advising the South Yorkshire coroner, Stefan Popper, throughout the inquests into the deaths of the 95.*

The police officer in question was Detective Superintendent Stanley Beechey. DS Beechey was seconded to the inquests in 1989, despite the fact his career had effectively been put on hold by the West Midlands Police, pending an investigation into the nefarious activities of the West Midlands Serious Crime Squad, of which Beechey was a former head.

In the 1970s and '80s, the Serious Crime Squad was responsible for over 30 unsafe convictions later quashed by the Court of Appeal. It was revealed that the squad had fabricated evidence; witnesses also told the court how officers had tortured them to extract confessions. The Serious Crime Squad was eventually disbanded in August 1989.

Beechey himself was never charged with a disciplinary offence relating to the Serious Crime Squad's misdemeanours.

* Tony Bland died in 1993.

However, as David Conn reported in *The Beautiful Game?*, Beechey began work on the preparation for the Hillsborough inquests in August 1989, despite the fact he had been transferred to 'non-jobs' by the West Midlands Police while the squad was under investigation. His chief constable, Geoffrey Dear, later told Conn that he was under the impression DS Beechey was merely studying the technical aspects of Hillsborough. 'We never deployed those officers [previously in the Serious Crime Squad] to do the serious bits of Hillsborough,' he said.

But as Phil Hammond, who lost his son Philip at Hillsborough, told Conn, during the inquests the coroner 'constantly referred to Beechey, asking him what evidence was coming next'. Hammond noticed how 'They used to go out for little chats, then come back in.' Beechey, Conn reported, was the second most senior officer in the West Midlands Police deputed to the inquests. He was present in June and July 1990, when the West Midlands Police interviewed Chief Superintendent David Duckenfield, Superintendent Bernard Murray and Sheffield Wednesday secretary Graham Mackrell, and he was praised for his invaluable work by coroner Stefan Popper.

The Hillsborough Independent Panel revealed that in February 1990, two months before the preliminary inquests got under way, Irvine Patnick wrote to Detective Superintendent Beechey at Nechells police station in Birmingham, on official House of Commons notepaper:

Dear Superintendent Beechey,

HILLSBOROUGH STADIUM DISASTER 15TH APRIL 1989

At your visit to the House of Commons on Monday 19th February, I undertook to supply you with further particulars and to this end I enclose (1) a copy of a report taken by Michael Shersby, who is the Parliamentary Adviser to the Police Federation (2) some photo-copies of correspondence from White's Newsagency. My own report, you confirmed, is already with you.

I do think that the South Yorkshire police's evidence was not fully taken into account at the [Taylor] Inquiry and as a common thread runs through the three reports I do so hope something can be done to rectify this. Should you require any further information that I am able to furnish please do not hesitate to come back to me.

Sincerely,

Here, finally, was confirmation of what the authorities had denied for so long, and what the likes of Phil Hammond and the other bereaved families had feared: a Tory MP colluding with the suspended former commander of a disgraced police squad to overturn the findings of the Taylor Report. Cocooned in that chapel, I was a journalist witness to a historic breaking news story, and a survivor who could only guess at how this was playing in real time outside.

For years, people had asked us: 'What is it you're after? What do you want when you chant "Justice for the 96"?' What we wanted was the truth – and for people to grasp why the truth is so much more than simply a step towards justice. As one man who survived a near-death experience in pen 4 said to me: 'Finding the truth is part of my struggle to retain my sanity.' The denial of the truth around Hillsborough caused severe damage to the mental health of many survivors.

Hillsborough is unique among the disasters of the 1980s – not least for the fact that its survivors were blamed for their own suffering, and for the deaths of their fellow victims.

This was the crude national narrative; but over 23 years, until the Hillsborough Independent Panel (HIP) report, the story played out more acutely on a personal level. There were countless mornings spent trying to walk off a nightmare from the night before. Breaking down, suddenly, in public – a particularly common symptom among survivors. Panic attacks on a packed train. And for me, looking at a map of the world for a country where they speak English and I might get a job, and wondering, 'Is it quiet there? Are the people good?'

The truth might have helped prevent this, might have nipped our trauma in the bud. But 'The Truth' as concocted by the British Establishment and published by Kelvin MacKenzie only heaped guilt or confusion upon trauma. The public looked away, or told us we had killed our own fans. This 'truth' was too much for some supporters, who – decades later – hanged themselves in the garage or jumped in front of a train.

What is it you want?

People can accept that terrible things happen, if truth and accountability follow; it is fundamental to the belief that you live in a decent society. But our truth was lost at the start, for in 1989 the people who came to visit me at home, to collect my truth, were the West Midlands Police. Two smart, plainclothes officers in my living room, July 1989. Telling my dad he probably wouldn't want to hear this . . . probably best to leave the room. Telling me that I was making serious allegations, and could I stand those up? Telling me things I claimed to have seen hadn't actually happened. That where I was in the stadium wasn't that bad: most people died in the next pen. Oh yeah, and in the tunnel. Yeah, and we've got to go now, because you haven't been much use as a witness, and we've got to go and talk to someone much more important than you. And we're not going to put you forward to the inquest, so you might as well just sign that statement and we'll be off.

This disaster was sufficient to reshape England's national sport, but those who survived it were not considered worthy by the state of an intervention themselves. We weren't asking for much: the traumatised need confirmation and reassurance, the tools with which to rationalise something grotesque. But we were denied these in the rush to create an alternative 'truth'.

By the early 1990s, many of us were struggling. Nightmares. *Not too bad where you were.* Rage. *Most people died in the next pen.* Breakdowns. *That didn't actually happen.* Truth at variance with 'truth'. I simply couldn't reconcile myself to the idea that, as the West Midlands Police had implied, I might have over-reacted, might have been a fantasist – it didn't fit with the consistent nightmares, and the pile of corpses. It was like Belsen. *Where you were wasn't that bad.*

By 1993 or '94, all I knew was that I didn't know what to think any more. Not until seven and a half years later did I realise the extent of the cover-up, when Jimmy McGovern's *Hillsborough* docudrama was broadcast on ITV, in December 1996. A lot of drink in those seven years. And two separate nights in a police cell, cooling off for my troubles, after kicking off at police officers in London . . . their uniforms provocation enough. And no little irony: arrested and charged, I simply refused to sign the charge sheet. The West Midlands Police had taught me the stupidity of that.

The second time I was arrested, I emerged sheepishly from the cells the following morning. I was a minor offender, not worth another hour's processing, so the duty officer gave me a cup of tea. Asked me what I was playing at. I told him. I began to rationalise my trauma to a policeman, and he listened. And he said, 'Well, I can understand that, but you can't carry on like this.' And I thought, 'That's fair of that copper, and he's right.' And I didn't carry on like this.

Sometimes, it's as simple as that.

It's largely overlooked that survivors and the bereaved experienced very different emotions following Hillsborough: the bereaved suffered intense grief; survivors bore the trauma. They are very different conditions, and require different treatments. Truth is perhaps the only remedy that can help to heal us both. On 12 September 2012, Margaret Aspinall, who lost her 18-year-old son James at Hillsborough, reminded the media that 'We will always be the losers in Hillsborough.' But as one journalist replied: 'Yes, but, Margaret, this is the first time I think I've ever seen you smile.'

That night, after attending the vigil in St George's Square, I joined Peter Carney, Damian Kavanagh and a group of other survivors in the Ship and Mitre pub in Liverpool city centre. David Conn, who has done so much to expose the lies around Hillsborough, was there too, along with Steve Rotheram and Andy Burnham, and Mick Jones, the legendary Clash guitarist, who has supported the campaign for justice in recent years. They kept a respectful distance, for in the centre of the pub the survivors were in full voice. This was our night, and the end, if you like, of a very long night. We might have got lost occasionally in the darkness, but we never gave up fighting – for truth, for affirmation, for our own sanity.

And on 12 September 2012, after 23 years, we won.

The report of the Hillsborough Independent Panel marked a watershed in the public's understanding of the disaster. Such was the outcry that, on 19 December 2012, the Lord Chief Justice of England and Wales, Igor Judge, quashed the original inquest verdict of accidental death, and set in motion the recent inquests. These were in preparation throughout 2013.

This book was due to appear in March 2014, to coincide with the 25th anniversary of Hillsborough. But on 10 March, the attorney-general, Dominic Grieve, warned that any comment in the media on the disaster from that day forward would risk being found in contempt of court. This despite the fact that the new inquests would not begin until 31 March.

While the attorney-general suggested that he had jumped the gun in an attempt to shut down irresponsible comment on social media, rather than responsible comment in conventional media, the ruling was so all-encompassing as to leave several books, TV documentaries, radio programmes and a feature-length film gathering dust. So it was that the 25th anniversary went largely unmarked. The families and survivors who gathered at Anfield were, once again, denied the right to have our say. But we had been assured the inquests would conclude before the end of 2014. We had waited 25 years; what were another six to eight months?

Besides, we were confident that justice would finally be done. For on the day the Hillsborough Independent Panel published its findings, David Cameron told a packed House of Commons that 'today's report is black and white: the Liverpool fans were not the cause of the disaster'. He was followed that day by the chief constable of South Yorkshire Police, David Crompton, who said: 'In the immediate aftermath, senior officers sought to change the record of events. Disgraceful lies were told which blamed the Liverpool fans for the disaster. These actions have caused untold pain and distress for over 23 years. I am profoundly sorry for the way the force failed.' Crompton also said that the South Yorkshire Police was 'a very different place in 2012' to what it had been 23 years earlier.

In December 2012, Lord Judge had stated that 'the families of those who died in this disaster will be vindicated' by the new inquests. He also made clear that the blaming of Liverpool fans was a 'falsity', and that allegations against them had been 'disappointingly tenacious'. And he advised: 'We should deprecate this new inquest degenerating into the kind of adversarial battle which, looking back on it, scarred the original inquest.'

Now exonerated by the highest authorities in the land, the survivors I knew declined to apply for legal representation at the new inquests. While John Beggs QC, counsel for the police match commanders, signalled he would argue that drunken fans had been a factor, we were confident the police had no evidence to substantiate such a case – all they had would have been presented to the panel, and there was nothing of concern in its report. So we sat back and waited for justice to take its course.

And we waited. And waited.

On 31 March 2014, the inquests began in a specially converted courtroom in Warrington. Few gave much thought to the fact that the most controversial inquests in British history were to be led not by a coroner, but by an appeal court judge deputed as a coroner. Sir John Goldring was the Court of Appeal's Senior Presiding Judge of England and Wales from January 2010 until December 2012. In his opening address to the jury, he said:

> I echo the words of the Lord Chief Justice, Lord Judge, that each death was, and remains, the source of anguish and grief to those to whom they were precious. I acknowledge that, for all that has been, or will be, said and written concerning the disaster, nothing will remove or lessen the private individual grief for those intimately concerned.

And yet Lord Justice Goldring appeared to have been selective in interpreting the ruling of Lord Judge, for on 1 April, in his opening address, he set out a number of core issues. Among them: 'What was the conduct of the fans, or some of them, excluding those who died? Did that play any part in the disaster?'

Survivors looked at each other askance.

In those early weeks, the survivors I knew discussed whether to apply for representation, but given that the other Interested Persons – those either implicated in or affected by the tragedy – had spent a year preparing their case, we were already a year behind them, and in a hearing forecast to last just six months.

We knew, too, that to apply for legal representation now might delay the inquests by several months, causing untold frustration for the families. It seemed pointless, simply to counter a charge so comprehensively dismissed already. What we hadn't grasped was that the coroner had been caught napping. As lawyers for some of the families told me: 'It was only a few weeks before the inquests began that the coroner realised the police teams were likely to blame the fans.' Now, it seemed to us that Goldring had left himself no option other than to let the police teams advance the case they had spent a year preparing. We now had to put our faith in Lord Judge's advice: if this were not to descend into an adversarial battle, surely the lawyers would be obliged to present only genuine evidence, and not unfounded allegations, before the jury.

Barely had proceedings got under way before Beggs, representing former Chief Superintendent David Duckenfield and former Superintendents Roger Marshall and Roger Greenwood, began making the same tired allegations of drunkenness and misbehaviour against Liverpool supporters. Here was the falsity revived: that they had arrived late to the stadium; a significant number were without tickets; drunkenness was rife; and the fans had been so unruly as to make the job of the police all but impossible. The allegations continued for months. Now, as lawyers for some of the bereaved told me, 'The coroner lost control of the process.'

On 30 June, it was the turn of structural engineer John Cutlack to give expert insight into the maintenance of Sheffield Wednesday's ground. Cutlack's was some of the most sophisticated evidence heard at the inquests, and would feature prominently in the coroner's summing up. In one exchange, Beggs said to Cutlack: 'I will go back . . . The period of early 1985, culminating on 29 May of that year at Heysel with 39 deaths, was a particularly bad crescendo period of football hooliganism, wasn't it?'

Cutlack: 'I think that is . . . you are choosing rather emotive words.'

Michael Mansfield QC, representing 77 of the bereaved families, stood to complain that the questioning was 'disproportionate'. When the coroner disagreed, Pete Weatherby QC, representing 22 of the families, pointed out: 'This is a structural engineer. We are now getting evidence put via a question about hooliganism in general.'

Counsel for the bereaved grew increasingly uneasy. As one of them told me: 'The coroner allowed himself to be bullied by the police teams' advocates into allowing evidence about Heysel and 1980s hooliganism to be adduced, under the very thin guise of relevance to the mindset of officers, and their alleged fear that what was happening at Hillsborough was a pitch invasion rather than a disaster.'

On 15 September, Rajiv Menon QC, representing ten of the bereaved families, finally lost his patience. After a survivor called Michael Hill was subjected to repeated questions from Beggs about Liverpool fans being 'the worse for drink', Hill, a chartered accountant, told the court how similar allegations had incensed him in 1989. When Menon produced a copy of the *Sun*'s infamous front page, Goldring moved quickly to stop him. 'I am not trying to shut anything out at all,' he said, 'but I think we just have to have an eye to what is actually of probative value for the jury's decision.'

Menon: 'Sir, I'm sorry . . .'

Goldring: 'Mr Menon . . .'

Menon: 'I am concerned about this because we have heard hours and hours and hours of evidence and questioning about drunkenness and ticketlessness.'

Goldring: 'Mr Menon, please . . .'

Menon: 'There has got to be some balance.'

It wasn't just Beggs, for the match commanders, who drew allegations of unruly fans, but Fiona Barton QC, for the South Yorkshire Police. Barton, who was ultimately instructed by David Crompton, as chief constable, had exposed the empty rhetoric of his mea culpa on the day of the panel's report.

Slowly, the group of survivors I knew realised that we were being sucked into a legal no-man's-land. Alongside the 96, we were the only people to be exonerated before the inquests began; now, having declined to seek legal representation, we were being implicated in our absence.

On 17 October, in the absence of the jury, counsel for some of the families submitted to the coroner that the jury should be told of the admission made by Chief Constable Crompton on the day of the panel's report; likewise the admission by the chief executive of Yorkshire Ambulance Service. As one lawyer for some of the families told me: 'Both SYP and YAS had previously admitted responsibility for their part in the disaster; and in the case of the police had also admitted there had been a cover-up. Had the coroner allowed the jury to hear this, it would have made it virtually impossible for the match commanders to take the aggressive stance they took of blaming the fans at every turn.'

The submission was rejected by the coroner. Consequently, as Weatherby told me: 'There was a risk that the jury might be being misled.'

By the autumn, a bizarre logic seemed in play. The body of evidence produced in court by South Yorkshire Police was drawn overwhelmingly from the evidence they had assembled in the immediate aftermath of the disaster. But this was cover-up 'evidence', designed to shift the blame onto Liverpool fans. (Much of this was at the instigation of Chief Constable Peter Wright, who told a meeting of senior officers at the Pickwick restaurant in Sheffield on 19 April 1989 that his force 'are preparing a defence and we had got to prepare a rock-solid story'.) At the same time, the findings of the Hillsborough Independent Panel – which led to the original inquest verdict being rendered unsafe, and which exposed the South Yorkshire Police as having falsified evidence on a colossal scale – were now set aside as inadmissible.

The coroner would later state that there was also evidence from 'local residents, club staff and some others' to the effect that Liverpool fans had misbehaved. But supporters researching the evidence on the Red and White Kop website discovered that one of the most vocal residents alleging misbehaviour was considered unreliable by a South Yorkshire Police officer in the original investigation; another was subject to a banning order at Hillsborough.* As for the club officials, they could hardly have been said to be impartial: Sheffield Wednesday stood accused of negligence. And 'some others' . . . it was far from a compelling case.

A further problem arose in that the inquests were held before criminal investigations into the police's conduct on the day and in the aftermath – led by Operation Resolve and the Independent Police Complaints Commission (IPCC) – had been concluded. This was at the request of the bereaved families: the inquest verdict was their crucial step towards justice, and must come first. But it meant that, in legal terms, there

* These researchers are not deluded amateur sleuths: they have given presentations to the Independent Police Complaints Commission.

had been no 'exhaustion of domestic remedies' – i.e. because the Resolve and IPCC investigations were still ongoing as the inquests progressed, those police officers under investigation were innocent until proven guilty. As Professor Phil Scraton explains: 'This meant that police officers and others who are under investigation could decline to answer questions put to them by investigators, anticipating they would be charged with an offence, yet they could come to the inquests and give their evidence, even if it was fabricated. The jury had no knowledge that some of those giving evidence had already been formally warned by investigators that they were being interviewed under caution.'

There was an even greater problem with much of the police testimony critical of Liverpool fans: the only truly incontrovertible evidence adduced at the inquests did not substantiate it.

Over 5,000 photographs had been taken, inside and outside the stadium, on 15 April 1989, by press photographers or police intelligence spotters. These images were made available to all the legal teams, and around 130 were put before the jury. And not one was produced in evidence by the police to indicate supporter misbehaviour.

Alongside these photographs was a compilation of 27 minutes of audio-visual footage that had been recorded outside the ground between 2.30 and 3 p.m., the crucial period when the police failed to control the build-up of fans on Leppings Lane. This footage was culled from various sources: a handheld camera operated outside by an undercover police team; a BBC camera; and a camera operated from within the police control box (PCB) inside the stadium. In those 30 minutes of footage, the lens on the PCB camera was either panned, tilted or zoomed no fewer than 59 times – meaning the police were capturing images from multiple angles from this one camera alone. In essence, this compilation footage was *the* evidence of how Liverpool supporters had behaved outside, and as lawyers for some of the families state: 'None of these police officers captured any evidence of the behaviour alleged by other officers.' And neither did the BBC camera.

The disconnect between the accounts of former officers and the AV footage and photographs was brought into focus in August 2014, when former police sergeant Philip Lomas took to the witness stand. Lomas had been part of the police unit closest to the Leppings Lane turnstiles between 11 a.m. and 3 p.m., and he claimed to have witnessed the arrival of 10,000–15,000 fans. In his opening exchange with Christina Lambert, counsel to the inquests, Lomas said: 'I have never seen so much alcohol consumed prior to a match as I saw on that day.' He alleged that the majority of the fans he witnessed arriving were 'worse for drink', that some were staggering under the influence, and that many were without tickets.

Lomas also claimed that 'Up until about 2.30, all the pedestrian flow was away from the ground and at 2.30 it was as if a switch had been flicked and the traffic started coming the opposite way.' When asked why most fans were walking away from the ground until 2.30 p.m., when they might more reasonably have been making their way inside, he explained: 'The understanding was that they were going for something to eat and something to . . . to get something to drink.'

In cross-examination, Brenda Campbell QC, representing the families of 12 men and boys who died, asked Lomas: '. . . you are telling this jury that somewhere between 5,000 and 7,500 people were the worse for drink obviously to you as an experienced officer?'

Lomas: 'Yes.'

Campbell: 'As an officer deployed on that day in a public order capacity within half a mile of Hillsborough stadium as three o'clock approached, what did you do about the fact that something in the region of 7,500 people the worse for drink were headed to this confined space?'

Lomas: 'I didn't do anything, because that wasn't my remit . . . That was somebody else's role.'

Reconvening the following morning, Lomas was shown video footage of the fans arriving at the stadium, taken from a camera looking down towards where he had been standing, outside the turnstiles. When he was unable to identify in the footage any misbehaviour, or drunkenness, or fans carrying alcohol, Lomas claimed that the cameras were taking images from an angle he could not have seen himself. But, Campbell suggested, 'You agree with me, don't you, though, that these fans are not a different species, are not a different breed than the fans that you will have seen?'

Lomas replied: 'Where I was standing, there were people carrying six-packs of lager, big bottles of cider, et cetera. I'm sorry, but you're putting in a different location there where I wasn't, where I can't comment on. I can't see any people on your footage at that location carrying alcohol, but I could see them where I was.'

Lomas's argument was reasonable enough, in principle. So Campbell then asked him to look at a number of photographs of supporters arriving after 2 p.m.

Campbell: 'Let me put these photographs into context for you, Mr Lomas. They were taken by a man called Michael

Warburton Lee . . . He was a photographer for the South Yorkshire Police. You didn't know him?'

Lomas: 'No.'

Campbell: 'Why would the police have photographers stationed outside football stadia?'

Lomas: 'At that time, I was . . . to gather evidence of football public disorder. That's the only thing I can think of, in 1989.'

Campbell: 'It would have been of interest to him, of course, to photograph these hordes of people carrying large volumes of alcohol, wouldn't it?'

Lomas: 'If there is issues around public disorder, and I re-iterate what I said earlier: I didn't witness any public disorder.'

Campbell: 'No, but you did witness, you say, large numbers of people carrying large volumes of alcohol?'

Lomas: 'Yes.'

Campbell: 'And much as it would be of interest to you, it would be of interest to the man who was behind the camera with an evidence-gathering function, wouldn't it?'

Lomas: 'One would imagine so.'

Campbell: 'So where the cameraman is positioned is some-where in front of the Leppings Lane turnstile area, but obviously on the road itself? . . . Anyone there carrying large volumes of alcohol?'

Lomas: 'Again . . . that is a different location to where I was. You're asking me to comment and make reference to . . .'

Goldring: 'I think if you just answer the question, I think it will be quicker.'

Lomas: 'No, I can't . . .'

Campbell: 'It is difficult to tell by a still, but is anyone there obviously staggering or being held up?'

Lomas: 'I can't see anybody being held up, no.'

Campbell then raised Lomas's allegation that fans hanging around outside must have been without tickets.

Campbell: 'Can you tell by looking at this picture whether any of these people have tickets?'

Lomas: 'Not at all.'

Campbell: 'No. Because you wouldn't be able to tell by looking at people whether any of them have tickets?'

Lomas: 'That's correct.'

Campbell then produced a photograph with a time stamp of 14:12.

Campbell: 'The photographer is looking in your direction, capturing those fans who have passed you by, and the majority of whom you have told us are the worse for wear for alcohol?'

Lomas: 'A static photograph does not show how people walk.'

Campbell: 'No, but it does show what they carry?'

Lomas: 'I agree.'

Campbell: 'And it does show if they are being carried?'

Lomas: 'Yes.'

Campbell: 'Yes.'

Lomas: 'I haven't said that thousands of people were being carried.'

Campbell: 'No, you haven't, that is quite right, but you have referred to people being carried?'

Lomas: 'I have, yes.'

Campbell: 'Now, where in this photograph are the people with the large quantities of alcohol that were coming from your position?'

Lomas: 'I have no idea.'

Campbell: 'No. You see, what is also interesting about this is it is at 14:12, and it is at a time when you have told us that all the flow was away from the stadium?'

Lomas: 'That's correct.'

Campbell: 'What direction are the vast majority of those people walking in?'

Lomas: 'If you told me that they're walking towards the ground, I will accept that. I don't know Sheffield area.'

Campbell put the question to Lomas a second time: 'Now show me in this photograph the majority of people who are walking away from the stadium?'

Lomas: 'That is at . . . if that is looking up there, I am up past the bus and the Middlewood Road area is . . . I am at that point. Those people are walking towards the ground.'

Campbell then asked: 'You are welded to your account, Mr Lomas, aren't you, that the majority of fans were worse for alcohol; that large volumes were carrying drink; that the flow was away from the stadium until half past two; and there was a large volume of ticketless fans?'

Lomas: 'I know what I saw, I know what I heard.'

To his credit, Lomas admitted that five days after the tragedy he had been advised on what to include in his statement by Assistant Chief Constable Stuart Anderson. Lomas told the court that Anderson 'wanted specific evidence regarding drunkenness . . . about the number of fans that were asking for tickets . . . That we shouldn't make mention about the radio . . . radios going down, the poor radio transmissions, because there was a reason for that and that would be addressed by an expert who could say that. And then also about we shouldn't make mention regarding the staffing levels at the turnstiles because, again, that was being addressed by people who were there who could explain it better than what we could see.'

In his summing up, the coroner reminded the jury that 'Mr Lomas said that Mr Anderson said to them [junior police officers] that people without a ticket stormed the turnstiles, which caused the crush, and that forced the gate to be opened, and then pushed down the tunnel, causing the crush. Mr Lomas said that fitted in with what he saw that day.'

And none of this is captured in a single photograph among 5,000, or in the crucial AV footage taken by the South Yorkshire Police themselves.

On 16 March 2015, midway through the inquests, I went to court to see David Duckenfield give evidence. It was his fifth day in the witness box, and my 45th birthday. Duckenfield was now 70. He had retired in 1990, aged 46, on the grounds of ill health, avoiding disciplinary charges for the disaster. He had spent 25 years on the south coast, on a full police pension, and was a notable figure at his local golf club. In all that time, Duckenfield had never accepted responsibility for the disaster, never admitted lying about the behaviour of Liverpool fans and never apologised to the bereaved or survivors. Now, in Warrington, he began to crack.

On 11 March, for the first time, former Chief Superintendent Duckenfield admitted he had lied when he told Graham Kelly there had been an 'unauthorised entry' of Liverpool fans into the stadium. Two days later, he apologised to the families for the first time. Duckenfield explained his long silence by claiming that he had only appreciated the enormity of the tragedy on the release of the Hillsborough Independent Panel report, in September 2012. Now, 'To the families, I say this, I am terribly sorry. It has now dawned on me what it means to you, and I am dreadfully sorry.'

But he was misleading the court, even now. For the next day, Pete Weatherby revealed that during an interview with Operation Resolve in March 2014, Duckenfield had stood behind the evidence he had given to the Taylor inquiry in 1989, in which he had sought to blame others. The problem for Duckenfield here was that the Resolve interview was held 18 months after the panel's report – and his supposed epiphany. As Weatherby said: 'The truth is that shortly before these inquests opened, you were still desperately trying to stick to denying any responsibility, Mr Duckenfield, weren't you?'

Duckenfield: 'Sir, I have said I was in denial.'

Weatherby: 'The truth is that you have followed these inquests, and you have seen the evidence that's emerged over the months, and you have seen that the writing is on the wall and you are now driven to accepting responsibility. That's the truth of it, isn't it?'

Duckenfield: 'Sir, I agree.'

The previous week, Duckenfield had sought to explain his lie to Kelly by claiming that it was not 'a conscious decision. I was busy . . . I gave him an answer at that time which was limited in information.' But this was undone by the revelation that it was information that BBC commentator John Motson had also been given prior to 3.13 p.m., when he was recorded talking off air to his producers about a gate being 'broken'. Furthermore, Tony Ensor, Liverpool FC's solicitor at the time and later a circuit judge, testified that Duckenfield repeated the lie to him and Liverpool chief executive Peter Robinson at an emergency meeting in the boardroom, at around 3.20 p.m.

Other issues remained unresolved. Duckenfield claimed that he could not recall what he was doing between 10 a.m. and 2 p.m. – a crucial period in the build-up to the match. As Christina Lambert QC, counsel to the inquests, suggested, this was a 'golden opportunity' to familiarise himself with the layout of the ground. Duckenfield said he couldn't remember if he had or not. To this day, no one has come forward to explain where he was.

In an earlier exchange, Rajiv Menon had put to Duckenfield that '[when it] suits you, you can't remember [but] when you want to assert something, your memory is absolutely fine'. To gasps in the public gallery, Duckenfield replied: 'This is one of the strange realities of post-traumatic stress disorder.'

He was, occasionally, candid. He admitted that his operational order was 'hopeless'. He was not fully abreast of whether it was the job of the police or stewards to monitor the pens, and couldn't remember if he had ever seen the safety certificate. And he confirmed that, two months after the tragedy, a memo he drafted for policing the stadium acknowledged the importance of efficient turnstiles, a filter cordon and good signage and ticketing arrangements – all either absent or deficient on 15 April 1989.

But still he sought to duck his responsibilities. He complained that he had been failed by his predecessor as match commander, Brian Mole, at the moment of handover on 22 March 1989: the only thing Mole was interested in talking about was how he could get tickets for the game, Duckenfield said.

He emphasised he was inexperienced, perhaps unfortunate to be burdened with responsibility for the match. But as lawyers pointed out, there were only five officers in the South Yorkshire

Police of higher rank than Duckenfield, and with high rank comes heavy responsibility. When it was put to Duckenfield that, if he felt unready, he should have asked that another officer command the game, he replied: 'If Mr Wright told you to do a job, you did it.' Moreover, his superior, Assistant Chief Constable Walter Jackson, 'gave me the impression, or assured me, that there would be no problem with the efficiency of the team that surrounded me, and I accepted that'.

But when Weatherby asked, 'Do you accept that control outside of the Leppings Lane entrances, police control, should never have been lost on that day?' Duckenfield replied: 'Yes, sir.'

Weatherby: 'Do you accept that once congestion at the turnstiles became apparent, measures should have been taken by [Superintendent] Marshall, and by yourself, to manage that situation so you never reached the position where exit gates were opened?'

Duckenfield: 'Yes, sir.'

Weatherby: 'And that that was possible, and that you and Mr Marshall failed so to do?'

Duckenfield: 'Yes, sir.'

Under questioning from the coroner, Duckenfield similarly accepted that, in failing to foresee where the 2,000 supporters would go after being admitted through exit gate C, he had not acted as a reasonably competent match commander would. Now, Weatherby asked: 'It must follow from all of that . . . I put it to you as carefully as I can, Mr Duckenfield, that the disaster resulted from your serious failures that day, as admitted by you before this jury?'

Duckenfield: 'Yes, sir.'

Duckenfield's failure to respond to the emergency in the

pens in front of him was also, finally, laid bare. He denied that a photograph taken of pens 3 and 4 at 2.59 p.m., showing fans attempting to escape, indicated that a major incident was unfolding, and that this should have been the moment for him to respond. He said that only when the match was abandoned, at 3.06 p.m., did he grasp the situation. He claimed to have declared a major incident at this point, thereby triggering the emergency response plan agreed between the police and ambulance services. But as Weatherby explained, 'Try as we may, looking at the recordings of the traffic between the control box and anybody else over the VHF radio or the telephone system, which is all recorded, there is no such declaration of a major incident at that time or, indeed, later.'

Duckenfield claimed it was an instruction he had fired off in a 'manic' control box, and that it may have got lost amid the other orders. But his real mindset was exposed by an order that was recorded on the radio transcripts: it came at 3.05 p.m. – a request for dog handlers. As distressed and injured fans began spilling onto the pitch, begging the police for assistance, Duckenfield was mobilising his officers for an outbreak of public disorder.

Crucially, 15 minutes elapsed before he requested the fire brigade to arrive with cutting equipment – which meant, as Weatherby said, 'police officers on the ground and supporters had to take those fences down with their bare hands, didn't they?'

Duckenfield: 'Yes, sir.'

Weatherby: 'Because no cutting equipment arrived in time to do it?'

Duckenfield: 'Yes, sir.'

Weatherby: 'It was a hopeless response to an emergency, wasn't it?'

Duckenfield: 'Yes, sir.'

A hopeless operational order, and a hopeless response.

Professor Phil Scraton, an expert in inquest law, later told me that Weatherby's was 'one of the finest pieces of advocacy I have ever seen'.

But the crucial moment of the entire two years of evidence came the following day. On 17 March, under cross-examination by Paul Greaney QC, for the Police Federation (which represents rank-and-file officers), Duckenfield finally admitted that he was directly at fault for the 96 deaths.

Greaney: 'Do you agree with the following, that people died in a crush in the central pens?'

Duckenfield: 'Yes, sir.'

Greaney: 'That if they had not been permitted to flow down the tunnel into those central pens, that would not have occurred?'

Duckenfield: 'Yes, sir.'

Greaney: 'That closing the tunnel would have prevented that and, therefore, would have prevented the tragedy?'

Duckenfield: 'Yes, sir.'

Greaney: 'That you failed to recognise that there was a need to close that tunnel?'

Duckenfield: 'I did fail to recognise that, sir, yes.'

Greaney: 'And, therefore, failed to take steps to achieve that?'

Duckenfield: 'I did, sir.'

Greaney: 'That failure was the direct cause of the deaths of 96 persons in the Hillsborough tragedy?'

Duckenfield: 'Yes, sir.'

*

It was effectively all over bar the shouting. Or so we thought.

By the summer of 2015, the inquests were more than six months behind schedule, and threatening to overrun by a year. The strain on the families was severe: one of the bereaved was struggling once more with post-traumatic stress disorder. The jury had lost 18 months of their own lives. They had sat through almost 200 days of harrowing evidence, while the bereaved sat solemnly, or disconsolately, just a few feet away. Concerns were growing over the coroner's time management.

On 6 July, the court heard of the final moments of Carl and Nick Hewitt, two brothers from Oadby, Leicestershire, who had died, aged 17 and 16. Carl was training to be a cabinet maker and was due to receive the Best in Class award. Nick was hoping to become an electrical engineer. Christina Lambert then announced that their mother, Brenda Hewitt, 'has recently died'.

In the last year of her life, Brenda might have clung to the hope that she would finally see justice for her sons. If the inquests had lasted their scheduled six months, she would have done. If they had run twice as long as expected, she would have done. But as lawyers for some of the families stated: 'The chief constable of South Yorkshire Police and the chief executive of the Yorkshire Ambulance Service have continued to deflect responsibility onto each other or the supporters. This has made the inquests far longer and more adversarial than they should have been.'

So Brenda Hewitt never got to see justice for Nick and Carl. And still the rest of us waited, and waited.

*

In August 2015, I take a call from Tim Knowles. Tim survived the crush in pen 3 but lost three of his friends: Simon Bell, 17, Gary Church, 19, and Chris Devonside, 18.

'I was 17 when I went to Hillsborough, and doing my A-levels,' Tim had told me when we first met. 'There were ten of us from my school in Formby who went to the match, and only seven of us came back alive.'

Tonight, the court is in recess. We have been following the inquests regularly for 18 months, and I am struggling with depression. Tim is a quiet, steady bloke, but tonight he sounds excited.

'Have you heard what's happened at the inquests this week, mate?'

I haven't, so he explains that, in the absence of the jury, barristers for each of the Interested Persons are making representations to the coroner about the evidence he should prioritise in his summing up, which is expected to begin around Christmas.

'Basically,' Tim says, 'Beggs has tried to argue that there should be a headline question put to the jury as to whether our fans contributed to the serious situation on Leppings Lane. Apparently, Goldring has knocked him back. I think there can't be enough evidence to consider it. We've won, mate,' he says.

I put the phone down, and almost fall over.

For the next few months, the court hears from some of the country's leading pathologists about the final moments of the 96: their medical cause of death, and the pathologists' assessment of the approximate time of death. Perhaps it is because much of this evidence revolves around the appalling scene in the gymnasium at Hillsborough, which became a temporary mortuary and remains the memory I struggle with the most, but for much of the autumn I put the inquests to the back of my mind.

In November, I learn that former Detective Superintendent Stanley Beechey has died, at 81. One of the chief suspects in the cover-up had lived out a long retirement, on a healthy police pension. Beechey was on the radar of the IPCC, and had become notorious among survivors for his conduct leading up to the 1990–1 inquests. He, like Brenda Hewitt, had died without meeting justice.

A week before Christmas, I arrange to meet Tim Knowles and three other survivors – Nick Braley, Richie Greaves and Pete Rankin – for a beer near Trafalgar Square. The five of us were lucky to escape from pens 3 and 4. We are joined by Jim Sharman, a redoubtable Hillsborough campaigner. We meet up every so often for a pint, and tonight we are marking what must, surely, be the final months of a 27-year campaign.

The lads are excited, too, that someone else is joining us for a pint: someone influential and highly respected; a man who has campaigned so long for justice; a man who knew exactly what was going on behind the scenes in Warrington; and a man whom we shall call the Man in the Pub.

We gather in a corner of The Chandos, on St Martin's Lane, by the dartboard. Around us Christmas revellers are growing flirtatious. We sip at our pints, contentedly, and give the Man in the Pub the floor. He sucks his lips over his teeth and gets straight down to business.

'Lads,' he says, 'I'm sorry to have to tell you this, but you might be about to get blamed all over again.'

Richie, Nick, Jim, Tim, Pete and I look at the Man in the

Pub, and at each other. Have we misheard him? He pauses only briefly, then says:

'You need to put a stop to this. Right now.'

On 26 April 2016, the jury of six women and three men in Warrington confirmed that the 96 football fans who died at Hillsborough (95 of them Liverpool supporters, one a Spurs fan) were unlawfully killed. They also confirmed that the 96, and all the survivors, were entirely blameless. The failings of David Duckenfield, his fellow officers, Sheffield Wednesday FC, their structural engineers Eastwoods, the South Yorkshire Metropolitan Ambulance Service and the licensing authorities were also laid bare.

In the days following the verdict, the families and their lawyers rightly, fulsomely, praised the jury. What the media were slow to recognise was that scarcely any of the survivors or bereaved extended their compliments to the coroner.

Alarm bells began to ring for both the families and survivors around Christmas 2015. On 14 December, Lord Justice Goldring confirmed to the Interested Persons the questions he would put to the jury, in consideration of their verdict. They have since been debated endlessly, but for survivors, one stood out:

Question 7: Was there any behaviour on the part of football supporters which caused or contributed to the dangerous situation at the Leppings Lane turnstiles?

The 25,000 Liverpool fans at Hillsborough would have no knowledge of this question until 25 January 2016, when the coroner would begin his summing up. But six of us had just been tipped off by the Man in the Pub.

In fairness, the coroner had indicated he might consider the role of the fans, as early as 1 April 2014. However, given that only evidence was meant to be admissible, and unfounded smear was not, we believed he had been more than generous in allowing lawyers for the police to have their say, but that he would rule there was insufficient evidence to warrant anything beyond a supplementary question for the jury to consider – under Q3, which addressed the performance of the police outside the turnstiles.

But a headline question on fan behaviour might lead to us being found causal, or contributory, in the disaster – and for the first time in an official hearing. After everything that had been seen and heard in court, the prospect was unacceptable. As Jim Sharman recalls: 'I just couldn't believe what I was hearing. I was totally baffled.' Nick Braley was 'a bit bewildered. Nothing made sense to me, given the legal teams seemed to have done an excellent job in exposing the South Yorkshire Police's case for what it is.'

The Man in the Pub was convinced the coroner had made a 'monumental mistake', and that we had to seek immediate representation on behalf of the supporters. We knew that many survivors were extremely vulnerable: 766 had been injured in the crush, and many of those, and countless others, had been damaged psychologically. We knew survivors who had attempted to commit suicide; and others, tragically, who had.

'You know,' I said to the Man in the Pub, 'if this question goes against us, there's a real risk that people will kill themselves.'

'I know,' he said, without hesitation.

We were now caught in a Kafkaesque situation. Liverpool fans, having been exonerated before the inquests began, had not sought legal representation, but now the only people affected by the disaster who had not been represented in court were about to be implicated – in their absence. While Goldring would later explain that the fact was aired in open court, he had not sought to directly approach survivors to notify them (it would have been very simple to contact either Liverpool FC or the fans' group Spirit of Shankly, but neither was approached). And with the evidence stage of the inquests closed, there was no opportunity for us to contest the dubious allegations the police were levelling against us.

Off Trafalgar Square, in the famous theatres, all sorts of dark and dreamy stories were being told: pantomimes, thrillers, comedies and farces. We were now caught in a nightmare of a drama. An influential contact meets us in a pub. Sips at a pint and asks us to prevent a potential miscarriage of justice on an historic scale. Disappears into the night. On the other side, a senior appeal court judge and knight of the realm, with the home secretary at his back.

We are, by now, three sheets to the wind, but the truth is breaking in waves. The question was all the more shocking for the fact that, if the jury found that supporters' behaviour had *not* contributed to the dangerous situation on Leppings Lane, they were being asked to consider whether 'there was any behaviour on the part of supporters which may have contributed to the situation'. As Richie said: 'What kind of question is "May have"? I mean, they've set the threshold so low it virtually invites the jury to find against us.'

We had been reliably informed that Goldring's overriding concern, not unreasonably, was to oversee a verdict that would not be challenged, because the Home Office was keen for this to be the last word on the disaster (criminal prosecutions were a separate matter). The suspicion is, however, that lawyers for the police had intimated that a judicial review of an unlawful killing verdict would arise if the question of fan behaviour were not put before the jury. We suspect that Goldring had walked into a trap of his own making: that he had erred in allowing Beggs to cast allegations for almost two years against supporters with insufficient evidence; now, Beggs could reasonably argue that the coroner must include his case before the jury, otherwise the inquests would be rendered unbalanced.

As Tim said, quietly: 'I might be blamed for killing my friends on the basis of a vague, theoretical possibility.'

The Man in the Pub had been unequivocal: it was down to us to put a stop to this. Tim, Nick, Richie, Pete, Jim and I were stunned.

'What can we do?' we asked. 'We're six blokes in a pub. We can't presume to speak up on behalf of 25,000 Liverpool fans.'

The Man in the Pub was unmoved. 'You've got to. No one else can do it.'

'But we need to canvass supporters' groups,' we said. 'If we do that, we could mobilise thousands of supporters and bring a powerful voice to bear.'

'You haven't got time,' he said.

And he was right. The evidence-gathering had now finished, after 22 months and close to 1,000 witnesses. Tens of millions of pounds had been spent on legal teams. The jury had sat on more than 200 occasions, and were themselves on the brink of burnout. The movements of each of the 96 who died had been pored over in excruciating detail by the country's foremost pathologists. The home secretary was hopeful that the inquests would finish soon, settling the dispute over Hillsborough once and for all.

And in a pub off Trafalgar Square, a week before Christmas, Nick Braley, Richie Greaves, Tim Knowles, Pete Rankin, Jim Sharman and I were now being asked to put a halt to the inquests.

In the first week of January we met again, at the offices of the *Guardian*, in King's Cross. Now, we were joined by Chris Lightbown, a former investigative journalist on the *Sunday Times* who has produced some excellent work on Hillsborough since 1989. He is also a good friend to some of the bereaved families.

Over the course of three hours, we realised we had to get the survivors' voice heard in court. We had two options. The first was to apply for Interested Persons (IP) status, on behalf of the survivors. This would see us appoint a legal team, paid for by the Home Office. The lawyers would have to get up to speed very quickly in order to get us onto the witness stand, so that we could both give and adduce evidence on behalf of the survivors. We would also demand the recall of a number of former police officers who had given evidence that was highly critical of the fans. As IPs, we would have access to all the material made available to the other parties, and we would be entitled to make a submission to the coroner over his summing up. If granted IP status, we would insist that Q7 was struck out, or substantially rephrased.

Eventually, we decided against applying for representation: we could not subject the bereaved families to even further delays. We knew, too, that any application would risk the wrath of the coroner, and that counsel to the police must have been delighted by the inclusion of Q7. If we took the stand as witnesses, with the aim of striking it out, they would throw everything at us. Like the families, we were almost out on our feet.

There was one option left.

On 20 January, Nick, Richie, Tim and I wrote to Lord Justice Goldring. In a four-page letter, we raised six key objections to the headline question being put to the jury on fan behaviour:

- we understood the High Court had, in quashing the original verdict of accidental death, recorded the innocence of Liverpool fans at Hillsborough. This was crucial in our decision not to seek IP status at the current inquest;

- if, at any stage of the proceedings, it had been anticipated that survivors might come to bear some blame for the disaster, then it should surely have been incumbent on the inquest team to point this out, thereby giving survivors the opportunity to defend themselves;

- there appeared to be no new evidence indicating the culpability of supporters for the dangerous crush on the Leppings Lane, or inside the stadium, other than oral testimony from police officers – testimony which had not been corroborated by either video footage or photographs, or by any other independent material;

- any alleged culprits among the Liverpool fans should be identified, questioned and given legal representation. (This was surely a matter of natural justice, but it appeared that no effort had been made to do this. In our view, this made an allegation against unnamed supporters unsustainable);

- we understood that the inquest was meant to be non-adversarial, but counsel for the police had resorted to mud-slinging;

- the most delicate argument we had to make now brought the 96 themselves into the debate. After obtaining the permission of prominent members of both the Hillsborough Family Support Group and the Hillsborough Justice Campaign, we pointed out that '. . . it appears to have been accepted by all Interested Persons at the inquest that none of the 96 people who died was to blame for his or her own death. While we concur with this argument, it nonetheless begs the question of how it could be possible to distinguish – or in any way separate – those who died from those around them who survived, in terms of culpability for the disaster. In our opinion, it is not possible to make such a distinction, since it has been estimated that at least 30 of the 96 people who died were in the crowd crushed against the turnstiles outside Gate C, and subsequently came through Gate C after 2.52 p.m.'

Furthermore, we wrote: 'It appears that no counsel has sought to make the case for why the grounds for exonerating the 96 do not apply similarly to the survivors.'

We also said: 'We would like to place on record that the possibility of effectively sharing the blame for the deaths of 96 people is an appalling prospect. It is all the more so because many survivors lost family members and/or friends in the disaster.'

We explained that we had no wish to delay the inquests, so we would therefore ask that he simply submit our concerns to the jury. The letter was shown by an intermediary to the families, to one of the country's pre-eminent QCs, and to other prominent campaigners. They all agreed we had a strong case for making a submission to the court.

We took a deep breath, and pressed 'Send'.

Two days later, we received a three-page reply from the solicitor to the inquests. Writing on behalf of the coroner, he explained, reasonably enough, that 'these are new inquests, not bound by any previous proceedings . . . the judgment of the Lord Chief Justice was not restricting the freedom of the Coroner in these inquests to hear evidence and make decisions based upon it'. He explained that there was indeed new evidence, as 'many new statements [were] taken and witnesses interviewed'. As to the question about supporters, he pointed out that arguments had been made both for and against its inclusion in the questionnaire, but that the coroner had decided that he should 'let the jury decide the issue so that it was publicly resolved'. There is, he wrote, 'sufficient evidence for the topic to be considered by the jury in their deliberations'.

He also stated: 'We do not accept that it was incumbent on the Coroner or his legal team to invite unidentified survivors to make applications for interested persons status, in the circumstances.'

In our view, his reply was weak, not least in response to our argument that it was legally incoherent to separate the survivors from the 96 in terms of our collective innocence. He ignored our point that counsel for the police should not have

404

been allowed to make this an adversarial process. And in stating that the coroner believed the conduct of the fans was a public issue that needed to be resolved, he appeared to have overlooked the fact that it already had been – by the Hillsborough Independent Panel, the prime minister, the chief constable of South Yorkshire Police and by the Lord Chief Justice.

We recognised his argument that these were new inquests not bound by former hearings; but surely, if the finding of Liverpool supporters' innocence were now to be overturned, there must be new evidence produced of their misbehaviour that should be sufficiently substantial as to set aside the conclusions of the highest judge in the land. In our view – and we were not alone here – it was not: the new evidence the solicitor had alluded to – from South Yorkshire Police, 'from local residents, club staff and some others' – was at best contentious, and in some cases highly dubious. That the coroner should consider this sufficient was alarming.

In explaining that the coroner had circulated the draft summing up to the bereaved families, he neglected to acknowledge that the families and their QCs do not formally represent the survivors. And one response in particular left us scratching our heads: 'It was not disputed by any legal team that the evidence of fan behaviour outside the turnstiles should be summed up to the jury.' This was true to the extent that the behaviour of the fans, whether good or bad, was material to many of the issues arising – no fans, no crush, of course. However, we felt he had underplayed the fact that the families' lawyers had made 'four strenuous submissions' to the coroner opposing the inclusion of a *question* on fan behaviour.

Tim, Richie, Nick and I – with the invaluable assistance of

Jim and Chris – were now working in parallel with the families. They had instructed their barristers to make representations to the coroner over his summing up, which was now under way and giving widespread cause for concern. This was perfectly legitimate – multiple parties did the same. Our submission was now before all the parties, and had reinforced many of the families' key arguments.

As survivors, we suspected that a question on fan behaviour had been inserted because of what we came to describe as 'the 5 per cent principle'. Many survivors believed Goldring had calculated that if the agencies implicated in the disaster were found to be 95 per cent responsible, few would protest if around 5 per cent of the blame were laid at the door of the supporters. We suspected the coroner had calculated that because no supporters would be named, this would be seen as a victimless attribution of blame. We were of the opinion that he had decided to throw a bone to the police, and we were having none of it.

In the final week of January, we wrote to apply for Interested Persons status on behalf of Nick, Richie and Tim. Although I helped draft the application, I had now to stand aside: I didn't want my position as an author, and the potential profile of this book, to have any bearing on the correspondence between the coroner's legal team and the survivors. We stated that 'There is evidence heard in court that Liverpool supporters have not had fair and sufficient opportunity to contest, which now seems set to be summed up in a manner that we believe is not balanced.'

Moreover, we said: 'Evidence has also been presented to the court by several police officers (either retired or still serving) who we know are currently under investigation by the IPCC for alleged criminal activity amounting to conspiracy to pervert the course of justice . . . If suspicious conduct by witnesses, designed to smear Liverpool supporters, results in adverse findings against a group who have not had IP status, this, in our opinion, would bring the entire process into disrepute.'

On 1 February, the coroner declined our application for representation. Nick, Richie and Tim did not fall into the categories of persons entitled to be granted IP status, wrote the solicitor to the inquests. 'Accordingly, you would each only be recognised as interested persons if the coroner considered that you had a "sufficient interest" in the inquest proceedings within the meaning of section 47(1)(m) (of the Coroners and Justice Act 2009) . . . You may be assisted by referring to the very full ruling of Lady Justice Hallett in the London Bombings Inquest, in which she considered the question of interested person status in detail and (among other matters) addressed applications by survivors for such status.'

But the survivors of the London bombings were not accused of causing that disaster. In our view, the inquest solicitor's argument was not analogous. He also stated that 'the fact that a person is a survivor of the Disaster does not, of itself, give him or her a sufficient interest to qualify for interested person status in these inquests'.

And here was the crux: survivors were on the brink of being implicated, but were not considered to have a sufficient interest in the proceedings as to merit a voice in court.

In early February, we appointed a legal team from London. Lochlinn Parker is head of the Actions Against the Police department at Irvine, Thanvi & Natas solicitors. He represents people seeking to hold the state to account, in particular in relation to the police and other detaining authorities. Parker instructed Martha Spurrier, a barrister from Doughty Street chambers, one of the top legal sets in the country. Spurrier – unbeknown to us – was already a rising star: three months later, she would succeed Shami Chakrabarti as the director of Liberty, at the age of 30.

As we sat in chambers, we realised we had exposed a serious flaw in these inquests. As Parker later confirmed: 'The usual approach of English and Welsh law through the ages has been that a person has the right to understand and defend themselves against allegations. In the old Coroner's rules there was more of an onus on the Coroner to identify interested parties, and even stop an inquest until that person has been informed, and arranged legal representation if they so wish. While those rules have changed, we suggested to the Coroner that the spirit of natural justice would require representation. In other inquests I have acted in, the Coroner has openly expressed concerns that evidence has emerged that could lead to a person being criticised, and has then taken steps to make sure that person is given a chance to make representations.'

In January 2016, Lord Justice Goldring, presiding over the most controversial inquest in modern times, declined to do this. And as Parker states: 'We believe this is the first inquest where a class of people who have not had representation could have been criticised for the deaths of others.'

On 3 February, Parker sent a Letter Before Claim to the Hillsborough inquest court, in which we challenged the refusal of the coroner to grant us IP status.

'As a matter of statutory construction and as a matter of

fairness at common law,' Parker wrote, 'the Coroner was obliged, at whatever time it became clear to him that a question might be left to the jury concerning whether the survivors caused or contributed to the deaths, to grant the claimants IP status and seek their representations. The Coroner's refusal to afford the claimants IP status is ultra vires . . . [outside the law].'

He also stated: 'If the claimants are not afforded IP status, and if question 7 remains, there is a real risk that the jury's conclusion will be unsafe. A "yes" answer to question 7, as it currently stands, would be unsustainable because, unlike the other IPs named in the questionnaire, the supporters who are being criticised, or at least a representative cohort, have not been allowed to be IPs so as to defend or account for their actions.'

Parker notified Goldring that 'Should this letter be rejected then we will advise our clients to seek an urgent rolled-up hearing in Manchester High Court by the close of business on 5 February 2016.'

Within 24 hours, the coroner rejected our application. His solicitor wrote: 'The coroner is not prepared to adjourn the inquests as you suggest, a course which would seriously disrupt his summing up to the jury.' He repeated an assertion he had made throughout our correspondence – that we were too late, and that as early as 1 April 2014, the coroner's opening statement had included the question: 'What was the conduct of the fans, or some of them, excluding those who died? Did that play any part in the disaster?'

This is entirely valid on his part. However, it was not the coroner's place now to wag his finger at us, given his failure, as we saw it, to oversee an inquest on the terms under which it had been prepared by the Lord Chief Justice. We had put our faith in him to do his job properly, and were far from alone in believing that he had come up short. As lawyers for some of the families told me, 'We have been thoroughly unimpressed with his performance.' Though there was time, even at this late stage, to make a short submission to the court on behalf of Liverpool fans, he had declined even to allow that.

Now, we feared the coroner was on the verge of presiding over an unsafe verdict. Should he do so, our case for an appeal was strong, and we had prepared the ground for thousands of survivors who might follow. Today, we had come as far as we could.

It was in the hands of the jury now.

After 27 years, justice came in a few short moments. At just after 11 a.m. on Tuesday 26 April 2016, Sir John Goldring took his seat in the specially converted courtroom in Warrington, to silence. There was no preamble from the coroner today; not even a perfunctory greeting. As the microphone sputtered into life, the most controversial inquests in British history were about to come to an end. After two years and nearly 300 days of evidence, from almost 1,000 witnesses, everything would rest on 14 questions – and on six women and three men from Warrington. The jury had given up two years of their lives to resolve this most bitter of disputes. Now, they were restricted to uttering a few simple words in response to the coroner. 'Yes', 'No' or 'It is'. But with those four words, they would rewrite history.

A few hundred yards from court, across the Birchwood industrial park, in building 401, I was one of 200 people – survivors, the bereaved and other campaigners – who filed into an annexe to watch a stream of the verdict, broadcast live. As we waited, quietly, a member of the inquest secretariat arrived to inform us that the annexe was technically a part of the courtroom itself; we should therefore show no emotion as the jury's determinations were announced. 'We ask you to be quiet and restrained,' she said. A few seats along from me, Damian Kavanagh, a friend and fellow survivor, muttered: 'We've been dignified for 27 years.'

Eventually, the camera wobbled into focus, and the face of Sir John Goldring appeared. Unseen, off camera, the forewoman confirmed that the jury had arrived at its determinations to all 14 questions. Within moments, the debate over Hillsborough would be settled, once and for all. Here it was, in front of us on a TV screen – justice, finally. Like a drip, intravenously – delivered drop by drop.

I was sat with my girlfriend, Deb, who was my girlfriend the day I went to watch an FA Cup semi-final at Hillsborough; she has seen me through years of anxiety and anger. In the seats beside and in front of me, other survivors. Damian survived the crush in pen 4, aged 20. He had obtained a ticket for the game for his friend, David Rimmer, who died in the same pen. There was Mike Bracken, who had been crushed outside the ground before trying briefly to stop 2,000 fans from pouring down the tunnel. And Tim Knowles, Nick Braley, Richie Greaves – none of them deemed worthy of making a submission to the jury.

Now, the jury begin. Their answers to the first five questions – on the multiple failures in police planning and the operation on the day – are resolved quickly. A formality. But all hinges on questions 6 and 7.

The coroner is unruffled. 'Are you satisfied, so that you are sure, that those who died in the disaster were unlawfully killed? Is your answer Yes?'

The forewoman's voice is calm and reassuring, and wears lightly the huge responsibility. With the faintest trace of a lisp, she says: 'It is.'

People scream, and jump to their feet. Mike's head begins to tremble in his hands. Richie turns towards me and punches the air. I turn slowly to Deb with tears in my eyes, and she smiles and rubs my back.

Then the moment is gone. For the coroner is on to Q7 – the question we fought so hard to strike out. This is not just a matter of truth now: people's lives are in the balance. The jury cannot know this, of course. I look around at Deb, at Richie, at Damian and Richie's wife Lou. No one looks at me.

The coroner: 'Was there any behaviour on the part of football supporters which caused or contributed to the dangerous situation at the Leppings Lane turnstiles? Is your answer No?'

'It is.'

People leap to their feet and punch the air. But again, momentary relief, for we are only halfway there. Now, having answered No, the jury are asked to step over that low threshold. The coroner: 'Was there any behaviour on the part of supporters which *may have* caused or contributed to the dangerous situation at the Leppings Lane turnstiles? Is your answer No?'

I am sitting down but my knees give way. Tears are falling either side of my nose. The woman with the reassuring voice says: 'It is.'

And the place erupts.

*

The opportunity to re-evaluate the truth about Hillsborough might be the occasion to re-evaluate the state of our nation, and our national sport. As Andy Burnham wrote in the *Observer*: 'the new generation in parliament must make Hillsborough a moment when Britain changed for the better'.

This tragedy, for so long regarded as a 'football disaster', is much greater than that: it has exposed deep failings in our legal system, our political class and our media. As Michael Mansfield QC told me last month: 'The most important legacy of Hillsborough is that it has revealed how the whole system failed miserably. Not just the corrupt source – the police. The system needs urgent reform in its entirety. We need proper democratic accountability.'

In the speech of his parliamentary career, delivered the day after the verdict, Burnham said the case had exposed Britain's 'flawed judicial system, which gives the upper hand to those in authority over and above ordinary people'. He asked if the home secretary, Theresa May, would work with him to insert a 'Hillsborough clause' into her policing and crime bill, 'ending the scandal of retirement as an escape route' for corrupt police officers, and of 'wrongdoers claiming full pensions'. He slammed the way in which the courts are loaded in favour of those in power, and argued for reform of the coronial system. 'This, the longest case in English legal history, must mark a watershed in how victims are treated,' he said.

But there is also a sense that the truth about Hillsborough is too much truth for those in power. As Professor Phil Scraton told me: 'Without doubt, Hillsborough points to the urgent need for reform in the procedures for handling complex and contested cases. This reform has to be far reaching and not confuse the role of "panels" with that of public inquiries.' But, he said, 'It is instructive that as the person who led the HIP's research, and took overall responsibility for its report, no one has approached me to discuss the potential of this unique and highly successful process. My concern is that on the coat-tails of its success, a watered down, non-critical process will emerge to be used at the discretion of governments.'

Elsewhere, some of the families have demanded that the director of public prosecutions, Alison Saunders, be held accountable for dismissing concerns, back in 1996, over the case of Kevin Williams, whose mother, Anne, had already done so much to expose the false account of his death.

The South Yorkshire Police, meanwhile, are in disarray. Chief Constable David Crompton was suspended the day after the verdict. His interim successor lasted less than 24 hours. The force's police and crime commissioner has been criticised for endorsing Crompton's aggressive stance during the inquests. At the time of writing, in early May, there are growing calls for the force to be disbanded, or merged into a greater Yorkshire force. But with question marks over North Yorkshire Police's role in the Jimmy Savile scandal, this in itself would seem insufficient.

It is surely time for a change in the culture, rather than merely the structure, of policing. In my opinion, as someone who watched in horror as police pushed escaping fans back into the carnage of pens 3 and 4, many of the rank-and-file officers on the pitch at Hillsborough got off lightly at these inquests. If this breakdown in trust between police and public is never to be repeated, I believe we need a truth commission – conducted outside the legal process – that would allow former officers, without risk of censure, to explain why they were so at odds with football fans by 15 April 1989. For years, the police hid behind allegations of hooliganism, but these have been debunked. It is time for them to delve a little deeper.

If one facet of our legal system is beyond reproach, it is the jury system. Six women and three men from Warrington succeeded where previously a coroner, a law lord and a High Court judge had failed. As Mansfield says: 'This verdict is a resounding endorsement of the jury system, which has regularly come under attack for being unable to assimilate complex, long cases and deliver reasoned verdicts. The real objection from the forces of darkness – which includes Labour governments – has been the jury system's democratic and challenging virtues.'

Perhaps this verdict should be adopted by pressure groups to resist the threat of secret trials, which – as Mansfield says – 'is what those in power really want, with no popular element and no lawyers; hence the legal aid cuts'.

The verdict also exposes the failure of David Cameron to implement the second-stage Leveson recommendations. As Mark Wheeler, professor of political communications at London Metropolitan University, argues: 'The Hillsborough lies were perpetuated by a combination of the police, justice and media systems. Therefore, while the common narrative has compartmentalised the relative influence of these forces, people need to take a holistic view – need to consider the complex interdependencies which shaped the agenda, and how they colluded.'

And so we come back to the modern game, which rose unchallenged from the wreckage of the Leppings Lane. As Wheeler says, 'The forces who ran football agreed with their political masters to frame Hillsborough in terms of "hooliganism". This was what we might call a "manufacturing of consent", and it was perpetuated by the worst excesses of the Murdoch press. In such a manner, opinion formers readied the public to embrace the commodification of football.'

Indeed. It was Hillsborough, and the false narrative that took hold around the disaster, that reshaped English football. The message of the whole new ball game was that traditional supporters could no longer be trusted, that the sport had to be rescued from 'the yob class', that the affluent middle-class consumer was vital to its revival, and that stadiums could no longer entertain supporters standing up. That standing was a disaster waiting to happen.

It wasn't. The clubs had merely to get their house in order, and the authorities to admit their failings around Hillsborough. Here was an opportunity for all interested parties to sit down around a table and draw up plans to revitalise the game, in which we might all have a stake, as the Germans would in 1992. But no; supporters would carry the can for Hillsborough, because the police wouldn't; because the police had become politicised under Margaret Thatcher, and because she had declared football fans an enemy of the state.

It is time, surely, for a rethink.

Various organisations could now be charged with manslaughter over the unlawful killing of 96 football fans. While they must all be held to account, the FA alone can make significant amends through football itself. But its response to the Hillsborough verdict offered scant hope. In an official statement, the FA said it 'reaffirms its deep sorrow and regret that these tragic events, which occurred at one of its fixtures, led to the loss of life of 96 football supporters on 15 April 1989 . . . While much has changed since 1989, the FA and English football in general must continue to recognise, remember and learn from the tragedy. In looking forward, it is important we never forget.'

I contacted the FA in the wake of the verdict, to ask whether – in a spirit of reconciliation – they might convene a football summit specifically in recognition of the issues raised by the inquests. Here, they could make the real legacy of Hillsborough, in 2016, a wide-ranging review of English football, to build on the earlier legacy of vastly improved stadiums. This review could be the moment not only to recover the purpose and integrity of the FA itself, but to involve all 92 league clubs, politicians of all major parties, social and community workers, the Football Supporters' Federation and Supporters Direct, in writing a new manifesto for the national sport, one which balances the need for a viable long-term commercial strategy with a recognition that the game can and should fulfil a unique social purpose.

In an email, an FA spokesperson replied: 'For the past year at least, along with the Premier League and Football League, the FA has been part of a Government Expert Working Group on Supporter Ownership and Engagement which looked at a number of key fan issues. This involved Supporters Direct and the Football Supporters' Federation. One of the outcomes was for the FA to assess how to best engage with representative supporter groups within its decision-making structures as part of its current review process.'

The FA is also funding a Supporters Summit at Wembley stadium on 16 July, organised by the Football Supporters' Federation and Supporters Direct. According to its spokesman, 'I believe a range of important fan-based issues will be addressed.'

While this is welcome, it was in the pipeline before the verdict was reached; it remains to be seen whether the truth about Hillsborough will encourage football's governing body to acknowledge that so much of the modern game was built on a falsehood.

And we have seen enough, in the 24 years since the Premier League arrived, to realise that it is not working – certainly not for the working-class, or 'subsistence' class; not for many of the communities which built these clubs; nor for so many of our young adults. Even Leicester City's remarkable title victory is not the fairy tale it is painted to be: the Foxes have their own billionaire foreign owner, and as David Conn pointed out in the *Guardian*, 'the Football League is still investigating the club's 2013–14 promotion season amid strong concerns from other clubs they may have cheated financial fair play rules'.

Andy Burnham is adamant the FA must take the lead in any review of English football, and that to do this they will have to reassert their right to govern the game over the interests of the Premier League. I asked Burnham whether there might now be a case for something more – government intervention, perhaps?

'Those people who say government and sport should be kept separate . . . it's not a logical argument,' Burnham said. 'On every level, government is involved in the regulation and funding of sport; sport is part of society, and government regulates television . . . all of these areas in which sport operates are properly the preserve of parliamentary politics. With football,' he said, 'it always came down from FIFA: there was an iron rule that if governments got too close, then FIFA would step in and remove the affiliation of FAs to FIFA. But this self-serving idea that governments shouldn't pay any attention has bred a sport that is rapidly becoming morally bankrupt. It has allowed excess and abuse to flourish. And nowhere is that more embodied than at FIFA. So I don't think that doctrine works.'

Burnham pointed to London 2012 as a prime example of how government can deliver. 'Look at the most successful sport in our country in terms of our performance on the world stage: it's Olympic sport,' he said. 'And that is very much down to a government model of investing in and structuring the sport. I'm not talking about government takeover [of football], but governments have flirted with it for too long: they talk about it, and then they don't do anything about it. What we have is vested-interest regulation, rather than proper independent regulation. Currently, the big and the powerful – i.e. the Premier League – regulate the whole of the game, because the Premier League basically decide what the policy of the FA will be. That is an unhealthy model. Ultimately, I think the government does have to enforce – or require in some way – independent regulation of the game, and have vested interests held to account by independent regulation. There has to be regulation in the interests of everybody, rather than in the interests of the most powerful.

'Ultimately,' he says, 'you can't run things just with the elite in mind: the game will die under the elite, and they'll be left standing on nothing. If football is to stay healthy, then the powerful have to give something up, and I'm afraid the leaders in our game are not prepared to do that. But if we leave things as they are, the dysfunctionality of football will increase.'

Football has not grown apart from society since 1989. The national sport has become dysfunctional as society has become dysfunctional. With wealth increasingly concentrated at the top, with inequality increasing, with clubs serviced on debt, and with foreign capital flowing in and out, English football is teetering on the same flimsy foundations as much of the English economy. And it suffers the same crisis of national self-confidence when it comes to asserting our right to own these institutions, and to manage them in our interests.

Supporters have a part to play here, in rousing themselves from a delusion that the game will surely correct itself one day – that their fortunes will come good again. Difficult, when this is the same faith that sustains their loyalty to a club through thick and thin. But for former Supporters Direct chief executive Dave Boyle, the Hillsborough verdict offers fans an opportunity to 'break down the policy prison' that has informed how the game has been run for these past three decades. 'In that time,' he says, 'we've seen much progress, but despite astonishing efforts on behalf of fans' interests, the position of supporters within the game has barely moved the dial. Resisting fans' representation at the top of the game is one of those few issues in which the FA and Premier League will reliably be in lockstep with each other. That is the policy prison.' Boyle sees something symbolic in the victory of the Hillsborough families: 'From day one, they set their sights on justice, and never let themselves be persuaded to accept a lesser goal as the best they could hope for in the real world. That triumph of optimistic spirits over pessimistic wills is what is needed now.'

Modern English football, born in the embers of the Thatcher era, is of a piece with the great economic and social reforms of her tumultuous decade. Many of those have been badly exposed in recent years, from the racketeering of the energy companies to the deregulation of the financial-services industry; from the housing bubble and the debt-driven economy to the decay that became entrenched with deindustrialisation in the north.

Football staggers on under the same free-market prescription: that financial transaction with our clubs gives us all the stake we need; that the only profit worth pursuing is on a balance sheet; and that competition is the best means of regulation. As the Premier League will tell us, if it sells, it must be healthy. There Is No Alternative to the market – because if there was, then the market would fail.

But the market is failing, and there is an alternative, and it is German. In the Bundesliga, football thrives at every level, while observing its social function. On the terraces at HSV and Schalke, at Dortmund and St Pauli, men and women are trusted to inculcate in their children a sense of social responsibility; to show them that the game can be a leveller in society, and that an element of risk brings its own reward; that there is reward, too, in an identity, and that football clubs are a precious community asset. And, of course, that there is nothing inherently wrong in being a man in a football shirt in a crowd.

As I stood on the terraces at Schalke with a beer in my hand, understanding intuitively what those lads were singing in German, I was reminded of a conversation I'd had with Barbara Ellen a few months earlier: 'There's nothing frightening about a crowd of men just because football is happening at the same time,' she said. 'The fear is the fear of them refusing to listen to you, and to continue doing what they want to do. And when they don't listen to you, they're a "mob".'

It's three years since Margaret Thatcher died. But the 'mob' that she and her henchmen once vilified, at Orgreave and at Hillsborough, are still here, and we have been cleared of all charges levelled against us.

Now, can we have our ball back, please?

Bibliography

Thanks to the staff at the national newspaper archive in Colindale, which – sadly – closed in November 2013.

CHAPTER 1

Aberfan: Government and Disasters, Iain McLean and Martin Johnes (Welsh Academic Press, 2000)

Annual accounts of Sheffield Wednesday FC, 1979–1988, c/o Companies House, London

Guardian, 13 April 2009

Hillsborough: Only Half-Remembered, Mick Hume, Spiked Online, 15 April 2009

Hillsborough: The Report of the Hillsborough Independent Panel (The Stationery Office, September 2012)

Hillsborough: The Truth, Professor Phil Scraton (Mainstream, 2009 edition; first published 1999)

Interim Report: The Hillsborough Stadium Disaster, Lord Justice Taylor (Her Majesty's Stationery Office, August 1989)

Newsnight, BBC2, 16/17 April 1989

Observer magazine, 15 March 2009

CHAPTER 2

Douglas Hurd: The Public Servant, Mark Stuart (Mainstream, 1998)

The Downing Street Years, Margaret Thatcher (HarperPress, 1993)

Hansard, 29 January 1990, minutes of the Commons debate on the Final Taylor Report

Hillsborough: The Report of the Hillsborough Independent Panel (The Stationery Office, September 2012)

Interim Report: The Hillsborough Stadium Disaster, Lord Justice Taylor (Her Majesty's Stationery Office, August 1989)

Mark George QC on Orgreave, quoted on the Justice Gap website, and the *Guardian*, 21 October 2012

Observer magazine, 15 March 2009

CHAPTER 3

All Played Out, Pete Davies (William Heinemann, 1990 edition)

Bobby Robson: Against the Odds, An Autobiography, Bobby Robson with Bob Harris (Hutchinson, 1990)

Football, Violence and Social Identity, edited by Richard Giulianotti, Norman Bonney and Mike Hepworth (Routledge, 1994)
The History of the World Cup, Brian Glanville (Faber & Faber, 2001)
InfoPlus statistics on World Cup viewing figures, compiled for FIFA

CHAPTER 4
The Blueprint for the Future of Football (Football Association, 1991)
Dished!: Rise and Fall of British Satellite Broadcasting, Peter Chippindale, Suzanne Franks and Roma Felstein (Simon & Schuster, 1991)
Glory, Goals and Greed: Twenty Years of the Premier League, Joe Lovejoy (Mainstream, 2011)
Hansard, 12 November 1990
The History of News Corporation, Funding Universe report online
Independent, 11 November 1990
Memorandum sent by Enders Analysis to Vince Cable, regarding proposed buyout of BSkyB by News Corp., August 2010
Murdoch, William Shawcross (Simon & Schuster, 1993)
Murdoch: The Great Escape, Richard Belfield, Christopher Hird and Sharon Kelly (Sphere, 1994)
One Game, One Team, One Voice: Managing Football's Future (Football League, October 1990)
Sky and Football: More to Pay, Less to Show, and Reduced Margin, Enders Analysis, May 2006
Sky High, The Amazing Story of BSkyB, Mathew Horsman (Orion, 1998)
Stick It Up Your Punter: The Uncut Story of the Sun Newspaper, Peter Chippindale and Chris Horrie (Pocket Books, 1999)
When Saturday Comes, various issues

CHAPTER 5
The Dawn of Dissent: The Complete Best of the Alternative Football Press as Printed by Juma (1985–1991), Martin Lacey (Juma)
Foul, October 1976
Four Four Two, December 2011
A Game of Two Halves?: The Business of Football, edited by Sean Hamil, Jonathan Michie and Christine Oughton (Mainstream, 1999)
Life in the Middle: The Untold Story of Britain's Average Earners (Touchstone/TUC, 2009)
Premier League Fan Survey 2001
Ripped and Torn, various issues
Sniffin' Glue, various issues
Terrace Talk, September 1983
When Saturday Comes, November 2012
Whose Game Is It Anyway? The Book of the Football Fanzines, compiled by Phil Shaw (Argus Books, 1989)

CHAPTER 6
The Brave Man in the Early Years (0–8): The Ambiguities of Being a Role Model, Dr Simon Brownhill (University of Derby, 2011)

Chavs: The Demonization of the Working Class, Owen Jones (Verso, 2012)

The Death and Life of Great American Cities, Jane Jacobs (Vintage Books, 1961)

'Fans und Sozialstruktur', by Gunnar Otte, in *Fans: Soziologische Perspektiven*, Hrsg. von Jochen Roose, Mike S. Schafer and Thomas Lux-Schmidt, 2010

The Football Supporter, issue 24

The Good Childhood Inquiry, research into childhood play by the Children's Society, 2007

Natural Childhood, Stephen Moss (National Trust, 2012)

New Economics Foundation report into happiness, 2004

No Fear: Growing Up in a Risk Averse Society, Tim Gill (Calouste Gulbenkian Foundation, 2007)

'The Numbers Game: FA Facing Participation Challenge', report by Dan Roan for BBC Online, 8 June 2011

One False Move: A Study of Children's Independent Mobility, Mayer Hillman, John Adams and John Whitelegg (Policy Studies Institute, 1990)

Outliers: The Story of Success, Malcolm Gladwell (Penguin, 2009)

Populus survey 2008/9 on Premier League fans' safety

Premier League fan survey 2002/3

Premier League fan survey 2007/8

Reaching out with Role Models (National Literacy Trust, April 2009)

Report Card 7: An Overview of Child Well-Being in Rich Countries (UNICEF, 2007)

Report Card 11 (Child Well-Being in Rich Countries) (UNICEF, April 2013)

Research conducted by ICM for Capital One into boys' football loyalties, and how they compare with their dads', August 2012

Research published by the German Home Office into the average age of German supporters, 2001

CHAPTER 7

Brand Finance: Football Brands 2012

Bullock Report: The Report of the Committee of Inquiry on Industrial Democracy, 1977

Deloitte Football Money League 1996/7

Football and Its Communities: Final Report, for the Football Foundation, May 2006

Football Mad: Are We Paying More for Less? Dave Boyle (High Pay Centre, 2012)

FT Weekend magazine, 28 April 2012

Harrington report, 1968

'Bayern Munich Embrace Anti-Nazi History after 80 Years of Silence', Raphael Honigstein, *Observer*, 12 May 2012

Red Men: Liverpool Football Club – A Biography, John Williams (Mainstream, 2010)

Report of the Committee on Football (aka Chester Report), Department for Education and Science, 1968

The Spectator, May 2010

www.mightyleeds.co.uk, for information on J. Hilton Crowther, Leeds City and Huddersfield Town

CHAPTER 8

Charter for Football (Labour Party, 1995)

Bibliography

Football in the Digital Age: Whose Game Is It Anyway?, edited by Sean Hamil, Jonathan Michie and Christine Oughton (Mainstream, 2000)
A Game of Two Halves?: The Business of Football, edited by Sean Hamil, Jonathan Michie and Christine Oughton (Mainstream, 1999)
The Journals of Woodrow Wyatt, Macmillan, 1999–2000

CHAPTER 10
Boomerang: The Biggest Bust, Michael Lewis (Penguin, 2012)
Tor! The Story of German Football, Ulrich Hesse-Lichtenberger (WSC Books, 2003)

CHAPTER 12
The Beautiful Game?: Searching for the Soul of Football, David Conn (Yellow Jersey, 2005)
Hillsborough: The Report of the Hillsborough Independent Panel (The Stationery Office, September 2012)

426

Index

Index

Sheffield Wednesday: and Hillsborough stadium, 5, 6, 8, 11, 378

Shersby, Michael, 371

Shoot! (magazine), 124–5, 129

Siefert, Christian, 337–8

Sir Norman Chester Centre for Football Research, 53, 162–3

Sky TV, 101–10; and 21st Century Fox, 90; and 2016–19 Premier League TV rights, 112–13; *see also* BskyB

Smith, Paul, 112–13

Snape, Peter (Lord Snape of Wednesbury), 55, 56–8, 90, 109, 216, 251, 255

Sniffin' Glue (fanzine), 128

Soccer Tots, 187

socialisation, football as, 166–71, 174–5

South Yorkshire Metropolitan Ambulance Service, 369

South Yorkshire Police: and Hillsborough disaster, 8, 14–24, 29; Hillsborough Independent Panel's findings, 368–9, 370–1, 376; Hillsborough Inquest, 380–8; internal discussions after Hillsborough, 34–8, 39; and miners' strike, 35; and other incidents at Hillsborough, 5, 7; and Stuart-Smith scrutiny, 258–9; and *Sun*'s coverage of Hillsborough, 94–5; and Taylor inquiry, 38, 40–4, 49–50

Southampton FC, 157

Spiegel, Thomas: on hooliganism, 341, 362, 364; on Schalke's board structure, governance and membership, 283, 285–91; on Schalke's finances and supporters, 287–92, 298–9

Spirit of Shankly, 309

stadiums: atmosphere on terraces, 297; campaign for safe standing, 169–70, 171–4, 195, 294–5; disabled access, 247, 249; German, 166, 172, 290–1, 297, 307–8, 323, 342, 348, 364–5; move to all-seater, 50–8, 147

Stone Roses, 69

Straw, Jack, 258, 259

Stuart-Smith, Murray, 258–9

Stuttgart football club, 304, 305, 330

Substance, 251, 262, 335

Sugar, Alan, 81–2

Sunderland FC, 164–5, 170, 195

supporters: average age and class, 162–9; change in identity, 117–18, 125–56; clubs' relationship with local communities, 196–237, 247, 280–4, 288–9, 292–3,

298–302, 305, 322–5, 328–9, 335–40, 354–63, 365; movements, 309–10, 315; ownership of clubs, 197–206, 280, 282, 302–5, 309–11, 315, 330–40, 350–3, 364–5; and politics, 213–15, 317–29; satellite TV's effect, 149–54; social engineering, 221–3; ultras, 173, 316–17, 319, 342–5, 360–1; young supporters, 161–75, 295, 297

Supporters Direct, 198–9, 203, 205, 249, 302, 320, 354, 417, 420

Swindon Town, 214

Swissramble, 112

Taylor, Graham, 80, 238, 241

Taylor, Lord Justice, 33; and Football Spectators Bill, 46; inquiry overview and Report, 7, 8, 12–13, 22, 38–43, 47–58; public reaction to Report, 43–5

Taylor, Rogan, 72–3, 117–8, 125–6, 145–9, 167, 168–9, 214, 247, 314–15; on Heysel, 220–1

television: early days of satellite, 101–5; and footballers' pay, 231–2; and kick-off times, 196; New Labour plans to investigate relationship with football, 245, 248, 249–50, 254–5; Premier League overseas viewers and effect, 206–8; and supporter narcissism, 240–1; Thatcher's relationship with BBC and ITV, 98–9; *see also* BSB; BSkyB; Sky TV

Terrace Talk (fanzine), 136, 142, 143

Thatcher, Margaret: attitude to football, 13–14, 40, 57, 145, 416; Brighton bombing, 139–40; and broadcast media, 98–9, 101; fall, 107–8; and health and safety, 10–11; and Hillsborough, 33–4, 35–6, 43–4, 45–6, 416, 421; and ID cards, 46–7; legacy, 244; and miners' strike, 35–6; and Murdoch, 107–10, 250; and police, 416; and Sky–BSB merger, 107–10; third government, 11–12; and World Cup 1990, 66, 70

ticket prices: England, 162, 221–3, 231–3, 252; and Football Task Force, 247, 252; and footballers' pay, 231–3; Germany, 162, 292, 298, 353

Tongue, Steve, 123, 124

Tottenham Hotspur, 5–6, 100, 126–7, 220, 221; and Tottenham Hotspur Foundation, 266–76

Triesman, Lord, 257

21st Century Fox and Sky, 89–90

433